IDENTITY AND NETWORKS

IDENTITY AND NETWORKS

FASHIONING GENDER AND ETHNICITY ACROSS CULTURES

Edited by
Deborah Fahy Bryceson, Judith Okely,
and Jonathan Webber

Berghahn Books
New York • Oxford

First published in 2007 by
Berghahn Books
www.berghahnbooks.com

©2007 Deborah Fahy Bryceson, Judith Okely,
and Jonathan Webber

All rights reserved. Except for the quotation of short passages
for the purposes of criticism and review, no part of this book
may be reproduced in any form or by any means, electronic or
mechanical, including photocopying, recording, or any information
storage and retrieval system now known or to be invented,
without written permission of the publisher.

Library of Congress Cataloging-in-Publication Data

Identity and networks : fashioning gender and ethnicity across cultures / edited by Deborah Fahy Bryceson, Judith Okely, and Jonathan Webber. -- 1st ed.
   p. cm.
Includes bibliographical references and index.
Includes a list of published works by Shirley Ardener.
ISBN 978-1-84545-161-5 (hardback : alk. paper) -- ISBN 978-1-84545-162-2 (pbk.)
1. Women--Identity. 2. Women--Social networks. I. Bryceson, Deborah Fahy. II. Okely, Judith, 1941- III. Webber, Jonathan (Jonathan Meir)

HQ1206.I54 2007
305.401--dc22
                          2007002609

British Library Cataloguing in Publication Data
A catalogue record for this book is available from the British Library

Printed in the United States on acid-free paper

ISBN-10: 1-84545-161-9   ISBN-13: 978-1-84545-161-5   hardback

Contents

Preface   xi

Introduction: The Artistry of Social Life   1
   Deborah Fahy Bryceson

Part I: Fashioning Identities

1. Changing Cultures, Changing Rooms: Fashioning Identities and Anthropological Research   21
   Sharon Macdonald

2. Identity at Play: Individuals, Characters, and Theatres of Action   38
   Kirsten Hastrup

3. Constructing Identities in a Post-Communist Society: Ethnic, National, and European   54
   Zdzisław Mach

4. Making Sense of the Past: Reflections on Jewish Historical Consciousness   73
   Jonathan Webber

5. A Sense of People and Place: The Chapel and Language in Sustaining Welsh Identity   91
   Gaynor Cohen

6. Towards an Ethnography of Colleagueship   103
   Hilary Callan

Part II: Gender Agency and Networks

7. Thinking the Unheard, Writing the Unwritten: Reflecting on Marginality, Ethnography, and Texts — 115
   Maria Jaschok in dialogue with Shui Jingjun

8. The Women's Movement: The Formative Years, 1850–1930 — 133
   Cecillie Swaisland

9. A Good Lady, Androgynous Angel, and Intrepid Woman: Maria Czaplicka in Feminist Profile — 146
   Grażyna Kubica

10. 'Ritual Sisters' or Female Rulers? Gender and Chiefship Revisited in Southern Africa — 164
    Gina Buijs

11. Revolting, Revolutionary, and Rebellious Women: Symbolic Disruption of Traditional Femininity and the Liberation of Femineity and Other Muted Identities — 179
    Rhian Loudon and Ronnie Frankenberg

12. What Women Really Want: Gender, Ethnicity, and Job Expectations on an Automobile Factory Assembly Line — 197
    Fiona Moore

13. Can You Call This Fieldwork? September in Venice — 214
    Lidia D. Sciama

14. Gendered Lessons in Ivory Towers — 228
    Judith Okely

Afterwords: In Celebration of Shirley Ardener

Gendering Oxford: Shirley Ardener and Cross-Cultural Research — 249
Janette Davies and Jacqueline Waldren

Shirley Ardener's Habitus **Jonathan Benthall**	260
Circumstance, Personality, and Anthropology **Tamara Dragadze**	261
Shirley in My Mind **Grażyna Kubica**	263
Titi ikoli in the Academy **Sharon Macdonald**	265
Going the Extra Mile **Sandra Burman**	267
Her Powers of Persuasion **Fiona Moore**	268
Shirley Ardener: Mentor and Friend **Paula Heinonen**	269
The African Connection in Oxford **Gina Buijs**	271
Shirley's African Roots **Cecillie Swaisland**	272
Returning to 'The Mountain' **Peter Geschiere**	273
Shirley's Magic **Jonathan Webber**	276
List of Published Works by Shirley Ardener	279
Notes on the Contributors	284
Index	292

SHIRLEY ARDENER, 2005
(Photograph courtesy of Bob and Carrie McIntyre)

The inspiration for this collection of essays is the life and work of

SHIRLEY ARDENER

to whom this book is affectionately dedicated

Preface

It has taken us more than three years to put this book together. We wanted to create a collection of new essays that would bring together some of the best work that has been done in the fields of ethnic and gendered identities, with special reference to the social study of networks. Our motive for this was straightforward – to honour the life and work of Shirley Ardener, who for more than fifty years has made an extraordinarily distinguished contribution to women's studies, studies of ethnicity and identity, and West African studies. Based in Oxford, Shirley has helped to launch many careers in all these fields, in particular through her work as the guiding spirit behind the establishment of the Centre for Cross-Cultural Research on Women, now known as the International Gender Studies Centre, at Queen Elizabeth House. In the past thirty years, since the publication of her pioneering, landmark book *Perceiving Women* in 1975, Shirley has convened and chaired not far short of five hundred seminars, in women's studies and in ethnicity and identity – an immense achievement, especially bearing in mind the originality of approach, the courageous venturing into completely new areas of research, and the capacity to throw startling new light on familiar topics that have always been the hallmark of her contribution to academic life. This collection of essays brings together a number of those who have spoken at Shirley's seminars or worked with her over the years, all of us indebted to her for her generous encouragement, her human warmth, modesty, and discretion, and her steady, non-confrontational intellectual influence.

This book, it should be said, can be taken as a tribute also to the unseen hand of the late Edwin Ardener, a social anthropologist of considerable creative imagination, who taught many of the authors of these essays. Twenty years after his death in 1987, his widow still maintains his legacy – by inspiring new generations of scholars to undertake innovative research and facilitating their seminars and publications. Shirley and Edwin began their professional life together as anthropologists in Nigeria and the Cameroons, and Shirley continues to divide her time between Oxford and West Africa to this day. These and other aspects of her remarkable personality are outlined in an Afterword to this volume – tributes and reminiscences by colleagues and friends that we feel compelled to call Afterwords.

As will be seen from her long List of Published Works, which appears following the Afterwords, Shirley has personally edited well over a dozen books (not to mention her editorship of more than one book series), and in that sense she has far more experience than we have. We hope nevertheless that (with the exception of Cameroonian studies, which would require a separate volume to itself) we have succeeded here in conveying something of the flavour of the wide range and cross-cultural expertise Shirley has demonstrated in her own work. Our grateful thanks are due to Robert Parkin, from the Institute of Social and Cultural Anthropology of the University of Oxford, for his inestimable help in compiling the list of Shirley's publications, to Bob and Carrie McIntyre for the frontispiece photograph of Shirley, and to Marion Berghahn (Publisher and Editor-in-Chief at Berghahn Books) for her support and encouragement in putting this volume together – even to the point of trying to keep the project confidential from its honoree (not at all an easy matter). Most of all, however, we are grateful to our two dozen contributors – not only for their essays but also for their support and patience while the volume was slowly assembled and edited. The modest number of people whose work could be included in one volume is no reflection of the countless others who would also like to have been associated with this book, and in their name too we offer it to Shirley with our humble thanks.

The Editors
Oxford, January 2006

INTRODUCTION
THE ARTISTRY OF SOCIAL LIFE

Deborah Fahy Bryceson[1]

Currently, much of anthropological literature on identity finds itself in unanticipated dialogue with other social science disciplines in a period of deepening global insecurity. The optimism of the last half-century, an era viewed as one of unparalleled economic progress for much of the world, is now being replaced by a profound pessimism in the West about the spread of social intolerance and terrorism in the twenty-first century. Even before the events of 11 September and the London bombings of July 2005, unease was surfacing. American political scientists took the lead in the cultural commentary, drawing attention to the decline in associational ties, trust, and 'social capital' in daily life (Fukuyama 1995; Putnam 1995a, b). Huntington (1996) argued that, at a global level, Cold War East–West political antagonisms had dissolved, to be replaced by misunderstanding and distrust between historically differentiated cultural blocs. According to Fukuyama (2000), the unravelling of familial social responsibility and the severing of social links in neighbourhoods, at workplaces, and within nation states at large were associated with individuals' quest for lifestyle freedom and women's feminist goals pushing women into the workplace, corroding time-honoured social norms, undermining existing social institutions, and atomising individuals.

This clutch of American political scientists deployed the concepts of cultural identity, individuality, and modernity to dramatise their findings. They borrowed from anthropological constructs, but normative political science informed their findings and conclusion. The picture that emerges from their work is one of Western societies and the world more generally becoming far less than the summation of its parts. Their vision is one of weakening associational ties, individual atomisation, and vacuous space where people collide with indifference. Terrorism and counterterrorism now fill this void with distrust and fear.

The chapters that follow take issue with this dejected view of humanity and social life. While we are indeed in an age of tumultuous questioning of individual identity and radical reordering of social institutions, which engender alienation, nonetheless the world is witnessing enormous social creativity. Collective identities are being reconfigured spurring new patterns of social networking. The concern of this book is to examine the ethnic and gender relationships and networks that congeal in the process of identity reformulation. A number of questions are posed. Under what circumstances does trust arise, paving the way for friendship, collegiality, national unity, or loyalty to leaders? How is social life constructed as a collective endeavour? Does the means towards sociality become its end?

Our inspiration for probing these age-old social conundrums is the work and persona of Shirley Ardener, to whom this volume is dedicated. A tenacious scholastic networker in the fields of gender and ethnicity studies in Oxford for more than four decades, her research and publications are formidable, repeatedly cited in the literature and continually influencing researchers. Yet Shirley rarely mentions her own work and instead uses her theoretical insights and broad empirical awareness to foreground the work of others around her. Her seemingly effortless way of bringing people together to debate the cultural patterns and peculiarities of the day has launched many academic careers, deep friendships and enduring collegial ties. Shirley's subtle hand in the artistry of social life is illustrative of how social agency can facilitate the widening and deepening of trust and associational ties. Through the nurturing of working relationships with people from a variety of backgrounds and interests, Shirley has catalysed new insights into the cultural intricacies of the world we live in.

The contributors to this volume are primarily anthropologists who have in one way or another collaborated with Shirley over the years, benefiting from her perceptive mind and enthusiasm for academic enquiry. I would like to note that, as a non-anthropologist, my engagement with anthropology over the past two decades has been largely prompted by Shirley's welcoming attitude to people of other social science disciplines participating in the seminars and forums that she has organised – a refreshing departure from so many social science circles where disciplinary allegiance becomes essentially tribal in nature with exclusionary territorial claims to the discipline's theoretical domain and deployment of terminology impenetrable for outsiders. While devoted to anthropological enquiry, Shirley has maintained an open-door policy towards non-anthropologists. This has afforded me and countless other non-anthropologists a deep appreciation of anthropology's insights into the social world around us.

This book is an acknowledgement of Shirley's inspirational role and our ongoing engagement with her numerous projects, edited collections, and zest for multicultural life. The collection illustrates the broad range of Shirley's comparative cross-cultural influence, spanning African, Asian and European case studies. Many of the authors have deliberately subjectivised their analysis, building on their fieldwork, teaching, and personal experience, not only in rejection of positivist objectivity per se, but also as a means of demonstrating the intersubjectivity of social life and cultural interpretation. All the chapters focus on public life, but not at the expense of its interconnections to private life. Social identities and networks at the workplace, in places of worship, amongst political leaders, and amongst urban residents and national citizenries are explored. This chapter considers the nature of different non-familial associational ties followed by the case-study chapters, which probe how shared ethnic, religious, and gender identities are collectively formed and serve as arenas for associational ties and ultimately social networks.

The authors in Section I explore the many facets of identity formation, be it cultural, social, political, or religious, traced through the popular media (Macdonald), Shakespearian theatre (Hastrup), nation building (Mach), religion (Webber and Cohen), and the formation of collegial ties (Callan). Section II examines gender agency in a wide variety of cultural contexts, with particular attention to the role of 'muted groups', a conceptual category that Shirley Ardener has deployed to cast light on the subtle, but cumulatively powerful, influence of women and other marginalised groups in bringing about social change. Women's agency sways the resolution of political, economic, or social dilemmas and, as Shirley Ardener (1975) argues, the relationship between dominant and muted groups in any society is always in flux, warranting theoretical enquiry into the interaction of the two and their respective internal dynamics. Thus, authors in Section II consider the agency and collegiality of women in the widely different settings of China (Jaschok and Shui Jingjun), early twentieth-century British feminist struggles (Swaisland), academia in Europe (Kubica and Okely), Southern Africa (Buijs), British Asian families (Loudon and Frankenberg), an English car factory (Moore), and Venice (Sciama).

The first section of this chapter explores aspects of associational relationships between people in public life, drawing from the case-study material presented in the following chapters. Social bonds of compatriotism, friendship, collegial professionalism and group leadership are considered. Thereafter, the relational substratum of these social ties, ethnicity and gender is discussed.

Fashioning Identity: Beneath Surface Appearances

Identity studies of Western societies during the twentieth century have been underpinned by the notion of self-destiny; birthplace, ethnicity, and class do not delimit one's identity. Postmodernist studies have emphasised the multiplicity of roles and the individual's 'divided self'. Both aspects point to the malleability of identity encapsulated in Hastrup's definition (chap. 2): 'identity is the means by which individuals can act consistently and convincingly within multiple plot spaces and change in the process'. The self is composite and – just because it is composite – it is malleable.

Using a 'theatre of action' motif, Hastrup draws attention to the reflexivity of individual identity and social context. The social nature of self and social agency of the individual are in Hastrup's words a 'character dialectic' expressed in individual speech and action, framed by a 'collectively endorsed illusion of society'. Through dialogue people create 'a world of shared understanding', which is transformational at the same time as it is an illusion. Hastrup argues that this comes about through humans sharing the ability to imagine one another. Shakespeare's characters take shape in relation to other characters. For example, honour and reputation are not inner qualities of the individual but rather lie in the recognition of others.

Her reflexivity argument contrasts with the dichotomy between individuality and sociality posited by the political scientists earlier cited. An anthropological perspective stresses the fluidity of individual and collective cultural identities. Social agency takes on multiple purposes and meanings. The political scientists commenting on cultural change see the individual as a maximising decision maker within a fixed cultural frame of reference reacting within a context of narrowing associational ties likely to generate misunderstanding or conflict upon contact (Putnam 1995a; Huntington 1996). In other words, atomistic individuals in hermetically sealed cultures gradually become more socially isolated and politically polarised. Fukuyama (2000), however, identifies a way out. Individuals, he argues, are essentially social beings and, despite the current moral and social degeneration, he predicts reconstruction through 'renorming' and individual acceptance of more social responsibility on the basis of a surge in religious belief and women's reprioritisation of work and family life. Social and moral values, in his view, are cyclical and will eventually become aligned with the political values of Western liberal democracies. This normative political science perspective, infused with the alleged cultural superiority of the West and now so influential, serves to underline the need for more reflected cross-cultural comparison of social agency.

National Compatriots

The study of national cultural cohesion is facilitated by the fact that the creation and perpetuation of nation states are the focus of historical record keeping and living memory. The cultural dimensions of collective identity go beyond the military battles and political power struggles that make their way most readily into the history books. The chapters by Cohen and Mach reveal how national cultural unity is enhanced by a common foe. For the Welsh this was the English, perceived as potential wreckers of the national language and culture (Cohen, chap. 5). In Poland, national cultural integrity was ironically safeguarded by the dual threat of invasion by the Germans as well as by the Russians during the first half of the twentieth century. Both invasions came to pass and the Polish identity endured, but at the cost of sacrificing its multicultural foundations, as argued by Mach (chap. 3). After decades of oppositional politics against German and later Soviet occupation, liberal-minded Poles now struggle to regain a sense of the cultural plurality that was lost on account of these invasions, military occupations, and changes of political frontiers.

Religion frequently merges with national identity. In Poland, Catholicism became a central pillar in the construction of Polishness, both symbolically and materially, in the minds of Poles in their struggle against foreign occupation, particularly during the nineteenth century. In so doing, Catholicism and Polish nationalism often became synonymous, thereby denying the Polishness of non-Catholics, notably Jewish and Lutheran Poles. Mach argues that identity may be context-driven, especially when the balance of political power may be such that the stronger party is able to impose identities on the weaker. Indeed, in the post-Soviet era, Poland faces a Catholic fundamentalism, which posits Poland as the cultural saviour of Europe fighting its liberalism and moral decay, once again undermining the Polish identity of non-Catholics. Cohen (chap. 5) traces how the community-based social values of Nonconformism fanned Welsh nationalism in the mining communities of Wales during and after the Industrial Revolution. The chapel provided an anchor in local societies undergoing a transformation from rural to urban lifestyles. Nonconformist chapel services were conducted in the Welsh language, nurturing the now-famous Welsh oratory and singing. Interestingly, more recently, the Welsh language has experienced a resurgence, whereas Western secular tendencies have dealt a heavy blow to Welsh communities' attendance at Nonconformist chapels. Now, even where chapels provide distinctive physical landmarks in the Welsh countryside, their form and function may be completely changed.

National and religious identities in China, by contrast, are oppositional. Jaschok and Shui (chap. 7) write of the tension that arises when the state refuses to sanction the religious identity of its nationals. China's Muslim population is accorded a 'minority status' and in fact constitutes a 'muted group' within China, along the lines identified by Edwin and Shirley Ardener. This is so even during the recent years of relatively less centralised state control. In the consolidation of the national identity of a people pushed into exile, Webber (chap. 4) shows how Jews' common religious identity and 'peoplehood' have been fostered, in the context of international diaspora and historical memory interpreted by rabbis through ritual observances which encourage and reinforce social apartness. Jewish historical memory entails making sense of a past of repeated persecutions and in particular of a 'holocaust that makes no sense'. The duty to remember is profoundly Jewish. Yet ritualised historical memory presents the world as changeless: it is posited as generating an active relationship with God. For secular or 'lapsed' modern Jews nowadays, however, history becomes a liberating experience, countering the power of the rabbis. The intellectual study of history affords Jews a common collective identity as a historical people, now politically affirmed by the existence of the Israeli state. Under these circumstances, the transnationalism of diaspora Jews can be acknowledged as well as their long-standing bifocal cultural vision, whereby, in addition to their Jewish identity, they are (and were) nationals in their lands of residence, with cultural preferences in food, clothing, daily rhythms, and associational ties dictated by the local environment. This bifocal cultural vision tends to be asymmetrical in favour of locality rather than religion for secular Jews.

Macdonald (chap. 1) provides a contemporary look at the nature of national identity through the comparative analysis of popular do-it-yourself house improvement television programmes in the United Kingdom (*Changing Rooms*) and Germany (*Tapeten-Wechsel*). In her exploration of national similarities, differences, and national stereotypes, she finds that the homogenisation of national culture through TV is evident in the programmes' format but, despite expectations to the contrary, globalised consumption patterns are not reflected in the participants' stylistic choices for their home decoration. The home becomes a metaphor for individual identity. Do-it-yourself decorating is a powerful statement about fashioning identity, at the same time as it embodies national aspirations and politics. German participants insisted on quality craftsmanship and conventional colour schemes, with a strong preference for wood grain surfaces, which Macdonald linked to the importance of forests in German symbolism. Meanwhile, the British programme, on a far smaller budget, relied more on bold colours and paint techniques to create eccentric or whimsical interior designs, whose saving grace may have been that they were made of less durable materials and would eventually have to be altered.

Changing Rooms appeared at the peak of Britain's DIY boom, following Thatcher's policies to encourage individual property ownership with the sell-off of council housing for private purchase. Unique interior designs reinforced the notion that someone's house was uniquely theirs. In Germany, on the other hand, the reunification of the East and West, merging two different national cultures and economic systems, inevitably sparked unease. Criticism of the spread of shoddy production from the East and the decline of (West) German manufacturing standards was one manifestation of this unease. *Tapeten-Wechsel*'s insistence on good craftsmanship and durable materials could be read as a reaction to these broader political and economic fears.

Political Leaders and Participation in Public Life

The construction of national identity is generally recognised as an ongoing historical process, whereas political leadership of nation states as well as other political groupings is commonly associated with the personality and 'leadership qualities' of men as opposed to women in most cultures to the present day. Both Buijs (chap. 10) and Swaisland (chap. 8) document the context and leadership paths of women. Buijs explores the nature of political leadership in patrilineal societies of Southern Africa who accord women ritual leadership roles as mothers or sisters of the male leaders, showing that these women hold far more real decision-making power than their symbolic positions suggest. They command respect from the populace and awe in their ritual role of rainmaking. Colonial officialdom was uncomfortable with their presence and attempted to dampen their influence. Despite these attempts, queen mothers and ritual sisters remain valued authority figures in many Southern African ethnic communities.

Swaisland (chap. 8) traces the background and career trajectories of some of Britain's early feminists, including Mary Kingsley, Florence Nightingale, and Jane

Waterstone, rebels against Victorian values of female subordination and economic dependence. Interestingly, most of them had close relationships with their fathers, who encouraged their access to education and careers. Their pursuit of independent work lives in the fields of education and health provided role models for later generations to follow and helped pave the way for the women suffragettes' demand for voting rights at the turn of the nineteenth century. Women's participation in the Boer War as nurses and administrative support gave their labour-force contribution more acceptance, setting the stage for their active labour involvement during the First World War. Swaisland stresses that although these early feminists achieved significant strides in education, educated women were not able to easily acquire jobs other than those in the health and education sectors until after the Second World War. Wars can dramatise the importance of female employment to the society as a whole.

In several other chapters, political leadership opportunities are denied women largely on the basis of their familial roles. Cohen (chap. 5) indicates that while women were the backbone of the Welsh Nonconformist chapel congregation, they were not afforded leadership roles other than as members of sisterhood support committees. Jaschok and Shui (chap. 7) indicate that Chinese women's marginalisation in politics and religion spurred them to establish women's mosques, where they could exercise female autonomy. Contrary to expectations, Islam in China uniquely granted women their own space to worship and their own female religious leaders. Loudon and Frankenberg's case study (chap. 11) of a young British Asian woman whose life was transformed when she became blind shows how her disability gave her more scope for participation in public life. Her family abandoned their attempts to find a suitable husband, freeing her to pursue further education and a career of her choosing.

Work Colleagues and Research Informants

Callan (chap. 6) draws our attention to a hitherto neglected field, the anthropology of colleagueship. She notes that colleagueship is both emotionally satisfying and culturally significant while being occupationally contingent and functional. By definition, collegial relations are vested with cordiality and positive outcomes. The issue of hierarchy and competition at the workplace and the antagonisms that they may engender can be smoothed over by reference to colleagueship. The salutation 'Dear colleague' resolves the tensions of hierarchy between different professional hierarchies. Furthermore, colleagueship gives co-workers the means to suggest professional interaction outside the workplace or beyond normal working hours and job descriptions. Alternatively, it is a tool for constructing work relations with others outside one's own workplace, as illustrated by Callan's personal experience of working in an international agency that was building an emergent group of professional experts with wide-ranging language and cultural differences. The bonhomie of colleagueship, symbolic as it was, nonetheless gave the group a stimulating, egalitarian atmosphere, encouraging the flow of information, ideas, and work output. Collegial relations are ambiguously poised on the cusp of cordial friendship and normative professionalism.

Jaschok and Shui (chap. 7) chart the nature of their collegial ties in the course of academic enquiry about Chinese women's mosques. Coming from markedly different social, political, and professional backgrounds, they found that their respective vantage points, skills, and contacts complemented each other. Nonetheless, there was always a need for them to consciously structure their collegial relationship in order to avoid allowing outside political and economic forces to shape their collaboration into one of hierarchical imbalance, as is too often the case in First and Third World collaborative research.

Are women more amenable to collegial relations of collaboration than men? Many of the chapters touch on the widely varying evidence of women's collegial ties. Kubica (chap. 9) follows the career path of the remarkable Maria Czaplicka, whose mastery of languages and encounters with cultures as a young Polish anthropologist did not accord with the strictures of the conservative, male-dominated, ivory towers of England at the beginning of the twentieth century. Kubica's analysis of Czaplicka's subjectivity reveals much about her collegial ties at a time when being a female anthropologist was very rare. In her fieldwork settings and working professionally amongst men, she was treated as an 'honorary man' but paradoxically without the camaraderie, opportunities, honours, and privileges normally accorded men in these contexts. Her suicide at the age of 37 may have been linked to the loneliness and ambiguity of her work position and lack of collegial relations. Kubica sees Czaplicka's androgynous persona as a logical outcome of her desire to succeed in a male professional world, in which emotion was sublimated to reason.

Okely (chap. 14) encounters a similar male-controlled ivory tower setting over sixty years later. As a female anthropologist, she contended with male colleagues, many of whom resented her attempts to put gender on the curriculum, research British subcultures rather than far-flung societies, and experiment with new lecturing styles. Her status as a woman with a male partner pursuing his own career elsewhere marginalised her from university housing opportunities and continually shifted her career prospects in unpredicted directions. Okely tells her story with humour and irony, drawing on the numerous collegial ties she has had with women and men through her career, both stimulating and comforting, which have triggered innovation and a sense of fulfilment in her work.

Moving away from the hierarchical pecking order of universities, Moore (chap. 12) examines the managerial hierarchy of a car factory, highlighting the collegial relations between factory workers that she directly experienced in her participant-observation fieldwork as a factory worker. Collegial ties amongst factory workers were solidified by the commonality of an 'us versus them' perspective. As the factory management persistently attempted to improve lines of communication between staff and management with newsletters, meetings, and channels for complaint, the workers continually tried to distance themselves from the management's gaze. Collegiality was ensured amongst factory workers by shared problems: the speed of the factory assembly line and the factory's demanding product quality controls. Nonetheless, there was a wariness on the part of women towards their male colleagues. Most of the women were loath to attract the sexual attention of their male colleagues. They chose to present themselves dowdily for work even though their verbal interaction with their female colleagues indicated keen interest in fashion (see also Barnes and Eicher 1994).

A variant of collegial ties, peculiar to social scientists especially anthropologists, is the relationship between researcher and informant. Sciama (chap. 13) was confronted with a dilemma when a student reported that her main informants were her mother as well as family members and friends. While her male colleagues disapproved, Sciama was confident that such informants would afford ready rapport and opportunities for data gathering, ultimately providing more penetrating insights. Loudon and Frankenberg (chap. 11) explore the subject/object focus of research and the transformative relationships that occur around this relational abstraction. Their collaboration began as a relationship between student and professor, which transformed into a working tie between two colleagues. As a medical doctor, Loudon was a direct participant in the healthcare process. So too, Loudon and Frankenberg's subject/object of study, an Asian woman adjusting to recent blindness, was in fact a participant in the study rather than an object or subject. Loudon and Frankenberg recorded her observations and insights over the course of the adjustment process. Acquiring a disability gave her social autonomy, escape from an enforced marriage, and a new-found freedom to study and seek a career, which could ultimately transform her relationship with her researchers from research participant to one of collegiality.

Callan (chap. 6), citing Hastrup (1987), considers the concept of researcher and subjectness from the perspective of participant-observation fieldwork, noting that the anthropologist's understanding of a newly encountered culture reaches a watershed when the anthropologist herself becomes a 'subject' in the eyes of her 'subjects'. This mutual subjectivity allows for exchange of meaningful information and deeper understanding. The complementarity embedded in Jaschok and Shui's collaboration (chap. 7) afforded them a 'fluid' field in which the boundaries between subject and observer became indistinguishable. They adopted a participatory research approach in which ongoing dialogue between themselves and with local people generated knowledge and understanding. Local people were as much analysts as subjects in this discourse.

Friends

Many of the chapters in this book self-consciously explore the subjectivity of anthropologists' interaction with their fieldwork, teaching, and professional world. Interspersed throughout these chapters is evidence of the serendipity of friendship in anthropologists' field and home settings. Indeed, anthropologists, as travellers across space and between cultures, may be in one of the most enviable settings for gaining not just the acquaintance, knowledge, and understanding of the places and people they visit but also the environment for 'falling into' friendships of mutual support, often of an enduring nature. It is in this light that Shirley Ardener and Margaret Niger Thomas's research in Cameroon during the 1990s 'meandered' into the rewarding path of serendipity, where their mutual trust and companionship provided the opportunity for delightful and unique research discovery. Sciama (chap. 13) highlights her friendship with her informant and the personal relationships that follow with other members of the informant's family over the decades. Callan (chap. 7) observes the enigma of friendship's two-way exchange of sentiment and meaning in which the meanings imparted to the friendship are elusive.

Happenstance has an important part to play in sparking friendship but anthropological field findings suggest that friendship is most apt to occur between people sharing either the same gender, ethnic group, class or age group – or in some cases religion. On the factory assembly line Moore observed (chap. 12), women of different ethnic groups compatibly interacted with one another, but social clusters during lunch and tea breaks tended to be mono-ethnic in composition. Cohen (chap. 5) writes of the tight-knit communities of Welsh Nonconformists, who saw each other as extended family members. They spent prayer time together and also sought to associate with one another in their wider daily lives. They chose their friends from their own ethnic group, class, and religion. There was also a preference to keep their commercial transactions amongst themselves. Nonconformists chose to shop at a butchery, bakery, or grocery owned by a fellow Nonconformist. The Welsh chapel thus functioned as a centre for networking and, in some cases, facilitated information gathering about employment opportunities during a period when jobs were scarce.

Weaving Networks

The preceding section has discussed individual and collective identity construction, exploring various categories of non-familial associational relationships. This section examines aspects of how these associational ties link to one another to form network patterns.

As the global mobility of people, commodities, and information has intensified over the last decade, diasporic peoples, hybrid cultures, and multilocational identities that bridge geographical space have kindled anthropologists' interest in networks (e.g., Appadurai 1996; Brah 1998; Bryceson and Vuorela 2002). Network theory is an area of interest for social scientists more generally, particularly geographers, sociologists, demographers and political scientists (e.g., Cohen 1997; Castells 2000; Buchanan 2002). Given anthropologists' sensitivity to cultural difference and the coherence of individual cultures, networks pose an epistemological challenge with their tendency to merge rather than accentuate cultural difference. It is worth asking what distinguishes the anthropologist's approach to social networks as opposed to those of other social science disciplines. This edited collection provides theoretical and empirical evidence of anthropological approaches to networks.

One of the major insights into the operation of networks in recent decades relates to the importance of 'weak ties' for extending network range and flexibility (Granovetter 1973). The strength of bonds between individuals is not uniform. Some bonds may be very frequent and strong whereas others may be far weaker and infrequent. Granovetter recognised a recurrent pattern in social networking. There is a tendency for an inverse relationship between the strength and number of bonds any one person has. Most people bond strongly to one another in clusters – based usually on age, ethnic group, gender, or religion, as noted above – but these clustered associational ties can be isolating in the absence of 'weak ties', namely between people who are mobile and gregarious and whose contacts are more numerous and varied, although their interaction is less frequent and hence deemed 'weaker'. The weak ties are vital to the connectivity of the overall network. Any one cluster constitutes a restrictive circle of people without the bridge provided by 'weak ties' capable of linking one cluster with another.

In the Oxford academic community, Shirley Ardener somehow manages to combine strong bonding within the gender, ethnic, and African clusters she belongs to with that key role of being a vital link between clusters. Social connectivity and intellectual inspiration amongst her colleagues have been Shirley's hallmark. Yet, unlike so many successful networkers who revel in the range and diversity of their contacts, Shirley emphasises the importance of the bonds she has cultivated within her collegial clusters. Her numerous between-cluster ties, which link so many people to one another, have greatly enhanced network connectivity in her chosen fields of interest.

Anthropologists are especially attuned to horizontal linkages. Their professional interest in remote pre-industrial communities has no doubt sensitised them to small tribal communities, many marked by inclusiveness and egalitarianism. Postmodernism has further enhanced anthropologists' interest in linkages but made them defensive about their traditional search for 'the exotic other'. Amidst anthropology's recent emphasis on cultural interconnectivity, we may now be witnessing a convergence of disciplinary focus or an inversion between anthropologists and non-anthropologists. Whatever the case, the relevance of the anthropological perspective for other disciplines is readily apparent.

Political scientists, sociologists and management and administration specialists have generally approached networks from the perspective of vertical hierarchies, tracing formal and informal chains of command in government bureaucracies, military organisations, corporations, etc., while largely ignoring the associational ties of civil society and everyday life. Now, however, non-anthropologists in the social sciences are increasingly focused on horizontal associational ties, which they see as the basic building blocks or essential glue of society (e.g., Fukuyama 1995; Putnam 1995a). Why have they turned their analytical attention to the close-knit, strong bonds of small clusters within the community? Putnam's concern was that these bonds were dissolving and causing alienation in the society at large. Nonetheless, the findings of Western security analysts suggesting that terrorist cells are small, strongly bonded clusters of a semi-autonomous nature, with weak connecting linkages, may ironically dispel this worry.[2]

Some of the case studies in this collection document people's desire to sabotage hierarchy and propagate associational ties on a smaller, more close-knit scale. Moore (chap. 12) describes the subtle ways that car workers undermined the factory management's attempts at managing them through 'participation'. They could ignore management's attempts at control because they had no career aspirations within the firm. In a period of low unemployment, their jobs were dispensable if they became dissatisfied with any aspect of them. Sciama (chap. 13) found that women from the outlying islands of Venice have been actively seeking new friends and acquaintances in the city. By extending their social networks, they have been able to bypass or overcome old barriers of hierarchy and social class. On initiating her research, she endeavoured to avoid being associated with any patron, knowing that building good rapport with her informants depended on horizontal egalitarian association with them.

However, the dichotomisation of horizontal as opposed to vertical networks is perhaps overstated and seen as too static by social scientists generally. Swaisland's case study of early British feminists (chap. 8) demonstrates how they realised their career goals as path-breaking women and built viable networks that helped win political voting rights. Women's acquisition of education at this time illustrates horizontal and vertical networking. Education provided the trellis upon which women's educational opportunities, their careers, and political activism spread.

In juxtaposing the strong bonds of the small group with the weak bonds linking groups, there is always the complicating factor of multiple identities that individuals hold and conflicting bonds that pull them in different directions. This is clearly illustrated in Cohen's biography (chap. 5) of Llywelyn Jones, Welsh chapel minister and personnel manager for a British oil firm. As unemployment deepened in his community, Llywelyn Jones felt compromised, wedged between the obligations he had to help his chapel members as opposed to his accountability to his administrative superiors in London and professional duty to ensure the firm's efficient management and profitability. A very far cry from the moral universe of Llywelyn Jones, suicide bombers nonetheless face not dissimilar dilemmas of identity and loyalty. They are likely to be torn between their cell membership and the bonds they have with their respective families and communities of origin, who rarely have any inkling of their terrorist associations.

Imagining Common Ground: Ethnic and Religious Collective Identities

Mach (chap. 3) considers the institutionalisation of Polish nationalism during the nineteenth century, when Poland did not exist as a sovereign state, and Webber (chap. 4) provides insights into the two millennia when Jews lived exclusively as a diasporic people and yet preserved a common identity. In both cases, identities were constructed on cultural foundations of a more or less religious nature. Cultural diversity was therefore threatening to these identities. Polish nationalism's allegiance to Catholicism pertained to a subset of the national population, alienating the rest. Over the centuries, rabbis had woven an elaborate ritual tradition based on key historical memory markers that served to reinforce Jewish identity within the cultural community. Emphasis on the theology of exile further detracted from identification with the nation state where they resided. Contrary to political scientists' notions of cultural network association as horizontal, both of these examples were hierarchical in nature, presided over by church and synagogue authorities. Before the current secularisation, rabbis cultivated a sense of alienation underlined by a notion of being surrounded by heathen impurity. In Poland, Catholic clergy and other nationalists popularised the theme of Poland's martyrdom for Europe and its ultimate capacity for redeeming Europe from the clutches of decadent Western liberalism.

Language is and has always been central to the formation of ethnic identity. The commonality of language generates a strong sense of solidarity in the face of language plurality. Cohen (chap. 5) documents the frustration experienced by those wanting to assert their identity as Welsh speakers who are hindered by work and school contexts where they are obliged to speak English. The forums in which Welsh was spoken became highly significant culturally. 'True religion' could only be taught in Welsh. People who lost their ability to speak Welsh or children who did not use the language sufficiently to make them proficient were marked as having lost their Welsh identity.

Increasingly, consumer preference has become a way of asserting one's ethnic identity. Whereas before clothing and housing styles were usually dictated by the ready availability of materials for producing such items, now, with the globalisation of consumer markets and the juxtaposition of different styles of material life in the minds of consumers through foreign travel, people can consciously exert their national identity through their sense of style. Macdonald's comparison of German and British consumers (chap. 1) shows that, even in a trans-European TV format, striking differences emerge, reflecting Germans' insistence on good craftsmanship and quality of materials as opposed to British 'expressive individuation' conveyed through bright colours and paint techniques.

Ethnic identities continually change. Negotiating history and historical memory may be a key aspect of redefining collective identities, even if technically there are many different types of historical principles involved: linear versus cyclical notions of understanding time, beliefs in the uniqueness of events versus the generalised patterns they represent, and the concern with both cause and meaning (Tonkin et al. 1989; Baumann 2002). But the use of historicisation, as in the case of modern Jewish identities discussed by Webber (chap. 4), is a good example of how such redefinitions can come about, using a completely new kind of historical principle, which is absorbed into contemporary Jewish culture.

Hastrup (chap. 2) makes a similar point commenting on the role of the Renaissance in attributing individuals with the power to shape their own destinies and influence history. The role of history in the reshaping of identities is an issue that Mach highlights (chap. 3). Under communism, minorities in Poland were presented in official contexts as survivors of pre-socialist historical formations; it was politically expedient to forget the Holocaust and maintain negative stereotypes of Jews as anti-Polish. What has happened since 1989 is a public process of reinterpreting Poland's national history as a basis for working out Poland's new identities, especially vis-à-vis Europe. Interestingly, the 'most spectacular change', to quote Mach, is the rapid growth of Polish interest in Jews – not necessarily to learn about Jews as such but for Poles to better understand their own Polish history. This is, of course, a liberal project; right-wing Poles see Polishness in danger and want to return to past simplicities and straight binary oppositions between essentialised ethnic groups. Thus today, to the extent that Polish identity is now seen within the framework of a multicultural society, the key marker is the contestation and debate over history. This national exercise illustrates what Hastrup (chap. 2) terms the 'philosophy of imagination', in which members of a collectivity explore their similarities and differences in the search for identity with 'all social worlds dependent on illusion for their wholeness'.

Finally, there are instances when ethnic identity is subordinated to class identification, a situation described by Moore (chap. 12) in her car factory case study. Workers, regardless of their ethnic affiliation, felt solidarity against the management's work output demands and rebuffed the German management's attempts to introduce a participatory style of management.

Trials and Triumphs of the Intrepid: Women's Gender Identity in the Twentieth Century

Several chapters in this volume confront the historical, cultural, and experiential outcomes for those seeking to move beyond the boundaries of gender ascription. Swaisland (chap. 8) shows how early twentieth-century British feminists started redefining women's occupational prospects through their insistence on greater formal education. Women were eventually allowed into key professions such as nursing, teaching, and medicine. Swaisland asks if the two thousand women who applied for teaching and nursing positions in South Africa during the Boer War were motivated by patriotism or simply a shortage of vocational outlets in Britain. In effect, these intrepid women were able to exploit the 'elsewhere' for careers beyond the domesticity of being a full-time wife. Her chapter documents the dramatic changes that took place during the first half of the twentieth century. Well into the mid-twentieth century some professions, including the civil service and some medical positions, were barred to married women. Those single women in these posts had to give up their professions upon marriage. When there were no formal restrictions, informal ones remained in place, as Okely's chapter reveals.

Kubica (chap. 9) explores the biography and work of Maria Czaplicka, the Polish contemporary of Malinowski, both of whom moved to England to study at the London School of Economics, but Czaplicka, constrained by the mores of the time, met with a far different fate from that of Malinowski. She strove to break free as an individual agent 'and yet remain anchored ... so as not to be discarded as mad'. The Western Enlightenment privileged the rational over the emotional, associating men with the former and women with the latter. Hastrup (chap. 2) argues that Shakespeare selects this historical period when 'individuals were attributed with the power to shape their own destinies' to enact his plays, pitting passion against reason. Kubica (chap. 9) describes how Czaplicka was fascinated with the problems of sex, love, and corporeality, viewing them in terms of a Cartesian body/mind dichotomy. Believing that emotion must be suppressed in favour of reason, Czaplicka became a model for androgyny, trying to avoid identification with femininity, which she feared would marginalise her in the public professional domain. Czaplicka's biography bears witness to an individual striving for innovation and for the professionalisation of women in anthropology to the point of personal tragedy. Whereas she could venture to Arctic Siberia for an extended period, it seems she could not survive the marginalisation afforded an 'intrepid' woman back in a British university.

There are parallels with the position of the female academic in the 1970s universities described by Okely (chap. 14). In early twentieth-century Britain, the female academic was seen as a sexless bluestocking, an image that persisted through the 1970s. The privileging of reason did not mean desexualising male academics, only females. Hilary Rose (1994) documents how this dichotomy persists amongst women scientists, who must appear gender-free and suppress all emotion at suspected exclusion.

The chapters by Swaisland, Kubica and Okely address differing historical and cultural contexts where women have attempted and sometimes achieved escape from prevalent definitions of womanhood through education. Like de Beauvoir, it seems that Czaplicka may have been downwardly mobile and without sufficient wealth for a dowry. Whatever the case, both women had to choose between extended education or marriage. This stark choice was in effect perpetuated in traditional collegiate universities, as illustrated in Okely's chapter and case studies of Cambridge and Oxford by Ardener and Sciama (see Ardener and Callan 1984).

The category of wife as opposed to sister and/or self-chosen spinster is found to be associated not only with Western academia but also with exported colonial systems in patrilineal societies, where women, treated as 'outsiders', were important mainly for their role as mothers of future leaders. Buijs (chap. 10) draws attention to the usually ignored political power and significance of the sisters and daughters of rulers in traditional Southern African societies. The political influence of headwomen and female chiefs resonates with the political prominence of women in South Africa today. Although it might be argued by some that influence is never the same as formal power, it is significant that the colonial authorities and missionaries were disturbed by the power relationship between African brother and sister in view of the prevailing Western notion of women's proper place in the family as that of wife.

The threat of the sister with hereditary political powers as opposed to a wife who owes her position to selection by a man has poignant parallels with the position of the spinster woman academic. She is presumed to be autonomous rather than individually selected by one man and controlled within a male-dominated power structure. Like the sister Buijs describes, she threatens the western European patriarchal tradition. Wives, on the other hand, without the autonomy accorded by birthright or educational qualifications, are dependents, subordinate to their husbands.

But the struggle for women's public and professional identity goes beyond the individual. Women consciously or unconsciously have worked together. In Callan's discussion of collegiality she refers to the negotiation of identities 'under construction' and the 'double vision/divided self', i.e., the observer self subordinated to engaged actor. In a coalescing world, she describes the very newness of the category and its rhetoric, which enable individuals to experience solidarity with each other, in opposition to the usual contrasts of language, personal occupational background, political culture, position in education, privilege, gender and age. In so doing, ethnic identities and nationalities are negotiated in new situations, especially where, as in the cases she describes, there is an absence of symbolic systems characteristic of mature organisations and established communities of practice, showing how in the real world the bridging of differences and building of solidarity are actually undertaken. Jaschok and Shui (chap. 7) provide a concrete example in China. Similarly, Loudon and Frankenberg (chap. 11) illustrate this, although in the case they document identity springs from unexpected and what might otherwise be considered tragic material circumstances.

Conclusion

Identity and network, the central themes of this book, have gained renewed significance in our global world of intensified cultural exchange, collision and recomposition. The chapters that follow were written to celebrate Shirley Ardener's contribution to the anthropological study of gender and ethnic identity and the intricate collegial networking she has engendered over the last four decades. The authors are friends and colleagues of Shirley Ardener, who readily and gratefully admit to Shirley's intellectual and social stimulus for their work. The 'Afterwords' of this book provide several reminiscences from her colleagues and outline the fruits of her creative energy – her numerous publications and institution-building activities.

Notes

1. This introduction reflects extensive discussions about the thematic content of this edited collection between Judith Okely, Jonathan Webber, and myself. I am grateful for their insights but take full responsibility for all of the chapter's shortcomings.
2. For example, see 'Comment and Analysis: The Ordinary Bombers', *New Scientist*, 23 July 2005, p. 18.

References

Appadurai, A. 1996. *Modernity at Large: Cultural Dimensions of Globalization*, Minneapolis: University of Minnesota Press.
Ardener, S. (ed.) 1975. *Perceiving Women*, London: Malaby Press.
Ardener, S. and H. Callan (eds) 1984. *The Incorporated Wife*, London: Croom Helm.
Barnes, R. and J. Eicher (eds) 1994. *Dress and Gender: Making and Meaning*, Oxford: Berg Publishers.
Baumann, G. 2002. 'Collective Identity as a Dual Discursive Construction: Dominant v. Democratic Discourses of Culture and the Negotiation of Historical Memory', in H. Friese (ed.), *Identities: Time, Difference, and Boundaries*, New York: Berghahn Books, pp. 189–200.
Brah, A. 1998. *Cartographies of Diaspora: Contesting Identities*, London: Routledge.
Bryceson, D.F. and U. Vuorela (eds) 2002. *The Transnational Family: New European Frontiers and Global Networks*, Oxford: Berg.
Buchanan, M. 2002. *Small World: Uncovering Nature's Hidden Networks*, London: Phoenix.
Castells, E. 2000 (orig. 1996). *The Rise of the Network Society*, Oxford: Blackwell.
Cohen, R. 1997. *Global Diasporas: An Introduction, Seattle*: University of Washington Press.
Fukuyama, F. 1995. *Trust: The Social Virtues and the Creation of Prosperity*, New York: Free Press.
——— 2000. *The Great Disruption: Human Nature and the Reconstitution of Social Order*, London: Profile Books.
Granovetter, M. 1973. 'The Strength of Weak Ties', *American Journal of Sociology* 78, pp. 1360–80.
Hastrup, K. 1987. 'Fieldwork among Friends: Ethnographic Exchange within the Northern Civilisation', in A. Jackson (ed.), *Anthropology at Home*, London and New York: Tavistock.
Huntington, S. 1996. *The Clash of Civilizations and the Remaking of World Order*, London: Simon & Schuster.
Putnam, R.D. 1995a. 'Bowling Alone: America's Declining Social Capital', *Journal of Democracy* 6 (1), pp. 65–78.
——— 1995b. 'Tuning In, Tuning Out: The Strange Disappearance of Social Capital in America', *PS: Political Science and Politics* 27 (4), pp. 665–83.

Rose, H. 1994. *Love, Power and Knowledge: Towards a Feminist Transformation of the Sciences*, Boston: Polity Press.
Tonkin, E., M. McDonald and M. Chapman (eds) 1989. *History and Ethnicity*, London and New York: Routledge (ASA Monographs, 27).

PART I
FASHIONING IDENTITIES

1

Changing Cultures, Changing Rooms: Fashioning Identities and Anthropological Research

Sharon Macdonald

Moving across and between cultures is at the heart of anthropology. Ethnography is an inherently mobile enterprise, involving the ethnographer literally moving across space, over time, and between the relatively familiar and unfamiliar. Although the idea of 'multi-sited fieldwork' has become fashionable recently, good anthropology has always entailed a degree of multi-sitedness, even if some of those sites might be called 'home' and some might be encountered vicariously. Good anthropological training entails learning about many peoples and parts of the world and going to seminars beyond geographical specialisms. The themed seminar and the edited collection, in which scholars are brought together to comparatively discuss sites that they know in depth, are particularly important forums and formats in anthropology, allowing as they do for the possibility of sensitive appraisal of commonality and difference and the developing of the 'meso-level' theorising at which anthropology excels.

Shirley Ardener's work has been exemplary in its recognition and realisation of the cross-cultural. Her own work has invariably contained sensitive and provocative comparative observations, as, for example, her superb research on sexual insult and female militancy, which considers not only a range of African examples but also cases from the Western women's movement (Ardener 1975b). And her quite remarkable editorial corpus – in which most volumes are the outcome of a participative themed seminar, allowing the contributors to refine their work in relation to that of other presentations – is evidence of collaborative anthropological work at its best. These volumes are multi-sited in a way that no one ethnographer could hope to achieve; and they are 'cross-cultural' in that they move far beyond being a collection of diverse instances to exciting speculation on the nature and complexities of similarity and difference.

In many ways, these volumes effortlessly deal with a subject that is currently the source of much consternation and debate in some parts of anthropology: that is, the question of how far it is possible or valid to talk in terms of 'culture' and to identify 'difference'. In a world of increased travel, movement, and mixing, how is an anthropologist to go about her task? How can we try to understand variability and difference without reifying these into fixed, bounded, homogeneous 'cultures'? And how can we be 'cross-cultural' without absolute cultural demarcations? All of this is also made still more challenging by our awareness of cultural change and its apparent rapidity. Where, and at what, is the anthropologist to look in the fast flow of fashion and innovation? Moreover, what are the implications for the notion of 'ethnicity'? Can we use 'ethnic' labels any more, and what should we expect them to be indicative of?

These are questions that I have also struggled with (and sometimes decided to sweep to one side) in my own work. In my fieldwork in the Scottish Hebrides, it was often hard to know whether what I was describing should be accounted for as 'Hebridean', 'local', 'Scottish', or even, perhaps, 'British', 'North European', or (most non-emic) 'Euro-American'; and, in my current work in Germany, I often struggle to decide whether to write, *inter alia*, 'German', 'former West German', 'North Bavarian', or 'Franconian'. When the individuals with whom we are working in these places may themselves identify as being from numerous other places, the difficulty is compounded. It is worth pointing out at the start, however, that these difficulties are not all equal. Talking of 'Germans' tends to feel especially risky, partly, no doubt, because Germany was politically and culturally divided for a chunk of the twentieth century, though also, paradoxically, because it is simultaneously easy to talk of 'Germans', so recognisable are their stereotypes. With relatives and friends (German as well as English), we readily fall into observations of particularities of 'the Germans' but, perhaps perversely, this makes it feel more problematic to do so as an anthropologist. Moreover, in a political context in which Germany tends to welcome the idea of an integrated Europe, pointing out 'Germanness' can seem like an affront.

In contrast, 'Scot' is easier to use because, unlike 'German', those who self-identify with this nomination generally want it to be acknowledged and even celebrated. Yet, in other ways, it is equally tricky. My own life experience and my anthropological work have made me acutely aware of different kinds of 'Scots', of semi-, lapsed, resurrected, and reinvented Scottishness, and of those who in some ways are quintessentially 'Scottish' but nevertheless wary of referring to themselves as such. And, while 'English' and 'British' are acknowledged to be particularly elusive categories, fieldwork in an official British institution – the National Museum of Science and Industry (London's Science Museum) – raised fewest difficulties for me in writing up, because the salience of the national label was taken as a given by those working there, even while it was consciously configured to include various 'cultures' with different histories.[1]

In this chapter, my aim is to explore some of these questions and observations further in order to discuss the relationship between culture, difference, and ethnicity, and to think about the implications of this for our research and writing on these subjects today. One of the things that makes Shirley such good company, as well as an insightful anthropologist, is her observations of, and curiosity about, everyday practices and popular culture. She has constantly embraced the serendipitous and followed leads thrown up by experience. Inspired by this, as well as by some of her particular writing (in this case, especially *Women and Space*), I have chosen to focus my discussion on an example encountered unexpectedly during my own recent fieldwork – beyond the 'official' boundaries of the topic that I was focusing upon. This was a television programme produced for Bavarian Television (Bayerisches Fernsehen) called *Tapeten-Wechsel*, literally 'Changing Wallpaper' and figuratively 'Changing Scenery' or 'Changing Surroundings'. Explicitly modelled on a BBC programme, *Changing Rooms*, the Bavarian version was at one level 'the same programme' and at another intriguingly different.

Changing Rooms

The BBC's *Changing Rooms* (produced by the independent company Bazal Productions) was launched in 1995 and rapidly became one of Britain's most popular early evening shows, regularly attracting ten million viewers and moving in early 2004 from BBC2 to BBC1, a marker of having attained thoroughly mainstream status. Such is the possible rapidity of media cycles, however, that it was then axed later that same year (see the Postscript below). It is acknowledged to have been the 'market leader' in 'lifestyle' television programming and to have spawned a whole gamut of similar programmes in Britain (Spittle 2002) – house and garden makeover series (such as *Home Front* and *Home Front in the Garden*) and personal makeovers (e.g., *Looking Good*, in which couples effect a kind of sartorial change on their partners) – as well as adaptations and imitations abroad, the format being sold to twenty countries (http://news.bbc.co.uk/2/hi/uk_news/magazine/4034503.stm). In 1998, Bavarian Television (or, more specifically, Gruner + Jahr Funk und Fernsehproduktion für den Bayerischen Rundfunk), with full acknowledgements to the BBC, launched its own version, *Tapeten-Wechsel*. Like its British forebear, the Bavarian *Changing Rooms* has become highly popular, reaching a record market share of almost 20 per cent in 2002 (http://www.medienkontor.de/2003/01/06/meldung01.html), though it does not seem to be part of such an extensive genre of similar programmes as in Britain and has not spun off the same paraphernalia of linked websites and books with DIY advice and titles such as *Jazz Up your Junk* (by Linda Barker, one of the designers on the British show). Nor have the interior designers who work on the show achieved the kind of cult status of many of their English counterparts, the latter appearing in numerous advertisements and magazine articles and having become sufficiently well known to be the subject of television impressionists. Interestingly, only the Bavarian 'handyman', Bastl Wastl (*basteln* meaning to make things, to handcraft), has come anywhere close to this generalised fame.

It is, of course, far from unusual for television programmes to travel across national or ethnic boundaries, and there is a growing body of studies of the ways in which the same cultural product may be received in different places, one of the earliest examples of this being Laura Bohannon's wonderful account of trying to explain *Hamlet* to the Tiv (Bowen 1966). The best works in this field, like Bohannon's, have been those that go beyond the study of the direct moment of reception – the viewing – into a broader understanding of other facets of life. Not surprisingly, this is a field in which anthropologists are particularly well placed to offer illuminating accounts (see, for example, contributions to Askew and Wilk 2002). Neither is it unusual that a television programme format will be adapted for different viewing publics. Programmes such as *Who Wants to Be a Millionaire?* and *Big Brother* have also been widely transnationally transported, and have somewhat different rules in different places, as well as their own locally distinctive programmes on the same basic model. The Netherlands-born *Big Brother*, for example, has been the inspiration for a variation in France in which literary figures are imprisoned together in a chateau, one typewriter between them. So very French, you could not make it up – but somebody did, and successfully sold the rights. In this way, programmes are adapted or created by drawing on ideas about the cultural market and, in the process, relaying these back to viewers, concentrated and amplified.

It is through such processes that distinctive identities are, if not created, at least reinforced. Cultural products like these are stories being told about ourselves, much of the time without us really noticing the fact. Categories such as 'German' or 'English' are ever present, even if not explicitly spoken, and thus are available for filling with various content (McDonald 1993). The process is itself, as Lévi-Strauss's concept of *bricolage* primes us to notice, rather like that employed by these home-improvement programmes. A basic structure, in this case the shell of a room and its contents, is altered, adapted and reordered in order to 'update' it and present it anew, while at the same time trying to capture and express the identity of its owners, making use of elements of the old, but perhaps 'jazzed up' and teasing at the limits of the acceptable. Yet, and here is where cultural difference comes in, the ways in which this is done may vary, if only subtly, as we can see in the case of the British and Bavarian versions of *Changing Rooms/Changing Wallpaper*.

The Format

The basic idea of the programme is that neighbours swap houses/flats and, with the help of a designer and the shared handyman (Bastl Wastl or the British 'Handy Andy'), redecorate one of the rooms. This always involves two people, generally a mixed-gender couple (though sometimes other combinations, such as flatmates, a gay couple, or a mother and daughter), from each household making the swap. They are not allowed back to their own homes until two days later, by which time the work should be complete.

Part of the dramatic tension of the programme relies on labouring against the clock: will they complete in time? Typically, though more so in the British case, things get increasingly frenzied as the deadline approaches. The other main element of dramatic tension concerns whether the owners will like what has happened to their home. Here, the neighbours are given a difficult task, that of trying to safeguard the taste and identity of their friends, sometimes in the face of what seems like (again, especially in the British case) rather irresponsible aesthetic experimentalism on the part of the designers (who have never actually met the people whose home they are redesigning). During the programme, cuts move from one house to the other, and we see the transformation of the spaces, the labour involved, the competition for Andy's/Bastl's time and talents, the worries of the neighbours over whether they are doing the right thing and, occasionally, their confrontation with the designer, the hassles, disasters, and triumphs.[2] After the deadline has arrived, designers are interviewed on how well they think things have gone, on how much they have actually spent and whether this is within budget, on their 'best bargains' and favourite items, and whether they think that the owners will like it.[3]

The denouement involves the programme presenter leading each couple blindfolded back to their own room, where all at last is revealed. In both the British and Bavarian versions, owners are typically nervous about seeing what has become of their space and possessions, and they sometimes have to be encouraged to remove their blindfolds. Watching the expression on their faces as they first see the transformation is a televisual high point, the viewer struggling to decipher what they really think as they almost invariably exclaim, 'Oh my God!' or, in Germany, '*Wahnsinn!*' (literally, madness). Sometimes tears and disappointment follow, but most often pleasure is expressed, either enthusiastically or more cautiously, coupled with comments about particular items. The programme ends, in a ritual marking both spatial change (Ardener 1981: 21) and the resolution of any conflict, with the pairs of neighbours reunited and sharing a glass of champagne. (Though Bastl, true to his Bavarian stereotype, sticks to beer.)

Differences

In some respects, the mapping of *Tapeten-Wechsel* onto *Changing Rooms* is very precise. Thus, not only do they share the basic formats, but there are other similarities, such as in the rhyming names given to the handymen – Handy Andy and Bastl Wastl – and the fact that both have marked regional accents (London, Munich). The basic 'social maps', as Shirley calls them (Ardener 1981) – that is, the structured hierarchies of relativities of dominance and muting that are played out (ibid.: 13) – are the same in both programmes. Thus the couples are equivalents, owning similar properties. During the makeover, the handyman and the presenter are the only ones permitted to cross the boundary between the two houses, moving through the temporarily redefined public and private and thus acquiring knowledge that the other parties would dearly like to have. The handyman acts as a kind of ritual clown or jester figure (made evident through the rhyming name and strong accent), theoretically of lesser status than the designer but possessing crucial knowledge, capable of enabling or preventing the designer's vision and often speaking the blunt truths that others dare not.

There are also various, apparently fairly minor, differences, however. Perhaps the most immediately evident of these is the difference in budget. In Britain, each designer may spend up to £500; in Germany the budget is equivalent to twice this. In both cases, the designers sometimes exceed their budgets, the latter doing so equally and sometimes even more spectacularly than the former, despite having a larger amount to play with. The reason for the bigger budget in Bavaria is not a consequence of the price of building and decorating materials or furniture, which are often more reasonable than in Britain. It is, rather, a function of a greater reluctance to 'jazz up junk' and to engage in what might be called 'going for surface over substance'.

While some items of furniture are redeployed, perhaps re-covered, in the Bavarian programme, there is much less of this than in the British. Instead, what takes precedence in *Tapeten-Wechsel* is good-quality work and to this end a considerable amount of joinery is undertaken, involving saws, hammers, and nails. Nearly all of this involves 'real wood' rather than the MDF (medium-density fibreboard – a wood substitute) that the British programme has done so much to popularise. In particular, the Bavarian programme frequently involves laying hardwood floors, something that the British budget cannot stretch to, meaning that other 'solutions' (a keyword of *Changing Rooms*) have to be found.

Indeed, *Tapeten-Wechsel* typically contains so much *basteln* – making things from scratch – that the designers and neighbours themselves take on many tasks that would in Britain be left to Handy Andy. In this, it should be noted, they are generally fairly skilled, reflecting a greater emphasis in Germany on having high levels of skills in *basteln*. (This is something that children are encouraged to begin at a young age. On several occasions during my time in Germany I happened upon events, such as a children's activity day at the town hall, at which children as young as two were wielding full-sized hammers in order to bash nails into planks of wood. In my six-year-old daughter's school report, the one subject that was listed of particular concern was her relatively low level of attainment in *basteln*.)

Where the German programme is characterised by high levels of dovetailing joinery, then, the English is much more so by 'paint effects', which appear in numerous rather esoteric forms, such as stencilling, sponging, rag-rolling, and poly-bagging (in which paint is applied with a scrumpled-up polythene bag). Creating a radically new appearance, often by redeploying existing items, is the leitmotiv of *Changing Rooms*. Where wood is the key substance in the German programme, paint – a material of surfaces – fulfils this role in the British.

The British programme is, in general, much more colourful than the Bavarian, literally and metaphorically. Rooms are often painted in loud colours – indeed, the gasp of shock when the neighbours see the colour chosen by the designer is another standard televisual moment – whereas in the Bavarian programme, white, typically dismissed as 'boring' by the Brits, is frequently used (wallpaper never being employed, despite the literal meaning of the programme's name) and colour schemes are rarely as bold or garish as in the British. In those few cases that I saw when bright colours were used in Bavaria, the owners were visibly upset, something that is perhaps related to Shirley Ardener's note that spaces are sometimes conceptualised as having inherent colours (1981: 23). Certainly, in the German case, white seems to be equated with 'light', something highly prized in modern living spaces and contrasted with a 'traditional' aesthetic and 'dark past'.

The designers themselves are also more visually and temperamentally sober in *Tapeten-Wechsel*, generally wearing casual jeans or stylish black (another cultural 'colour inherence'?). None is as outlandish as Britain's Lawrence Llewelyn-Bowen, now having graduated to be programme presenter, with his long curling hair and colourful rococo-inspired suits. In contrast to the calculatedly eccentric or even 'wild and wacky' British designers, the Germans are more thoughtful and measured, more concentrated on the task, and less busy playing to the cameras. It is hard to imagine them deciding to base a room design on a pair of frilly knickers, as was the case in one, not uncharacteristic, design for *Changing Rooms*. They are also less likely to persuade the neighbours to accept ideas against their better judgement and more willing to see their task as working with them. And, while in both programmes there is plenty of joking and of worry about the fast-approaching deadline, in the British everything possible is done to actually meet it, work being shoddily performed if necessary just to give the appearance of completion.[4] In the German, if all is not ready, extra time is allowed or the couples even return home knowing that there is more to be done. Quality, or substance, is not allowed to be compromised (or not to the same extent) for appearance.

Fashioning Identities

Shirley reminds us that '[a]ttention has … been drawn to the capacity of human beings to enrich life by placing great significance on seemingly trivial events. … The human spirit, it seems, creates its own visions of heaven and its triumphs as well as its own damnations and failures, even in apparently unpromising environments' (Ardener 1981: 22). In some ways, the business of redecorating houses is an apparently fairly trivial matter – even an unpromising environment – and, likewise, some of the differences between the British and German programmes may seem rather minor. Yet it is to the awareness of the potential significance of such matters that both anthropology and feminism have contributed so much. As Shirley has written specifically on the subject of domestic space, 'the home, far from being an arid arena deprived of rich significance compared with the world outside, may render up spiritual meanings lacking elsewhere' (ibid.: 22–23).

One way of looking at home improvement programmes such as *Changing Rooms* and *Tapeten-Wechsel* is as lessons in the art of fashioning identities, a matter which could indeed be seen as to a degree 'spiritual', its reliance on hammers and glue notwithstanding. The great proliferation of such programmes, and their gardening and personal appearance counterparts, might be seen as part of an alleged change in ways in which self-identities are coming to be conceptualised and realised in what is sometimes called 'late modernity' (or various near synonyms). Drawn on here too is a more long-standing and widely resonant cultural deployment of the home as a metaphor for the individual – and especially for female subjectivity – and vice versa.[5] The popularity of such programmes, according to this perspective, lies at least partly in the fact that they are not 'just' about painting and decorating but about what is conceived as the more fundamental but increasingly tricky matter of how to fashion the self, especially, though not exclusively, the female self. If education, migration and social mobility have meant that identities are no longer so ascribed by the circumstances of birth, so embedded in relations of kinship or so tied to place, then individuals can be increasingly free to 'make themselves up', to decide who they want to be (Giddens 1991). This has been called DIY culture – a culture of do-it-yourself identities and making up your own rules and practices (e.g., Dürrschmidt et al. 1997; MacKay 1998). In some forms, this can also be characterised by a greater reliance on 'reading signs' and surfaces (a consequence of less actual direct knowledge about people) and a proliferation of techniques for altering appearances.

Living spaces have, of course, long been one of the signs by which a person's identity could be read: that is, we could know something of who somebody is by where they live and the type of property that they inhabit. This persists but it is also accompanied by an increased (though not necessarily all-pervasive) conceptualisation of the home as an arena for change and for expressing self-wrought identities. Literal DIY, then, has added resonance as a technique for helping not merely to manifest but to perform DIY identity. As Shirley observes in *Women and Space*, 'changes in belief [can be] deliberately paralleled by changes in artefacts and in spatial arrangements' (Ardener 1981: 23). Redesigning homes can be seen as a deliberate parallel to changing understandings of, or beliefs in, identity possibilities.

DIY Identities

DIY identities can be theorised as highly individualised and 'disembedded' from 'traditional' social relations and constraints, though they might also involve constructing new forms of social ties (Giddens 1991; Dürrschmidt et al. 1997). Anthropological studies of the home, including home decorating in the late twentieth century, cast doubt on the extent to which these processes are, in fact, disembedded and radically novel. As is clear from the studies in *Women and Space*, as well as in more recent collections (e.g., Birdwell-Pheasant and Zúñiga 1999, Chapman and Hockey 1999, Cieraad 1999; and especially Miller 2001a), the home is also a space in which perhaps conventional social relations are played out and in which culturally understood functionality has to be allowed, and this strains against pure 'expressivity'. Home design needs to incorporate accepted ideas about the organisation of social activities (ideas that, as *Women and Space* showed, may vary cross-culturally), living with heirlooms and even unwanted gifts, and making space for collections of, say, cuddly toys or allowing for serious home-brewing. Moreover, what Miller (2001b and especially 2001c) calls the 'agency' of the home is also implicated here, compromising the agency of the home decorators, who may feel themselves constrained by the existing state of their homes and, variously, lack of sufficient money, time, and skills. The message of a programme such as *Changing Rooms*, however, is that rather little of these are needed – only vision and will.

None of this is to say that viewers of *Changing Rooms* necessarily fully accept this idea or its metaphorical implication that identities may be radically reflexively self-redesigned, even with relatively few means. Moreover, both the British and Bavarian programmes temper the idea of total redesign, though they do so in interestingly different ways. Relatedly, they also have somewhat different 'takes' on the individuality that is generally seen as the goal of expressive DIY.

Changing Rooms does celebrate the individually different. Designers strive to create something that will not look like anything that has existed before, even while they enjoy the idea of 'the theme', deriving inspiration from, say, the medieval castle or South Sea island. 'Customising' the mass-produced is a key technique here, items being 'rescued' from the world of sameness and turned into individual pieces (Miller 1988). At the same time, existing items of furniture are also used but refashioned to look different. In *Tapeten-Wechsel* there is also a degree of such rescuing and refashioning but, in contrast to the British programme, there is less of this. Moreover, finished rooms look a good deal more similar to one another (at least, to my British eye). Where *Changing Rooms* plays up and even exaggerates an 'expressive individuation' (as Charles Taylor (1989) more specifically characterised what is sometimes called 'individualisation'), the *Individualisierung* ('individualisation' – a keyword in some German social science theorising (e.g., Beck 1998) that has also been influential in Britain) of *Tapeten-Wechsel* does not seem to need to be proclaimed at surface level in quite the same way. Rather, the individualisation in the Bavarian case seems to be rooted more in the individualised nature of the process, the serious handcrafting, than in a highly individually differentiated 'look'.

Gender Identities

The central area of exploration of *Women and Space* is the gendering of space, especially of the home. While certain parts of the house may have particular gender associations or be deemed the space of one gender more than another (see also, for example, Carsten and Hugh-Jones 1995), in Western Europe in particular, the home tends to be seen as women's space to a greater extent than it is men's (Steedman 1982, Brydon and Floyd 1999). Here, women are not only prone to spend more time than men, but are also more likely to be responsible for the home as an expression and, consequently, to see the home as an aspect of their own self-fashioning – or, at least, to be more conscious of the fact that their home will be regarded as a reflection of their own tastes and personalities (Clarke 2001). If *Changing Rooms* and *Tapeten-Wechsel* can be seen to some extent at least as scripts for fashioning identities, then how is gender played out? And is this different in the two countries?

As described above, the programme generally entails mixed-sex couples decorating each other's homes, the participation of both male and female partners being presented as a kind of ideal type. The script here is one of the home as a collective project for couples to fashion their joint identities, men being drawn into the shaping of this 'private' space along with women, in what might be regarded as a statement of gender equality and a denial of the idea of the home as especially the preserve of women. In the detail of more specific cases, however, more 'traditional' gendered differences emerge, in particular, in the tendency for the men to defer to the women's opinions on decoration, so affirming the idea of women as especially responsible for matters of taste and the home. In many ways, what is also on screen in *Changing Rooms/Tapeten-Wechsel* is the drama of 'coupledom', as couples negotiate both the designers and their own tastes and habits in a space that traditionally has been especially women's sphere of creativity and is now, alongside the DIY boom, increasingly witness to the male homeowner's tastes and skills too.[6]

While the performance of coupledom seems to be equally the case in the British and the Bavarian programmes, creativity itself seems to be more feminised in *Changing Rooms*. This is connected to the differing aesthetics described above. The German emphasis on handcrafting solid materials relies on skills that are more often seen as masculine in Germany as well as in Britain, and the greater weight accorded to form and function has also been regarded in design circles as relatively masculine. In contrast to *Tapeten-Wechsel*, *Changing Rooms* involves designs that are more likely to be associated with feminine styles, such as the use of more decoration, colour, and soft furnishings. The *Changing Rooms* designers themselves are also more likely to self-present as feminine or to a degree effeminate, interior decoration being an occupation more likely to be regarded as women's work in Britain.

Gender is also played out in the work conducted. In both programmes, there are often attempts made to flout the usual gendered associations of work tasks by setting men at the sewing machine or handing women the drill. These, however, act paradoxically, for they serve to remind at the same time of the more usual gendered associations and skills (especially where those charged with the tasks are clearly not competent).[7] Moreover, although there are higher levels of skills in general in *Tapeten-Wechsel*, both Bastl Wastl and Handy Andy clearly possess superior knowledge and as such they act as icons of traditional masculine skill. (Neither is ever seen at the sewing machine.) Through their quips and joking, as well as their greater capabilities, they often highlight the inadequacies of the other participants when it comes to the work that in German is described as *das Grobe*

– the rough stuff. When the going gets tough, the message seems to be, we need a real man after all. However much we might like the idea of playing with identities and refashioning them, we cannot do without the capabilities represented by the working-class, local, and traditionally masculine character of Andy/Bastl. If the home and men are being feminised by interior decoration, and if identities are increasingly being presented as up for refashioning, Andy and Bastl serve as playful reminders of some of what might be lost along the way.

Conclusion

Both *Changing Rooms* and *Tapeten-Wechsel* produce a kind of commentary upon matters that are about far more than the painting of walls and stuffing of cushions. Both produced to the same template, at virtually the same time in history, within the same broad geographical area (Europe), it is not surprising that they possess many similarities. Matters such as identity fashioning, the role of the home, and gender relations are broadly the same in the two countries.

The programmes, however, also reveal subtle differences, as we have seen. To some extent these differences seem to fit relatively familiar stereotypes that each country holds of the other. The depiction of Germans as creating products that are good-quality and reliable, but perhaps a bit boring, is well known. (Think Volkswagen.) Germans, according to this stereotype, are very, and perhaps obsessively, sensible and rational, though sometimes also highly stylish in a cool, hard-edged kind of way. (Think Pögenpohl kitchens.) The stereotypical German aesthetic is relatively masculine, privileging line, form, function, and quality. (Think *Vorsprung durch Technik*.) Germans watching *Changing Rooms* would also be likely to have some of their existing stereotypes about Brits confirmed: shoddy quality and often poor taste, with a puzzling predilection for garish colours and unsuitable materials, though perhaps also a strangely admirable eccentricity and lack of concern about what others might think of them. German friends would express (feigned?) surprise after visits to Britain over the cramped room sizes, hideously unmatching decor, lack of double glazing, small and lumpy beds, and the peculiarly unhygienic practice of having carpeted bathrooms. These impressions were generally based on bed-and-breakfast establishments, the domestic interiors most often encountered by visitors from other countries.

What is partly going on here is that, as both Malcolm Chapman (1982) and Maryon McDonald (1993) have elegantly argued (drawing on Edwin Ardener's ideas about language and reality (1989: chap. 11)), labels are being populated with that which fits pre-existing ideas. We easily seek confirmation of the views we already hold. This is one reason why anthropologists have cause to feel suspicious of such a process, and why we might want to point out instances that do not confirm such preconceptions. Much important anthropological work has indeed challenged stereotypes on the basis of a first-hand knowledge of the people involved (as many contributions to volumes edited by Shirley show; see, for example, Okely 1975).

At the same time, however, the same basic reinforcing process is carried out by self-identifying groups in relation to themselves. *Changing Rooms* has been produced for a British audience by a British broadcasting company and *Tapeten-Wechsel* adapted for a Bavarian audience by a Bavarian company. Such a process contributes to the production of cultural differences between groups of various sorts, especially those separated by language and/or national boundaries and possessing shared institutions capable of producing representations. The representations and cultural forms created may or may not include features that also support stereotypes held by outsiders. Thus, for example, a visitor to Bavaria may note some cultural differences that conform to prior expectations (e.g., the rows of sauerkraut in the supermarket) and others that do not (e.g., the popularity of doner kebab). The good cultural critic will explain the latter as well as the former (Çaglar 1995; Richter 2002). Certainly, within either Britain or Bavaria there will be a good deal of variety, resulting not least from ethnic and cultural mix.

Yet, as both Shirley and Edwin Ardener have pointed out, what we are dealing with here are not exclusive categories with clear-cut boundaries but the ways in which these work in use (e.g., S. Ardener 1975a; E. Ardener 1989: 168). There will be variety but this can coexist with what Edwin called 'semantic density' (1989: chap. 11) – relatively 'core' meanings, those most often employed and perhaps most likely to be recognised as familiar by those who use them, even if that familiarity means that they are rendered unremarkable or invisible. Trying to grasp the 'semantically dense' is a key aspect of the anthropological attempt to grasp 'cultural difference'. Social psychologist Michael Billig has devised the term 'banal nationalism' to describe the ways in which nationality may be 'flagged' simply by being mentioned in numerous contexts in daily life (1995). What the Ardeners alert us to goes beyond this: it is not just about employing certain terms (and certainly not just self- or other-labelling) but concerns all kinds of practices and what Edwin called 'materiality'. That is, it is about such matters as uses of space, bodily movements, dress, drinking, home decorating, and other topics of the kind covered in series edited by Shirley and colleagues, and their differential patternings. Indeed, the material and practical expression of cultural difference is what accounts for the apparently incontrovertible and sometimes 'obvious' nature of such difference even if we cannot at first quite put our finger on what is involved.

In *Women and Space*, Shirley draws attention to the 'correspondence between the so-called "real" physical world and its "social reality"' (Ardener 1981: 11). As she argues, this should not be understood as 'simple one-way "cause and effect"' (ibid.: 12) but as the outcome of cumulative 'both-way' interaction that has resulted in 'simultaneities' (ibid.; see also E. Ardener 1989: 168). Putting it a bit crudely, social uses and practices shape uses of physical spaces and, simultaneously, the latter shape the social uses and practices, and so on. The cumulative nature of this is important and can involve processes such as those identified by Lévi-Strauss in his discussion of *bricolage* (1963). The emphasis on wood in *Tapeten-Wechsel* is an example. This is not simply a novelty produced in this programme but draws on long-standing ideas in Germany about the importance of forests as sites of the German spirit (*Geist*) (see, for example, Schama 1995: chap. 2) and on wood as a material that in some sense indicates 'home', there being a preference, as Drazin argues for Romania, for leaving wood grain on show (Drazin 2001). What is involved here might even be thought of as a 'cumulativity'. It is also evident in such matters as children being encouraged to handle and work with wood at early ages: they are given wooden toys, and these are perceived as more wholesome than playthings made from other substances. Indeed, wood can, I suggest, stand for substance over surface, as emblematic of a relationship that is authentic, natural, and solid.

I have suggested above that in the two programmes there seems to be a tendency in the Bavarian to emphasise substance and in the British to emphasise surface. In part, this is a function of cumulativities of the sort discussed in relation to wood as a substance. But it may also show simultaneities with other kinds of ongoing identity processes. On the one hand such programmes can be seen as linked to the spread of ideas of DIY identities but, as I have suggested, not perhaps in quite the same ways in the two countries. This prompts the question of whether, in addition to different inflections rendered by cumulativities, the differences might also be related to simultaneities with wider identity processes.

Changing Rooms was launched at the peak of the DIY boom, a phenomenon that, as various commentators have noted, flourished under Thatcherism (e.g., Tomlinson 1990; Clarke 2001: 23). Ideas of individual entrepreneurship, of making something of oneself, of origins being unimportant, and of practical activity were all characteristic of the neoliberal conservatism and general DIY ethos espoused by Thatcher. Her selling off of council housing for private ownership epitomised her view that private ownership would produce better results than would state ownership, as well as manifesting the Conservative celebration of the home and individual property. The Labour government that came to office in 1997 largely adopted the same philosophy. Moreover, its attempts to give the nation a new face and, in particular, to present it as 'young and dynamic' (two concepts cast as linked) chimed well with the idea of *Changing Rooms*. 'Cool Britannia' was the term created by the PR firms employed, and it was manifest in such things as Britart and Prime Minister Tony Blair posing with hip new pop bands and meeting ministers from other countries in rooms with funky designer furniture. Brits were to be presented as lively and different, even while at the same time there was a rhetoric of this always having been part of being British even if it had not previously been given official imprimatur and proper space to flourish.

While Germany in the 1990s also saw first a conservative government and then a nominally socialist one, and while it broadly shared a neoliberal climate, its principal concerns were to some extent different. In particular, the major national post-unification task was to dovetail the former East and West. Those from the former Democratic and Federal Republics generally continued to see themselves as culturally distinct, there being talk of a cultural wall remaining even though the physical *Mauer* had gone. One difference, from the perspective of Wessies (those from the former West), was that Easterners (Ossies), having only been able to purchase poor-quality goods in the socialist period, would accept and maybe even cause a spread of the shoddy.[8]

In Bavaria, as a wealthy former Western state bordering on the former East and recipient of significant migration from it, such fears were particularly marked; and this may also have contributed to *Tapeten-Wechsel*'s emphasis on high quality and high cost and eschewing of the 'something-for-nothing' motif of *Changing Rooms*. Moreover, in the decade after unification it became increasingly recognised that what was needed was to put something in place that would be a good foundation for the future and that would last. Quick fixes would not do. In this post-euphoria period it was also increasingly clear that the real work of unification would take much longer than had originally been envisaged. So, in contrast to the usual images of German efficiency and punctuality, a new tendency to overrun deadlines, often remarked upon by Germans themselves, became widespread in the public sphere. As in *Tapeten-Wechsel*, finishing late became regarded as a lesser evil than doing a poor job.

In some areas of theorising (albeit not generally anthropological) 'culture' is thought of as a kind of 'surface' – an epiphenomenon of more substantial matters (especially economic). There is also a tendency, perhaps especially in popular thought, to regard culture and difference as 'in themselves', disconnected from all else, as confirmation simply of difference per se. In this essay, I have tried to argue for the validity of a focus on cultural difference even in the face of variability and change, and have attempted to point out why we should not be surprised to find differences consolidating around national or ethnic identities. In doing so, I have drawn on the theorising of Shirley and Edwin Ardener in order to present an alternative to the perspectives of culture as surface effect or as hovering autonomously. To be sure, their own works make these points more fully and elegantly. Nevertheless, through a brief account of two versions of the 'same' television programme, I hope to have been able to show some of the purchase of the cross-cultural and some of the work of identity fashioning in a world of changing cultures, rooms, and wallpaper.

Postscript

In September 2004 the BBC announced that no new series of *Changing Rooms* would be made. According to the BBC, this was just the inevitable end of shelf life and the decision to bow out at a high point. In the words of presenter Laurence Llewelyn-Bowen, the programme had 'done everything there is to do' and was ending 'on a high note' (http://news.bbc.co.uk/2/hi/uk_news/magazine/4034503.stm). Others, however, suspected that mounting criticisms of the programme, in particular of the botched work that it often entailed and that was increasingly being 'outed' in the media, were largely to blame (e.g., "'The curtains were nailed on, it was all resoundingly naff'" (*Daily Mail*, 29 Sept. 2004)). Some newspaper reports suggested that there were more fundamental and gendered shifts at work by bringing the news of the demise of the programme together with results from a study commissioned by Standard Life that showed that British men seemed to be becoming increasingly less likely to be willing to undertake DIY (e.g., *Daily Telegraph*, 24 Nov. 2004). Working longer hours than anywhere else in Europe, nine out of ten of the five hundred men questioned said that they would not attempt any DIY at all, 67 per cent of them agreeing that they were 'not up to the job' and 27 per cent that they were not interested (ibid.). Moreover, the reports implied, the experience of the DIY boom and *Changing Rooms* itself had revealed that DIY often led to shoddy work and personal injuries, 100,000 people a year requiring hospital treatment for DIY injuries (Department of Trade and Industry figures, ibid.). Spurred on by seeing the havoc that *Changing Rooms* could produce, British men preferred to leave the job to a professional – like Handy Andy. Time will tell whether this heralds shifting 'simultaneity' and a deeper rejection of the quick fix.

Acknowledgements

Mike Beaney was responsible for making me watch *Tapeten-Wechsel*. For this, and for discussions of it, I thank him, as well as Tara, Thomas, and Harriet, who also offered insightful observations. Thanks too to Judith Okely, Ronnie Frankenberg, Jeanette Edwards, and Simone Abram for encouraging comments and helpful suggestions.

Notes

1. References to some of this work include Macdonald 1997, 2002, 2003.
2. For further discussion of the content of the programme see Spittle 2002.
3. 'Owners' as used here may include those renting or otherwise inhabiting, though in Britain it is almost invariably the case that those on the programme are homeowners. In the German case, those involved are less likely to actually own the properties that are being renovated, long-term renting being much more common in Germany than in Britain. In some ways this serves to highlight even more the differences between the two countries, in that doing a high-quality job – which as I argue below is a significant difference between the programmes in the two countries – would be less likely in a rented than in an owned property in Britain.
4. The fact that getting things completed may also involve other members of the production crew than those actually shown on camera and that work may be even more poorly completed than it appears on camera has been a mainstay of a set of accusatory 'revelations' about the programme that have gathered over the years.

5. The idea of the home as expressive of identities and of the bourgeois home as a materialisation of a new conception of individuality rooted in notions of interiority and privacy is generally said to have emerged in Western Europe in the eighteenth century. See, for example, Steedman 1982; Brydon and Floyd 1999; Maleuvre 1999.
6. Another 'home' programme that began on British television, called DIY SOS, is dedicated to trying to help households in which repairs are urgently needed. The need for repair is almost always due to men's hopeless botch jobs, taking on tasks for which they were insufficiently skilled, or which they never managed to complete or simply got utterly wrong. Women on this programme are typically presented as modern-day damsels in distress, possessing the vision but lacking the necessary accompanying male skill to put things right – until the DIY SOS team arrives, knight-like, to the rescue.
7. A survey in 2001 reported that in Britain gender differences remained in the domain of DIY: 'It's amazing to note that sexism about DIY in the U.K. is alive and well! If it comes to the crunch, it's still the men who have to get the job done. Of the sexes, 65 per cent think men are better at DIY. And in these times of supposed sexual equality, 60 per cent of women still think that men are better at DIY than them. (Well, that's the excuse anyway!)' (http://www.prnewswire.co.uk/cgi/news/release?id=65587).
8. By the end of the 1990s, however, Ossies had become increasingly unwilling to accept the idea that all of their goods had been of lesser quality than those produced in the West. Consequently, a market for former Eastern goods, and the resumption of manufacture of some of them, has grown up. For a discussion of some of the changes in housing, especially in East Germany, since unification, see Weinthal 2002.

References

Ardener, E. 1989. *The Voice of Prophecy and Other Essays* (ed. M. Chapman), Oxford: Blackwell.
Ardener, S. 1975a. 'Introduction', in S. Ardener (ed.), *Perceiving Women*, London: J.M. Dent & Sons, pp. vii–xxiii.
——— 1975a. 'Introduction', in S. Ardener (ed.), *Perceiving Women*, London: J.M. Dent & Sons, pp. vii–xxiii.
——— 1975b. (orig. 1973). 'Sexual Insult and Female Militancy', in S. Ardener (ed.), *Perceiving Women*, London: J.M. Dent & Sons, pp. 29–53.
——— 1981. 'Ground Rules and Social Maps for Women: An Introduction', in S. Ardener (ed.), *Women and Space: Ground Rules and Social Maps*, London: Croom Helm, pp. 11–34.
Askew, K. and R.R. Wilk (eds) 2002. *The Anthropology of Media: A Reader*, Oxford: Blackwell.
Beck, U. 1998. *Das Zeitalter des eigenen Lebens: Die Globalisierung der Biographien*, Frankfurt: Suhrkamp.
Billig, M. 1995. *Banal Nationalism*, London: Sage.
Birdwell-Pheasant, D. and D. Lawrence-Zúñiga (eds) 1999. *House Life: Space, Place and Family in Europe*, Oxford: Berg.
Bowen, L. 1966. 'Shakespeare in the Bush', *Natural History* (August–September), pp. 28–33.
Brydon, I. and J. Floyd 1999. *Domestic Space: Reading the Interior in Nineteenth-Century Britain and America*, Manchester: Manchester University Press.
Çaglar, A. 1995. 'McDöner: Döner Kebap and the Social Positioning Struggle of German Turks', in J.A. Costa and G.J. Bamossy (eds), *Marketing in a Multicultural World: Ethnicity, Nationalism and Cultural Identity*, London: Sage, pp. 209–30.

Carsten, J., and S. Hugh-Jones (eds) 1995. *About the House: Lévi-Strauss and Beyond*, Cambridge: Cambridge University Press.
Chapman, M. 1982. '"Semantics" and the Celt', in D. Parkin (ed.), *Semantic Anthropology*, London: Academic Press.
Chapman, T., and J. Hockey (eds) 1999. *Ideal Homes?*, London: Routledge.
Cieraad, I. (ed.) 1999. *At Home: An Anthropology of Domestic Space*, Syracuse: Syracuse University Press.
Clarke, A.J. 2001. 'The Aesthetics of Social Aspiration', in D. Miller (ed.), *Home Possessions: Material Culture Behind Closed Doors*, Oxford: Berg, pp. 23–45.
Drazin, A. 2001. 'A Man Will Get Furnished: Wood and Domesticity in Urban Romania', in D. Miller (ed.), *Home Possessions: Material Culture Behind Closed Doors*, Oxford: Berg, pp. 173–99.
Dürrschmidt, J., D. Purdue, R. O'Doherty and P. Jones 1997. 'DIY Culture and Extended Milieux: LETS, Veegie Boxes and Festivals', *Sociological Review* 45 (4), pp. 645–67.
Giddens, A. 1991. *Modernity and Self-Identity: Self and Society in the Late Modern Age*, Cambridge: Polity.
Lévi-Strauss, C. 1963 (orig. 1958). *Structural Anthropology*, New York: Basic Books.
McDonald, M. 1993. 'The Construction of Difference: An Anthropological Approach to Stereotypes', in S. Macdonald (ed.), *Inside European Identities*, Oxford: Berg, pp. 219–36.
Macdonald, S. 1997. *Reimagining Culture: Histories, Identities and the Gaelic Renaissance*, Oxford: Berg.
——— 2002. *Behind the Scenes at the Science Museum*, Oxford: Berg.
——— 2003. 'Trafficking in History: Multitemporal Practices', *Anthropological Journal on European Cultures* 11, pp. 93–116.
MacKay, G. (ed.) 1998. *DIY Culture: Party and Protest in Nineties' Britain*, London: Verso.
Maleuvre, D. 1999. *Museum Memories*, Stanford: Stanford University Press.
Miller, D. 1988. 'Appropriating the State on the Council Estate', *Man* 23, pp. 353–72.
——— (ed.) 2001a. *Home Possessions: Material Culture Behind Closed Doors*, Oxford: Berg.
——— 2001b. 'Behind Closed Doors', in D. Miller (ed.), *Home Possessions: Material Culture Behind Closed Doors*, Oxford: Berg, pp. 1–19.
——— 2001c. 'Possessions', in D. Miller (ed.), *Home Possessions: Material Culture Behind Closed Doors*, Oxford: Berg, pp. 107–21.
Okely, J. 1975. 'Gypsy Women: Models in Conflict', in S. Ardener (ed.), *Perceiving Women*, London: J.M. Dent & Sons, pp. 55–86.
Richter, S. 2002. 'Food and Drink: Hegelian Encounters with the Culinary Other', in A. Phipps (ed.), *Contemporary German Cultural Studies*, London: Arnold, pp. 179–91.
Schama, S. 1995. *Landscape and Memory*, London: Harper Collins.
Spittle, S. 2002. 'Producing TV, Consuming TV', in S. Miles, A. Anderson, and K. Meethan (eds), *The Changing Consumer. Markets and Meanings*, London: Routledge, pp. 56–73.
Steedman, C. 1982. *The Tidy House*, London: Virago.
Taylor, C. 1989. *Sources of the Self*, Cambridge: Cambridge University Press.
Tomlinson, A. 1990. 'Home Fixtures: Doing It Yourself in a Privatised World', in A. Tomlinson (ed.), *Consumption, Identity and Style*, London: Comedia, pp. 57–73.
Weinthal, L.R. 2002. 'Domestic Spaces: Homes in the Heimat', in A. Phipps (ed.), *Contemporary German Cultural Studies*, London: Arnold, pp. 102–16.

2

IDENTITY AT PLAY: INDIVIDUALS, CHARACTERS, AND THEATRES OF ACTION

Kirsten Hastrup

Identity categories are at the core of anthropological practice, in terms of both individual identities (or notions of the self) and collective identities (or notions of ethnicity). In this chapter I shall deal primarily with the interface between the self and the collectivity in order to discuss identity as a response to multiple actualities rather than a fixed frame of subjectivity. This tallies with other attempts at understanding the self as composite and malleable (Cohen 1994; Rapport 1997). It also in its own way reflects the insight of relational identities provided by scholars of gender such as Shirley Ardener (e.g., 1975, 1978, 1992) and Judith Okely (1996). I shall make my case by drawing on material provided by players of Shakespeare on their building a character through their actions. Through the prism provided by play-acting we may arrive at a new understanding of the profoundly social nature of the self, being a result both of 'character dialectic' and of individual action being framed by a larger and collectively endorsed illusion of 'society'.

It is worth noting that in what follows I am not using Shakespeare's theatre as an analogy of the social; rather I see it as a 'theatre of action' in its own right, to use a term suggested by Edwin Ardener (1989: 25). This notion was introduced by Ardener to deal with a semiotic system that – in the absence of language – depended upon perception by the human participants of contextually defined relations among themselves in space. Often the spatial relations match those of gender (S. Ardener 1981). I would argue that the contextually defined relations are operative also in the presence of language – the latter seen not so much as an expression of relations but rather as co-constitutive of them. The theatre of action in this sense is an apt analytical object for anthropology, highlighting the simultaneity of language, action, social relations, and topographical features (Hastrup 2003a). Far from simply being literature on stage, theatre is a world of players and actions and of rules and reflections on the plot that are as real as anything and that takes place in a concrete, socially defined space, within a set time frame. In a couple of precursors to this chapter I have argued that all social worlds are dependent on an illusion for their wholeness (Hastrup 2000), and, further, that a social space has no ontological status apart from what is collectively attributed to it and made manifest in action (Hastrup 2004). In the present context, my focus is on the individual acting within a particular social space and therefore contributing to the realisation of both self and society.

The procedure here will be: first, to discuss the sense of self that emerged in the Renaissance and which is still with us; secondly, to show how this self acts in character within a particular social space; and, thirdly, to discuss the social space as an imaginatively sustained plot. This will finally lead me to some concluding remarks about identity and the multiple actualities that the individual must negotiate – and thereby to questioning some of the more tenacious implications of 'individuality'.

Self: The Birth of the Passionate Individual

The Renaissance horizon, which is an important 'historical' element in Shakespeare's plays, is also a diacritical feature in their longevity. While in the Middle Ages people had seen themselves as embedded in a universal world order, presided over by God, who had allotted humans and other species a fixed and permanent position in the cosmos, in the Renaissance people were being torn out of this order. The creative power of humans was affirmed within a new philosophy of imagination that insisted on 'the primacy of anthropological over onto-theological truth' (Kearney 2001: 155). Within the new historical horizon (which evidently had its forerunners), individuals were attributed with the power to shape their own destinies and to influence history. We are still very much operating under this horizon in anthropology.

History and biography became mutually implicated; history was the result of human action. This idea furnished Shakespeare with dramatic material, and in turn Shakespeare's plays contributed to the exemplification and establishment of an integrated sense of history and of the self. While in the later Enlightenment this would give rise to an idea of an autonomous self, entirely governed by reason and will, in the Renaissance the self was much more ambiguously, and – I believe – more truthfully, portrayed as a character deeply embedded in a social world. Shakespeare's plays provide rich sources for the emergent anthropology – and also for the new philosophy of imagination itself.

From Shakespeare's point of view, art itself is instrumental in bringing out the nature of the social world – as implied in the transformation of Hermione from stone to flesh in *The Winter's Tale* – and art therefore is itself an agent in history (Kermode 2000). The plays demonstrate how history unfolds between order and chaos – and the force of Shakespeare's plays is that they show this at the level of concrete events and individual actions and destinies. The players of Shakespeare *performed* the new philosophical insight, as they still do. They bring a particular anthropology to life for the audience to experience.

The view of the self as a historicised and historicising individual placed people (rather than God) at the centre of the world, and made the centre as frail as the humans embodying it. A major source of frailty was the drama *within* the individual, a drama between passions that pull in diverse directions. Passion was one side of the newly discovered individuality of the Renaissance. The 'new' individuals were in some sense freed of authorities, but they were the more slaves of their passions, as we know from a good many tragic and/or heroic characters.

The ambiguity of individual characters in Shakespeare's plays in many ways is a reflection of the Renaissance crack in the moral mirror, as is the distinction between heroes and villains, which is never absolute. There is no longer a view of an absolute standard for good or bad, but rather a recognition of ambiguity in action. Shakespeare shows the audience the consequences of particular choices and courses of action, for individuals and for society, and leaves it to the audience to judge for themselves. In *Othello*, to take one conspicuous example, the juxtaposition of Othello and Iago is also a contrast between the old order and the radically new view of the world. While Othello cherishes absolutes, including absolute honesty, Iago defies it:

O wretched fool,
That liv'st to make thine honesty a vice!
O monstrous world! Take note, take note, O world,
To be direct and honest is not safe.

(*Othello* III. iii. 379–82)[1]

The old order may be virtuous and yet it is also fragile; deception and jealousy may overturn it. In other words, passion has been let loose in a world populated by people who are subject to a complex mass of emotions (Sløk 1990). In medieval philosophy, passion was known, of course, but it was not seen as a historical force, as it came to be in the Renaissance, where people were seen as principally ruled by their passions, either negatively or positively. As Hamlet says to Horatio:

Give me that man
That is not passion's slave, and I will wear him
In my heart's core …

(*Hamlet* III. ii. 69–71)

Passions drive people to excellence, as Henry V's passion for England makes him an almost mythological soldier, but they may also drive people to evil, like Macbeth's passionate wish to become king. In each case, Shakespeare shows us how the passion propels the drama along, quite often because the individual's passions are fraught with contradiction and ambiguity.

The life history of any one individual, therefore, does not proceed in an even manner, nor does it allow a uniform sense of progress – either in biography or in history. Lived time is different from measured time in this sense, too. And it cannot always be 'expressed'; it can only be acted. As Hamlet himself says to Horatio:

> There are more things in heaven and earth, Horatio,
> Than are dreamt of in your philosophy.
>
> (*Hamlet* I. v. 166–67)

Remembering now that Hamlet and his like were not characters in history but characters in particular plays, we may return to the question of how passions drive the play in an often quite irrational manner. Dover Wilson has suggested that a 'strain of sex-nausea' runs through many of Shakespeare's plays, but – in answer to T.S. Eliot – he does not associate this with 'some mysterious complex' (i.e., the Oedipus complex) 'but with the more commonplace derangement known as jealousy, jealousy of the same kind as, if not identical with, that described so savagely in the *Sonnets*' (Wilson 1996: 306). Jealousy is the mainspring of several plays, notably *Othello*; in the case of the Moor we can readily see how his feeling is completely irrational. He demands evidence of Desdemona's infidelity because he really has no reason to suspect it. Only Iago's persistent lies finally convince him of the truth of the claim. All the way through, Iago uses rational (but false) arguments to achieve his goal. He even deceptively warns Othello against the jealousy he has staged for him:

> O, beware, my lord, of jealousy;
> It is the green-ey'd monster, which doth mock
> The meat it feeds on. That cuckold lives in bliss
> Who, certain of his fate, loves not his wronger;
> But, O, what damned minutes tells he o'er
> Who dotes, yet doubts, suspects, yet strongly loves!
>
> (*Othello* III. iii. 169–76)

The 'green-eyed monster' is operative in a good number of Shakespeare's plays and it is one of those passions that are more often than not quite irrational. In this respect, jealousy is like love itself: it may strike at all times, unexpectedly and uncontrollably. There is no reason beyond passion itself, as exemplified by Emilia when she comments on Desdemona's firm conviction that Othello cannot be jealous because she never gave him any cause to be so. Emilia says:

> But jealous souls will not be answer'd so;
> They are not ever jealous for the cause,
> But jealous for they are jealous. 'Tis a monster
> Begot upon itself, born on it self.
>
> (*Othello* III. iv. 160–63)

One could argue that the main passion at play in *Othello* is neither the love between Othello and Desdemona nor its companion, jealousy, but the passion within Iago, demanding that he destroy the happiness of the lovers. It is the ultimate 'unreason', the utmost irrationality. While Richard III's destructive passions could be explained by the fact of his ill-fated birth and grim physical appearance– as Shakespeare lets Richard soliloquise about – Iago's passion is not explained by Shakespeare; it 'remains a passion seeking in vain for its own reason' (Sløk 1990: 80). As Emilia said about jealousy, it is a monster 'begot upon itself'.

Still, we cannot judge Iago or other individuals who act destructively as unambiguously evil. Iago himself is trapped between lust and reason, as are other humans, and he is very eloquent in his appraisal of this opposition:

> If the beam of our lives had not one scale of reason to poise another of sensuality, the blood and baseness of our natures would conduct us to most prepost'rous conclusions. But we have reason to cool our raging motions, our carnal stings, our unbitted lusts …
> (*Othello* I. iii. 326ff.)

Individuals incarnating this duality cannot be measured on an absolute scale of value, even if they can still be declared either good or evil. In the words of Hamlet, 'there is nothing either good or bad, but thinking makes it so' (*Hamlet* II. ii. 248–50). In some cases, we sense the disastrous consequences of the lack of moral standard, as when Macbeth himself declares that after he has murdered Duncan there is no longer anything of worth in the world:

> Had I but died an hour before this chance,
> I had liv'd a blessed time; for, from this instant,
> There's nothing serious in mortality –
> All is but toys; renown and grace is dead;
> The wine of life is drawn, and the mere lees
> Is left this vault to brag of.
> (*Macbeth* II. iii. 89–94)

Having destroyed the old order, Macbeth has also destroyed himself. Henceforth there is no hope of grace. Whether the Elizabethan audience actually saw it that way or not is of less moment than the inherent point that the world expanded with the birth of a new kind of individual responsibility.

What I am aiming at is a more general point that in the actions of Shakespeare's characters there is a latent fusion of historical dynamics and individual passion. The plays incarnate what seems to be a poignant ethical rule, not only in his world but also maybe in the world in general, that, under certain circumstances, the individual is not necessarily the *primum mobile* in committing a particular deed. This applies more particularly to human reason, which was later to be hailed as the locus of self and subjectivity by Enlightenment philosophers. Circumstances could – and can – overthrow both individual reason and responsibility.

As Vernant has said about the world of Aristotle's dramas, the individual who commits a crime is also its victim:

> The action does not emanate from the agent as from its source; rather it envelops him and carries him away, swallowing him up in a power that must perforce be beyond him since it extends, both spatially and temporally, far beyond his own person. The agent is caught in the action. He is not its author; he remains included within it. (Vernant 1992: 44)

This, I would suggest, is also true for Shakespeare's characters, with the difference, however, that the classical view of the daemonic influence has been replaced by the Renaissance view of individual passion as the force of development. Shakespeare helped people know themselves as part of a larger history that was not preordained but a result of a passionate human engagement in the world.

The newly found sense of self in the Renaissance gave rise also to a set of human sciences, born 'when man constituted himself in Western culture as both that which must be conceived of and that which is to be known' (Foucault 1994: 345). Although Shakespeare was not a scholar, he was actively engaged in making people know and conceive of the self, as a person fraught with ambiguity and subject to shifting historical allegiances. He – more that anybody – embodied the new philosophy of imagination. He also foreshadowed the postmodern anthropological view of identity having less to do with fixity than with movement (Rapport 1997). The confined space of the actual stage should not deceive; the theatre of action – as imaginatively presented on stage – expanded vastly in both history and geography, and the individual agents came to life through their movements within it.

Character: The Dialectic of Subjectivities

Shifting now from the Renaissance horizon of Shakespeare to the world of Shakespeare players, the emphasis also moves from the notion of self to the notion of character. The notion of 'character' already indicates that persons are formed within particular dramas, life histories, and social plots, in which they participate and to which they contribute. It is tempting to quote George Herbert Mead, who in 1934 suggested something similar: 'As a man adjusts himself to a certain environment he becomes a different individual; but in becoming a different individual he has affected the community in which he lives' (Mead 1965: 215–17). The individual and the social evolve in a subtle interplay; the self is visible only among others.

This does not mean that one is totally at the mercy of others' perception for one's own sense of character. We know perfectly well from gender studies, for instance, that women may be muted (E. Ardener 1975) and that wives may be incorporated (Callan and S. Ardener 1984). They are still persons, however, with a certain amount of power at manipulating their destiny (S. Ardener 1992). As social persons, people may seem to be prefigured, so to speak; yet as characters they are not reducible to elements in a system. Character – in the sense I use here – is the result of action and is reducible neither to a social position nor to the application of individual will. If the self is ambiguous, the character emerges in the wake of the actions undertaken by the self – partly in response to passions of various sorts, partly in response to the presence of others in the theatre of action.

A well-known theatre theoretician, Constantin Stanislavski (1950), has discussed the 'building of a character' at some length. Too often, this notion is taken to imply a mind-body dualism and to reflect an idea of the player's subject taking control over the object, the body. It is difficult to evince this dualism from the notion of acting because the very rhetoric used to represent the building of a character all too often gives the impression that the character is an object logically constructed in the mind and then put into the body. There is little, if any, discussion of the process by which the character actually gets incorporated (Zarilli 1995). This can only happen by way of acting – in character.

Evidently, the formation of a character in play-acting is to a large extent a matter of technique, of the wilful and talented transformation, even distillation, of real life. The actor Geoffrey Hutchings playing Lavatch in *All's Well That Ends Well* recalls his experiments in living the somehow crippled or disfigured character:

> I launched boldly into a character whose shambling gait and incoherent diction made Quasimodo seem like the Queen Mother. This became eventually modified into a recognizable human being as I began to draw on sense-memories. As a boy in Dorset, I often used to see a farmer taking his milk churns from his farm on a cart: a small figure with a stick, walking by his horse, his back bent and his legs bowed with age and labour. I remember from his knees to his boots he wore very shiny leather gaiters. Other such memories of people I had known or seen helped me to establish a kinaesthetic picture in my mind of how the character moved and felt. I have been asked if the germ for the idea of making him a 'hunchback' had come from his line on leaving for the court, 'I am there before my legs.' I can only say that it did not. Such was the organic growth of the character that I hadn't perceived this as being funny in that way until I actually did it before an audience. I'd thought it a witty line purely in terms of its word-play and not connected with his physical appearance. (Hutchings 1989: 85)

The important thing here is to note the real-life source of the character, on the one hand, and the organic growth of the character, on the other. It takes an imaginative effort and a husbanding of impulses to get to this point of creativeness, and the more so because the physical characterisation is not always given by the play itself. Playing King John, the actor Nicholas Woodeson tells how none of the countless physical characterisations seem any more justified by the script than others, and how he was interested, not 'in demystifying Shakespeare's kings, but discovering the inside of this one, how he was different from others. If I could sense a little of how he functioned, how he felt, then that emotional cast of mind would create its own appropriate physical characterization' (Woodeson 1993: 91). Physicality and emotion go together.

In spite of technical sophistication and skills, acting is not reducible to something that can be learnt intellectually. The main thing is still to be able to act convincingly, not simply to understand. The director Peter Hall says something to that effect when he ponders over his own acting skills, or his lack of them: 'I never could act. In my performances, I merely drew diagrams of acting – indications of how a performance could be shaped and what it should mean. I was giving a lecture on the part; I wasn't being it. Nonetheless, the lecture was clear, some people mistook it for acting ...' (Hall 1993: 55).

Studying the players' notions of their making of a character, one soon realises that in finding one's own path 'into' the character, mind and body cannot be separated. There is no distinction between 'self' and 'other', subject and object, along the lines of mind and body. The fusion of player and character is a precondition for acting convincingly. This relates to the notion of double agency, which I have also dealt with elsewhere (Hastrup 1998, 2003a) – implying the momentary fusion of the skilled player and the portrayed character into a 'third' person. This is known also from ethnographic fieldwork (Hastrup 1987). Incidentally, this fusion of player and character also points to the limitations of the by now venerable distinction between sex and gender (Hastrup 2003b).

Quite apart from the individual player finding his or her own feet to stand on, what is of particular interest in the present context is what one could call the dialectic between characters. One is not alone in establishing one's identity on the stage. It is constantly modified by the presence and expectations of others, as the players know and are able to relate in some detail. The dialectic is very much part of the players' experience during rehearsal, when they gradually 'find themselves' in the play in relation to others. Speaking of *Hamlet*, actor Philip Franks recalls from the production of Roger Mitchell that after having discussed the text among the entire cast, two or three people would gather and fill in their own picture of the characters' past history and inner life, and he continues:

> The input was threefold, and my own insights and discoveries started to be tempered by those of other people apart from Roger. This was particularly surprising when it came to investigating parental relationships. Bob Goody was creating a crippled, agonised, asthmatic Ghost, doubled up with pain and begging for revenge with, as it were, his last gasp. I had never thought of the part like this, yet suddenly it seemed to make perfect sense. Hamlet constantly refers to the Ghost in compassionate terms: 'Alas, poor ghost', 'ay, thou poor ghost', 'this piteous action', 'tears perchance for blood' – all these phrases leapt into prominence and with them a more complicated set of responses than I had anticipated. To see a strong, authoritative father brought so low and desperate provoked a far deeper unease and guilty responsibility than a mighty armed Commendatore figure would have done. Seeing misery and, more important, weakness in a parent for the first time is profoundly unsettling. I found it a valuable addition to all the other horrors of the scene, and I also found it very moving. Indeed, I was moved to tears by the scene almost every time we played it. (Franks 1993: 193)

Another actor, Michael Pennington, in his recollections of playing Hamlet, also indicates that the nature of the relationship between the main characters plays a vital role in the formation of the play, and he adds that this primary character dialectic 'is further refined at four crucial moments into Hamlet's purest and most distinctive encounters, those with his audience. These form the character's most confidential relationship; and in practice it meant preparing to meet the audience on terms as open and mutual as possible' (Pennington 1989: 119).

Hamlet's encounters with the audience are his soliloquies, being a means to communicate directly with the audience. When Hamlet poses his question of 'to be, or not to be', he is not simply telling us about his misery: he is sharing his thoughts with the audience. The audience, in general, is the ever-present 'third' party to the character dialectic, just as 'society' is the ever-present backdrop of any communication between people outside the theatre. If nothing else, it is present in language – functioning only because, by being public, it allows us a sense of *shared* understanding.

The character dialectic is related to a process of subjectification that takes place by way of self-objectification; as we have often heard, one becomes a self through the gaze of the other. If we believe that this is a new insight – owing to Merleau-Ponty (1962) and others to whom we refer today – we may like to think of Shakespeare's Brutus who states succinctly that 'the eye sees not itself / But by reflection' (*Julius Caesar* I. ii. 85), a point that is slightly more elaborated in a dialogue between Ulysses and Achilles on how one is mirrored in the other's gaze:

> The bearer knows not, but commends itself
> To others' eyes; nor doth the eye itself
> That most pure spirit of sense, behold itself,
> Not going from itself; but eye to eye opposed,
> Salutes each other with each other's form;
> For speculation turns not to itself,
> Till it hath travell'd and is mirrored there
> Where it may see itself. This is not strange at all.
> (*Troilus and Cressida* III. iii. 95–111)

In a manner of speaking, what we have here is an early expression of reflexivity and a profound insight (in the context of *Troilus and Cressida*) into the fact that such features as honour and reputation are not inner qualities but lie in the recognition of others (Kermode 2000: 89). People are positioned within a social 'field' in the sense suggested by Bourdieu (1990), implying also that they acknowledge their relative positioning.

This is another way of articulating the collective characterisation that happens all over the place. Individuals are in some important sense always accessories to each other's acts, as the villain Richard III claims for Anne Neville; admitting to having killed her husband and volunteering to kill himself for the love of Anne, Richard (Gloucester) continues:

> This hand, which for thy love did kill thy love.
> Shall for thy love kill a far truer love;
> To both their deaths shalt thou be accessory.
>
> (*Richard III* I. ii. 189–91)

This again is an important general point: no characters act in a void. We are surrounded by people whose actions exert influence upon the social space and which are therefore, directly or indirectly, party to our characterisation. In that sense, characterisation is always collective. Because character emerges in action and because people are never alone on a particular stage and therefore constantly engaged in character dialectic, we may now say more generally that human agents are accessories to each other's destinies. So, while individuality may imply uniqueness, it does not entail absolute self-fashioning. Quite the contrary: subjectivity is achieved through a process of (self-) objectification that is largely mediated by the presence and actions of others.

Society: A Theatre of Action

To recapitulate the argument so far: Shakespeare reminds us that 'individuality' is subject to internal, often passionate, conflict between desires that cannot be kept in check by reason; further, we have seen how his characters take shape in acting and in relation to other characters. The relative position of individual characters (being one source of their identity) is a function of a particular theatre of action; this concept firmly links the individual to a particular (social and topographical) space and makes it impossible to deal with agency as a matter of a disengaged reason applying free will to the world. 'The subject' is a simultaneity of body, thought, and social position. It is this combined, integrated, and embodied self that acts and responds to other actions. In the process of responding to multiple experiences, each individual may be said to be constituted by a variety of personhoods (see S. Ardener 1992).

The reason why I stress the embodiment of agency is the Western tradition of separating body and mind, object and subject, and locating reason and agency exclusively in the mind, seen as engaged in a more or less futile battle against the occasional eruption of less worthy drives. Rationality, in our world, has been disembodied and, accordingly, the self has been perceived as disengaged (Taylor 1989). The mastery of one's self implies not being slave to passion. *Willing* one's acts has been the hallmark of individual breeding, while collective domestication of passion and desire and of bodily drives has been cast as a prerequisite to a civilisation, the history of which is the history of increasing distance between mind and body (see Elias 1978). This is at odds with the Renaissance view of the self, and with human experience in general. Not only do we act upon implicit and only partly understood desires, but we also act upon an anticipation of a particular (social) drama – an imagined plot (Hastrup 2004).

There is no way to act meaningfully if we have no sense of participating in and contributing to a particular plot, a 'whole', in which we play a part. Social wholes, however temporary and fleetingly acknowledged, link people together as characters in a particular plot space, a social space in which everybody plays a part (Hastrup 1997). I want to emphasise the notion of playing a part, which is not the same as simply playing a role, although the theatrical metaphor in anthropology has often been used to signify just that. It is to be distinguished on two grounds. First, playing a part presupposes a whole – whether a story, a plot, a play, or a culture – without which no part is meaningful. Secondly, playing a part means becoming a true character, not pretending to be somebody else. The continuity between theatre and the world is profound; it is not simply a convenient allegory for social scientists to play with. The arenas may be of different scale and vitality, and yet they are mutually constituting elements in a reality that we can neither do without nor simply reach – except by an act of imaginative projection, implicating the knower as well as the known (see Shweder 1991). Realities are emergent and contingent upon action and imagination.

The notion of plot structure is originally owed to Aristotle, who in his work on drama simply defined it as the organisation of events (Halliwell 1987). The plot 'is the first principle and, so to speak, the soul of the drama' (ibid.: 38). One could argue that the plot is also the soul of the self, conceivable only in narrative form. In the words of Ricoeur, who has elaborated on Aristotle's notion of the plot, identity is narrative. We are narrators of our own stories but we are not, therefore, the authors of our own life (Ricoeur 1991). 'In place of an ego enamoured of itself arises a self instructed by cultural symbols, the first among which are the narratives handed down in our literary tradition. And these narratives give us a unity which is not substantial but narrative' (ibid.: 33). In narration we are always in the process of becoming who we are (see Nietzsche 1991). The very notion of narration gives impetus to the idea of society forming the ever-present third point in conversation. Language cannot be private and still make (social) sense.

Again, I think we are at a point where we can see that acting on stage is not set apart from social action in general. All theatres of action are closely tied to a vision of plot, to the anticipation of a story, a line of future development. It is a profound matter of *responding*, response being made within a moral horizon and within a social context that we interpret and project forward as we go along. Without a sense of plot, meaningful action would be precluded. The sense of plot is what integrates individual actions into a larger vision of the world, filled out imaginatively and acted upon. In that sense any social action is a creation, contributing to a history that outlasts (and outwits) our imagination. This is one reason why all meaning is emergent, as are those social spaces that anthropologists have incorporated while studying them (Hastrup 1994).

Society itself is thus implicated in individual action and character building. It pre-empts neither action nor characterisation. Rather it is constantly renewed or challenged by actions that were not previewed but were also not precluded by previous realisations of the social space. Individuals always – if to different degrees

– present discontinuities within it. 'Individuals experience and can generally only express what their world-structure registers, yet individuals can, as it were, "step out" of the structure under certain conditions, or perhaps individuals are not equally automatised by the structure' (E. Ardener 1989: 148). We all know how some individuals are always experimenting with expression or action. They are the first ones to stretch old language to fit new experiences, and vice versa.

What is at stake for social agents is the degree to which they can free themselves from the social and yet remain anchored in it so as not to be discarded as simply mad. History is made by human agents, who are in some sense always in contrast to their worlds from which they can never entirely free themselves (see E. Ardener 1989). This 'contrast' has been dealt with by Anthony Cohen:

> The opposition of individual to society may well be a figment of the anthropological imagination, rather than a consequence of their irreconcilability. There seems little reason to suppose that sociality and individuality must be mutually exclusive, nor even that behaving in a 'social mode' requires a person to mask his or her selfhood. The axiomatic juxtaposition of these modalities might be seen to reveal an overemphasis on the superficial dogmas of cultural theory, neglecting the more substantial reality. (Cohen 1994: 54)

This is not to deny, of course, that any society may want to cast itself as social in a particular way, using all sorts of devices to distinguish the collective from the individual. However, collectivism and individualism are inevitably two sides of the same coin. They are implicated in each other. This also applies to the individual who 'steps out' of the self-evident but who remains a challenge from *within* the social space, a creative element in the theatre of action.

Conclusion: Identity and Multiple Actualities

On the basis of the above, I would like to terminate this chapter on some general observations on identity as they present themselves though the prism of Shakespeare's plays. When Shakespeare claimed that the world was a stage, there was also an element or a vision of the artist transforming and multiplying experiences by imagination, and he 'may even come to think that what is true of his art will be true of the world it mirrors' (Granville-Barker 1927: 5). Few will fail to recognise some general truth in this; the world always partly becomes as we conceive of it. Definition and discovery merge. Action is never simply a reaction to what has already happened; it is also a mode of acting upon anticipation. The plot unites the actions within the play into one composite, whole action – the play itself. This is not necessarily a metaphysical point; it could be purely practical. With Shakespeare we are rarely left in doubt about the primacy of action and the need to get the play going by way of poetic emplotment: 'whatever the exigencies of its performance are to be, the play itself is an indivisible whole. It was the telling of a story; its shape would be dictated by the nature of the story and the need to make it dramatically effective' (Granville-Barker 1993: 41). In the drama, the representation of action (the act) and the organisation of the events (the plot) fuse and make one whole play, a world.

If drama works by its creation of a whole, it is noteworthy that we only become aware of it when it is gone: 'It is only when the drama is over that actions take on their true significance and agents, through what they have in reality accomplished without realising it, discover their true identity' (Vernant 1992: 36). I would argue that theatre allows us the luxury of experiencing a whole story, of seeing action in its total context, and thereby enabling us to understand the nature of motivation, which our daily life does not. So far from simply mirroring life at this level, theatre shows us what life never is: a whole. Only when life is over are we able to fully assess a person's character. At the same time, theatre shows us that identity is profoundly malleable and responsive to circumstance. The self is integrated mainly in its consistent response to new experiences (Ricoeur 1992).

This further enables us to understand both identity and agency as fundamentally social. The socially motivated body is not only the locus of agency (Hastrup 1995) but also the site of character, and thus the inevitable meeting point between the one and the many. The theatres of action – on stage and elsewhere – are the sites for the 'acting out' of authoritative cultural texts in more than one way (see Charnes 1993: 151) – and thereby confirming their authority. Language plays an important role in this. Not only because speaking is an act in its own right, but also because language never simply reflects the world, it deals with it, just as Hamlet deals with his own situation in his soliloquies. Once the words have been spoken, the world has changed.

At another level, the fusion of self and character stresses the need to acknowledge the *undivided* experience of action and meaning. Further, it substantiates the claim that being is *becoming* (Nietzsche 1991). By playing one's part, the whole changes – as does the player. Identities are thus both a precondition and a consequence of particular acts and are elements in an ever-emergent drama, featuring diverse characters in an open-ended plot. With the loss of 'culture' as a fixed frame for an understanding of the individual act, we are faced with a problem of recognition (see Taylor 1995). Recognition implies a kind of dialogue, which is more than a mere 'talking across' difference and creating a world of shared understanding. The idea of sharedness is always debatable, and it is certainly not a logical prerequisite of dialogue. Dialogue is not a matter of levelling of difference, but remains a relationship of considerable tension (Crapanzano 1992). This is why it has a transformational aspect: we talk across a perceived difference between you and me, other and self, and are transformed in the process. Yet, at the same time, the distinction may be affirmed. As a speech passing between two who are in some ways opposed, the dialogue is antagonistic, live, and dramatic.

The antagonism is due to the different contexts of the interlocutors. By their embodying different points of perception, their respective framings of the talk always vary to a greater or lesser extent. While we may be engaged in a talk on a mutually understood theme and converse meaningfully within a common vocabulary, the sense of unity is of necessity an illusion. What happens in dialogue is not a creation of conceptual unity, but rather a temporary fusion of horizons within a space of intersubjectivity – a space that is also the basis of anthropology (Jackson 1998). This space is of necessity more comprehensive than the narrow circle of the self, but the selves are not thereby dissolved.

The politics of recognition thus implies an acknowledgement of multiple views of the world or cultural difference, of tension, on the one hand, while also engaging in a serious talk across the void, on the other – on the basic assumption that if nothing else, then humans do share the ability to imagine one another (Shweder 1991: 18). It is in the tension between people, world views, cultures, or realities that something radically new may take place, affecting multiple actualities within a single plot space. In the process of dialoguing, we come to share the experience of relativism, and this experience is, paradoxically perhaps, what takes us beyond the claim of incommensurability.

Individuals must always negotiate diverse actualities; identity is the means by which they can act consistently and convincingly within multiple plot spaces and change in the process. Conversely, the social is a space created by individuals who coordinate their actions and horizons of expectation, all while putting their identity at play. If society is an ontological illusion, so is individuality.

Notes

This essay is written as a tribute to Shirley Ardener, whose generosity, wisdom, and scholarship have been important sources of inspiration for me over a period of thirty years.

1. All quotations from Shakespeare are from the edition by Alexander (1994). I follow the convention of giving act, scene and lines.

References

Alexander, P. (ed.) 1994. *Complete Works of William Shakespeare*, Glasgow: Harper Collins Publishers.

Ardener, E. 1975 (orig. 1972). 'Belief and the Problem of Women', in S. Ardener (ed.), *Perceiving Women*, London: Malaby Press, pp. 1–27.

——— 1989. *The Voice of Prophecy and Other Essays* (ed. Malcolm Chapman), Oxford: Blackwell.

Ardener, S. (ed.) 1975. *Perceiving Women*, London: Malaby Press.

——— (ed.) 1978. *Defining Females: The Nature of Women in Society*, London and New York: Croom Helm and St Martin's Press.

——— (ed.) 1981. *Women and Space: Ground Rules and Social Maps*, London: Croom Helm.

——— (ed.) 1992. *Persons and Powers of Women in Diverse Cultures: Essays in Commemoration of Audrey I. Richards, Phyllis Kaberry and Barbara E. Ward*, New York and Oxford: Berg.

Bourdieu, P. 1990. *The Logic of Practice*, Cambridge: Polity Press.
Callan, H., and S. Ardener (eds) 1984. *The Incorporated Wife*, London: Croom Helm.
Charnes, L. 1993. *Notorious Identity: Materializing the Subject in Shakespeare*, Cambridge, Mass.: Harvard University Press.
Cohen, A. 1994. *Self-Consciousness: An Alternative Anthropology of Identity*, London: Routledge.
Crapanzano, V. 1992. 'Dialogue', in *Hermes' Dilemma and Hamlet's Desire*, Cambridge, Mass.: Harvard University Press, pp. 188–215.
Elias, N. 1978. *The Civilizing Process: The History of Manners*, Oxford: Blackwell.
Foucault, M. 1994. *The Order of Things*, London: Tavistock.
Franks, P. 1993. 'Hamlet', in R. Jackson and R. Smallwood (eds), *Players of Shakespeare 3: Further Essays on Shakespearean Performance by Players with the Royal Shakespeare Company*, Cambridge: Cambridge University Press, pp. 189–200.
Granville-Barker, H. 1927. *Prefaces to Shakespeare*, First Series, London: Sidgwick & Jackson.
––––––– 1993 (orig. 1937). *Preface to Hamlet*, London: Nick Hern Books and the Royal National Theatre.
Hall, P. 1993. *Making an Exhibition of Myself: The Autobiography of Peter Hall*, London: Sinclair-Stevenson.
Halliwell, S. 1987. *The Poetics of Aristotle*, London: Duckworth.
Hastrup, K. 1987. 'Fieldwork among Friends', in A. Jackson, ed., *Anthropology at Home*, London: Tavistock, pp. 94–108.
––––––– 1994. 'Anthropological Knowledge Incorporated', in K. Hastrup and P. Hervik (eds), *Social Experience and Anthropological Knowledge*, London: Routledge, pp. 224–40.
––––––– 1995. *A Passage to Anthropology: Between Experience and Theory*, London: Routledge.
––––––– 1997. 'Teatrets Rum: En analyse af scenen i Shakespeare's teater', *Tidsskriftet Antropologi* 35–36, pp. 75–88.
––––––– 1998. 'Theatre as a Site of Passage: Some Reflections on the Magic of Acting', in Felicia Hughes-Freeland (ed.), *Ritual, Performance and Media*, London: Routledge, pp. 29–45.
––––––– 2000. 'Menneskelig handling: Illusionen som dramatisk grundvilkår', *Tidsskriftet Antropologi* 41, pp. 5–22.
––––––– 2003a. *Action, Anthropology in the Company of Shakespeare*, Copenhagen: Museum Tusculanum Press (Copenhagen University).
––––––– 2003b. 'Desire and Deception: A Discussion of Gender, Knowledge, and University Education', *Arts and Humanities in Higher Education* 2 (3), pp. 231–48.
––––––– 2004. 'All the World's a Stage. The Imaginative Texture of Social Spaces', *Space and Culture* 7 (2), pp. 223–36.
Hutchings, G. 1989. 'Lavatch in All's Well That Ends Well', in P. Brockbank (ed.), *Players of Shakespeare 1: Essays in Shakespearean Performance by Twelve Players with the Royal Shakespeare Company*, Cambridge: Cambridge University Press, pp. 77–90.
Jackson, M. 1998. *Minima Ethnographica: Intersubjectivity and the Anthropological Project*, Chicago: University of Chicago Press.
Kearney, R. 2001. *The Wake of Imagination*, London: Routledge.
Kermode, F. 2000. *Shakespeare's Language*, London: Allen Lane, The Penguin Press.
Mead, G.H. 1965 (orig. 1934). *Mind, Self and Society*, Chicago: University of Chicago Press.
Merleau-Ponty, M. 1962. *Phenomenology of Perception*, London: Routledge.
Nietzsche, F. 1991. *Ecce Homo: How One Becomes What One Is*, Harmondsworth: Penguin Classics.
Okely, J. 1996. *Own or Other Culture*, London: Routledge.

Pennington, M. 1989. 'Hamlet', in P. Brockbank (ed.), *Players of Shakespeare 1: Essays in Shakespearean Performance by Twelve Players with the Royal Shakespeare Company*, Cambridge: Cambridge University Press, pp. 115–28.

Rapport, N. 1997. *Transcendent Individual*, London: Routledge.

Ricoeur, P. 1991. 'Life in Quest of Narrative', in D. Wood (ed.), *On Paul Ricoeur: Narrative and Interpretation*, London: Routledge, pp. 20–33.

—— 1992. *Oneself as Another*, Chicago: University of Chicago Press.

Shweder, R. 1991. *Thinking Through Cultures*, Cambridge, Mass.: Harvard University Press.

Sløk, J. 1990. *Shakespeare. Renaissancen som drama*, Copenhagen: Centrum.

Stanislavski, C. 1950. *Building a Character*, London: Methuen.

Taylor, C. 1989. *Sources of the Self: The Making of the Modern Identity*, Cambridge: Cambridge University Press.

—— 1995. 'The Politics of Recognition', in *Philosophical Arguments*, Cambridge, Mass.: Harvard University Press.

Vernant, J.-P. 1992. 'Myth and Tragedy', in A.O. Rorty (ed.), *Essays on Aristotle's Poetics*, Princeton: Princeton University Press.

Wilson, J.D. 1996 (orig. 1935). *What Happens in Hamlet*, Cambridge: Cambridge University Press.

Woodeson, N. 1993. 'King John', in R. Jackson and R. Smallwood (eds), *Players of Shakespeare 3: Further Essays on Shakespearean Performance by Players with the Royal Shakespeare Company*, Cambridge: Cambridge University Press, pp. 87–98.

Zarilli, P.B. (ed.) 1995. 'Introduction', *Acting (Re)Considered*, London: Routledge, pp. 7–21.

3

Constructing Identities in a Post-Communist Society: Ethnic, National, and European

Zdzisław Mach

The long and complicated process of social, economic, and political transformation of central and eastern Europe, which began in 1989, is still far from complete and needs much more research to be fully understood in its many aspects. The decomposition, construction, and reconstruction of collective identities constitute one of the dimensions of this transformation that has been widely debated, but which still causes controversy and must be better understood. Contemporary central and eastern Europe is thus a very productive place to study – a social laboratory ideal for researchers interested in social change.

In this essay I intend to discuss some aspects of the transformation of social identity in Poland – a large central European country, which, because of its size, history and the complexity of its internal and external relations, seems to be a good case to study. I shall try to analyse some aspects of identity construction on different levels – from ethnic through national to European.

Identity as Symbolic Construction

Identity is a symbolic construction, an image of ourselves, which we build in a process of interaction with others. It is therefore contextual and dynamic, developing through dialogue and through the different ways in which people negotiate the meaning of the variety of the symbols that constitute their cultural environment and their social relations. Landscape, material culture, history, language, literature and art, ritual and myth, indeed, the totality of the cultural heritage of all the partners involved in the interaction – all these and many other symbolic constructions play a role in the process of the creation of images, serving as the material out of which these images as well as boundaries between groups are created (A. Cohen 1974; A.P. Cohen 1985). The construction of the identity of one's self and of others involves not only building symbolic images but also power relations, which must always be taken into account. Where there is an unequal balance of power between social groups, the process of mutual symbolic identification assumes the character of maintaining and legitimising the status quo through creating and re-creating the identity of all the participants in that social context. Changes in the balance of power result in changes of symbolic identification and models of identity. But symbolic images also play an active role in social relations, contributing to the transformation of the balance of power (Elias and Scotson 1965). Often the creation of an image of others, their model of identity, is an act of imposition (Ardener 1989). It may result in the acceptance of this imposed identification. An individual or a group may often come to accept their identity as it has been constructed by their partners in social interaction, especially if these partners occupy a stronger position in the social structure. An imposed identity can indeed thus be accepted and then belong to the self-image of an individual or group (Elias and Scotson 1965; Mach 1993).

Identity may therefore be considered as the effect of two factors: the social relations of power and the symbolic image of the world. The first factor includes the internal power structure in the group as well as relations with other groups. If, for example, the power structure is such that a particular social group is oppressed or incapacitated, then its chances freely to develop those activities in which its identity is formed and transformed can be impaired. The second factor – the symbolic model of the world – is the conceptual basis for these activities. The model of the world provides members of the group with images of themselves and others, concepts of social relations, ideas, prejudices, stereotypes, ideologies and beliefs. It motivates people to action and generates these actions, giving them their ideological and emotional dimensions (Turner 1967).

National Identity of Poles: The Construction of Unity

Despite now being largely homogeneous in ethnic terms, Poland has a long tradition of multiculturalism. The current situation is the result of ethnic cleansing, changes of borders, deliberate social engineering, and genocide. However, until the late 1940s, a large percentage of the Polish population was ethnically, linguistically, and religiously non-Polish and even non-Slavonic. The Polish state prior to the partitions in the late eighteenth century was called the 'republic of two nations' – i.e., Polish and Lithuanian – although its population in fact consisted of many more ethnic groups, such as Ukrainians, Germans, and of course Jews. The Polish Republic created after 1918 was also multicultural, the ethnic Polish population constituting merely 65 per cent of the total. The twenty years of Polish political sovereignty (1918–39) was dominated ideologically and symbolically by the slogan of unity: politically it was imperative for the new state to unite the three parts that had been controlled by Austria, Prussia, and Russia for the previous 123 years. Unity of the nation was the main theme of state-controlled education, and was strongly present in literature, art, state rituals, and the symbolically constructed public landscape (street names, the symbolism of public buildings, etc.). The historical background of the symbolic campaign to create this image of national unity took place during the nineteenth-century partitions of Poland, when the Polish nation was constructed by the intellectual, artistic, and 'spiritual' elite in the absence of a sovereign national state – in fact, in opposition to the existing states, which had divided up between themselves the Polish historical and ethnic territory (on the history of Poland, see, for example, Davies 1981).

The construction of Polish national identity was dominated by the interpretation of history as a process of continuous struggle against two neighbours: the Germans and the Russians. Other neighbouring countries and peoples were mentioned only marginally, while the meaning of relations between Poles and their two big 'significant others' and their respective images in relation to Poles dominated Polish national history as it was presented in literature, art, and school education, as well as in numerous myths and certain elements of the public landscape, such as historic buildings, monuments, or street names. The concept of history constructed around the dichotomy 'us' versus 'them' made the development of the Polish nation meaningful, justified past victories, and gave hope for the future.

In the absence of a Polish state and its institutions, it was the traditional 'spiritual' elite who assumed the role of constructors of the national identity. The Polish nobility and the Roman Catholic Church played the leading role in this process. Prior to the partitions, the nobility, or rather the gentry class, more numerous than elsewhere in Europe (more then 9 per cent of the population (Davies 1981: 215)), had had the monopoly of political and economic power, but had also been the only stratum of Polish society in possession of a national identity as such. They took on the responsibility to spread the feeling of belonging to a national community and national identification over to the rest of Polish society. Elementary education, which included national history and some national literature, became a powerful instrument in this attempt, while at the same time the state administration of Prussia, Russia, and to a lesser extent Austria, which controlled most of the territory that was historically Polish, tried to incorporate the Poles into their nations by assimilating them to their national cultures – through language, formal education, and careers in administration or military service. The Polish elite was supported by the Roman Catholic Church, which identified Polishness with Catholicism, in opposition to Russian Eastern Orthodoxy or German Protestantism. In the sixteenth century Protestantism had been increasingly popular in Poland, but the wars against Sweden in the mid-seventeenth century led to this gradual identification of Polishness with Roman Catholicism and to the representation of non-Catholic religions as inseparably linked to enemies of the Polish nation. Hence, in the nineteenth century, after the partitions of Poland, a combined national–Catholic symbolism dominated Polish national culture and made a strong impact on the perception of the position of the Polish nation in relation to its neighbours. This symbolism constituted the core of the representation of Polish national identity and dominated the national high culture. Such essential books as works by Henryk Sienkiewicz (a Nobel Prize-winner), Eliza Orzeszkowa, Bolesław Prus, Adam Mickiewicz, Juliusz Słowacki, and Cyprian Norwid, visual art (paintings by Jan Matejko, Artur Grottger, and many others), and also music (Chopin) have been dominating the Polish national imagination till the present (Mach 1994). These works had as their main theme the 'us vs. them' concept, while the interpretation of national history, as offered in school education, told the story of the nation seeking its identity in the complicated process of its relations with its neighbours, particularly the 'significant others', namely, Germans and Russians.

The idea of national unity was a powerful instrument in the struggle for the development and preservation of national identity and eventually for national sovereignty, finally achieved in 1918. The national culture was the main point of reference in the process of the construction of national identity, especially in the absence of the national state and of its institutions, administration, currency, national army, and other core elements on which a national identity is usually focused in nation states. Poland was then not a nation state: it was divided into three states, none of which identified with the Polish national cause, and it was the Polish national literary and artistic culture, as well as education and religion, that replaced the state in its role of national identity constructor. But it was essential that the model of national identity was presented to the Poles as well integrated, undisputed, and in complete agreement with the 'historical truth', social and moral justice, and religious faith. Any attempt to present Polish society as riddled with divisions and conflicts, or any suggestion that there might be different interpretations of Polish history, traditions, and culture, was considered to be anti-national, even subversive, and in the interests of the political enemies of Poland. Poles should be united behind their history, culture and religion. Suggestions questioning the official national orthodoxy, attempts to deconstruct and discuss national mythology, were attacked as anti-Polish (Mach 1993).

This model of 'united nation' put the minorities in Polish society in a difficult position. If there had been a Polish state, then there would have been a Polish citizenship as a basic category on which feelings of belonging and common identity could have been constructed. In the absence of the Polish state, the boundaries between 'us' and 'them' were constructed out of cultural symbols dividing those people who were presumed to share Polish ethnic culture from those who were classified as cultural minorities, because of their religious or linguistic differences. Therefore Jews, despite having lived in Poland for centuries, were 'others', as were Ukrainians, Byelorussians, and all non-Catholic, non-Polish-speaking inhabitants of the lands that were ethnically or politically dominated by Poles. The division of Polish society between ethnic Poles (Polish-speaking Roman Catholics) and minorities or ethnic others – members of the population who did not in this sense belong to the nation – became a founding construction of Polish national identity and Polish nationalism. This was strengthened by the reluctance of many members of these minorities to join the Polish national resistance movements aiming at political sovereignty. This tendency was particularly visible in the Austro-Hungarian part of Poland, where minorities enjoyed a relatively high degree of freedom in the multinational Habsburg monarchy. Minorities had every reason to be afraid that if Poland gained independence, it would emerge as a nation state dominated by nationalism, which would be less tolerant to minorities than Austria. There was therefore little reason for them to join the Poles in their national liberation movements. But the Poles understood this reluctance as a sign that they were refusing to show solidarity with them, even a sort of national treason. This feeling was particularly strong towards the Jews: because they lived in a condition of diaspora, lacking their own state or national territory in Europe (or a piece of land that might become the setting for their own nation state, as in the case of the Ukrainians), it was imagined that they could become loyal members of the Polish nation. There thus arose the concept that Jews were not to be trusted, that they were not loyal to the Polish national cause; it became an important element of Polish nationalism.

Poland indeed regained independence in 1918, and the following twenty years were spent on the consolidation of Polish territory and Polish national culture, together with the (re)construction of Polish national identity. The tradition of classifying people into 'us' and 'them' along ethnic boundaries remained very much alive. According to nationalistic Poles, ethnic others, in spite of being citizens of the new Polish state, did not have the right to Polish national identity. This logic led to the assassination of the first Polish president, Gabriel Narutowicz, who had been elected by the Polish parliament largely because of the support he received from MPs representing ethnic minorities; he was therefore denied legitimacy by Polish nationalists and ended up being assassinated by one of them. Of course, not all Poles shared such extreme views. The state attempted to create the unity of the nation through education and through a range of symbols, including those of military, religious, artistic, and literary significance. The young generation was educated in an extremely patriotic manner, although this process involved only those who attended Polish state schools (including many members of the ethnic minorities). Large segments of the peasant class remained substantially unaffected by this national culture and patriotic ideology (in 1921 more than 38 per cent of peasants over the age of ten were illiterate), and those members of the minorities who did not choose to join the Polish education system were also outside the symbolic system of Polish nationalism. In addition, some young Polish intellectuals rebelled against the orthodox version of Polish national identity and in their literary and artistic activity proposed an alternative, liberal view, in the direction of multiculturalism and a pluralism of world views. This was often associated with socialist ideas, very popular among young people, intellectuals, students, and some workers.

The Second World War, which opened with the combined German and Soviet occupation of Poland, led to the strengthening of Polish national identity in its traditional, nineteenth-century version. This view of the world, according to which Poland had always had two enemies, i.e., Germany and Russia, fighting against whom had determined the Polish fate and the identity of Poles, found its dramatic confirmation. Communism was installed in Poland by the Soviet army in 1945, and this further contributed to the strengthening of the Polish national identity and nationalism based on the model 'Poles against their enemies'. The old slogan 'unity of the nation' was paradoxically constructed from both sides of the political and ideological boundary, dividing Poles into communist supporters and anti-communist opposition. For the communists, the unity of the nation meant one, communist ideology, loyally followed by the entire society and leading to its 'glorious future', as directed by the Communist Party. To the opposition, the unity of the nation was understood as solidarity in opposition to the state and faithfulness to the national tradition, including (in some interpretations) the Catholic faith. Any attempt to demonstrate divisions within society and to argue that society was not united but divided in many ways (for instance, according to religious, gender, ethnic, or class divisions) would be considered as weakening the national cause and thus playing into the hands of the 'other side', i.e., the enemy.

Both the communist state and the leaders of the anti-state opposition (principally the Catholic Church) constructed their own symbolic model of the Polish nation, its culture and its identity, using a variety of symbols. The regime tried to present itself as a truly national government, representing the interests of the nation, albeit in alliance with the Soviet Union. Therefore the state used national symbols very extensively (Mach 1993; Kubik 1994), and tried to combine them with communist symbols of the working class and revolution (such as red flags, revolutionary songs, pictures of Lenin or of Marx and Engels). But on all state occasions the public space was full of national symbolism, from national flags and emblems to national music (such as Chopin), patriotic songs, and symbols associated with the glorious past, especially victories over the Germans (the battle of Grunwald of 1410, when Poles defeated the Teutonic Knights, was a particularly popular symbol of national history conveniently associated with anti-German ideology). The anti-communist opposition also used a full range of national symbols, but in combination with religious ones, such as the cross and, especially, pictures of the Virgin Mary from a national shrine in Częstochowa (Mach 1992).

National Identity in Post-Communist Poland

The collapse of communism in 1989 was the beginning of the end of this polarised model, which had been easy to comprehend and convenient to use in situations of political conflict. Gradually it became clear that the former ideological and symbolic polarisation oversimplified social reality and concealed divisions and conflicts in society. Step by step, various groups started to express their views, often not in agreement with traditional national ideas. In particular, it became obvious that Polish national history would have to be reinterpreted. It was not enough that one could now freely discuss past and present Polish–Russian relations, which had been strictly forbidden under communism. The entire Polish national history would have to be told anew; relations with neighbours and others would need to be re-evaluated. The new generation of schoolchildren and students demanded a less biased, more balanced, and multidimensional story of their nation and how it stood in relation to others. Instead of concentrating attention just on relations with Germans and Russians, the collapse of the Soviet Union resulted in the emerging awareness of new neighbours of Poland – Ukraine, Byelorussia, and Lithuania – whose place in Polish national history had to be reconsidered.

Perhaps the most spectacular change was a rapid growth of interest in the role of the Jews in Polish national history and culture. The former, official, communist antisemitism had led to the total elimination of this subject from public discourse, education, and the media. Now the public (especially young people) demanded information about Jewish history in Poland, not only in order to learn about the Jews as such but also to understand better their own history and identity.

However, many Poles still continue to think in terms of the old, polarised world and are nostalgic for its simple and easily understood model, where everybody knew who was a friend and who was an enemy. The plurality and ambiguity of the new world view, as presented nowadays by the liberal media and liberalised education, is more difficult to understand and requires much more effort. Therefore, many people continue to see the world in the old way, divided into the dichotomy of good and evil, and construct a symbolic system which is in effect a continuation of the old, communist system of thinking. The right-wing, nationalistic political parties, often fundamentalist Catholics, construct a very traditional image of Polish history, relations with neighbours, and the national identity of Poles, the essence of which is Catholicism and moral as well as political conservatism. The new, liberal political and cultural reality is for them a major threat to the well-established traditional system of norms and values. They try to defend the traditional interpretation of Polish history, with the old images of the 'eternal enemies of Poland'. The openness of the new, post-1989 Poland is from their point of view a disaster, because through the newly opened borders new ideas, ways of life, values, and world views freely come and 'infect' the minds of their fellow countrymen. Polishness is in danger, symbolised by the concept of liberalism – a word that in itself has become the symbol of a new, dangerous, and evil political and social reality. The essentialist concept of national identity, ethnic nationalism, and the close link between Polishness and Catholicism dominate this radical and noisy option. Many, though not all clergy and bishops of the Polish Roman Catholic Church share this view and sympathise with its proponents. The best-known example of this is Radio Marya, an influential, extremely conservative broadcasting company owned by a Catholic monastic order, which caters for those members of Polish society who feel threatened by the political, social, and economic change after 1989, and who feel lost in their attempt to adapt to the new situation and believe that a return to the past simplicity of the polarised world would bring back their secure life once again.

The alternative is the liberal option, which argues that the future of the Polish nation requires that its identity should be reconsidered in order to be more open, more inclusive and tolerant, without the essentialist element of the traditional nationalistic version. This option is represented mainly by intellectuals and liberal media, and also by a large segment of the Catholic Church of a liberal and intellectual flavour. They reject stereotyped views of relations between Poles and 'others', encourage debates about the Polish past, and acknowledge the ambiguity of meaning of national symbols. These two orientations fight for the hearts and minds of Poles, especially the young, many of whom feel lost and who distance themselves from such themes as national history, national identity, and patriotism. The public discourse is full of discussions about national symbols and ideas, while very many Poles are alienated and disappointed and withdraw to private affairs. It would seem, on balance, that the discourse is still in effect dominated by the old, nineteenth-century conceptual model of 'us' versus 'them'. The liberal view sees this as old-fashioned and no longer relevant, as well as being destructive of the present attempt to integrate Poland into the family of European societies – but it is not widely seen as a convincing alternative. Polish national identity is still dominated by the old generation of Polish intellectuals, people brought up and educated in the 1930s, whose thinking about the position of Poland in Europe is constructed along the lines of 'us and our enemies', where Poland is still seen as permanently threatened in its sovereignty by enemies, and the only significant question is whether we can defend ourselves or whether we will be defeated and deprived of our freedom yet again. Such questions as 'What could Poles achieve together with others?' or even 'What danger does Poland create for others?' are rarely asked; the only question here is, 'Who is attacking us this time and how can we survive?' Polish history has provided enough examples of such ways of thinking, and indeed this is how Polish national literature and art in the nineteenth century created the image of Polish historical identity.

The new generation of Polish intellectuals, in creating an alternative, liberal view, certainly expresses reservations about this model but has yet to construct a rival one. Meanwhile, the school curricula and the history and literature textbooks still propose the same old image: Poles versus their enemies. It is true that after the collapse of communism, the enemies are now somewhat different: there has been some attempt to eliminate the fierce anti-German propaganda that dominated the historical discourse before 1989. Also, Russia has been presented as an enemy at least as dangerous as Germany. But the logic remains the same. It is simple and convenient, providing easy answers to the question 'Why have we not achieved the success which we deserve?' and a scapegoat, when needed. But there is no new, fresh view on Polish identity in relation to other European nations, a view that would be a good basis for building a Polish position in the enlarged Europe.

Ethnic Minority Identities in Poland

Polish national identity, as developed in the nineteenth century and consolidated as a political ideology in the period between 1918 and 1939, also determined the position of ethnic and religious minorities in Polish society, as noted above. The boundary between ethnic Poles and 'others', as constructed in the nineteenth-century system of linguistic, religious, and historical symbols, pushed to the margins of Polish national society all those who did not belong to the culturally defined nation – even if they lived on Polish territory, contributed to social and economic development, and, when Poland became a state again after 1918, accepted Polish citizenship. In the Polish Second Republic (between the two world wars), the situation and rights of minorities were the subject of much political controversy. Nationalists argued for a policy of assimilation, wishing to create a Polish nation state, without minorities, on Polish ethnic territory and dominated by Polish national interests. This option was most prominently represented by the National Democratic Party. The opposite view was presented by socialists, whose leader was Józef Piłsudski, the hero of the war for independence against the Bolsheviks. He proposed creating a federation in which ethnic Poles would live together with other nations and minorities, notably Ukrainians, Byelorussians, and Lithuanians.

The Jewish minority was a separate issue. This large group (at that time more than 8 per cent of the population) was very heterogeneous, consisting of a wide range of people, from Orthodox Hasidic to assimilated Jews. There was, however, much distrust towards Jews in Polish society, as described briefly above. In the 1930s, antisemitism grew, partly due to internal Polish conflicts and partly as a result of the diffusion of extreme nationalism from Germany. Some Poles, no doubt, would have been happy to see the 'Jewish problem' solved, although the precise form such a 'solution' was to take in German-occupied Europe could not, of course, have been predicted. Nationalist Poles saw Jews mainly as their economic competitors and accused them of supporting one another against Poles, of being greedy and ruthless in business relations, and (following the nineteenth-century concept) of lacking loyalty to the Polish national cause. Nevertheless, the Jewish communities of interwar Poland constituted a strong element of Polish social and economic life; they enjoyed enough freedom (despite many instances of discrimination and even violence) to develop economically and politically; and Jewish education and culture were an important element of the multicultural mosaic of the country at that time. The main problem was the relative isolation of the two (Polish and Jewish) communities. They lived largely side by side rather than together, their mutual contacts were limited (other than in the case of assimilated Jews), and the knowledge of an average Pole about traditional Jewish culture and religion was very limited. This was especially true in the areas where Hasidic communities lived next to Polish peasant communities. There was economic cooperation, but little beyond that in terms of social relations. Research carried out in the 1980s on the memory of Polish peasants of the Jewish communities — their neighbours from fifty years before — revealed an extremely low level of knowledge and understanding of Jewish culture.[1]

The most numerous minorities in interwar Poland were Ukrainians (14 per cent of the total population), Jews (8 per cent), Byelorussians (3 per cent), and Germans (3 per cent). The situation of the Ukrainian and Byelorussian minorities was closely related to the problem of the eastern borders of the Polish state: they lived in the eastern provinces of Poland, while on the other side of the border there were the vast territories inhabited by their compatriots in the Ukrainian and Byelorussian Soviet republics. These borders were a constant source of tension between Poland and Soviet Russia, while the relations between Poles and Ukrainians and Byelorussians were dominated, on the one hand, by the memory of atrocities committed in the years after the First World War and, on the other hand, by centuries of Polish cultural domination.

Germans lived not only in western and northern parts of Poland, close to the border of Germany, but also in the big cities. The presence of Germans in Poland goes back to the Middle Ages, when settlers from German lands were invited to Poland to bring know-how and help to Westernise Poland. However, the thousand years of history of Polish–German relations is also remembered as the process of German cultural, economic, and often political domination, which (as mentioned above) became the leading theme of Polish national identity. The ambiguity of Polish–German relations is reflected in the stereotype of Germans held by Poles, containing a mixture of positive and negative elements: efficiency, good organisation, high culture, technical superiority, but also cruelty, ruthlessness, the tendency to dominate, even aggression. However, due to the high economic and social status of the Polish Germans, they did not suffer from discrimination and were well integrated into Polish society.

The Second World War changed the multi-ethnic character of Polish society completely. The Jews were murdered in the Holocaust. The Ukrainians and the Byelorussians remained on the eastern side of the new Polish–Soviet border, established roughly along the ethnic boundary separating them from Poles. Those Ukrainians who lived in territories that were predominantly ethnically Polish were deported to the Soviet Union or to the western Polish provinces, where they were scattered over very large areas in order to prevent them from organising themselves as minorities and to facilitate assimilation. The final destruction of Ukrainian communities in Poland was the result of the crushing of Ukrainian military resistance in 1946 by the Polish army. The entire German community who remained in Poland after 1945 was deported to Germany. All these were classic cases of large-scale ethnic cleansing, as we would call it now, although at that time it was generally accepted by international opinion as an understandable rearranging of ethnic relations following the end of the war and the new border arrangements.

The communist ideology that dominated Polish politics after 1945 created the image of an ethnically homogeneous nation. Minorities were presented as survivals of pre-socialist historical formations, which would disappear with the development of a classless socialist society. As mere survivals from the past, minorities were not supposed to be supported or recognised as elements of a modern society. Minorities were eliminated from the public discourse; school education never even mentioned their existence, let alone their contribution to the cultural heritage and economic development of Polish society. The image was that of Polish history belonging entirely to the Poles. The only expression of the existence of minority cultures in public was folklore, which was presented and even celebrated on the occasion of festivities, in museums, or at folk-song and folk-dance competitions. But it was out of the question that minorities should represent themselves politically or otherwise communicate their identity. In socialist society, minorities should simply dissolve – such was the official interpretation of Marxism–Leninism.

The Jewish minority was a particularly sensitive issue in communist Poland. Some of those few Jews who survived the Holocaust joined the Communist Party or even the secret police, and thus confirmed the image held by many Poles that Jews were not to be trusted and that they were in fact enemies of Poles. On the other hand, Jewish Holocaust survivors who returned home after the war often found that their property had been taken over by Poles, who refused to give it back. There were pogroms and instances of violence, of which the infamous Kielce pogrom is just one example.[2] Poles had to confront the question of their moral responsibility for the Holocaust: their pre-war antisemitism was seen in a different light after the genocide, committed by the Germans but with the passive and indifferent attitude of more than a few Poles. The memory of antisemitism and of the Holocaust was very difficult and troubling. It was more convenient to forget and to maintain the stereotype of Jews as anti-Polish. The Communist Party of Poland used this sentiment in 1968, after the Israeli–Arab war, when the Soviet Union and its allies supported the Arabs and condemned Israel. The Polish regime declared that all the many political and economic problems of the country were due to the subversive activities of Jews living in Poland, who were then all expelled. What then followed was a total silence about anything connected with the Jewish cultural heritage or even their very presence in Polish history; generations of young Poles were brought up and educated in total ignorance of the Jewish component of the history of Poland. Private, family channels were the only source of information, and they were full of stereotyped views. Independent public communication did not exist, while the only institution relatively free of communist domination – the Catholic Church – was not interested in teaching the public about Jewish people and their culture. For many church representatives, even very high-ranking ones, Jews were evil and not to be trusted, and certainly not worth remembering in Catholic Poland.

The German minority officially did not exist in communist-dominated Poland. Since all the Germans who lived on the territory of post-war Poland were supposed to have left, following the Potsdam Treaty, there could not officially be any German minority left in the country. If anyone declared German identity, he or she would have to leave Poland. Some Germans, however, did remain in

Poland, mainly in Silesia, and they tried to preserve their cultural identity in close family circles, but without any institutional framework or any public manifestations of ethnic identity.

It should be emphasised that under communism no local community, whether or not that of an ethnic minority, was able to organise itself; no form of self-government was allowed. The only institution truly independent of the state was the Roman Catholic Church, but it was closely linked to Polish national identity and used its power to protect and maintain it.

There were some non-Catholic and non-Christian religious organisations active in communist Poland, but they did not enjoy any power or independence even remotely resembling that of the Roman Catholic Church. They were, however, important for the identity of their believers and in some cases were central for their ethnic or regional identity. Good examples of these are the Polish Lutherans and the Polish Greek Catholics (Uniates).

The Lutherans are scattered in several big towns, but their main region is in part of Silesia near the city of Cieszyn, close to the Czech border. For centuries they have maintained their Lutheran religion as the main symbol of their separate identity, as opposed to Catholics or Jews. Dominated by a German-speaking Catholic community, they developed over many generations a world view in which to be Polish was identified with Lutheranism. It was only after unification with other Polish lands that they discovered that most Poles identified Polishness with Catholicism. Lutheranism then became the main symbol of regional identity in the Catholic-dominated country (Mach 1993; Kubica-Heller 1996).

Uniate Greek Catholics were Ukrainians or ethnic communities culturally related to Ukrainians, such as the Lemkos. Their religion developed in the sixteenth and seventeenth century as some Eastern Orthodox people accepted the authority of the Pope and some dogmas of the Roman Catholic Church, but retained the liturgy, symbolism, and ritual structure of Orthodoxy. In this way the Roman Catholic Church broadened its power and spiritual influence in part of the Eastern Orthodox domain. The new religion became a national church of those Ukrainians who wished to create a boundary separating them both from Russians and from Roman Catholic Poles. In communist Poland the Ukrainian minority was subject to repression because of the nationalist guerrilla fighting immediately after the Second World War and the deportations that followed. Those Ukrainians who managed to remain in their ethnic lands in south-east Poland were able to practise their ethnicity only through folklore, but without any chance to organise themselves politically. The Uniate church was unable to function freely, although it was not officially delegitimated, as was the case in the Soviet Union. Greek Catholic services were organised by the Roman Catholic Church, who chose to help the Uniates in order to prevent the Ukrainians from converting to Orthodoxy and to oppose the state policy towards the Ukrainian population (Hann 1985).

Ethnic Minorities after 1989

The process of liberalisation and democratisation of the Polish state and society that began in 1989 had a considerable influence on the situation of ethnic minorities. First of all, the minorities acquired the right to organise themselves in any legal way they wished and to manifest publicly their existence and their identity. Secondly, mainstream society began to develop an interest in the cultural pluralism of the past and present, an interest that was as much a matter of simple curiosity as the need to understand better the Polish social and cultural identity in its multidimensional and historically constructed character.

This new openness towards minority problems was particularly visible in relation to the Jewish presence in Polish society. Since 1989, there have been countless events in Poland devoted to Jewish history, culture, and identity: festivals, concerts, books, art exhibitions. Practically everything that is published concerning Jewish history and culture arouses extreme interest, particularly among the youth, who apparently not only wish to close the gap in their ethnographic knowledge, but primarily to try to reconsider their own identity, now seen within the framework of a multicultural society. Unfortunately, the actual Jewish minority in Poland is very small, not more than a few thousand people. There are a few functioning synagogues, where a handful of locals mix with numerous Jewish visitors, who come from all over the world to see the country of their ancestors or to revive the memory of their own past, tragic though it usually was. There are a few Jewish periodicals and some Jewish restaurants and cafes, though they obviously also cater for a non-Jewish clientele.

However, the most significant change from pre-1989 times is the presence of newly created monuments commemorating the Holocaust. In many towns and villages where Jewish communities had lived before they were murdered by the Germans, plaques and statues are being erected to pay homage to the victims and to stigmatise the murderers. There have been many debates concerning the actual wording of the commemorative texts attached to these monuments, debates involving survivors as well as different groups of Polish intellectuals and politicians: nationalists, liberals, post-communists, and the Roman Catholic Church. Perhaps the most prominent setting for such debates is Auschwitz, focusing much ideological discussion and strong emotions (Kapralski 2000). Some of them, such as the conflict over the proper or improper location of a Catholic convent in a building next to the former concentration camp or the struggle of a Polish extreme-right activist to erect crosses on the outskirts of the camp, became widely known and commented on in the world media. Among many aspects of these discussions and conflicts, there was also the question of ownership and the control of symbols. Who owns these symbols? Who has the right to say what their proper meaning is? Such questions were new to institutions in Poland not used to public debates of this kind, such as the Roman Catholic Church. A curious and often unpleasant competition between various groups of people who suffered from the German occupation over the question of 'who suffered more' added to the heated atmosphere of these discussions. Nationalistic Poles and some Jewish political activists were particularly active in this contestation, interpreting all aspects of the past to suit their political aims. One important dimension here was the role of Poles in the Holocaust, their responsibility for the fate of the Jews during and, especially, immediately after the war. The forgotten memory of these disturbing events was brought back to public attention and stirred emotions, but in particular it caused fresh debates among Poles about their history, historical myths, relations to other nations, and moral aspects of the past events. The memory of the pogrom in Kielce and the recent discussion about the murder of the Jews of Jedwabne by their Polish neighbours became symbols of Polish identity in all its complexity in relation to the Jews – the 'significant others' vis-à-vis whom Poles have themselves constructed their identity over many centuries.

The new, post-communist Poland became a place for more than one minority to rediscover and reconstruct its collective identity. The Germans were finally able to represent their identity in public, to organise themselves politically, and to begin the debate on who they really were: Germanised Poles, local Silesians, or just Germans. They soon became the best-organised ethnic minority in Poland, with representation in the Polish Parliament and with considerable influence on the politics of the region of Silesia where they lived (Rabagliati 2001). The whole region, traditionally squeezed between Polish and German nationalism, has been the scene of complicated processes of identity construction for several generations. Additional problems were created by the fact that a wave of immigrants from central and eastern Poland came to Silesia in the late 1940s to fill the place of the deported Germans (Mach 1998). After the communist period of artificially imposed silence, the debate about identity broke out with new strength, involving such symbols as language (local German, standardised German, local Silesian Slavonic dialect, standardised Polish), religion (some shrines, such as the Mount of St Anne, were claimed by more than one group as their own symbols of identity), and history (in particular the memory of the anti-German Silesian uprisings, which led to the splitting of Silesia in the 1920s) (Szmeja 2000).

Ethnic revival has also been experienced by the Ukrainian minority, who not only now organise themselves politically, but also try to regain their property confiscated in the late 1940s, including the shrines of the Uniate Church. This has caused a series of conflicts with local Polish communities, who had been using the buildings and, indeed, had often altered their appearance to make them look more Polish (as in the case of a church in Przemyśl, where a cupola, normally identified with the eastern rite, had been removed) (Hann and Stępień 2000; Nowak 2000).

The symbolic aspect of the ethnic revival has been strong in all cases. Often conflicts over symbols are the results of conscious attempts to monopolise the meaning or to dominate the symbolic space. Sometimes they are simply the result of ignorance or lack of sensitivity. Lech Wałęsa, the first democratically elected Polish president after 1989, always used to pin to his jacket a picture of the Black

Madonna of Częstochowa – the patron saint of Poland and a national symbol for Catholic Poles. He continued to wear the symbol after becoming president. This irritated Polish Lutherans, who felt alienated and excluded from the Polish nation by the fact that the President of the Republic should choose publicly to display the symbol of division between the Lutheran and the Catholic community (this is the role the Virgin Mary has been given by the two communities).

The Construction of European Identity

An important aspect of the political and social transformation of the Polish (and other central European) society after 1989 was the question of participation in European structures and European identity. The opening of the Polish borders after the collapse of communism was also the beginning of a long debate about the Polish place in Europe, Polish European identity, and relations between Poles and other Europeans.

For centuries Europe has been present in Polish national mythology. The history of Polish conflicts with the eastern neighbours, especially Russians, Ukrainians, and Turks, has been interpreted in terms of Poland playing the role of defender of the frontier – which has different names, depending on the context: Christianity, civilisation, the West, or Europe. This mission of protecting Europe from barbarian enemies became a core element of the Polish national/Catholic identity, together with the myth that presented Poland as a martyr who suffered and perished but through her sacrifice saved the world from evil. This mythology has survived till the present day and is very much alive in the world view of Polish nationalistic, right-wing political parties and the media.

For the educated, upper- and middle-class Polish elite, Europe was a dream and a heritage during those many years when Poland did not exist as a sovereign nation state and when Poles could not freely construct their identity. Polish literature in the nineteenth century is perhaps the most central element of the national heritage and the vehicle of national mythology. The poetry and drama of Polish Romanticism (the works of Adam Mickiewicz, Juliusz Słowacki, and others) and of the neo-Romantic period of the turn of the nineteenth century (Stanisław Wyspiański) created a powerful image of a Poland that died (that is, lost its sovereignty) but would be reborn thanks to her spiritual and moral virtue and would then redeem other nations. The popular novels of the nineteenth century, which shaped the view of the world of many generations of Poles (especially the works of Nobel Prize-winner Henryk Sienkiewicz), described the history of Poland in terms of its heroic struggles against barbarians from the East. The crowning achievement of the Polish protection of Christian Europe was the Battle of Vienna, when the Polish king Jan Sobieski led the Polish army to rescue Vienna from the Turks. Poles are very sensitive about this victory, the last one in Polish history, and always protest, to this day, if anyone interprets the battle in a way that does not give full credit to the Poles. After this historic battle, no more victories came, and Poles could fulfil their duty of protecting Europe only spiritually, by fighting evil forces with moral strength. The next chance to fight came after 1918, when Poland defeated the Bolsheviks on the outskirts of Warsaw. This battle is presented by Polish historians and authors of school textbooks (except those written during the period of communist domination) as a decisive victory, which prevented the Russians from exporting revolution to western Europe and thus destroying European culture and identity.

For the Polish elite, their belonging to Europe and participation in European culture were beyond doubt. They believed that having done so much for Europe – belonging to it culturally, as Christians, and as a people competent in Latin culture – the one thing they felt that nobody could deny them was their right to be Europeans. Such a sentiment was particularly strong under communism, when Poland was largely isolated from the West, and when educated Poles found it particularly difficult to accept not being able to travel and not having access to Western culture. Neither Polish membership of Europe 'as of right' nor the readiness of Poles to integrate with Europe was ever in doubt. At the same time, most of the ordinary Polish population remained indifferent to these matters. In the nineteenth century, peasant communities had no identity other than local, regional, or religious. Neither the nation nor Europe had any meaning to them. Also, in communist Poland, where only about 7 per cent of the adult population had university-level education, the elite concept of Europe and Polish European identity had little significance. However, in communist-dominated Poland, 'the West' represented not only freedom and high culture but also economic prosperity, and this aspect had a lot of attraction also for those Poles for whom access to European culture had little significance.

These two images – of a free, democratic western Europe and of the communist-dominated east – were, of course, antithetical to each other. The model was polarised: Europe versus communism. Europe became the symbol of freedom and prosperity, high culture and progress, while communism was seen as backward and oppressive. In this view, propagated in Poland by the anti-communist elite and by the Roman Catholic Church, the true place of Poland was in the West, in Europe, while communism was only an artificial, imposed construction, kept in place by force.

One of the first things that the new, democratic political elite did in Poland after the change of 1989 was to declare 'the return to Europe'. It was a very powerful symbol: Poland was to return to her proper place, to regain the status of a European nation. However, it soon became clear that different segments of the Polish society understood the idea of return differently. For some, especially the right-wing, orthodox Catholic conservatives and their political representatives, Poland has always been in Europe, understood as a moral entity, the essence of which has always been Christian values and the Catholic religion. In this view, Poland not only has always been in Europe, but has represented the core of Europe, being more European than other countries, where decadent people have forgotten the Christian essence of their heritage. The contemporary Europe in the

West, organised in the European Union (EU), is in this view very far from the original and authentic European Christian civilisation. It is, as it has sometimes been expressed, dominated by the 'culture of death', allegedly propagating euthanasia, abortion, drugs, and sexual perversions. This moral decay, Polish right-wing activists say, presents a grave danger to Poles, whose moral integrity and cultural purity are threatened. Only isolation can protect them. Therefore Poland should not join the EU. Now that this has already happened and Poland is a member of the EU, it is her duty to bring Christianity back to Europe, to play once again the role of the saviour of Europe, to protect her this time not from eastern barbarians but from the internal danger of atheism and liberalism. Among the symbols most commonly used by this conservative option are, of course, Polish national symbols, combined with Catholic ones, and images from Polish history, carefully selected and interpreted in such a way that the picture is unambiguous. To generate negative feelings towards western Europe, old anti-German resentments are recalled, such as the historic battles against Germans or literary and artistic symbols of the German domination of Poland.

The democratic liberal option, which also has a strong representation in Polish politics and the media, constructs a very different picture of Europe and of Polish European identity. In this concept Poland has traditionally belonged to Europe and to its Latin culture, but has been separated from this heritage by unfortunate historical developments. In their construction of Europe, liberals point not only to such traditions as the Enlightenment, the democratic revolution, and civil society, but also to the welfare state, individual freedom, and human rights, of which the right to choose is among the most central. The liberal construction is not against the Catholic tradition as long as this is interpreted as open and inclusive, represented by more liberal and tolerant, democratically oriented branches of the church. Poland has indeed a liberal Catholic orientation in the church, for example in its representation in highly respected periodicals such as *Znak* or *Tygodnik Powszechny*, and their supporters among the clergy include some very influential and respected bishops. In this way the Roman Catholic Church can be said to participate in the European debate, and the entire continuum of options, from very pro-European to very anti-European, is to be found among the Polish clergy.

The liberal option also offers a very different picture of Polish history, trying to deconstruct some historical myths and to destroy black-and-white, polarised images. It is more critical of Polish traditional values and the role of Poland in European history, more realistic about the evaluation of Polish chances in Europe, and less arrogant in its approach to the West and its contemporary culture. The central value of Europe, as represented here, is dialogue, openness, and the gradual construction of mutual understanding and cooperation among all European societies – with respect to cultural differences and also in the search for the common foundation of negotiated values. In this kind of Europe, Poland may not only rediscover her identity but develop it to create a modern civil society (Millard 1996; Mach 1997).

Of course, the two radically opposite views are only the two ends of the continuum of images of Europe and Polish European identity. Most Poles try to find their place in the new, European identity of the Polish state. This process is characterised by many dreams and hopes, but also by a lot of fear and anxiety. Poles know that in many ways they are different from the average western European, that the decades of communism left their trace. They have doubts about their competence, their chances to compete, to achieve success, to find a place in Europe. But nevertheless Europe is gradually becoming a place of reference and another level of Polish collective identity – not replacing other levels but adding to them. Although at this stage European identity has not yet been solidly constructed in the mind and symbolic world view of most Poles, and although the nation is still the most obvious and 'natural' basis for identity, a plurality of world views and symbolic images has become a reality of Polish culture.

Notes

1. The project consisted of interviews with Polish peasants and was carried out by a team of researchers from the Jagiellonian University led by Professor Andrzej Paluch.
2. Kielce is a provincial town in central Poland where, after the end of the war, about two hundred survivors of the Holocaust were to be found. On 4 July 1946 there was a pogrom in the course of which forty Jews were killed and over eighty wounded; there were also two non-Jewish Poles among the victims. The pogrom happened after rumours spread – following a libel that dates back many centuries – that Jews had kidnapped a Gentile child in order to use his blood to make *matza* (unleavened bread for the Passover festival). While the pogrom may have been provoked by the communist secret police – and indeed it was the police who started the killings of these Jews – they were joined by the Polish mob, who killed many Jews as well as a couple of Poles who tried to help the victims. The pogrom in Kielce ended hopes of any large-scale reconstruction of Jewish life in Poland after the Holocaust, and it became a symbol of antisemitism in Poland.

References

Ardener, E. 1989. *The Voice of Prophecy* (ed. M. Chapman), Oxford: Blackwell, pp. 211–17.
Cohen, A. 1974. *Two-Dimensional Man*, London: Routledge & Kegan Paul.
Cohen, A.P. 1985. *The Symbolic Construction of Community*, Chichester and London: Ellis Horwood and Tavistock.
Davies, N. 1981. *God's Playground: A History of Poland*, Oxford: Clarendon Press.
Elias, N. and John L. Scotson 1965. *The Established and the Outsiders*, London: Frank Cass.
Hann, C. 1985. *A Village without Solidarity*, New Haven and London: Yale University Press.
Hann, C. and S. Stępień 2000. *Tradycja a tożsamość*, Przemyśl: Południowo-Wschodni Instytut Naukowy.
Kapralski, S. 2000. 'Frontiers of Memory: The Jews in the Changing Landscapes of Poland', in S.C. Pearce and E. Sojka (eds), *Mosaics of Change*, Gdańsk: Civic Education Project, pp. 27–41.

Kubica-Heller, G. 1996. *Luteranie na Śląsku Cieszyńskim*, Bielsko-Biała: Głos Życia.
Kubik, J. 1994. *The Power of Symbols against the Symbols of Power*, University Park, Pennsylvania: Pennsylvania State University Press.
Mach, Z. 1992. 'Continuity and Change in Political Ritual: May Day in Poland', in J. Boissevain (ed.), *Revitalizing European Rituals*, London and New York: Routledge, pp. 43–61.
―――― 1993. *Symbols, Conflict and Identity*, Albany: State University of New York Press.
―――― 1994. 'National Anthems: The Case of Chopin as a National Composer', in M. Stokes (ed.), *Ethnicity, Identity and Music*, Oxford: Berg, pp. 61–70.
―――― 1997. 'Heritage, Dream, and Anxiety: The European Identity of Poles', in Z. Mach and D. Niedźwiedzki (eds), *European Enlargement and Identity*, Kraków: Universitas, pp. 35–50.
―――― 1998. *Niechciane miasta*, Kraków: Universitas.
Millard, F. 1996. 'The Failure of Nationalism in Post-Communist Poland 1989–1995: An Historical Perspective', in B. Jenkins and S.A. Sofos (eds), *Nation and Identity in Contemporary Europe*, London and New York: Routledge, pp. 201–22.
Nowak, J. 2000. *Zaginiony świat? Nazywają ich Łemkami*, Kraków: Universitas.
Rabagliati, A. 2001. *A Minority Vote*, Kraków: Nomos.
Szmeja, M. 2000. *Niemcy? Polacy? Ślązacy!*, Kraków: Universitas.
Turner, V. 1967. *The Forest of Symbols*, Ithaca and London: Cornell University Press.

4

MAKING SENSE OF THE PAST: REFLECTIONS ON JEWISH HISTORICAL CONSCIOUSNESS

Jonathan Webber

Making sense of the past ranks among the key intellectual activities of any society and indeed of any individual. Not only must we learn to select those social and personal events with which we have had direct or indirect experience, make connections between these events, smooth out inconsistencies, establish meanings, construct narratives, mask out uncertainties, and develop an aesthetic appreciation of our historical understanding of things; we also seem to be able to do it all the time. We know how to adapt previous interpretations to suit new circumstances, and we are capable of remodelling our memories of the past when, for one reason or another, we need to find fresh ways of seeing the world.

The human capacity to make sense of the past, and to do so in accordance with present perceived needs, would seem to be an intellectual universal, similar, for example, to the ability of a child to learn a native language and to do so in such a way as to be eventually able to understand utterances it has never heard before and indeed to construct intelligible sentences it has never uttered before. But, as we know, the totality of a grammar of a language is an abstraction, for it cannot be altogether brought to consciousness. Likewise, the culture we are conscious of is never the whole of culture. Our capacity to make sense of the past is not at all the same thing as the totality of our historical consciousness. On the contrary, it would seem that any definition of historical consciousness should include the notion that it is subject to change.

Just as there are countless possibilities for dialects even within a single language, often governed by quite different kinds of rules and structures, so too are there many different ways of being aware about the past, even within a single culture, or for that matter within the mind of a single individual. These variations in apprehending and presenting the historical past can be accounted for at many diverse levels: for example, by variations in concepts of time, in the stability of personal and social experience, in the presence or absence of trauma, or in developmental changes in narrative aesthetics. One suspects that in most cases, however different the results may be, it is always that sense of inner coherence which is the desired effect, if not also the prime mover. Historical memory must define a special relationship with what belongs to one's own experience of time. The act of memory is, at least notionally, to keep that past alive, to shape the personal and social self with a sense of continuity and consistency. But the techniques by which this is done vary greatly.

Here I follow through some thoughts about this with respect to the Jews – a people, a religion, a nation, an ethnic minority group (there are many definitions). Given the variety of historical and historiographic strategies to which I have just referred, there is, of course, no such single thing as 'Jewish historical consciousness', despite the title of this chapter. Nevertheless, the phrase does suggest at least some sense of a bounded entity, which I would like to explore in the sections that follow.[1]

Jewish Historical Consciousness: The Classical View

The phrase 'making sense of the past' has one particularly strong resonance in today's Jewish world, especially among academic Jewish historians – and that is the Holocaust. The reason is quite simple: the Holocaust is fundamentally a past that does not make sense; it is an unmastered past, to cite the phrase of Saul Friedlander (1993: 123, 102–16), one of the senior professional Jewish historians who have specialised in this field. The Holocaust is an unmastered past, even an 'unmasterable past' (Maier 1988), because it is historically incomprehensible. It is extremely difficult to account for it – whether, in seeking its causality, one identifies such generalised features of collective agency as the nature of bureaucratic modernity, the collective German psyche, or the history of antisemitism. Many senior non-Jewish scholars would agree. Jörn Rüsen, probably Germany's most important philosopher of history, writes that the Holocaust has altered the basic understanding we have of our own humanity. The reason is that this problem of adequately identifying its causality poses almost insuperable problems for the writing of history. Or, as Rüsen puts it (1997: 116),[2] 'the Holocaust calls into radical question the very character of what is historical': the enormity of the deeds of the perpetrators does not permit its inclusion in a continuity of historical development. Strong words, indeed. But the result is that the professional historians are unable to provide a master narrative, in effect (amongst other things) to provide that past with a sense of closure.

The professional historians' intellectual distance from the world of ordinary Jews poses additional difficulties. In particular, the dominant empiricist model of Western historiography, in its reliance on recording objectively 'true facts', the past 'wie es eigentlich gewesen ist' (as it actually happened), has meant in practice a questioning of the historical reliability of the many hundreds, even thousands, of published memoirs by Holocaust survivors. The historians see them as a deluge of uninformed informants – chaotic, unstructured, nothing more than the outpouring of feelings. How can such texts be incorporated into the narrative produced by the historian, how can the historian impose rationality upon them? Of course, this can indeed be attempted, and the seminal work of Martin Gilbert (1986) is a well-known example. But the gap between historians and survivors is unquestionably an important part of the ethnography. For what the survivors are doing, almost invariably, and often highly self-consciously, is quite another exercise. *They* want to make sense of the past, and they have only one strategy at their disposal to confer meaning to the emptiness, the meaninglessness, and the purposelessness of the murder of six million people in cold blood. Their strategy is simply, as they put it, to remember what happened. They say it is a sacred duty to remember, and they say that when they witnessed their neighbours and their loved ones dying in the mass graves in the forests, at public hangings, or during the atrocities of the concentration camps, they heard one voice from them: do what you can to survive and tell the world what happened.[3]

Hence, today, the public meetings (often on the anniversaries of important events during the Holocaust), the lectures to schoolchildren, the filming of return visits to Poland and elsewhere, in which the Holocaust survivor sits on the podium, grants an interview, or is the one chosen to light the candles or recite the memorial prayer. It is, of course, easy for the anthropologist to poke fun at the historian for not knowing what to do with all these supposedly uninformed informants. However, Friedlander remarks in one revealing passage (1993: 133–34) that in displays of popular Holocaust Judaism, it is ritual that may offer a sense of closure and in effect keep watch over absent meaning.

There is no doubt that the trauma of these survivors and more generally of the Jewish people following the Holocaust would be utterly destabilising for any fixed, continuing model of Jewish historical consciousness. Recalling the past in the present in this case means drawing out those dangerous, menacing, negative, and disturbing historical experiences that would usually be pushed away from the memory, preferably into the world of the undifferentiated other. In that sense, ethnographically speaking, one might have predicted massive interference with any identity model inasmuch as it perforce relies on a coherent view of the past. But the survivor's 'sacred duties' and their enactment often in a stylised ritual environment in fact rest on an important set of continuities and evoke deeper cultural considerations. For the duty to remember, the duty even to nurture a historical consciousness at all, is profoundly Jewish, and, indeed, in the opinion of many leading authorities is at the very heart of the entire Jewish cultural system. Hanging on to memory would in this perspective constitute the survivors' last stand at keeping their Jewish self-image, if not also their self-respect.

But how, it might be asked, can one generalise about the entire Jewish cultural system? The dominant discourse from within the system relies on the vast corpus of texts, beginning with the Bible and continuing with the Talmud and its commentaries, as the normal representation of classical Jewish culture. The ethnography of ordinary Jewish life is usually passed over in silence (though I will come back to this later, in the last section of this chapter). From the standpoint of the texts, however, the insistence on history and memory is very clear. The opening books of the Hebrew Bible or Torah present themselves unambiguously as the history of the people, set in the context of world history beginning with the creation. The duty to remember the past described there is repeated so very often that it is not difficult to argue, as did Momigliano, that whereas the ancient Greeks liked history but never made it the foundation of their lives, for the biblical Israelite, on the other hand, 'history and religion were one' (cited in Shavit 1997: 361).[4] The Oxford Old Testament scholar James Barr came to a similar conclusion (Barr 1961: 11). As the distinguished Jewish historian Yosef Haim Yerushalmi put it, the distinctive feature of the rituals described in the text are not mythic stereotypes but relate to events located within history (1982: chap. 1). The world view of the Five Books of Moses is firmly anchored in chronological, historical realities without being encumbered by legend (for example, Abraham, who lived several centuries before Moses, is in this sense correctly shown, historically, as being unaware of the Law of Moses), and the result is that the Hebrew Bible, says Yerushalmi, is a coherent narrative of the whole of Israelite history (ibid.: 14).

Yerushalmi's argument has remained very influential during the twenty years since it was first published. One enthusiastic version of his ideas can be found in a recent book by the British Chief Rabbi, Prof. Jonathan Sacks:

> The prophets of Israel were the first people to see God in *history*. The ancient world [on the other hand] … saw the presence of the gods in *nature*. … The revolution of ancient Israel was to see God not in nature but above it, utterly transcendent … Monotheism was not the only great Israelite discovery … Jews were the first to make the momentous claim that history has meaning. It is not merely a sequence of disconnected events, but the long story of humanity's response to, or rebellion against, the voice of God as it echoes in the conscience of mankind. (Sacks 2003: 27–28; emphasis in original)

And he goes on to say again that:

> Where other faiths, ancient and modern, saw religion as the flight from history into a world without time, Judaism saw time itself as the arena where God and mankind met … The historical books of the Bible are the first of their kind by several centuries, long before … Herodotus, … known as 'the father of history'. Yet the biblical narrative is never mere history, a recording of what happened because it happened … It is nothing less than the sustained attempt to see events through the prism of faith, as the ongoing interaction between heaven and earth. (Ibid.: 28–30)

According to the Chief Rabbi, what Judaism is fundamentally all about is the maintenance of this culture of memory: 'history is information. Memory, by contrast, is part of identity' (ibid.: 29). And it is through re-enactment of the rituals prescribed in the Bible that Jews can live again the events of ancient times as if they were happening now.

The Chief Rabbi's text is a highly coherent statement of what amounts to an essentialist view of Jewish culture: consistent, unified, establishing a sublime order of things, at the pinnacle of the developmental potential of all humanity, while the diverging cultures of other peoples and faiths are, again in classical essentialist fashion, comprehended as merely rudimentary prototypes or imperfect products of faulty development. 'Our' society is characterised by dynamic history, while that of others is characterised by stagnation, a world without time, where presumably hardly anything seems to change or move and basically would seem to lack history altogether.

Such, then, are the claims made for the Jewish concern with history as a fundamental defining feature of the ancestral culture and, by extension, for historical consciousness as the basis of Jewish identity, transmitted through the generations. Joseph Hertz, a predecessor of Jonathan Sacks as the British Chief Rabbi, came to a similar conclusion in commenting on a difficult passage in the book of Exodus (33: 18–23). Moses asks God if he can gaze at him: 'Show me, I pray thee, thy glory.' To which God replies, 'You cannot see my face, because a human being cannot see me and remain alive.' But then God has a suggestion: 'I am going to place you [Moses] in a cleft of a rock and will pass by in front of it. You will see my back, but my face will not be seen.' In a commentary published in 1936, Hertz makes an interesting interpretation of this somewhat enigmatic biblical passage (Hertz 1978: 363, ad loc.): the idea of understanding God not frontally but 'from the back' suggests that just as a ship moves through the sea leaving its wake behind, so God is known by his divine footprints in human history. One can glimpse God, so to speak, only through a consciousness of the past. It is just a cleft in the rock, but enough of a glimpse to obtain a sense of the larger picture. God leaves his traces in the world, and that is why the spiritual challenge to the Hebrews is to nurture a sense of history.

There are a great many examples that can be cited from the Bible in support of this view. Perhaps the clearest case concerns the observance of the sabbath, which, apart from being one of the Ten Commandments, is treated as one of the central rituals of Judaism. The biblical text, at different points, supplies three reasons why the Israelites should observe the sabbath. All of them rest on some sense of the need to be aware of the historical past. The first reason, which is given in the Ten Commandments in the book of Exodus (20: 8–11), is that God created the world in six days and rested on the seventh – therefore his people should do the same. By observing the sabbath people are to recall the entire process of the divine creation of the world. In the book of Deuteronomy (5: 15) the text supplies a second reason: 'Remember that you were slaves in the land of Egypt and that God brought you out from there ... therefore the Lord your God instructed you to keep the sabbath.'[5] By observing the sabbath the people are also to recall their national history, their spiritual independence from slavery and, thereby, their freedom from materialism.

These two reasons for the sabbath are clearly two historical master narratives, each of which can be treated homiletically as inspiring additional scope for ritual activity and spiritual meditation. But in addition there is a third reason given in the text – also historical but this time more of a folk nature. When the people escaped from the slavery in Egypt they arrived in a desert, which was totally without any source of food. To solve the problem, God sent down a bread from heaven known as manna, which the people had to go out and gather (see Exod. 16: 11–36). The story says that this manna came down from heaven only six days a week. Moses made it clear that gathering on the sabbath was in any case a form of work that was forbidden (ibid.: 23–30). It is as if, in later recollection of the event, the Israelites were saying: 'Long ago, when our ancestors escaped from slavery in order to become a free people, we established the tradition that we did not go out into the fields on the sabbath day to collect food. That is how it was then, and that is why we do not do it now.'

These three historically based interpretations suggest quite different conceptualisations of the sabbath but all arrive at a single ritual conclusion, the observance of the sabbath, by urging the need for historical reflection. All three concepts appear at various points in the sabbath liturgy, clearly reinforcing the insistence of the biblical text on the commemorative, historical depth of the sabbath as a central Jewish ritual.

But whether all this is to be called 'history' as such is a much more doubtful matter. It looks strongly like an anachronism, based on Western scholarly ethnocentrism. For example, the Bible has no word for history. Nor are events laid out in systematic chronological order with a coherent dating scheme – even if the text appears chronological and occasionally supplies dates. As the rabbis later asserted in the Talmud, 'ein mukdam ume'uchar batorah' (there is no chronology in the Torah).[6] The Bible may resemble history, but it is neither disinterested history nor a complete account. Too many events in the Bible seem to happen out of nowhere – 'once upon a time' or 'and it came to pass' – without obvious historical causes or consequences.

The creation story in the book of Genesis is not history in the modern Western sense. It is better understood as a conceptual handbook to the nature of reality, placed at the beginning to differentiate categories that are needed later on in the system for ritual purposes, such as for distinguishing the sacred and the profane (e.g., the existence of differences between certain kinds of animals or between the sabbath and the other six days of the week). The supposed historicity of the creation story is a vehicle or narrative strategy for making important cultural statements about the nature of the world, for establishing fundamental truths and for depicting what is changeless in the cosmos. God's promises to Abraham and the other ancestors that their progeny would be blessed is, again, not disinterested history but rather an explanation of the idea of the Hebrews as a 'chosen people'. This is not because they have inherent virtue but because they are who they are – descended from ancestors to whom those promises were made.

This also explains the tie with the so-called Promised Land, to which the Hebrews were foreigners, since Abraham came from what is now Iraq. They are to possess an existential link with Palestine, conditional on their agreement to observe the word of God. The narrative proposes these and many other such ideas as statements about the nature of reality. They are by no means intended simply as historical facts. Their significance does not lie in the past. The past as past, or knowledge about the past for its own sake, is irrelevant. On the contrary, these are presented as eternal truths, not at all as 'history'. The world is basically changeless, and everything in it was brought into being at the beginning of time. By definition, there can be nothing new. Hence the well-known phrase from the book of Ecclesiastes (1: 9), 'There is nothing new under the sun.'

So what, then, about memory? What can be said about the observation that the text insists so much on the need to remember?[7] The short answer to this is that 'remembering' is not about isolated historical facts or historical events. On the contrary, remembering is a metaphor for the active relationship between the people and God. Remembering is not an end in itself but a prerequisite for some other form of action, just as the image of forgetting means the abandonment of the relationship and the absence of action. In my own studies of the text I have noticed that the word to remember almost always comes with a predicate action; for example (to go back to the sabbath once again), the Ten Commandments in the book of Exodus say 'Remember the sabbath day in order to keep it sacred.' It is as if memory is the conceptual strategy for triggering effective ritual action. In Deuteronomy we have the same thing: the instruction 'Remember that you were slaves in the land of Egypt' is followed immediately by the statement 'therefore the Lord your God instructed you to keep the sabbath'. All this remembering is hardly disinterested in character: quite the reverse. As ever, biblical memory is goal-oriented, at the service of present needs – in this case the identity of the Hebrews as being in a covenantal relationship with God and in fulfilment of the necessary rituals. There are many other such cases scattered through the biblical text.

The annual Passover ritual, which commemorates the Israelite departure from Egypt, celebrates it as the key foundation event and master narrative of the Jewish tradition. It is clear from the biblical story how the representation of the event has been structured in the original narrative so as to become memorable. Even before the Israelites have left the country, the text is busy describing in detail how the future festival will be conducted to celebrate the event that has not yet happened. The narrative thus includes within itself a sense of its own futurity, and in particular how there will be, once a year, a ritual retelling of the story. Unleavened bread will be eaten during this future festival, because this will have been the food that the Israelites will have eaten during their departure.

In one extraordinary passage in Exodus chap. 10, God says to Moses that he is going to perform miracles in Egypt 'in order that you will be able to tell your children and your grandchildren what I accomplished there'. If one believed that the Bible is a history book, this statement would seem particularly bizarre, if not perverse – that the history is concerned with its own future, or that the ten plagues which paved the way for the departure from Egypt took place only so that future generations would have something to talk about. But if one starts from the assumption that historical memory in any case structures itself for present-day needs, then the text can be seen in fact as totally transparent here. Since the commemorative ritual is deemed to re-enact the past and make the past present, then of course the awareness at that past time that there was something historic going on can certainly be attributed to the original event. In other words, *that* historical present can be deemed to remember its own future. This would surely seem to account for the way in which the narrative has been written. The narrative describes the events not as they originally happened but rather proposes a story that is to be memorised and treated as culturally memorable. The narrative describing the original historical event was specifically structured with the needs of the future ritual in mind.

It should come as no surprise, then, that the Passover liturgy explicitly includes an injunction about the correct state of mind that performance of the ritual requires: 'In every generation all individuals are obliged to regard themselves as if they personally had actually gone out from Egypt.' This statement is not merely an invitation to private spiritual meditation regarding the personal relationship of the self with the material world (represented by the escape from slavery in Egypt); it is the assertion that the present-day participant in the Passover ritual did in fact take part in the original historical event because, as the text states explicitly, the original event took place with these future participants of the ritual in mind. Hence the roles can be exchanged. This is how historical consciousness – not history as such – can govern present-day identities. The narrative and its ritual have restructured the past in such a way as to deprive it of its essential pastness. It is now its essential presentness and futureness that matter. The past here is simply the medium of expressing these ideas. It is certainly not the message.

The Passover liturgy draws attention to the fact that the Jewish textual tradition extends far beyond the Bible. It also encompasses a vast post-biblical, talmudic, and diasporic experience, which I would like to comment on next.

Diasporic Ahistoricism

All these biblical memories needed to be remodelled when Jews began to experience their great national catastrophes and when memory, in the service of the present, had to take account of new social conditions. The first catastrophe happened in the sixth century BC, when the sovereign Jewish state was defeated in battle, the Temple in Jerusalem was destroyed, and the people were forcibly exiled to Babylon. A couple of generations later the Jews were permitted to return to Palestine and reconstruct their society. Five centuries after that, in the year 70 AD, the Jewish state was defeated again, this time by the Romans, the reconstructed Temple in Jerusalem was destroyed, and again the people were exiled. This second exile lasted nearly two thousand years, reversed only some sixty years ago with the establishment of Israel as a Jewish state.

The sociology of exile presented a variety of challenges, not least the constant remodelling and renegotiation of historical memory in the construction of Jewish identity, finding fresh ways of seeing the world in a coherent manner under new circumstances. It would be an exaggeration to claim that the cultural production of historical meanings became the highest priority, but it certainly suffused a wide range of activities and generated new narratives, as well as offering substantial scope for the restructuring of older narratives with new types of exposition. It would seem that it was during the period of loss of statehood and exile that the totality of the Bible came into its own as the founding document of the people. The rabbis, who now became the spiritual leaders of Jewish communities (as opposed to the priestly clan, who had at least notionally occupied this role during Temple times), slowly began to develop principles of biblical hermeneutics, seeing the text as free from error, fully comprehensive, and containing nothing superfluous. The Hebrew Bible thus became, quite literally, the textbook of the culture and for the culture. Whatever needed to be said had to be read into it or read out of it. And indeed, now that many of the biblical rules could no longer be practised (especially given the loss of the cultic centre in Jerusalem), study of the Torah and its commentaries, together with a new interest in mysticism, slowly became the religious and spiritual focus of what in effect was a new faith, founded on what came to be known as the Talmud. It was thoroughly text-based and, as such, saw itself as in continuation with the old scriptures.

Talmudic writings were accompanied by an intense effort to assert the historical continuities. What the rabbis collectively succeeded in doing – with some brilliance in the construction of this new culture – was to make analogies to match the new with the old, the unknown with the known, so as to exert symbolic power over new phenomena, put new things in their place, and domesticate them to the familiar and the mundane. The historical vision of the Torah still lived on, in other words, not only despite but because of the new realities.

Certainly, in memory of the catastrophes, new rituals of loss and mourning were added to the liturgical calendar, but the rabbis carefully accorded them a lower ritual status compared with the main observances specified in the Torah, protecting the Torah (as they put it) by restating the cultural attachment to that world which had been destroyed. Indeed, in reconstructing the details of just what had been destroyed, the rabbis introduced the regular liturgical recitation of the texts they had composed on these subjects, specifically to emphasise the idea that the previous system, now gone, could nevertheless live on in the collective memory – as if nothing had happened at all. Exile thus stabilised itself culturally. New historical memories were accepted into the system, but at the same time, in a manner surely comparable with many other diasporas, such newer memories coexisted with much earlier ones of peaceful life in the lost homeland.

With this powerful new emphasis on the lost homeland and the respecification of the historical memories associated with it, we can now better understand how those beliefs in the centrality of memory arising from the biblical tradition gained vigour and, indeed, came to be used as an emblematic banner to summarise Jewish culture. After all, once the Jews became a transnational diaspora whose members came to live far apart from each other, the very notion of membership in a single peoplehood became more and more of a construct, relying specifically on this memory of historically shared experience and common inheritance of a scriptural tradition. Having now become enclaves of minority groups in many different lands, the Jewish sense of cultural difference had to be constantly negotiated and renegotiated, place by place, generation by generation. In the context of the cultural hybridity that marks most, if not all, diaspora communities, the rabbinical leadership needed constantly to regenerate the sense of apartness and its raison d'être. The discourse they established included a sense of guilt and shame (it was because of sin that the homeland had been lost), a sense of alienation (God had simply departed from the people), and a sense of being surrounded by heathen impurity. Exile was one long dark night, which would be redeemed only at the end of time itself, at a messianic moment of God's choosing. Prominent reference was given in the daily liturgy to the sentiments of Psalm 137: 'By the rivers of Babylon, there we sat down and wept when we remembered Zion. … How can we sing the Lord's song in a foreign land?'

Now one fundamental consequence flowed from this view of the world: if the people were in exile and the spirit of prophecy had departed from them, then history was no longer dynamic but was in a state of stagnation. Time had become motionless. The idea of motionless time was, of course, known at one level from within the system, most especially from the usage of cyclical time, in determining the finite set of meanings of the rituals of the annual calendar, for example. Non-cumulative repetitiveness in this sense is not negatively loaded. It simply means that nothing new is added into the system. The calendar is full, and new historical events are merely repetitions of old events. Indeed, the rabbinic commentaries on the Bible relied heavily on this concept: all the important historical events had already happened; later events were prefigured in earlier events. The full meaning of history, why events happen at all, is fundamentally hidden from view, certainly to the ordinary mortal lifespan. But, to the extent that one is able to probe more deeply into the meaning of those earlier events, one can then understand the later ones. Time in this sense is an illusion, but mortal human beings in any case have only a very limited vision of time, circumscribed as it must be by the linear time of their own lifespan. Only the past is accessible for the understanding of events in the present.

It was this kind of approach which meant that the rabbis had no interest in investigating the way in which the life of the present systematically differed from the life of the past: all that is needed to know about the present is to study the past. The rabbis did not care about the chronology within their world. Even to this day, Talmud is studied with the help of commentaries that are not dated, even though they may have been written centuries apart from each other. On the contrary, all the commentators belong to one timeless world and are sitting in the same room discussing Talmud with each other.

History was not studied in the talmudic seminary and still is not, to this day. The rabbinic view of historical consciousness was that there was little place for new external events during the time of exile, other than for the writings of new rabbinical commentaries. When the Chmielnicki massacres of the mid-seventeenth century destroyed hundreds of communities in eastern Europe (mainly in what is now Ukraine), the greatest catastrophe that the Jews had known since the destruction of the Temple, the reaction of the leading rabbis of the time was not to acknowledge this as a new event by introducing a new fast day or other mourning rituals. It was said that the massacres were simply a continuation of the pogroms, by the Crusaders and others, that had taken place in Europe five centuries earlier (see Yerushalmi 1982: 48–51).

In the book of Genesis, when the Pharaoh of Egypt asks Joseph to interpret two dreams of his, Joseph said that the Pharaoh may indeed have had two separate dreams, but they were simply repetitions of the same basic idea (Gen. 41: 25–26). This reference to Joseph was the response of the Chief Rabbi of Cracow in 1650, when he wrote about the massacres (Yerushalmi 1982: 50). It was all one and the same: 'pogroms we know already'. The episode well sums up how the Jews did not develop new structures of historical consciousness in the Middle Ages. In fact, there are some today who say that the twentieth-century Holocaust also falls into this 'one and the same' event type: Auschwitz is not unique according to this view.[8]

It would be a mistake to suppose that this type of motionless time and historical forgetfulness should necessarily be characterised as faulty transmission or badly remembered history. On the contrary, the view of the Chief Rabbi of Cracow exemplifies an approach that is capable of recording only certain types of event, distilling the events of the past and present to fit pre-existing categories. Or, if one wished to ascribe rationality to it, one could say it is a conscious strategy, part of the whole rabbinic structure of memorability in shaping Jewish reality in the specific context of exile.

Another way of characterising this system is that it had little interest in the historical present (i.e., the present that needed to be recorded for the future), while having an immense respect for the memorability of the past as a category informing Jewish law, an area of everyday life that concerned the rabbinic system. Case law was largely governed by precedent and customary law. Ancestral custom, particularly local custom, was one of the most important legal mechanisms used by the rabbis of the exile. Given that, over the centuries, Jewish communities came to differ from each other in the understanding of many of the details of the received tradition, the rabbis in effect lent their support to the safeguarding, codifying, and consolidating of local diasporic identities by asserting their validity under customary law.

The principle of ancestral custom derives from the Talmud, which ordained that when the original reason for a custom no longer applied, nevertheless the custom must still be maintained. One astonishing example of this was the institution, during the early period of the diaspora, of celebrating a biblical festival not only on the specified date in the calendar but on the following day also. Before the Jewish calendar was fixed in the fourth century AD, diaspora Jews had observed two days of each festival instead of one, on the grounds that they were deemed to be uncertain of the correct date used in faraway Palestine when the festival would be being celebrated. But after the calendar was fixed, thereby removing any source of doubt about the precise calendrical date, nevertheless the Talmud ruled (tractate *Beitsah* 4b) that the previous rule of observing a second day remained valid since it was 'ancestral custom', and therefore should continue to be observed – it still is, to this day. It is a remarkable ritual statement of the special status of diasporic Jewish identity: its past, by definition, authenticated its present. Maybe, for the rabbis, the diaspora did not have much in the way of its own history; but that is very far from saying that diaspora communities had no historical consciousness of their own status as diasporic.

The Rediscovery of History

But what about the non-rabbinic, ethnographic realities of diaspora life? In describing Jewish life, the rabbinic law-books, to this day, consistently use the present tense: 'On Passover, Jews eat unleavened bread, on the Day of Atonement they fast, on the carnival of Purim they drink alcohol, on the ninth day of the month of Av they sit on the floor and mourn the destruction of Jerusalem.' This use of the present tense, coupled of course with a normative view of Jewish practice and the sense of motionless time, became over the centuries such an established usage that even today most ordinary Jews, when representing Jewish life to themselves or outsiders, still rely on it. There is really no tradition of an ethnographic discourse in the Jewish world, which would distinguish, for example, between what Jews eat on Passover and what Jews *actually* eat on Passover. It is true nowadays that some people would add the word 'practising', noting that practising Jews eat unleavened bread on Passover or that 'it is the custom' for Jews to do so. But these would really amount only to cosmetic improvements: the truth of the matter is that traditional Jewish society has completely disintegrated over the past two hundred years and is now structured on quite different lines from before. Today, the broad masses of secularised and assimilated Jews do not necessarily eat unleavened bread on Passover, though of course they might. Regardless of actual practice, the old text-based discourses are still dominant, in the sense that the new Jewish ideologies of modernity still lack a developed vocabulary other than that inherited from the classical tradition.

An important source for the problem of identity for many modern Jews derives from the absence of any significant ethnographic discourse about Jewish life in the diaspora, and especially Jewish history. Certainly there were always realities of life in diasporic exile other than what the rabbis recorded of their feelings of the long dark night. Perhaps the best way to put it is that, of course, the ordinary people in the lands of their dispersion were able (at least selectively) to construct a sense of being at home. The historical fact is that the exiles in Babylon in the sixth century BC did not all return to Palestine when, two generations later, it became possible for them to do so. To paraphrase the prophet Jeremiah (29: 4–7), they built houses, planted gardens, and prayed to the Lord for the peace of the city where they were in diaspora. This first Jewish diaspora was not only the result of forced migration but a voluntary one also. But much of this sense of at-homeness in exile was culturally invisible to the male rabbinical establishment, whereas it was probably a quotidian reality for many women.

Jews certainly spoke the local languages, grew fond of the local landscape, adopted local folk music, cooked using local recipes. For twenty centuries Jews did not try to return en masse to the Land of Israel. On the contrary, a multilingual, cosmopolitan, decentred, and transnational diaspora with its own internal networks constituted vernacular Jewish identity (Boyarin and Boyarin 1993), and indeed they spread further and further, even to India and China, and more recently to South Africa, Australasia, and South America. God would decide when the return would be, in the indefinite future. The *longue durée* of exile was not so bad as the so-called lachrymose view of Jewish history, dominated by incessant pogroms and antisemitism, would have it. As the distinguished Polish-born Jewish historian Salo Baron (1952) has emphasised in his monumental eighteen-volume social history, Jews often flourished materially and spiritually in diaspora. They were ideologically in exile but existentially at home.[9]

This simultaneity is surely a central point in understanding the bifocal cultural vision of diasporas, as I have argued previously with reference to the Jewish experience (Webber 2003). Whether this emerges, following the anthropologist Gerd Baumann (2002), as dual discursive competence or, following the Palestinian scholar Edward Said (cited by Clifford 1994: 329 n. 9), as 'contrapuntal' dialogic tensions or Paul Gilroy's 'double consciousness' with its 'syncopated temporality' (discussed ibid.: 317), the process of balancing the simultaneity of at least two coexisting discourses is the fundamental challenge, and the stimulus also, for the construction and negotiation of identity among diasporic groups. It is not enough, however, to recognise the existence of these simultaneities. The important thing is that there is a lack of symmetry between the discourses. They do not necessarily compete on equal terms.

But the relationship between the discourses changed very substantially for the Jews in modern times, when the hegemonic rabbinic discourse and its fundamental lack of concern with the social history of the diaspora came to be decisively redressed. The process began in the nineteenth century in Europe, at that time home to 90 per cent of the world's Jews (DellaPergola 1994: 62), when Jews slowly obtained political emancipation and were granted equal rights as national citizens. The long-term internal effects of these developments were dramatic, conventionally known today to Jews as the rise of assimilation and secularisation. Institutionally speaking, the synagogue and the talmudical seminary slowly collapsed as the principal public domains of Jewish life, to be replaced by the rise of Jewish recreational, philanthropic, sporting, political, and cultural associations and private societies for the exclusive recruitment of Jews rather than the pursuit of specifically Jewish aims or cultural goals as traditionally defined. New Jewish socio-political ideologies also came into existence, most notably an interest in socialism and communism, as well as the Zionist nationalist movement. But what provided perhaps the most influential aspect of this cultural revolution was a completely new interest in history. The movement started out on the initiative of new types of Jewish scholars, principally those who were university-educated.

Contrary to the model of motionless time and eternally valid religious law presupposed by the traditional rabbinic leadership, the first secularising European Jewish scholars, mainly in Germany, came to believe that history was a better guide and source of inspiration than traditional Jewish law. History slowly became the ideological starting point for the route out of religious practice, suggesting that Jewish culture had originated in the context of the primitive ideas of 'ancient times' which were no longer relevant. Change, not timeless eternity, was the true reality. Historical consciousness could now mean that Jewish culture had itself undergone historical development under the influence of changing conditions. It followed that contemporary Jews could equally legitimately adapt their lifestyles to the habits of modern civilisation.

History, first in scholarly forms and then later in more popular forms, became the medium for arriving at new definitions of Jewish identity. History slowly became the new religion of lapsed or lapsing Jews and it has remained so to this day. It is important to note that there was no attempt to cut Jews off from their past. On the contrary, the discourse of evolutionary historical development made it possible to restate continuities with the past. Making sense of the Jewish past, then, means precisely seeing it as the historicised past and a means for arriving at fresh ways of working out identities in the present. It is indeed a good example of similar processes observed in other societies (see Baumann 2002) of how renegotiating history and historical memory may be a key aspect of redefining collective identities. Many Jews find all this highly exhilarating. The sense of reclaiming hitherto neglected aspects of the Jewish historical past has given Jews a new feeling of empowerment, not only vis-à-vis the rabbinic leadership, which lost its monopoly of control, but also as part of Jewish ethnic assertiveness in the countries where Jews live. This has enabled Jews to repossess their own histories and, furthermore, to provide a Jewish historical counter-narrative to official state histories, in which they had hardly appeared at all.

The intellectual challenge for today's Jew is thus conceived in this approach as nothing less than 'the return into history' (thus, for example, the striking title of Fackenheim 1978). Following the establishment of the State of Israel in 1948, 'back to history' is now a political reality as well: Jews are no longer powerless, eventless, and historyless. They can re-identify themselves as a historical people. Whereas, under the old dispensation, history was the medium but not the message, history today is both the medium and the message. Jewish historians now confidently set out to reconstruct and restore forgotten diaspora histories. The Jewish public can now avidly consume their products in lectures, films, theatrical productions, oral histories, historical novels, and leisure trips to former diaspora homelands such as Poland, India, Morocco, and elsewhere. This type of historical past no longer obliges people. It does not have to be re-enacted or be made ritually present.

On the other hand, these new realities tell us something important about the nature of historical consciousness and its contribution to the shaping of culture. The new Jewish attitudes to the past may lack that inner sense of coherence and cosy familiarity which the process of making sense of the past should normally accomplish through smoothing out inconsistencies and masking uncertainties. Perhaps, in the explosion of new histories in the context of the steady democratisation of memory, too much is taken on as relevant. In the Polish historical heritage tours, for example, the visitor encounters a highly tangled web: Holocaust sites alongside the old pre-war graves of the saintly rabbis, the nothingness of destroyed cemeteries, the silences of market squares in small towns once densely populated with Jews, windows flapping in the wind in the abandoned former Jewish quarter of Cracow. All of these real places are also places of the historical Jewish imagination. Visitors coming away from these tours say they are simply numb. They cannot absorb what they have seen. It corresponds to nothing else they can operationalise in their lives. One has to ask: is this really making sense of the past?

The professional historian would answer that understanding the past, even within the Western tradition, has not been unified and has often contained within itself many opposing trends – for example, the reliance on both linear and cyclical histories, an interest in both the unique specificity of events and the generalised patterns they reflect, or a concern with both cause and meaning. The scholarly world can accommodate the uneasy coexistence of such differences and of course be invigorated by it, but the rediscovery of history for the Jewish world has led not merely to very substantial internal cultural debate about the new meanings attributed to history but also to considerable factionalism. The new historical consciousness has come to shape new competing identities: traditionalist, reformist, nationalist, and secularist, all in many varieties.

No new master narrative or meta-historical vision has been found to accommodate the totality of the recovered Jewish experience, including also the Holocaust. The introduction of the historicising principle was basically foreign to traditional Jewish culture and has played an important role in deeply unsettling it. Reconstructing the forgotten past for its own sake is quite a new idea for Jews, whether this is in the field of biblical criticism, the sociology of the Talmud, or the archaeology of the Holy Land. As a counter-commentary, it has sponsored radical re-evaluations of identity and, as such, has demonstrated, yet again, the cultural vigour with which attitudes to the past explain the present. It may even impart the sense that the people are living in important new times. Perhaps it is the existence of the debate that in many ways has become the intellectual homeland of many contemporary Jews: making sense of the past has become the medium for drawing people in and give them the wherewithal to construct their sense of cultural belonging. They want to be part of the same peoplehood, even though they may fundamentally disagree about what this means in practice. *This* is the heart of the paradox regarding the uses of the past – the point where the simultaneity of the coexisting discourses expresses itself most clearly.

But perhaps it was always like this. So let me end with a quotation from the Talmud (tractate *Berakhot* 27b, cited in Stern 1994):

> R. Zera said, quoting an opinion that R. Assi had said, in turn quoting an opinion that R. Elazar had said, in turn quoting an opinion that R. Hanina had said, in turn quoting an opinion that Rav had said: at the side of this pillar R. Yishmael ben R. Yose used to recite the prayer of Shabbat [Sabbath] on the eve of Shabbat.

So far so good, you might think: how seriously the Talmud here attempts to record Jewish history, but the passage continues:

> When Ulla came he said: it was at the side of a palm tree and not at the side of a pillar; and it was not R. Yishmael ben R. Yose, but R. Elazar ben R. Yose; and it was not the prayer of Shabbat on the eve of Shabbat, but the prayer of the end of Shabbat.

To which I suppose the comment must be that Ulla should have added: 'But yes, and on all other points the original story is historically entirely correct in all the details.'

Notes

1. I am deeply grateful to Shirley Ardener for her encouragement, over many years, of my work in Jewish studies, and so it is with enormous pleasure that I dedicate this essay to her. An earlier version of it was first delivered in May 2003 as the Marett Lecture, given at Exeter College, Oxford.
2. Cited in Eaglestone 2004: 137.
3. For a convenient survey of the relevant published sources for this, including the sacred duty to remember, see Wollaston 1996, especially her chap. 1 ('Why Remember?'). The Nazis were determined to leave no trace of their destruction of the Jews, causing two of the best-known Jewish survivors, Primo Levi and Elie Wiesel, to describe the Holocaust as a 'war against memory' (ibid.: 13). Giving testimony about what happened became in this sense an act of resistance, an obligation to the dead, and an act of mourning.
4. For a detailed review of the scholarly debates surrounding the comparison between the respective attitudes to time and history of the Greeks and Hebrews, see Shavit 1997: chap. 12.
5. The full text of the Ten Commandments occurs twice in the Hebrew Bible: once in the book of Exodus and once in the book of Deuteronomy. The two versions, though certainly very similar to each other, are not identical, and the two different reasons for observing the sabbath are one striking difference. The Talmud explains (tractate *Shavu'ot* 20b; for an English-language edition of the whole Talmud, see Epstein 1961) that the two versions were uttered simultaneously, perhaps as a mystical hint at the multidimensional nature of the divine revelation (cf. Ps. 62: 12, 'God spoke one utterance, [but] I heard it twice [or 'in two versions'], since that is [the nature of] God's strength'). Critical scholars would probably prefer to see such textual variants as evidence of rival traditions and/or authorships.
6. The talmudic reference, frequently quoted by later commentators, is tractate *Pesachim* 6b. The particular case under discussion that gave rise to the aphorism (which has wide

application in talmudic literature) was that the book of Numbers opens in chap. 1 with events identified as taking place in the second month of the second year of the departure from Egypt, whereas chap. 9 describes events taking place a month earlier.
7. Yerushalmi (1982: 5) and Sacks (2003: 29) say that the word *zachar* (remember) in one or other of its forms or declensions occurs 'no less than 169 times' in the Hebrew Bible. This is true: according to my reckoning, Mandelkern's magisterial concordance (1967: 353–55) lists precisely 223 occurrences of *zachar* as a verb and a further forty-five as a noun. Whatever the actual number, the idea that Judaism is fundamentally a memory culture has been taken up by many Jews nowadays as an emblematic position, even including secular Jews who feel that the duty to remember the Holocaust is thus authentically Jewish, being based on strong biblical foundations. It is not the whole truth, however. Traditionally – that is, in the perspective of rabbinic law – Jews are not obligated to remember everything that happened in the past, but merely certain key points: remembering the sabbath, for example, remembering the exodus from Egypt, remembering the revelation at Mount Sinai, remembering the attack on the Jewish people by the Amalekites, and so on. There are altogether just six such topics of memory, all of which derive from the Bible, and these are listed in the traditional daily prayer-book. The duty of reciting regular memorial prayers for the dead, as well as a particularly powerful liturgy of remembrance that is recited on the Jewish New Year, does, however, serve to fill out the self-image of Judaism as a memory culture.
8. See for example Solomon 1991: chap. 7 ('Shoah and Theology of Suffering'), which, after a detailed survey, comes to the conclusion that the Holocaust 'does not appear to have posed radically new questions for [Jewish] theology. The questions were there all the time. The Shoah [Holocaust] has focused our attention on them as never before, but they are the same questions' (p. 197). Most of the answers, moreover, are the same as those to be found in earlier sources, though some modernist Jewish theologians, acting in the interests of contributing to contemporary debates over the nature of religion and belief more generally (i.e., unrelated to the specifics of the Holocaust itself), have, of course, argued for new styles of explanation. Traditional theologies of suffering were in any case not particularly satisfactory, a view expressed even in the Talmud itself, in the Mishnah tractate *Avot* 4: 19 (see Solomon 1991: 198–200).
9. The phrase is that of Yerushalmi, in an important recent article (1997) arguing the case for at-homeness. It is true, however, that Jews have consistently complained of their suffering in exile. Indeed, it was a common theme of both rabbis and chroniclers, although in modern times it became known even for secular Jewish historians to accept Max Weber's characterisation of the Jews as a 'pariah people'. This view was encouraged by Zionist political philosophy, which (amongst other things) predicated from the outset (long before the Holocaust) the need for a Jewish state on a highly pessimistic attitude to Jewish prospects in modern Europe. Baron disagreed with this view (1952: vol. 1, 297). Such a flat, 'lachrymose conception of Jewish history', as he called it, was in contradiction with the objective facts. Furthermore, Jews may have experienced suffering (on account of sin), but at no time did they regard themselves as inferior or as a pariah people. But the lachrymose view, emphasising social distance, if not alienation, from the local environment, overpowered alternative histories, with the result that a more balanced historical anatomy of the sociology of Jewish exile, stressing the simultaneities, is not widely available. Some Jewish historians have recently begun to take up Yerushalmi's lead on this, but the dominant discourse within Jewish society still continues to give prominence to outbreaks of antisemitism.

References

Baron, S.W. 1952 (orig. 1937). *A Social and Religious History of the Jews*, 18 vols., 2nd edn, Philadelphia: Jewish Publication Society of America.
Barr, J. 1961. *The Semantics of Biblical Language*, London: Oxford University Press.
Baumann, G. 2002. 'Collective Identity as a Dual Discursive Construction: Dominant v. Demotic Discourses of Culture and the Negotiation of Historical Memory', in H. Friese (ed.), *Identities: Time, Difference, and Boundaries*, New York: Berghahn Books, pp. 189–200.
Boyarin, D. and J. Boyarin 1993. 'Diaspora: Generational Ground of Jewish Identity', *Critical Inquiry* 19 (4), pp. 693–725.
Clifford, J. 1994. 'Diasporas', *Cultural Anthropology* 9 (3), pp. 302–38.
DellaPergola, S. 1994. 'An Overview of the Demographic Trends of European Jewry', in J. Webber (ed.), *Jewish Identities in the New Europe*, London: Littman Library of Jewish Civilization, pp. 57–73.
Eaglestone, R. 2004. *The Holocaust and the Postmodern*, Oxford: Oxford University Press.
Epstein, I. (ed.) 1961. *The Babylonian Talmud*, 18 vols., London: Soncino Press.
Fackenheim, E.L. 1978. *The Jewish Return into History: Reflections in the Age of Auschwitz and a New Jerusalem*, New York: Schocken Books.
Friedlander, S. 1993. *Memory, History, and the Extermination of the Jews of Europe*, Bloomington and Indianapolis: Indiana University Press.
Gilbert, M. 1986. *The Holocaust: The Jewish Tragedy*, London: Collins.
Hertz, J.H. (ed.) 1978 (orig. 1936). *The Pentateuch and Haftorahs*, 2nd edn, London: Soncino Press.
Maier, C.S. 1988. *The Unmasterable Past: History, Holocaust, and German National Identity*, Cambridge, Mass.: Harvard University Press.
Mandelkern, S. 1967 (orig. 1898). *Veteris Testamenti Concordantiae Hebraicae atque Chaldaicae*, 7th edn, Jerusalem: Schocken.
Rüsen, J. 1997. 'The Logic of Historicization' (trans. W. Templer), *History and Memory* 9, pp. 113–44.
Sacks, J. 2003. 'Essays on Passover', in J. Sacks, *The Chief Rabbi's Haggadah*, London: HarperCollins, pp. 1–136.
Shavit, Y. 1997. *Athens in Jerusalem: Classical Antiquity and Hellenism in the Making of the Modern Secular Jew* (trans. C. Naor and N. Werner), London: Littman Library of Jewish Civilization.
Solomon, N. 1991. *Judaism and World Religion*, Basingstoke: Macmillan.
Stern, S. 1994. 'Attribution and Authorship in the Babylonian Talmud', *Journal of Jewish Studies* 45 (1), pp. 28–51.
Webber, J. 2003. 'Notes Towards the Definition of "Jewish Culture" in Contemporary Europe', in Z. Gitelman, B. Kosmin, and A. Kovács (eds), *New Jewish Identities: Contemporary Europe and Beyond*, Budapest: Central European University Press, pp. 317–40.
Wollaston, I. 1996. *A War against Memory? The Future of Holocaust Remembrance*, London: SPCK.
Yerushalmi, Y.H. 1982. *Zakhor: Jewish History and Jewish Memory*, Seattle and London: University of Washington Press.
——— 1997. 'Exile and Expulsion in Jewish History', in B.R. Gampel (ed.), *Crisis and Creativity in the Sephardic World, 1391–1648*, New York: Columbia University Press, pp. 3–22.

5

A Sense of People and Place: The Chapel and Language in Sustaining Welsh Identity

Gaynor Cohen

Within Britain, the Welsh language is often presented by the English media as controversial. In some cases it is seen as the instrument through which the minority, namely Welsh language speakers, impose their will on the majority. Promoters have been accused of encouraging linguistic racialism in Wales in the context of bilingual education policy. Yet few would deny the importance of language in a person's identity: 'For a man to speak one language rather than another is a ritual act, it is a statement about one's personal status; to speak the same language as one's neighbours expresses solidarity with those neighbours, to speak a different language from one's neighbours expresses social distance or even hostility' (Leach 1954 cited in Fishman 1966: 7). Identity, language and religion have been central themes in the edited book collections and seminar series organised by Shirley Ardener at Oxford University since the 1970s. This chapter discusses the role of the Welsh language and the chapel in sustaining Welsh cultural identity during the growth of mining and industrialisation in the Welsh countryside over the nineteenth and twentieth centuries.

Outsiders often dichotomise Wales's identity and culture relative to that of England. This can lead to a false picture of a homogeneous and cohesive community, which does not exist in reality.[1] This dichotomy is also operative within Wales. For many Welsh people, being Welsh means being different from the English. The majority of the population are conscious of the need to affirm their Welsh identity in relation to the English, their powerful neighbours, whom they perceive as potential perpetrators of cultural genocide.

The Welsh language is an obvious means of presenting this difference, although it is not the only or even necessarily the main mediator for 'Welshness'. Fiona Bowie (1993) analyses conflicting interpretations of Welsh identity. In Gwynedd, Welsh speakers are perceived by the English as the working-class locals living around the slate mines. Using examples, she argues that social class is often linked with Welsh identity and in some situations may manifest itself in aggression by locals towards the English.

In the South Wales area, to which my case study refers, there is ambiguity today over the definition of 'Welshness'. During the nineteenth and first half of the twentieth century, the definition of Welshness was closely linked to the Welsh language and the chapel. This chapter traces the Welsh sense of identity back to this period and then throughout the twentieth century through the eyes of my father, Llywelyn Jones, who lived from 1900 to 1986, in Llansamlet, a village situated between Swansea and Neath in South Wales. He lived and worked in two cultures: as an accountant in a British oil firm and as a local Welshman serving as the secretary of the local Welsh chapel. Much of the material for this chapter was collected by my husband, Abner Cohen, from 1965 to his death in 2001, who conducted long interviews with my father during our numerous visits to Llansamlet, South Wales. He appreciated the historical and anthropological insights my father provided regarding the transformation of the Welsh countryside from a land of agrarian producers to industrial wage labourers working in the mines. Later sections consider the influence of the Welsh language on children's educational standards and the decline and current regeneration of the language with schools' new bilingual policy. Finally I turn to the role of women in the maintenance of the Welsh identity before concluding.

The Building of Bethel Chapel in the Industrial Heartland of South Wales

The building of Bethel chapel in Llansamlet illustrates the link between the chapel, the family, and the community. During the eighteenth century, Nonconformism grew in strength in Wales. In 1740 a small group were meeting informally in the front room of a house in Llansamlet. Peripatetic preachers travelled substantial distances to link this house and village with others in the area. The Reverend John Davies was one of these preachers, travelling miles to homes in Neath and Skewen, Ystalafera, Swansea, Llansamlet, and Pontardawe. Once a month he held communion for a number of believers at his home in Mynyddbach. Eventually he persuaded the people of Llansamlet and members of Mynyddbach to get together and build Bethel on the site where it stands today. A wealthy coal-mine owner contributed money and land towards the building. The combined membership of farmers and miners who constituted the religious community came to about eighty. The chapel's opening ceremony was held in 1818.

The cost of the building was £352. In 1839 the community added a small gallery with stairs outside the chapel leading to it, so that services would not be disrupted by those climbing to the gallery. Within thirty years this building was too small for its congregation and a larger chapel was built in 1850 with a capacity for five hundred. After the lapse of some years, a committee made up of chapel members and officials met to decide on the size and plan for a new chapel that could accommodate nine hundred people. It was completed in 1880 at a cost of £3,057 and it took until 1915 for this sum to be paid off by the members.

This long-term chapel-building effort was undertaken by a small dissenting community with little surplus wealth. Bethel chapel offered a place of worship suited to the needs of families struggling in difficult circumstances as a self-sufficient, independent, religious community. The minister was chosen and paid for by the congregation. In the nineteenth and even the early twentieth century, many ministers were the sons of miners and had received only an elementary education. They empathised with the congregation and relied more on appeals to their hearts than to their minds. The best of them knew how to stir their congregation to great emotional heights with their distinctive oratorical style known as the *hwyl*. It has no exact English translation but would approximately mean 'soul'. It was a style closer to singing than speaking, rising to a crescendo at regular intervals, and guaranteed to move the most insensitive of listeners to fever pitch.

The whole family was likely to attend the evening service, after which the sermon would be the subject of discussion around the supper table in members' homes. The language of the home and the chapel was Welsh and continued to be so during Llywelyn's lifetime.

Llywelyn's Family

Llywelyn Jones was one of seven children brought up on a farm in Llansamlet. They were the Joneses Tai Esther, as the Welsh custom was to identify families by the names of the farms on which they lived. Llywelyn's father, David, had been expected to run the farm together with his brother but the soil was too poor to support two families, so David moved into wage employment as a miner in a local pit. The same pattern was true of other families in the area, who supplemented their farming income with wage employment from the mines or from other industries that had grown up in Llansamlet in the late nineteenth century, such as tinplate or copper smelting.

David married Sarah, a girl from another local farm. Of their seven children, four were girls. Two of the girls had children but Llywelyn was the only boy to marry. He met and married a woman from the neighbouring town of Morriston and I was their only daughter. As the only one of his family to have employment, Llywelyn delayed his marriage until 1936. South Wales had experienced a severe depression, when members of his own family as well as other chapel members were unemployed.

The years between 1914 and 1936 were bleak in South Wales. Once again, the chapel was needed as a haven. It was a time when the chapel gave as well as received donations. When the unemployed could not maintain their donations, they received five shillings each from the chapel funds. Llywelyn recalls: 'If we hadn't done that it would have been like taking bread from the babies' mouths.

No no, the very least we could do was to give them a little to tide them over. That's what the chapel's supposed to be for isn't it? Giving to those in need' (interview with Llywelyn Jones, Cohen field notes, 4 April 1965). Historians have claimed that the Nonconformist emphasis on thrift, self-help, sin, repentance, and temperance provided an anchor in a society undergoing transformation from rural to urban lifestyles (Williams 1985).

Chapel Organisation: The Deacons

Bethel, as an *Annibynwyr* (Congregational institution), had no centralised authority or regional structure, unlike the Methodists. Chapel elders were the deacons supported by two officials: a secretary and a treasurer. Four committees administered the chapel, those of the minister and deacons, the trustees, the cemetery, and the organ. In Llywelyn's day, deacons occupied a coveted position. Elected by the congregation for their high moral standards and leadership qualities, they were known to be ready and able to assist the chapel when there was need and to contribute slightly more financially than other members. Their standards of literacy in Welsh too were usually above average, although this was not a specified requirement.

Chapel membership was divided into six districts, with one deacon responsible for each. Every member was given a small envelope with a letter written on it signifying the district and a line underneath for the member's name, leaving room for each to write the amount of their donation. Every Sunday evening, after the sermon and before the last hymn and the secretary's announcements, the organ played hymns. This was a cue for the four deacons downstairs and two upstairs to walk slowly down the aisles carrying the donation plates. They would wait patiently for each plate to be passed from member to member, gathering each person's envelope. There would be no talking between neighbours during this process. The stately organ music added to the solemnity of the occasion.

After the service the district secretaries assembled in the deacons' room, at the back of the pulpit and the *sêt fawr* (big seat). The donations were then checked and counted and given to the chapel treasurer, who took the money home for safe keeping on Sunday night before paying it into the bank on the following morning. The treasurer was insured against theft or loss by the chapel. The house of one particular treasurer, who had been very nervous about the responsibility of the money, was broken into one Sunday evening. The thieves left empty-handed as the treasurer had hidden the money under his pillow.

Chapel Secretary

All the children of Tai Esther were faithful chapel members and good Welsh speakers. Llywelyn spoke Welsh to me, his daughter, but only until I was four. His

Sustaining Welsh Identity

concern for my later education encouraged him to use English as well as Welsh when we spoke. As in other such cases the language of the majority won over the minority language. Llywelyn finally spoke only English within our home. This caused me many problems when my mother and I visited my uncles and aunts, my father's brothers and sisters. They would always address me in Welsh. Over time I increasingly replied in English as my Welsh deteriorated. My aunts and uncles became angry and accused Llywelyn of allowing me to lose the language: 'Mai wedi colli'r iaith' (she's lost the language). In their eyes, this linguistic lapse was synonymous with losing my identity.

Despite leaving school at fourteen, Llywelyn, thanks to the years of extramural studies he followed, was the best educated of the family. The year he left school he became a chapel member. By the age of thirty, he was the chapel secretary, a function that became more onerous as the chapel started to decline in Llywelyn's later years. The secretary's main task was to organise preachers on those occasions when the chapel's regular minister was not available. Every Sunday he would have to get up on his feet at the end of the service to make any announcements – deaths, illnesses, births, marriages, recent and forthcoming events, and the name of the minister for the following Sunday service. If he had been unable to find an appropriate substitute for their regular minister, then as secretary he would have to preach himself. In later years, as the chapel lost their regular minister and had to rely on visiting preachers, these occasions became frequent. Llywelyn spoke excellent Welsh, which he constantly updated through his Bible readings in preparation for his regular Sunday school class, which he led.

The Chapel and Employment

The peak of the Nonconformist movement in Llansamlet coincided with Welsh industrialisation during the late eighteenth century. The rural Welsh-speaking Nonconformist movement had spread from the west, while industrial growth, bringing in non-Welsh, English speakers, spread from the east. Welsh cultural symbols were reinforced or even created at this time.

Eisteddfodau (verse competitions) were revived in 1858 when an annual National Eisteddfod was established, alternating venues between North and South Wales every other year. Locally, the chapels took over from the pubs in hosting the events. Some of the finest hymns were written during this time and the Welsh national anthem, *Yr hen wlad fy nhadau* (The Land of My Fathers), was composed by two weavers from Pontypridd in 1858. Music flourished and *Gymanfa Ganu* (singing festivals) were held annually in chapels, including Bethel. These were frequently supplemented by concerts given by invited artists and choirs. Many Bethel members belonged to choirs attached to other chapels or to clubs such as the rugby club.

There was evidence of growing national pride as industry expanded. In Llansamlet iron, tinplate, and copper were manufactured. The River Tawe, flowing west into Swansea, ran red with copper. Many Bethel members were employed in such industries as well as in the mines.

This period of prosperity in South Wales was short-lived. The conditions of the workers, especially the miners, became appalling. Trade unions to protect the workers' interests had not developed and, despite severe pit accidents, no compensation was given to the injured. Children and adults worked long days for low wages. Lloyd George, the first Welsh prime minister, agreed to import coal from Germany as part of the reparations for the war, creating a crisis in the coal industry as manufacturers in the Midlands and the North were reluctant to pay higher prices for British coal. This led to semi- and in some cases even total starvation for working-class families in South Wales.

Llywelyn was one of the lucky ones. In his evening classes he had studied and gained qualifications in accountancy. When, in 1921, a large oil refinery opened at Llandarcy, Llywelyn was employed as head of the wages department. As they did not then have a trained personnel manager, this responsibility was added to Llywelyn's employment profile. As many of his acquaintances and some from his own family were unemployed at that time, Llywelyn's post as personnel officer gave him a golden opportunity to find jobs for them. He frequently found himself under considerable pressure to use his position to the advantage of other Bethel members. In the early days of his marriage, fellow members of the chapel would come to his house in the evenings to plead their case. Many had reason to be grateful to him for their livelihood.

Employment at Llandarcy again provided cross-cutting ties between members of the congregation, although their workplace had a significant effect upon the use of the Welsh language. Bethel members spoke Welsh as their mother tongue, while most senior members of the Llandarcy refinery had been recruited from London and spoke mainly or exclusively English. Gradually Welsh became a medium reserved for use with close friends or in the home and the chapel.

As a senior staff member Llywelyn was automatically part of the management team and was expected to side against the workers in their union disputes:

> I never felt really comfortable in those negotiations you know. Especially if they involved men I knew, like Bethel people; even if I knew they were in the wrong. You are forced to take the management's side. I couldn't help feeling I was letting the family down. Because that's what it felt like. Men I've known all my life, who speak my language and pray with me every Sunday; they're like my family. (Interview with Llywelyn Jones, Cohen field notes, 9 September 1977)

The associational ties of Bethel chapel helped generate local employment for its members. Ivor Sims owned the sawmills that produced wood which chapel members purchased. Idwal Clements ran a funeral service that Bethel's ageing congregation used. There was one shopkeeper and one greengrocer whom Llywelyn urged his wife to patronise: 'I keep telling Doris it's important. They must be able to rely on Bethel members for support. It's like supporting your own family' (interview with Llywelyn Jones, Cohen field notes, 10 September 1977). For Llywelyn, the chapel members were in effect an extension of his own family. Their daily welfare mattered to him. Another important feature of this family was the common language they spoke.

Learning Welsh

Llywelyn, like other members of Bethel, began his education in the chapel. There they learnt the alphabet in English and Welsh, the foundations for developing their reading and writing. The Bible had been translated into Welsh in the sixteenth century. Throughout Wales chapel Sunday schools were training grounds for reading, writing and discussion of the Bible in the Welsh language. In the late nineteenth century Welsh writing flourished, both in Welsh newspapers and in literary efforts. The Welsh language lent itself to poetry as is evident in the focus on poetry writing at the national and local *eisteddfodau* and in the hymns still sung today.

Sunday schools provided a strong base for most people's education, especially in Welsh. In the early part of the nineteenth century, education in Wales was fragmented and elementary. Many children had no schooling outside the chapel. The national schools, supported by the Anglican church, found it difficult to recruit Welsh children, as Nonconformist families feared the influence of the Anglican church upon their chapels, their language, and their culture.

The Westminster government, concerned about education in Wales, sent three commissioners in 1844 to inquire into the issue. The three were young, male, Anglicans who sought advice from the Anglican clergy. Their reports, published as 'blue books' and which became popularly known as *Brad Y Llyfrau Gleision* (The Treachery of the Blue Books), became notorious throughout Wales (HMSO 1847). The reports attacked the medium of education, the Welsh language, which was presented as a stumbling block to learning. To people who believed that true religion was only capable of being taught in Welsh, any attack on the language was an attack on their beliefs. One writer saw the study of Welsh in the Sunday schools as essential because it was the best way to raise spirituality (Evans 1883).

The reports of the commissioners were thorough and mixed in their reactions to the chapel, the language, and Sunday schools, which appeared to evoke a sense of wonder:

> The Sunday Schools are an institution of peculiar character. ... They are composed of the congregations of different places of worship which meet on Sundays, not only for worship, but also for the instruction of the young, and for a systematic discussion of religious topics, which goes on concurrently with the instruction. The adult classes choose one of their number as a teacher, or rather as a sort of leader of the discussion. (HMSO 1847: 52)

The chapel Sunday schools, as institutions, were not the subject of criticism. It was their teaching of the Welsh language that was blamed for the flaws of education in Wales. The Welsh language was not simply presented as an obstacle to learning and progress but also as a vehicle of immorality and backwardness. In the wake of the reports the English press called for the extinction of the Welsh language and teachers were encouraged to punish the use of Welsh on school premises. Even as late as 1910 Llywelyn remembered having the 'Welsh Not' hung around his neck for unthinkingly reverting to his mother tongue while on the playground. This attack on the language led the Welsh to stigmatise the reports as treachery and engendered a passionate divide, which to this day lingers on.

The passage in the reports that gave the greatest offence to the Welsh was the declaration that Welshwomen were almost universally unchaste. In Wales 'mam', the mother of the family, had significant influence and in many homes, including Llywelyn's, had been instrumental in ensuring that the children attended chapel and Sunday school regularly. The consequences of the reports might have been irredeemable were it not for a young Welsh civil servant called Hugh Owen.

In 1843 Owen addressed his 'Letter to the People of Wales' (Owen 1843). An ardent believer in education as the way forward for the Welsh, he urged them to take advantage of any official government money available for education and argued his case with the mastery of the skilled senior civil servant that he was. His knowledge of Westminster and the 'corridors of power' was of the greatest assistance to his Welsh compatriots in their dealings with a Parliament representing Tory, Anglican interests. It was because of Owen that primary and then secondary schools were set up, creating in turn a demand for teachers. The establishment of training colleges for teachers and the University of Wales at Aberystwyth followed. These institutions had grown on the back of Nonconformist Wales.

Women's Role in the Chapel

Although I have not systematically gathered data on women's role in the chapel, no article dedicated to Shirley could not at least make some reference to women.

Llywelyn praised the faithfulness of women in the chapel. As early as 1965, he complained about dwindling membership and attendance at services. In a conversation with Abner Cohen he reminisces:

> *Llywelyn*: When I was young we had twice as many members. ... I must say that we have now more women than men members ... if it wasn't for the women the chapel wouldn't function.
> *Abner*: So why are there no women deacons?
> *Llywelyn*: They are entitled to become deacons and even ministers. In other churches this is the case. Strangely enough, in Bethel women are reluctant to elect other women. The number of women here now is 60 to 40 male members. They're always willing to

give a hand when needed. They're prepared to come and clean if need be. We pay 35 shillings a week for a woman to clean one day a week. If there's a special event on, then we ask for extra help from women members. (Interview with Llywelyn Jones, Cohen field notes, 12 September 1977)

Women had their own service in a sisterhood on Monday evenings. The sisterhood aimed to develop an autonomous group that contributed to the life of the chapel, with a president, secretary, and treasurer. Their president was the minister's wife who invited either men or women to address the sisterhood. They arranged outings for children and Sunday school tea parties. They spoke Welsh with each other and with other chapel members.

Llywelyn felt that the sisterhood had achieved its objective and helped women develop self-confidence. Even so, until 1975 there were no women deacons. Could that be an example of a 'muted group', to use the concept coined by Edwin and expanded by Shirley Ardener? In this instance, the women may have been described as muted because they lacked authority and power within the chapel, even though they were active in every part of chapel life and, as Llywelyn had observed forty years earlier, were its pillars. Today this is more evident than ever before, as the chapel struggles to survive, even as others in the area succumb to secular pressures and close down. Abner Cohen described a typical Welsh scene in 2000[2] in his notebook:

It is a wet cold morning in February 2000 in Bethel, a chapel in Llansamlet in the Swansea area of South Wales. The service should begin in five minutes but the mighty organ remains silent because of the cost of maintenance. The thin, tinny music now comes from a harmonium temporarily placed to the side of the *sêt fawr*. Five women and two men make up the morning congregation. They sit, not in one area, but are scattered in different pews, each the preserve of a different family, with the amplified sound of loudspeakers piercing the cold emptiness. For many weeks now the congregation has been without a professional minister because their appointed minister has been ill and now has to share his time between three chapels … the remaining congregation are struggling hard to protect the chapel from closure. Their techniques include abandoning their insistence on Welsh as the sole medium for the service, combining with the congregations of three other chapels for each service, and lowering the stringency of some rules such as the frequency of communion services.

Continuity of the Chapel Networks and Survival of the Welsh Language

The chapel is now kept alive by about twenty active members. The dwindling membership could possibly be explained within the context of the general decline in attendance at Christian religious institutions. The Welsh language, though, has suffered since Bethel chapel was originally built, by a strengthening of Nonconformism. Nevertheless, the chapels have provided the basis for sustaining and even strengthening the Welsh language through their networks and their support for bilingual education.

The foundations for bilingual education were laid at the beginning of the twentieth century. The impetus for growth came from wider political and socio-economic trends taking place throughout Europe (Hechter 1974; Khleif 1979). The first designated Welsh-medium school appeared in 1948. By 1982 their number had vastly increased, with the education service itself generating demand and offering support to Welsh-language teaching in the face of subsequent changes in socio-economic and political trends. Major reports, such as the Gittins Report (Gittins 1967), recommended the effective teaching of Welsh as a first or second language in both primary and secondary schools. In 1977, a consultative document, *Education in Schools* (United Kingdom, Department for Education and Science 1977), stressed the importance of the Welsh language in the life of the nation and the fact that the use of Welsh as the medium of teaching had no harmful effect on attainment. It therefore encouraged more Welsh learning by both Welsh- and English-speaking children and better language planning by Local Education Authorities.

The result is that there has been a rise in the number of young people speaking Welsh.[3] The Welsh language has also gained from the increased popularity of the National Eisteddfod, where it is the main medium of communication. During the National Eisteddfod's lifetime the Bardic chair[4] was consistently won by a man, frequently a Nonconformist minister. Three years ago the chain was broken when a young woman became the first to win the Bardic chair.

Other Welsh-language organisations have grown from chapel roots. Organisations such as *Merched Y Wawr* (Daughters of the Dawn) were women's movements established to foster the language. In 1999–2000, they had 277 branches and 7500 members from all over Wales. The 277 branches, which hold at least ten meetings a year, have received a grant from the Welsh Language Board and have opened clubs for younger people to socialise through the medium of the Welsh language.

Conclusion

Drawing on the biography of Llywelyn Jones, I have stressed the importance of the chapel in the life of the Welsh community. Llywelyn was born when Nonconformists were a strong force in Wales. Struggling to advance in a difficult and rapidly changing environment, they built chapels like Bethel to support Welsh-speaking communities. At that time, the chapel was an extension of the Welsh-speaking family, training the children in their own language and with cross-cutting ties created by employment, friendship and kinship.

By the time of Llywelyn's death, the chapel's influence had waned. The community did not have the same needs for nurture and comfort. The British welfare state and a developed education system had replaced those requirements.

Chapel membership dwindled in the face of strong competition from developments such as the mass ownership of television, motor cars and telephones and the exodus of younger generations in the search for employment in England and elsewhere.

The Welsh language suffered concurrently. Nevertheless, the foundation provided by the chapel has been the source from which language networks have recently grown. The language is now being taken forward through Channel 4C (the Welsh radio channel), the National Eisteddfod and the Welsh Assembly, which has taken over from the former Welsh Office. Bilingual education is now officially supported and increasing numbers of people are communicating in Welsh on a daily basis. Chapels remain important landmarks in the landscape, but the spread of the Welsh language currently is more likely to come through the influence of television and radio rather than public worship. Welsh identity and language have a strong post-industrial foundation. The mines are largely gone, but Welsh culture moves on.

Notes

1. I was employed as an education adviser for the Department of Education and Employment between 1983 and 1997. When Welsh advisers rose to speak about schools in Wales I used to hear my colleagues jest: 'Trust those two to stick together. They went to the same nursery school' and 'Can't tell whether it will be accurate or not. They can pass it on in a different language.' The jokes were good-humoured but could not have been more inaccurate. The Welsh advisers usually spoke no Welsh and came from different parts of the Principality.
2. My husband, Abner Cohen, died in 2001, his illness having deprived him of the opportunity to finish his Welsh study.
3. At a recent conference (May 1999) organised by the Welsh Language Board, Professor Colin Baker, a world expert on bilingualism and bilingual education, praised the Welsh-medium education sector on increasing dramatically the number of children and young people able to speak Welsh.
4. The Bards are the heirs of the Druids, those with spiritual and poetic gifts forming the gorsedd, a governing body of Bards. At the National Eisteddfod, the Druids/Bards, dressed in white robes, follow their leaders on to the eisteddfod platform, where a carved chair is placed. The Archdruid, in a traditional ceremony, crowns the winner of the verse competition, who is seated in the Bardic chair. One writer has called this 'the only national ceremonial order in the world based upon cultural merit' (Vaughan-Thomas 1985: 192).

References

Bowie, F. 1993. *Discovering Welshness*, Llandyssul: Gwasg Gomer.
Cohen, A. 1965–2000. Unpublished field notes.
Evans, Rev. D. 1883. *The Sunday Schools of Wales*, London: The Sunday School Union.
Fishman, J.A. 1966. *Language Loyalty in the United States*, The Hague: Mouton.

Gittins, C.E. 1967. *Addysg gynradd Cymru*, London: Department of Education/Central Advisory Council for Education.

Hechter, M. 1974. 'The Political Economy of Ethnic Change', *American Journal of Sociology* 79, pp. 1151–78.

HMSO 1847. *Reports of the Royal Commission of Inquiry into the State of Education in Wales, appointed by the Committee of Council, Chairman Kay-Shuttleworth*, vol. 1, London: HMSO.

Khleif, B.B. 1979a. 'Ethnic Awakening in the First World: the Case of Wales', in G. Williams (ed.), *Social and Cultural Change in Contemporary Wales*, London and Boston: Routledge & Kegan Paul, pp. 102–19.

Leach, E. 1954. *Political Systems of Highland Burma*, London: Thames & Hudson.

Owen, H. 1843. 'Letter to the People of Wales published August 26 1843', Caernarfon Civics Society, County Hall, www.caernarfononline.co.uk/civic_society/page16.html

United Kingdom, Department for Education and Science 1977. *Education in Schools: Consultative Document*, London: HMSO.

Vaughan-Thomas, W. 1985. *Wales: A History*, London: Michael Joseph.

Williams, G.A. 1985. *When was Wales? A History of the Welsh*, Harmondsworth: Penguin Books.

6

Towards an Ethnography of Colleagueship

Hilary Callan

> Not only can one never be fully aware of who one is in a relationship with, since the self is less a thing than a process, but one can never be entirely sure what definition of 'self', situation, or relationship the 'other' has created. (Crick 1992: 176)

In this short essay I focus on two issues relating to colleagueship and anthropology. First, I look at a case drawn from my own occupational experience and recent analytical work, where it seems to me that colleagueship is germane to an understanding of institution building and the negotiation of identities in a particular environment. Secondly, using the same material, I consider the 'colleague relationship' as a context and a tool for ethnography. The designation of this relationship is, inevitably, imprecise, but perhaps no more so than others that have been much discussed as a basis for the production of anthropological knowledge, such as those of sojourner to host, enquirer to informant, or friend to friend. In its most general sense, colleagueship implies reciprocity and a shared engagement in a common pursuit; and in this sense, of course, it has frequently been argued[1] that forms of co-authorship and hence of colleagueship lie at the heart of ethnographic production, whether or not this is recognised. Here, I take a less inclusive view and examine colleagueship in a more everyday, contemporary sense – referring, roughly, to a relation of co-workers between whom a common occupational orientation of some kind is being emphasised.

Colleagueship in this sense has been neglected as a relationship providing a context for anthropological understanding. This is no doubt attributable partly to its provenance as a relatively recent construct tied to largely contemporary occupational conditions. Yet it is a construct capable of carrying great subtlety[2] in the negotiation of self and identity. It is a relation of assertion as well as of description: to claim colleagueship is to make a statement about a structure. Its edges are ambiguous: at one pole, it slides into representations of friendship, at another, into those of hierarchy. But it can also be oppositional to these. Sometimes, as in the standard 'Colleagues and friends' salutation at the beginning of speeches, the categories are purposefully conflated; at other times, they are differentiated, as where colleagues are represented as becoming, being, or not being friends. Again, claims to colleagueship can stand as a suppression of hierarchy even where it is present; yet such a claim is notably more likely to be made in a 'top-down' than a 'bottom-up' direction. A manager is more likely to speak of his 'colleagues' on the shop floor than the latter to theirs in the boardroom. Gender too adds a dimension: there are situations in which the assertion of colleagueship can either counter or reinforce gendered relationships and roles.

The analytical neglect of colleagueship is surely surprising in an anthropology that has been for some years both open to ethnography 'at home' (Jackson 1987) and collectively engaged with issues of reflexivity, autobiography, and the positioning of the self in analysis (Okely 1992). It has become orthodox (but not trivial) to recognise the relationship of author to academic colleagues and audiences as a condition of the production of anthropological knowledge. Davis (1992) has usefully discussed some of the methodological and ethical criticisms of a tradition in which colleagues are incorporated in a community of discourse – a 'we' within which discussion takes place about 'them'. A self-conscious anthropology should surely find nothing strange in taking colleagueship, at least within academic communities, as an object of interest. Extension of this interest to colleagueship in other environments should not be too great a step.

My own interest in colleagueship as a social form began with an attempt to understand the negotiation of 'professional' identities and performances in an environment of international higher education (Callan forthcoming 2007), which also forms the ethnographic context of this chapter. This was not a situation of fieldwork in the normal sense. I was not in this environment to study it and produce an academic analysis; I was engaged in it as a salaried employee over some ten years, seven of them as director of the European Association for International Education (EAIE, hereafter referred to as the Association), based in Amsterdam. During that period, therefore, I was in the same position as others with training and experience as actors in academic anthropology, working in parallel or applied fields to which they seek to bring an anthropological consciousness.[3] Elsewhere (Callan 1984 and forthcoming 2007) I have discussed ways in which such a situation may encourage the cultivation of a double (sometimes multiple) vision and a divided self. In this case, however, as I have also stressed, I held responsibilities that required my observer self to be subordinated at the time to that of fully engaged actor; only in retrospect have I been able to become, in some degree, an ethnographer once more. Throughout the period in question, the person I needed to be was deeply involved in the negotiation of identity intersubjectively with others who were doing the same thing from their own standpoints in the intersecting structures that constitute international higher education.

If this can be thought of as a dance, colleagueship was one of its basic steps; another was professionalism; a third was internationalism. How did these 'steps' move together, and what kinds of 'flourishes' did they allow? The Association had been founded in 1989 as a non-profit, non-governmental professional body to represent an expanding occupational group – that of (mainly) junior to mid-level staff employed by universities throughout Europe in the management and administration of international programmes of academic exchange and cooperation. The forces behind its creation and rapid growth in the early years are described more fully elsewhere (Callan forthcoming 2007). Most relevant here is that over a relatively short period of time in the late 1980s and 1990s, and with a perception of urgency derived from a desire by European governments and universities to ride the 'bandwagon' of EU programme development and funding (itself, of course, driven by political and economic imperatives), a new kind of occupational grouping began to take shape and its members began to think of themselves as 'international education professionals'.

In 'Identities under Construction' (Callan forthcoming 2007) I stress the power of constructions of internationalism and professionalism, as well as a somewhat idiosyncratic notion of 'culture', as binding values for this emergent group. Highly variable in their application over time and space, these constructions are nonetheless invoked in very specific and standard ways. I argue that they contribute to a rhetoric which in turn enables individuals to experience a solidarity in opposition to their many contrasts of language, personal occupational background, political culture, positioning in national educational systems, relative privilege, gender, and age: the list is long. This solidarity is, of course, material as well as symbolic; claims to professionalism in a recognised area of 'expertise' are here, as elsewhere, an important means of securing advancement and honour. I suggest also that a simplified, essentialist notion of culture and cultural difference is attractive partly because it lends itself to precisely these aspirations to professionalism and expertise. I go on to argue that where individuals experience structural isolation in their conditions of work, as is frequently the case for a number of reasons, alliance outside the institution provides an alternative support system, along with reinforcing symbols and values. To simplify and slightly modify Mary Douglas's terms (Douglas 1978; see also Mars 1982), common cause with those perceived as co-professionals provides an experience of 'group' to counter too much 'grid' in their working lives. The binding values for this group are made all the more powerful by the very newness of the occupational category they have entered and by the absence of what I term 'the governing metaphors, the classifications of reality and the symbolic systems that are characteristic of mature organisations and communities of practice' (Callan forthcoming 2007). I want now to consider ways in which colleagueship is experienced and negotiated in this environment.

The word itself is ubiquitous: a standard term of address and reference in both written and spoken communications on Association business.[4] 'Dear colleague' is the salutation used in virtually all messages such as cover-letters, e-mails and faxes addressed to unnamed or multiple recipients. It contrasts with the variety of forms of address and reference found in differing national academic traditions, where etiquette may require particular honorifics to be used ('Professor Dr X…'). It thus provides a solution to the problem of address across these 'frontiers of courtesy' without downgrading anyone's position. Its counterpart in personalised communication is the use of first names, which again is universal even among those who, at 'home', would not necessarily expect to be on first-name terms. Its usage flattens hierarchy and stresses an idiom of informal, egalitarian relationships, which may or may not obtain on different ground.

This can have odd consequences and lead to misreadings where differing usages come into conjunction. An example is the Association's annual conference, a large-scale affair held in a different European city each year, and jointly organised by Association staff and international committees and by a local team normally drawn from a consortium of host universities on site. This local team will have members with many areas and levels of responsibility, all of whom will be 'colleagues' in the eyes of those dealing with them from the 'centre'; but relations may be very differently configured on the ground. The lead time for organising each conference is more than a year, during which distance communication between the teams is constant, everyone is a colleague, and working relationships become close. The extent to which people are code switching between different modes of communication may only become evident at a late stage of conference organisation, when on-site meetings bring actors face to face. I recall one conference in a certain city where, throughout the planning process, from the perspective of the 'centre', the idiom of colleagueship had been sustained equally in dealings with the heads of the International Offices of the local participating universities and with their administrative staffs. Only on site was it apparent that this idiom did not obtain locally: the International Office heads had not met at all until the conference project created the occasion for them to meet, and relations with support staff were handled in a formal and distant style with only surnames used. In such a situation, code switching around a meeting table can be fairly dramatic, with colleagueship perceived simultaneously as a mode of relating to others and as a polite fiction.

In the context of the Association, then, colleagueship provides a defining framework within which individuals can construct an identity that may stand in opposition to others available to them or required of them. It also makes possible, and reinforces, a style of governance that facilitates the Association's own survival and success. Within the Association's governing bodies, whose members are by design drawn from as multinational a field as possible, very wide differences can be bridged by acting out a shared notion of colleagueship. Needless to say, the bridging is never perfect and there are divisions and conflicts; but colleagueship offers a powerful performative construct in resolving these. Hence it plays a significant part in the institution building that is in turn perceived as part of a wider European educational project. The equivalent could, of course, also be said of many other occupational groups or institutions, and similar questions could be raised.

I turn now to the question of colleagueship as a relation for the creation of ethnographic understanding. Do relations perceived as obtaining between colleagues yield distinctive kinds of understanding? Does this relationship have epistemological implications? Once again, I take as a case my own experience within the Association. It is relevant that this experience was of being, ostensibly, in charge; no doubt a different narrative would result had I written from any other place in the system.[5] Watching the workings of a structure while exercising a degree of control and being in an audit sense accountable for it is a standpoint rather different from either the 'studying down' or the 'studying up' that are more conventional in ethnography. Lest this seem self-regarding, I instantly add that any sense of control was inextricably tied to that of being controlled – by operational necessities, by the workplace needs of others, and by the performative dances in which we were all engaged.

A seminal paper by Kirsten Hastrup (1987) has the significant title 'Fieldwork among Friends'. In it Hastrup uses the notion of friendship in a sophisticated and many-layered way, invoking not only personal attachment between herself as a Danish fieldworker and the Icelandic communities she studied, but a richness of historical and linguistic associations that lead the two peoples to classify one another as friends. Her focus in the paper is on the gender of the fieldworker and the experience of time, but in the course of her analysis she describes her own participation in the arduous labour of milking cows, recovering sheep from high summer pastures, and (at a different stage) fish filleting. This participation was not just a matter of practicality (gaining access to work groups, avoiding becoming a burden) but an instrument of study in a deep sense. Hastrup negotiates around self and gender, in her own eyes and those of other actors, and becomes a particular kind of subject in relationship to the subjectness of others: 'it seems to me that the most potent point of departure for solving the puzzles of local culture is the point where the locals actually "see" your presence. Only there can the anthropological encounter turn into an exchange between subjects.' From this mutual seeing is created a kind of 'third culture', that of the ethnographic exchange or cross-cultural dialogue, which Hastrup describes as:

> the truly privileged position for ethnographic work. It is not solely a matter of both participating (assuming the role of *you*) and observing (keeping my professional aims intact) but also, and more importantly, to let go of both and live, feel and experience from the position of the third person. Here, the silences of both you and I are heard, and the blank banners are readable. (Ibid.: 105; author's emphasis)

Hastrup, in her Icelandic fieldwork, moves through the sharing of physical work and the negotiation of a shifting self to this kind of readability, in a setting of anthropology conducted in a culture closely akin to her own. Despite the many differences, I suggest that her analysis offers a way of seeing the relation of colleagueship as, also, a route to a particular ethnographic readability. My work sharing with others in the Association was not physical in the sense of Hastrup's hard labour, although the constant international travel and lengthy meetings throughout the year certainly took their toll. Yet, here too, relationships were conducted and defined as holding between *colleagues*, in highly embodied ways. On one occasion, as part of the preparation for a conference held in southern Europe, I had obtained funding from the European Commission for the Association to administer a programme of travel grants to enable selected individuals from the countries of lowest participation in the European educational programmes (Spain, Italy, Portugal, and Greece) to attend the conference. One of the Commission's conditions for the funding was that the Association require the grant recipients, before receiving their money, to provide undertakings countersigned by their universities that proof of conference attendance, hotel receipts, and travel ticket stubs would be supplied and forwarded to the Commission with the final account. Because, at that time, e-mail was not in general use in those countries and post and telephone were unreliable, the grant conditions had to be communicated by fax – several pages per fax – to some forty individuals at different universities in the four countries. This boiled down to my spending a full Saturday and Sunday in the office sending the faxes manually, with the help of an office manager, who certainly could not have been asked to do this but was led to it by her construction of *colleagueship* with me, with others in the office and the Association, and with the *colleagues* who would benefit from the grants.

In this scenario of two women struggling over those two days with the fax machine and the unsteady connections with southern Europe was embodied a nest of parallel and contrasting notions of colleagueship: her self-assertion as a co-actor in the proceedings; our joint despair at the 'bureaucracy' of the Commission's requirements and what we saw as its indifference to real working conditions in universities in southern Europe; issues of trust and accountability between the Association, the Commission, and the recipient grant holders – all of whom were represented nonetheless as *colleagues*.

On another occasion, a major annual meeting of the Association's governing boards was being held in Ireland. Preparation for these meetings was always very labour-intensive, with a high volume of paperwork. Because those involved often had complicated travel schedules and were not necessarily in touch with their offices, a great deal of redundancy had to be built into the preparations to ensure that everyone had the right papers in the right order for the meetings. This was particularly important since the meetings were held in English, which for most was a second or third language. Our practice was to prepare individually addressed envelopes (about fifty) with everyone's papers, which my deputy and I would carry in our suitcases from Amsterdam and deliver to the hotel on site for individuals to collect on arrival. My deputy, with whom I had a particularly close working relationship, was responsible for preparing all the budget and other financial papers and presenting them at the meetings. The plane journey was our opportunity to go through the file together and make last-minute preparations for handling the issues coming up at the meetings. On this occasion, on the plane to Ireland with the individuals' envelopes out of reach in the hold, we discovered that one of the budget documents contained financial assumptions that could not be justified and that, even if corrected, would mislead the board as to the Association's financial position. Since no replacement could be prepared without office facilities, the only option was to remove the offending paper from everyone's package.

The scene this time, then, is of two women in a hotel bedroom at midnight with fifty document packages spread over the bed, extracting a paper from each, reordering the rest and resealing the envelopes before stealing furtively down to reception to deliver them in time to be collected by our *colleagues* before breakfast. The colleagueship the two of us acted out with much hilarity that night (a photo records the episode) was a collusive one; but at issue also was an unspoken negotiation of our own colleagueship in relation to our obligation respecting the management of information towards the governing bodies – also our colleagues – to whom we were *professionally* responsible.

These anecdotes (I could, of course, have chosen many others) illustrate my contention that facets of the Association as a social complex are rendered ethnographically readable, in something like Hastrup's sense, through attention to colleagueship as it is constructed and enacted. I have been interested in the ways in which core notions relating to professionalism and internationality furnish a rhetorical apparatus within which individuals are able to build and negotiate identities or 'selves' important to them. The lived enactment of colleagueship, in my own consciousness, that of others with whom I worked, and theirs with others refracted back onto my awareness constitute an intersubjective field on which my ethnographic account substantially rests.

Thus my formal account of the ways in which a particular notion of 'culture' and 'intercultural competence' intersects with those of professionalism, expert knowledge, and internationality rests on a history of the negotiation of colleagueship in many contexts. These include, for example, heated arguments over whether a *professional* section of the Association should have the title 'Languages and intercultural communication for mobility' or 'Languages for intercultural communication and mobility'. The language-teaching specialists wanted to assimilate 'culture' and 'language' and claim expert ownership of both. The dissenting view – which prevailed – was that 'intercultural communication' was a requirement and possession of the 'international education profession' at large.

Again, my ethnographic account (Callan forthcoming 2007) draws on my own intellectual unease with and criticism of the essentialist notion of culture taken for granted by those involved in the Association's *professional* training courses in 'intercultural communication for international educators'; my attempts to communicate and explain these criticisms to others within a relation of colleagueship; and their response to me, including what they made of their knowledge that I was an anthropologist (another kind of cultural expert) as well as a director. Even where, as in this case, there is no acknowledged ethnographic relationship between fieldworker and 'subjects', a form of ethnographic understanding can be embodied in and emergent from dialogues and performances of colleagueship.

Jimènez (2003) has recently argued that 'the language and imagery of labour have become part and parcel of what makes a person today (i.e., of our definition of personhood) which ... calls for a reconsideration of what an "anthropology of labour" might have to say to anthropology at large.' The colleague relationship is integral to this language and imagery, intersecting in complex and shifting ways with other component imageries, as I have indicated above. Beyond the particular case illustrated in this chapter, I suggest that by highlighting the construct of colleagueship, we can shed additional light on the anthropology of organisations and occupations and offer a more general contribution to understanding the relations within which ethnographic knowledge can be generated in a contemporary environment of work. It is particularly fitting that the suggestion should be made within a collection dedicated to the work of Shirley Ardener, in whom the designations 'colleague' and 'friend' indeed come together.

Notes

1. See most notably the discussions of polyphony and polyvocality in Clifford and Marcus 1986, and the many later commentaries on these.
2. An example from diplomacy: until well into the 1970s, under published procedures, U.K. diplomats in a post were to refer collectively to co-nationals serving anywhere as 'colleagues'. Those of other countries serving in the same post were to be termed *chers collègues*. The switch of language served as an ironic marker of an alteration in trust among those who at one level could serve conflicting national interests, while at another they constituted a 'community' of practice. I am not aware, however, of the distinction being much used on the ground.
3. From the perspective of 'mainstream' anthropology, those in this situation have shown many of the features of 'muted' groups (Ardener 1975). Various attempts over the years to theorise and integrate into the mainstream(s) the anthropological understandings generated through practitioner (but qualified) experience have not been particularly successful. There are, however, signs of change, at any rate in U.K. anthropology. For example, the Royal Anthropological Institute and Association of Social Anthropologists have made a strategic commitment to strengthen organisational links and intellectual cross-fertilisation between university-based anthropologists and those working outside academic institutions.
4. This practice transcends language. The Association has no official language; for convenience, English is its usual working language, but, unlike some of the specialised vocabulary of international education, 'colleague' actually translates rather readily – at least superficially – into the major European languages.
5. This requires some qualification. My post was that of Executive Director which, as in many organisations, means that I held administrative responsibility for the office, staff, finances, external representation, and servicing of the elected governing bodies. I was accountable to these bodies for the implementation of policies laid down by them. In practice, my responsibilities in setting policy became larger than my job description, mainly because my post carried a continuity of tenure absent in the elected bodies.

References

Ardener, S. 1975. 'Introduction', in S. Ardener (ed.), *Perceiving Women*, London: Malaby Press, pp. vii–xxiii.

Callan, H. 1984. 'Introduction', in H. Callan and S. Ardener (eds), *The Incorporated Wife*, London: Croom Helm, pp. 1–26.

────── forthcoming 2007. 'Identities under Construction: The Case of International Education', in S. Ardener and F. Moore (eds), *Professional Identities: Policy and Practice in Business Bureaucracy*, New York and Oxford: Berghahn Books.

Clifford, J. and G.E. Marcus (eds) 1986. *Writing Culture: The Poetics and Politics of Ethnography*, Berkeley: University of California Press.

Crick, M. 1992. 'Ali and Me: An Essay in Street-Corner Anthropology', in J. Okely and H. Callaway (eds), *Anthropology and Autobiography*, London and New York: Routledge (ASA Monographs, 29), pp. 175–92.

Davis, J. 1992. 'Tense in Ethnography: Some Practical Considerations', in J. Okely and H. Callaway (eds), *Anthropology and Autobiography*, London and New York: Routledge (ASA Monographs, 29), pp. 205–20.

Douglas, M. 1978. 'Cultural Bias', Royal Anthropological Institute Occasional Paper no. 35, republished 1982 in *In the Active Voice*, London and Boston: Routledge & Kegan Paul, pp. 183–254.

Hastrup, K. 1987. 'Fieldwork among Friends: Ethnographic Exchange within the Northern Civilisation', in A. Jackson (ed.), *Anthropology at Home*, London and New York: Tavistock (ASA Monographs, 25), pp. 94–108.

Jackson, A. (ed.) 1987. *Anthropology at Home*, London and New York: Tavistock (ASA Monographs, 25).

Jimènez, A.C. 2003. 'Working out Personhood: Notes on "Labour" and its Anthropology', *Anthropology Today* 19 (5), pp. 14–17.

Mars, G. 1982. *Cheats at Work*, London: Allen & Unwin.

Okely, J. 1992. 'Anthropology and Autobiography: Participatory Experience and Embodied Knowledge', in J. Okely and H. Callaway (eds), *Anthropology and Autobiography*, London and New York: Routledge (ASA Monographs, 29), pp. 1–28.

PART II
GENDER AGENCY AND NETWORKS

7

THINKING THE UNHEARD, WRITING THE UNWRITTEN: REFLECTING ON MARGINALITY, ETHNOGRAPHY, AND TEXTS

Maria Jaschok in dialogue with Shui Jingjun

England

Jaschok

At the core of my last years of research – indeed, all-pervasive in its implications – is the ongoing dialogue with my Chinese–Hui research collaborator, co-author and friend, Shui Jingjun. One of the prompters of this enduring conversation, begun over nine years ago, was my correspondence with Shirley Ardener, then not known to me in person. It was about 1994, when conducting fieldwork in Henan Province, in the interior of China, that I wrote to Shirley about the relevance of issues addressed in *Perceiving Women*[1] to problems arising from my own cross-cultural and collaborative research. And I wrote of the challenges of developing a reflexive, feminist ethnographic fieldwork methodology in the context of Chinese state repressive treatment of ethnic and religious minorities, of whom Shui is a member. (I was then less eloquent on another issue, which concerned the nature of a working relationship of collaborators situated in unequally situated positions of power, resources, and knowledge.) Shirley Ardener responded generously to the unknown letter writer, thoughtfully and with pertinent questions, encouraging me to rethink and develop some of my 'problems' into tools of critical thinking.

One of the most influential concepts to have come out of the work of anthropologists, to different degrees associated in the 1970s with the Oxford Women's Studies Committee, was that of 'muted' groups. First elaborated by Edwin Ardener in the 1970s (Ardener 1975: 1–27),[2] this concept had widespread ramifications for the understanding of how dominant systems, or patriarchal structures of authority, may co-opt the very groups it 'mutes' into an internalised acquiescence to 'the way it is', ensuring reproduction and maintenance of the arrangements that constitute the status quo. The theory of the 'influence of dominant male systems of perception' to diminish alternative, that is women-centred, ways of perception and social expression served to challenge essentialist notions of women's nature and capacities. As Shirley Ardener pointed out in her introduction to *Perceiving Women*, this understanding of the structural roots of women's under-representation in symbolic, cultural, and socio-political domains has an application also to the theorisation of other kinds of inequalities (1975: xii). My intention here is to explore the relevance of these insights for my own research and fieldwork methodology among Chinese Muslims, contrasting emerging research priorities in scholars' treatment of issues of gender, difference and marginality with abiding neglect of their implications for ethnographic practice.

Only in recent years, as the American anthropologist Susan Blum notes in her state-of-the-field article, revealingly entitled 'Margins and Centers: A Decade of Publishing on China's Ethnic Minorities' (2002), have the ideological and cultural implications of the structural dominance of the Chinese Communist Party/state for 'muted' marginalised groups emerged as a central area of investigation. Discussing a list of seven recent anthropological studies, Blum identifies certain common features that challenge entrenched hierarchies of 'centre and margin'-derived thinking, so long implicit in China scholarship, to question both the (highly politicised) nature of this relationship and also its continued validity for posing questions over centre/Han/Chinese identity. She takes it as an achievement of the books at the heart of this trend to have dismantled the construct of a homogeneous and Han-centred 'Chinese/ness'. A new openness, she suggests, allows for exploration of cultures and lifestyles, histories and notions of the meaningful, which thus reposition and centre hitherto peripheralised peoples, the designated ethnic minorities of Chinese society. Blum 'celebrates' as she cites the achievement of this scholarship as a testimony to disengagement from the all-too-close relationship between a political status quo in China and its officially sanctioned academies and academic projects, both national and international.

One of the books Blum listed is *The History of Women's Mosques in Chinese Islam*, which I co-authored with Shui Jingjun (2000a; revised Chinese edition, Shui and Jaschok 2002). Blum notes the subject matter of our investigation, female religious culture as evolved through the history of Hui Muslim women's mosques in central China, and applauds the attention paid to a neglected area of Chinese women's history. It is interesting to note what she fails to address in her review of the role of marginality in China scholarship: our collaborative relationship in fieldwork, in research, in the continuous process of interpretation as well as in the writing of the final text; perhaps the most perplexing stage was grounded in a realisation of our differences and of the presence of boundary markers of cross-border communication. We sought to preserve our ongoing conversation, our dialogue, between two very different, individual voices – one not only a Chinese academic but also a member of an ethnic/religious minority, the other a Western academic — by agreeing not to merge the conversation into one authorial voice. For this we had to acknowledge our respective approaches: Shui more of an essentialist in her close linkage of ontology and knowledge, in which superior education and imagination might facilitate (however, at best, only a partial) transcendence of fate of birth and divine will, while in my case the approach of social constructivist relativism, carried by a lifelong habit of relocation and transience.

We had decided to make the situated identity of the two co-authors the fault lines of our differing interpretations, through which could be gleaned and allowed our divergent perspectives, concerns, commitments, audiences. Blum's discussion welcomed the dismantling of rigid centre/margin binaries in political and academic discourses and the disengagement of academia from a state agenda, no less potent for being scarcely noteworthy. But she bypassed what feminist and reflexive anthropology has sought to address, namely, our bringing of the person of the researcher into the frame of investigation. It is a most topical and urgent dilemma.[3] A few years ago, at an international conference at the University of Westminster, a well-known China scholar declared that the removal of her Chinese collaborator from the authorship of the final text reflected a pragmatic decision brought about by the 'theoretical distance' between the collaborators. Yet, in her presentation of the oral histories of central informants, the guiding intervention of the Chinese colleague was all too apparent. But, whilst she had been essential to the 'writing down', she was excluded from the process of 'writing up' and from the authority of authorship.

Chinese studies as a whole still adhere to the 'scientific' pursuit of knowledge accumulation and objectivity in research method and written presentation. Recently published works in our field, whether by Allés (2000) or by Gillette (2000), still exclude from their writing the relationships on which their fieldwork interviews and access to informants and information, or lack of access, were based.

In the course of research work, together with my Chinese collaborator Shui Jingjun, I have sought to step back from time to time so that we may address each other more directly, using the texts of our joint writing to attempt a 'personal anthropology'. Such an approach, so Judith Okely says, borrowing from Pocock, 'recognises and explores a person's assumptions about his [sic] own society, embedded in written texts and recorded interaction with another people' (Okely 1996: 41).

In one article (Jaschok and Shui 2000b), after completion of our first jointly authored book (2000a), we asked ourselves how 'mutedness' played into our relationship built on different kinds of subordination and inequalities. We recognised Shui's ethnic (Hui) classification and religious (Islamic) faith in Chinese society, thus her 'minority status'. We identified the marginalisation of Hui history and Hui scholarship in Chinese-sanctioned mainstream academia. We acknowledged the larger context of a historical East–West asymmetry as a legacy and challenge for our relationship and for our relationship with informants and audience alike. Conversations and a dialogic presentation to a workshop on feminist methodology[4] preceded the conceptualisation and writing of the article, which left editing and translation as my responsibility.

We described our collaboration as a dynamic, sometimes volatile, process of slow mutual discovery, as the interplay of personal relationship and ethnographic involvement with the communities studied. We maintained that even in the area of reflexive anthropology, such an alternative was still under-theorised when compared with critical writing on the more ubiquitous outside researcher relationship with 'native' informant, wherever geographically situated. Thus we wrote:

> We feel that through our collaboration, we have started to respond to [Kamala] Visweswaran's challenge to (Western) feminist ethnography to rethink its one-directional epistemological and methodological traditions. We related to the other as a source of stimulation and testing of theory, facilitating more 'experimental' conversations during field visits. In the course of our conversations, disagreements and differing emphases expanded our field of observation in response to each other's personal narratives, and sensitised us to the multiplicity of factors which inscribe personal, but also family and collective histories. Both collaborators were forced to confront each other's precariously, sometimes painfully, fragmented and contradictory natures. (Jaschok and Shui 2000b: 36)

In 2003, at a time when we were commencing a new research project, we followed this up with another dialogue on our work together, this time in Chinese. Shui had been encouraged by editors of the review journal *Bolan Qunshu* to take the initiative for such an undertaking, arguing that such a long-term collaborative relationship as ours was rare enough to create general curiosity in Shui's 'home' audience. Like the previous English-language publication, the article was co-authored, continuing discussion of our continuous preoccupation with formulating what we consider a reflexive and morally responsible ethnography. But this time, by mutual consent, editorial responsibility was taken on by Shui, shaping our conversation, 'translating' my writing, responding to a Chinese audience of publisher, editors and the journal's readership.

Conversation and Readerships[5]

China

Jaschok

Books originate in and are nurtured by conversations. The very process of knowing, observing, and participating, which becomes knowledge production, is facilitated by conversations: those between author and other academics (and specifically between author and academics who are members of the community studied), between author and informants, between author and editors. In the case of our joint research, conversation occupied the central place, which allowed for constant scrutiny of personal and ethnographic identities and of their interconnectedness. In other words, a dialogic relationship had come into being, which shaped all stages of our joint project: the field trips together, but also the times when we worked apart (continuously in touch, thanks to modern technology), the different phases of research, conceptualisation, and theorisation, writing and translation (translations that included conceptual and cultural terminologies), the final stages of editing and re-editing, and so on.

In presenting the book[6] as an outcome of what Hastrup (1992) refers to as the creative space of 'intersubjectivity', it becomes necessary to present ourselves, the two partners in the enterprise, and to relate the origin of the ethnographic project, the questions asked, and the responses interpreted to the biography of the researcher herself. 'By locating the researcher in the same critical plane as the subject studied, the class, race, culture, gender assumptions, beliefs, and behaviour of the researcher her/himself become visible. "Thus the researcher appears to us not as an invisible, anonymous voice of authority, but as a real, historical individual with concrete, specific desires and interests"'(Hom and Xin 1995: 10).[7] Moreover, the partnership implied in such a conversational model of 'the anthropological project from singular to communal venture' (Gudeman and Rivera 1990: 4) makes the choice of collaborator a choice of distinct positions, perspectives, and questions that shape the entire outcome of fieldwork.

I am by training a social historian, anthropologist, and sociologist of Chinese modern society. My professors at London University were not only academics but also political activists (some self-proclaimed Maoists), strongly committed to the ideals of a strong and dignified Chinese nation. It was their influence on me as a student during the 1970s, an era in which European university campuses were hotbeds of social and political movements and of vigorous feminist activism, which inspired me to spend many years in various parts of China – teaching, researching, and writing. To me the involvement with 'China' (a complex construct of shifting and changing dimensions) has thus also always been associated with my personal life history, beyond my identity as an academic. Moreover, the topics I chose to pursue have also always related to questions that I can trace both to my home culture (Europe) and to my family history.

Shui

I had begun to interview *nü ahong*[8] at women's mosques in the early 1990s when I met Maria Jaschok in a women's mosque. It was 1994, and because of our common interest we began to work together on a project that in 2004 is still ongoing.

Laura Newby, when reviewing (2001) the English version of *The History of Women's Mosques in Chinese Islam*, said that it is very common for Western and Chinese scholars to collaborate together. Apart from such a convenient academic division of labour, the result of the joint labour of research and thought also symbolises the ideal of cooperation. However, what happens to arguments, to disagreements over questions to be asked and interpretations? Ordinarily, the convention of privacy conceals what is seen as non-academic matter and of concern only to the collaborators. What the readers see tends to be only the final product in all its harmonious and homogenised glory, shaped by the dominant party. In regard to our book, Newby observes that some of the most interesting chapters are those which clearly reveal the intellectual tensions that were left unresolved between the authors. And because of their trust and the readers' trust, Newby writes, Jaschok and Shui write in a format in which their contrastive voices are heard, where the readers are given to understand that differences over interpretation remain unresolved.

Laura Newby spells out the characteristics of our joint product. The Chinese version of this book is the second product of my collaboration with Jaschok. It maintains the fundamental characteristics of the English version, but we have made the necessary amendments, additions, revisions and editing adjustments in order to suit the Chinese context and readership. In our preface we explicitly inform the readers of our shared assumptions and (sometimes) different interpretations. Because readers are informed, they can participate in our dialogue. It is by means of dialogue, according to Zhuo Xinping, that human beings share their wisdom. It is the best way to increase our understanding and communication. And we hope for our part that this can more generally facilitate communication among different cultures, different ethnic groups, different religions, and different genders.

England

Jaschok

In the dialogue addressed to Western feminist scholars (Jaschok and Shui 2000b), it was my contextualisation of Shui's biography and place in Chinese academia that served to measure 'distance', the cultural trajectory to be travelled in the course of collaboration. In other words, her story became part of 'the native' field, allowing for fieldwork experience as personal and most involving interaction. The editorial role in which I was placed, largely for the sake of expediency – given the use of English and publication in the U.K. – shaped the intellectual excursion that our dialogue was to illuminate, quite imperceptibly, one dominated by my issues.

In the Chinese publication, the interrogative gaze was directed at me. It was my story that was unfolded in order to illustrate the cultural distance and achievement entailed in its joint explorations. And it was now Shui's role to act as mediator of interpretation between myself and the readership, and I, the European, became the figure in the distance.

China

Shui

Talking about her mother culture, Maria Jaschok's background must be seen in the context of European culture. She was German-born, but she completed her academic education in England (both undergraduate and doctoral). Moreover, when she writes in the English language, she identifies with European culture, not specifically with English or German culture. When I place the word ying (England) in front of her name, which ordinarily signifies nationality, this refers to her academic context and her current country of residence. This interesting multifaceted identity is representative of a European lifestyle that is much more fluid than is the case with Chinese intellectuals.

England

Jaschok

This reversal of conventional ethnographic relationships (Western academic as foreign investigator and Chinese academic as local informant/research assistant/interpreter) was made possible in 1998, when I organised Shui's first trip abroad to present with me a preliminary account of our research findings in central China to an audience of Australian feminist academics. Shui was provided with an opportunity to visit and interview diverse ethnic female Muslim communities in Melbourne and Sydney. I performed the role of interpreter and mediator, i.e., what is commonly the task of the native informant (despite the fact that I have only intermittently been in Australia). Such other opportunities arose in subsequent years when it was Shui who was in the role of the investigative scholar gathering knowledge for her home institution and readership, thereby shifting the balance of power in subtle ways. Information flow, contacts and academic networks, and direct experience of the other's 'home' culture (although first impressions needed revising over time, and refining) became a part of both partners' travel record. Our conversations benefited from the broadening of knowledge of the other.

The world we inhabit, and our understanding of our place in this world, derive to a certain degree from our understanding of space and time and of their crucial part in constructing both social order and subjectivity (Grosz 1995). The way in which this understanding is complicated by cultural crossings formed the subject matter of many conversations, whether in relation to our collaboration or in relation to the subject studied.

The complex issues that confront the ethnographer in the historicising of the fieldwork, on the one hand, or in the spatialisation of time, on the other hand, are well explored (Hastrup 1990; Strathern 1990; Tsing 1993). Due to the continuous and dialogic nature of the fieldwork methodology we evolved in the course of collaboration, Shui's narrations of her personal and family history became interwoven with accounts of Muslim women we interviewed, each cross-referencing and illuminating the other, opening up ever new thematic threads for ethnographic questions and investigation. Shui's memories of family history, in particular of the fate of female kin, facilitated conversations on women's historical and tortuous trajectory from outsider status to rightful religious participation. It took many generations of Chinese Muslim women, including Shui's own relatives, to lay claim to their own site of learning, worship, and spiritual congregation, known as women's mosques (Jaschok and Shui 2000a).

It was Shui's overriding concern to reinsert women's religious individual and collective creativity into the canon of Hui scholarship. In turn through a reinvigorated Hui scholarship the aim was to facilitate critical appraisal of Chinese Han historiography and its muting of peripheralised peoples, both ethnic and religious (Harrell 1996).

China

Shui

In the current ideological climate of Chinese society, the secular has primary status over the idea of the sacred. In the ongoing modernisation of China, we are faced with questions concerning the legitimacy of religion and of the status, position and identity of believers – indeed, whether believers have rights entitling them to the legal protection of individual and collective religious practice. This problem, as far as Chinese scholars are concerned, is both old and new. It is old in the sense that China has never been a society anchored in one dominant religion, new in the sense that discourses on modernisation have problematically positioned religion. Misunderstanding in regard to religion has always existed. In recent years religious believers have often been treated as a distinct social group – as the Other – and Chinese society has derogatory notions about them. Popular discourse reflects this prejudice. Indeed, although more attention is paid now in Chinese academia to religious culture and to gendered life experience, a scholarly consideration of subjectivity in Chinese culture is absent. In this context, ordinary believers are rendered a muted people. We have little knowledge concerning their ideas, emotions, and values – about their spiritual and worldly lives. There is especially little known about the negotiation of the dual impact of religious and secular cultures.

As far as women believers, above all, are concerned, current Chinese culture is governed by a secular orientation. The religious culture that determines their lives and subjectivities leads to a marginal social and academic position of women believers. They are invisible in the public (secular) spheres of society. Their impact on the mainstream secular women's movement, represented by the All-Chinese Women's Federation, a mass organisation set up by the Chinese Communist

Party, is at best peripheral. The history and socio-political status of Muslim women have to be seen in this context of religious repression, which is compounded by their ethnic identity.[9] Until we began our study of the emergence and history of women's own mosques under a female leadership, a history of more than three hundred years (Jaschok and Shui 2000a; Shui and Jaschok 2002), this major contribution of women to the development of Chinese Islam was unknown. Women were even missing from the chronicles of Hui scholarship on Islam in China.

Yet we have discovered that Muslim women constitute an active religious group, enriching both the history of Chinese Muslims and Chinese history at large. Silence or absence is not equal to non-existence or to an incapacity of their own voice. In their material constitution and spatial positioning, women's mosques display their own unique history, an impressive testimony to a uniquely female religious culture, and a long journey from gender segregation to women's autonomy.

England

Jaschok

Shui is describing the silenced history of religious women. Furthermore, she is remarking on the silence of *zhishi fenzi* (the educated elite), who are betraying a long and sacred Confucian tradition, she writes, which demands that knowledge and privilege must serve the cause of the people, particularly the most marginalised and neglected among them. Intellectuals must be prepared to challenge the dominance of privileged power systems (*pingtianxia*), and shoulder responsibility for all humanity (Tu 1992). Whereas Shui's precarious situation as a Hui Muslim scholar, a political predicament all too common in the post-1949 Chinese Communist Party-dominated academic establishment, has limited her power to intervene in society, nevertheless she is imbued with a distinct sense of obligation and responsibility to members of her ethnic and religious community. In Shui's own words:

> The sensitivity I have felt towards my identity as both a researcher and woman made me explore in greater depth the world of *qingzhen nüsi* (women's mosques) and *nü ahong*. But no sooner had I decided to 'return', than I felt the urge to escape. My mind is torn by a conflict more complicated than the one described by Qian Zhongshu in his famous novel *Weicheng* (A Fortress Besieged). To me, it is not simply a matter of getting in or out of the fortress. Born in a fortress, I have never really been out of it, and yet it is hard for me to get perfectly settled in it. It seems that I have been divided into different parts: some are kept inside while others are left outside. Those outside mean to get in, while those inside yearn to get out. None is to enter or escape completely. (Jaschok and Shui 2000a: xvii)

I have realised that the contradictions Shui refers to, as Muslim, as Hui, as an intellectual, as a woman, are articulated issues from conversations about representations to Western audiences, contradictions that also surfaced in my editorial deliberations over the directions that our writing should take. This area of discussion is absent in our Chinese-language writing, when Shui assumes overall responsibility. There, oblique references at most touch on political and ideological constraints in religious scholarship.

Space and time are important determinants of what and how we speak. The intellectual space created by our constant and close conversation opened up possibilities for transgression and for circumventing the boundaries set by state controls upon those who work in politically sensitive areas. But it was the shift to a Chinese site of our knowledge production that demonstrated how circumscribed the transgression had been, and it was largely confined to 'my' side of the boundary.

In the unilinear time frame of Chinese Communist developmentalist ideology, religion is anchored rigidly in the 'feudal phase', in 'pastness' and 'traditionalism'. On the back of this, an aggressively modernising Chinese state has defined its modern credentials, as well as its legitimacy as a party, by ushering in women's liberation as the antithesis of religiously determined stasis (see also Harding 1991). I have written elsewhere on how the ambiguities in the use of the term of *zongjiao* (religion) are expressive of the volatility of the relationship between party/state and religion over more than fifty years of Communist rule (Jaschok 2003: 664). The dehumanising process of the stereotyping of religious believers also froze my colleague Shui into 'pastness', into a rigid association with backwardness, left behind in the inexorable march of history towards secular progress. Her dilemma is expressed in the above citation, which she wrote before publication in 2000.

The following extract, written about four years later, reflects changes of a personal nature, in the way that I too changed in the course of our long collaboration. But the more liberal Chinese government attitude towards academic dissent (which, however, is also never to be taken for granted) has shifted Shui's position. It has moved from the expression of deeply felt existential perplexity and ambivalence to a more assertive advocacy of the official tolerance of diversity, pointing to the benefit of religio-cultural diversity for a society. She is also asserting the invaluable contribution Chinese Muslim women can make to international discourses on justice and equality, given their unique and remarkable standing in Islam.

China

Shui

Following the historical investigation of women's mosques, we are now able to make a coherent academic investigation of Muslim women as well as of the unique culture of the Chinese women's mosque. And we have discussed gender politics, women's rights, modernisation and tradition, and the construction of multiple identities. We have also discussed the impact of Islam on mainstream social culture. Although we have constructed a history of Chinese women's mosques and Muslim women, we believe that the significance and insights of our study go beyond the world of Chinese Muslim culture.

Any type of religion is an important component of the spiritual culture of human beings. It is the spiritual space for people, men and women, to transcend their limitations. If we can allow for different perspectives in the understanding of religion and beliefs, then we can better understand that the pursuit of sacredness is part of the pursuit of self-betterment. Personal life experience, thoughts, inspiration and action not only raise the level of believers themselves but also enrich culture for the benefit of all Chinese. Women's mosques and their spiritual culture, evolved over many generations of believers, are an innovation that comes from Muslims' effort to accommodate their way of life to mainstream Han Chinese culture. The women's mosque culture provides a good illustration of how a foreign religion enters a local space and becomes indigenised and how during this process of localisation the construction of ethnic religious identity takes place. It can help us to understand the relationship between mainstream and non-mainstream cultures, enhancing our understanding of the circumstances that assist a harmonious coexistence of cultures in all their diversity.

Many feminist theologians, as well as academics, are themselves believers. Much of their work engages with other theologians over the impact of patriarchy on women's spirituality and over the value of critical reinterpretations of canonical scriptures for all believers (Shui and Jaschok 2002). But it is also important for religious women to engage with secular feminism in debates over shared concerns.

Where Muslim women have established their own mosques with their own culture, women discovered their own strength and raised their level of consciousness in religious pursuit. I believe, in line with many feminist theologians, that frequent contact with the spiritual world does not necessarily make women weak. It can make women stronger. Should we not consider the possibility of agency among women who seek liberation in the pursuit of religious practice and the transcendence of self?

Our current research and oral history investigation of the nature of women's religious life and practice in local Chinese cultures is ongoing. Already we can measure our success by the many conversations that have over the years engaged communities of believers and non-believers, religious leaders and official cadres, religious scholars and secular feminists. However, most important and at the centre of our work is the dialogue between the two of us. This is the catalyst of change and source of inspiration.

Jaschok

Intellectually speaking, I have always been interested in the problem of marginal identity in relation to mainstream culture, in particular issues of identity in which class, ethnicity, education, status, and the like are criss-crossed by gender construction. I had never previously written about the 'lives as lived' and those aspired to by religious women. Then the first sightings of women's mosques and female Muslims in Zhengzhou, Henan, when I was engaged in other research in the early 1990s, changed my course of investigation. It became ever more apparent to me, especially after my meeting with Shui Jingjun, in a Zhengzhou women's mosque, that historians of the recent history of Chinese women had failed to acknowledge the diverse 'little religious traditions'. In these, so many women had created for themselves spaces of learning, individual contemplation, and collective prayer. In other words, we began to develop an investigative focus which argued that, side by side with scholarly interest in an increasingly active national culture of women's organisations, addressing the many urgent issues derived from an industrialising society, closer academic attention also needed to be paid to the richness of local cultures. There should be renewed examination of the part women have played in transmitting and sustaining faith and ideals through collective action, often in the process engendering change, not only for themselves, but also for the larger community. The institution of women's mosques – its complex evolution, geographical and ethnic distribution, its unique characteristics and significance to so many ordinary Muslim women – presented an irresistible challenge.

But my personal biography and family history are no less relevant as the source of my intellectual curiosity and questions. If the spiritual quest and religious identity of informants are the subject of my work, alongside more secular identities, then the strong religious affinities of members of my family and their affirmation of belief as a part of their social identity in modern Europe must account for specific academic emphases as much as influences from scholarly trends.

Reflections on Self, Ethnography, and Text

England

Jaschok

Fieldwork is embedded in social relations and in the cross-cultural encounter. The key themes of anthropology reveal themselves in the etymology of autobiography as 'self+life+text', says Judith Okely (1996), the more complicated for being played out across different national, cultural, academic, and religious boundaries. We believe however that a genuine collaboration, if constructed as a dialogic partnership, widens and enriches the scope of anthropological enquiry on which we may build our interpretations. In such a strategic dialogue, dominant discourses can be more critically examined and the enquirer subject herself to constant self-examination. Influenced by standpoint theory developed by feminist thinkers such as Patricia Hill Collins (1990, 1991) and Dorothy Smith (1987, 1990), Nancy Naples argues that a dialogic approach to ethnographic relations addresses issues of inequalities and the insider/outsider divide through an understanding of the 'interactive' process of fieldwork (Naples 1997: 75–76). In such an approach, the multifacetedness of identity construction and the dynamic of change, altering consciousness as well as material circumstances, are taken into the reflexive conversation and interpretations.

> Collaboration is the act of two or more people working together in a relationship that is characterised by equality, sharing of responsibilities, and trust. Collaborative research begins with identification of shared issues, data collection procedures and implementation, analysis and publication. The results of collaborative research are variously described 'as joint interpretation of meaning' or 'unpredictable discovery based on intersubjectivity'. Some feminist theorists suggest that collaborative work is more feminine than masculine because women are more able and willing than men to collectively share knowledge and emotional experience. (Hom and Xin 1995: 48, quoting Maggie Humm)

We are developing the epistemological and theoretical implications of a dialogic model of research even further in our current research. While Hill Collins (1991) argues for the importance of biography as a source of knowledge for those in the margins of academia, we take this to be important also for the study of a community from an outsider perspective.

Our collaboration also shaped the divergent questions we ask in our book and the audiences we addressed. Whilst collaborative models in research and fieldwork are not uncommon, their application to the final text is still quite rare. We sought to preserve our individual voices, thus our dialogue, in the book; and we shall develop such an approach still further. Our contrastive 'situated' identities are most starkly expressed in the publication of the book first in English (Jaschok and Shui 2000a) and two years later in Chinese (Shui and Jaschok 2002). This was to take seriously our commitment to our respective 'home' audiences so that the text should indeed be accessible to them.

We have had many objectives: to recover women for history, and to recover history for women (the classic feminist cause); to add to the history of all Chinese women the narratives of local collective traditions, in all their specificity and manifold interdependencies; to tell of the varied local cultures that constitute the great umma of international Islam and of the contribution that women have made to render China's Islam one of the most remarkable instances of female religiosity.

'There is an administration of knowledge,' Foucault (1980: 28) says, 'a politics of knowledge, relations of power which pass via knowledge and which, if one tries to transcribe them, lead one to consider forms of domination designated by such notions as field, region and territory.' And, as Judith Okely (1996) has pointed out, the very fact of geographical distance has made it too easy in anthropology of distant cultures to equate remoteness from the observer's homeland with her capacity for objective detachment. Objectivist approaches were countered by Western feminist ethnographers with what a number of postcolonialist critics have come to see as the pitfalls of a politics of identification with their subjects. Thus Kamala Visweswaran warned of the erasure 'of difference through the logic of identification' (Visweswaran 1997: 615, 616). Spivak castigated the perpetration of a 'new Orientalism' with 'marginality', the prescription for jaded Western feminism in need of a reinvigoration (1993), and Leela Gandhi maintained that the 'voyeuristic craving for the colourful alterity of native women seriously compromises the seemingly egalitarian politics of liberal feminism' (Gandhi 1998: 85; see also seminal texts in Bulbeck 1988; Trinh 1989; Tsing 1993). But what all of these devastating criticisms of Western feminist appropriations have in common is the assumption of particular relationships that makes the 'field' forever one of foreign (Western) researcher and native (to-be-inscribed) informant.

What is more rarely taken into the critical lens is the emergence of 'native' reflective voices, and how, for example in Chinese women's studies, these have been changing the nature of relations in which scholarly discourse is embedded. Representative of this development are Hong Kong cultural critic Rey Chow (1993), the foremost Chinese theoretician Li Xiaojiang (1999), and members of the influential American-Chinese diaspora, such as the historian Wang Zheng (1999). Collaboration in the field jointly engaged in by scholars foreign and local, with each granting the other's right to a hearing, shapes an ongoing conversation and fieldwork project beyond the unidirectional model. Indeed, the ethnographic methodology that Shui and I have come to favour is characterised by a long-term commitment to the community of informants, by an ongoing, multiparty conversation, which returns the published (where necessary, translated) text to the people studied, and which then, in an act of 'reappropriation', engenders renewed challenges to our research process, findings, and outcomes.

This is not to suggest that the very fact of cross-border conversation and reflexive methodology levels difference. Such a claim would be to misunderstand the insight brought by the constructionist conceptualisation of knowledge as socio-politically embedded in and intimately connected to power and interest (Chopp 1996). The Chinese version, over which Shui had editorial control, although faithful to the English-language original, is also different in a subtle way. The difference points to our situatedness within specific constellations of the author/publisher/readership nexus. When the Chinese edition emphasises women's contribution to Islam, the audience is both Islamic patriarchy and Communist Party organisation. The importance is both of religious and of political import, explaining and lauding the institution of women's mosques as uniquely Chinese and therefore worthy of establishment support. Shui makes the argument a forceful one, namely, that women's culture is emerging within Islam as doctrinally pure and within Chinese socialism as ideologically faithful. In the English edition the framework of reference is Arabic Islamic orthopraxy and global Muslim feminist movement towards a widening of debate. Within this context Chinese Islam is a reference by which a diverse and complex global Islam can be measured.

We speak from different positions to different audiences and to varying agendas. Only when the dialogue, verbal and written, also reflected the specificity of knowledge and power, publication and readership, and became anchored in two successive stages in the U.K. and in China were the full implications of our collaboration visible to us.

Hastrup (1992) has situated the locus of fieldwork, of dialogue and engagement, in the 'betweenness' of intersubjective engagement of researchers. It is here that the drama of discovery plays into processes of definition and into production of knowledge, in turn informing the approach to discovery. But because this methodology imbricates both of our biographies and identities, the multiply constituted negotiation of I and Other (Jaschok/Shui) and of We and Them (researchers/researched) makes this drama of discovery by its very nature ever open-ended.

Our mode of collaboration has now been assigned a formal place in the history of feminist ethnography. The German sinologist Mechthild Leutner presented in a recent paper a periodisation of the history of collaboration between German and Chinese scholars based on criteria of hierarchy and equality in their working relationships (2004). Distinguishing three historical phases (1887–2004), Leutner identifies two trends in the current phase, the 'neoliberal mainstream' scholarship and, in contradistinction, the 'emancipatory minorities position' represented by our collaboration.[10] She notes that 'new trends have developed in the direction of a minority position that promotes egalitarian transnational cooperation and working relationships. These new positions make recourse to modes of self-reflection initiated in gender studies as well as postmodern approaches in social anthropology, both of which developed from marginalised positions within the global scientific community' (2004: 16). Leutner argues that, whereas earlier generations of scholars, most prominently Richard Wilhelm, feared 'fragmentation of identity' as a result of closer collaboration with Chinese colleagues, issues of identity 'are solved by Jaschok and Shui via an understanding of identity not as a fixed (nationally determined) monolith, but rather as "fluid". They define identity after Moore [1994] not by means of the other, but in conjunction with the other' (2004: 17).

If our collaboration indeed merits a place as 'emancipatory' ethnography, then much is due to the legacy of critical feminist scholarship, importantly Ardener, on which today we can build and develop. Shirley Ardener has voiced, and lived, the central conviction that – to use the title of this volume – 'fashioning identities' and 'weaving networks' across boundaries of competing knowledge and power constructions are interdependent processes. They are mutually beneficial and are the conditions for the coming-to-voice and rupturing of the complicity of 'silence' that political and gender hegemonies anywhere require for their perpetuation.

Notes

This essay elaborates on a reflexive dialogue Shui and I wrote for a Chinese academic review journal, *Bolan Qunshu*, Beijing (June 2003), entitled 'Kua jie yan shuo: shuxie chenmode lishi' [Speaking across boundaries: Writing muted history].

1. *Perceiving Women* (1975), *Defining Females* (1978), and *Women and Space* (1981), publications all edited by Shirley Ardener, now form part of the canon of feminist-inspired anthropology and had been my earliest introduction into anthropology as a site of some of the most interesting debates in women's studies.
2. The term 'muted groups' was first coined by the anthropologist Charlotte Hardman, who was associated with the Women's Studies movement in Oxford (Ardener 1975: xii).
3. This is not to say that all reviewers were oblivious to the 'conversational' model of anthropology we adopted: see Laura Newby (2001), Mechthild Leutner (2002), Zvi Azis Ben-Dor (2003). Blum's state-of-the-field article, least sensitive to reflective issues, is published in the foremost influential journal in Chinese studies, *The Journal of Asian Studies*.
4. 'Fields of Knowing' workshop, organised by the Centre of Women's Studies and Gender Research, Monash University, 4–8 Sept. 1998.
5. Our article was published in June 2003. Written for a Chinese audience, we reflect on the personal and research histories we bring to the ethnographic partnership, and on how our respective commitments to communities 'at home' and abiding ties beyond the completed project with these communities have shaped gestation, translation, and mutual learning.
6. *Zhongguo Qingzhen Nüsishi* (Shui and Jaschok 2002). The purpose of our article was to give publicity to the book we had just published in Beijing.
7. Quoting Sandra Harding 1987: 9.
8. The reference is to a female religious leader, usually resident at a women's mosque, with a position often tantamount to that of an imam; thus it is a highly contested term of address in Islamic orthodoxy (see Jaschok and Shui 2000a).
9. The Muslim population in China officially consists of ten ethnic 'minorities' (with estimates of the total Muslim population ranging from eighteen to twenty-five million, or more). Islam in China is popularly referred to by non-Muslims as *xiaojiao*, that is, a 'minority religion' (see Gladney 1991).
10. Leutner defines the following phases: (1) the colonial period when 'hierarchical relations of subordination were prevalent'; (2) the postcolonial phase, featuring 'a gradual transition from hierarchical relations to a relation of presumed equality'; (3) the phase of globalisation, distinguished, first, by a 'neoliberal mainstream position', based on hierarchy of Western theory and Chinese empiricism, and, secondly, by the 'emancipatory minorities position' (Leutner 2004: 2–3).

References

Allés, É. 2000. *Musulmans de Chine: Une anthropologie des Hui du Henan*, Paris: Éditions de l'École des Hautes Études en Sciences Sociales.

Ardener, S. (ed.) 1975. *Perceiving Women*, London: J.M. Dent & Sons.

——— (ed.) 1978. *Defining Females: The Nature of Women in Society*, London and New York: Croom Helm and St Martin's Press.

Ardener, S. (ed.) 1981. *Women and Space: Ground Rules and Social Maps*, London: Croom Helm.

Ben-Dor, Z.A. 2003. 'The History of Women's Mosques in Chinese Islam: A Mosque of Their Own' (review), *Arab Studies Journal* 10 (2)/11 (1), Fall 2002/Spring 2003, pp. 140–43.

Blum, S. 2002. 'Margins and Centers: A Decade of Publishing on China's Ethnic Minorities', *The Journal of Asian Studies* 61 (4), pp. 1287–1310.

Bulbeck, C., 1988. *One World Women's Movement*, London: Pluto.

Chopp, R. 1996. 'Eve's Knowing: Feminist Theology's Resistance to Malestream Epistemological Frameworks', in *Concilium 1996/1: Feminist Theologies in Different Contexts*, Maryknoll, New York: Orbis Books, pp. 116–23.

Chow, R. 1993. *Writing Diaspora: Tactics of Intervention in Contemporary Cultural Studies*, Bloomington: Indiana University Press.

Foucault, M. 1980. *Power/Knowledge. Selected Interviews and Other Writings, 1972–1977* (ed. Colin Gordon), New York: Pantheon Books.

Gandhi, L. 1998. *Postcolonial Theory. A Critical Introduction*, Edinburgh: Edinburgh University Press.

Gillette, M. Boyd 2000. *Between Mecca and Beijing: Modernisation and Consumption Among Urban Chinese Muslims*, Stanford: Stanford University Press.

Gladney, D. 1991. *Muslim Chinese; Ethnic Nationalism in the People's Republic*, Cambridge, Mass.: Harvard University Press.

Grosz, E. 1995. *Space, Time and Perversion: Essays on the Politics of Bodies*, London: Routledge.

Gudeman, S. and A. Rivera 1990. *Conversations in Colombia: The Domestic Economy in Life and Text*, Cambridge: Cambridge University Press.

Harding, S. 1987. *Feminism and Methodology*, Bloomington: Indiana University Press.

────── 1991. 'Representing Fundamentalism: The Problem of the Repugnant Cultural Other', *Social Research* 58, pp. 373–93.

Harrell, S. 1996. *Cultural Encounters on China's Ethnic Frontiers*, Hong Kong: Hong Kong University Press.

Hastrup, K. 1990. 'The Ethnographic Present: A Reinvention', *Cultural Anthropology* 5 (1), pp. 45–61.

────── 1992. 'Writing Ethnography: State of the Art', in J. Okely and H. Callaway (eds), *Anthropology and Autobiography*, London: Routledge.

Hill Collins, P. 1990. *Black Feminist Thought: Knowledge, Consciousness, and the Politics of Empowerment*, Boston: Unwin Hyman.

────── 1991. 'Learning from the Outsider Within: The Sociological Significance of Black Feminist Thought', in M.M. Fonow and J.A. Cook (eds), *Beyond Methodology*, Bloomington: Indiana University Press, pp. 35–59.

Hom, S. and Xin, C.Y. (eds) 1995. *English Chinese Lexicon of Women and Law*, Beijing: China Translation and Publication Corporation.

Jaschok, M. 2003. 'Violation and Resistance: Women, Religion, and Chinese Statehood', *Violence against Women* 9 (6), pp. 655–75.

Jaschok, M. and Shui Jingjun 2000a. *The History of Women's Mosques in Chinese Islam*, Richmond, Surrey: Curzon.

────── 2000b. '"Outsider Within": Speaking to Excursions across Cultures', *Feminist Theory* 1 (1), pp. 33–58.

Leutner, M. 2002. *Review of the History of Women's Mosques in Chinese Islam*, Berliner China-Hefte (Berlin), Autumn Issue.

────── 2004. 'Interaction as Hierarchy or Equality? Patterns of Collaboration between German and Chinese Scholars, 1887–2004', paper presented at the conference 'China's

Interactions with the World: Internationalisation, Internalization, Externalization', Peking University, 18–20 June; also presented at the European Association of Chinese Studies conference, Heidelberg, 25–29 August.

Li Xiaojiang 1999. 'With What Discourse Do We Reflect on Chinese Women's Thoughts? On Transnational Feminism in China', in M. Yang (ed.), *Spaces of Their Own: Women's Public Sphere in Transnational China*, Minneapolis: University of Minnesota Press, pp. 261–77.

Moore, H. 1994. *A Passion for Difference: Essays in Anthropology and Gender*, Cambridge: Polity Press.

Naples, N.A. 1997. 'A Feminist Revisiting of the Insider/Outsider Debate: The "Outsider Phenomenon" in Rural Iowa', in R. Hertz (ed.), *Reflexivity and Voice*, London: Sage, pp. 70–94.

Newby, L.J. 2001. 'The History of Women's Mosques in Chinese Islam' (review), *Journal of Islamic Studies* 12 (3), pp. 378–81.

Okely, J. 1996. *Own or Other Culture*, London: Routledge.

Shui Jingjun and M. Jaschok 2002. *Zhongguo Qingzhen Nüsishi*, Beijing: Sanlian Chubanshe, Harvard-Yenching Academic Library Series.

——— 2003. 'Kua jie yan shuo: shuxie chenmode lishi' [Speaking across boundaries: Writing muted history], *Bolan Qunshu*, Beijing, June issue.

Smith, D.E. 1987. *The Everyday World as Problematic*, Toronto: University of Toronto Press.

——— 1990. *Conceptual Practices of Power*, Boston: Northeastern University Press.

Spivak, G. 1993. *Outside in the Teaching Machine*, London: Routledge.

Strathern, M. 1990. 'Out of Context: The Persuasive Fictions of Anthropology', in M. Manganaro (ed.), *Modernist Anthropology: From Fieldwork to Text*, Princeton: Princeton University Press, pp. 80–122.

Trinh, T.M.H. 1989. *Woman, Native, Other*, Bloomington: Indiana University Press.

Tsing, A.L. 1993. *In the Realm of the Diamond Queen*, Princeton, New Jersey: Princeton University Press.

Tu, W.M. 1992. *The Confucian World Observed: A Contemporary Discussion of Confucian Humanism in East Asia*, Honolulu, Hawaii: Instititute of Culture and Communication, East–West Centre.

Visweswaran, K. 1997. 'Histories of Feminist Ethnography', *Annual Review of Anthropology* 26, pp. 591–621.

Wang Zheng 1999. *Women in the Chinese Enlightenment: Oral and Textual Histories*, Berkeley: University of California Press.

8

THE WOMEN'S MOVEMENT: THE FORMATIVE YEARS, 1850–1930

Cecillie Swaisland

In early 1902, following the Report of the Fawcett Commission, also known as the Ladies' Commission, sent to South Africa by the British Government to investigate conditions in the Boer War concentration camps, an appeal was made for teachers and nurses from Britain and Canada to serve in the camps. Two hundred women were needed but two thousand applied. Were the women motivated by patriotism, or did the response reflect a shortage of vocational outlets for women in these professions?

The year 1900 may be described as a watershed in the struggle of British women to achieve, as of right, a legal persona, a serious education, a professional training leading to recognised qualifications and, eventually to enfranchisement. The campaign had gained momentum throughout the Victorian period, but it was only in the early years of the twentieth century that the efforts of many women in many spheres began to bear the fruits of formal recognition.

If we consider the formative years of certain middle- or upper-class women whose influence was of vital importance in improving the status of women, the scope and difficulty of the problems facing them become apparent. The problems of working-class women were no less real but of a different kind and will not be dealt with in this essay.

Before the days of formal schooling for girls, most acquired their education in the home with the help of governesses. Some boarding schools, like 'Mrs Goddard's' in Jane Austen's *Emma*, were often of poor standard in both education and health. The school to which Patrick Brontë sent his daughters, and on which Charlotte Brontë based 'Lowood Institution' in *Jane Eyre*, caused the deaths from neglect of her sisters, Maria and Elizabeth (Gordon 1994: 14–19).

An important factor in the early lives and education of the Victorian women who made the greatest impact on their fellow women was the influence of their parents, particularly of their fathers. Some mothers proved to be remarkable women who had a profound influence on their daughters, but many were so frustrated by their social and domestic roles that, in their frustration, they resorted to the panacea of invalidism and spent their days confined to the chaise longue. Anne Elliot's sister Mary in Jane Austen's *Persuasion* amply illustrates this escape mechanism.

The role of the father, provided he was interested in the education and development of his daughters, could be profound, as he was often in a position to bring the world into the family domain. Indeed, Jane Waterston, the first woman doctor in South Africa, claimed in 1884 that a distinguished father often had clever and ambitious daughters who might rebel against boring domesticity and seek fulfilment outside the family (Bean and van Heyningen 1983: 27).

The role of parents could, however, have a profoundly deleterious effect on the lives of many Victorian daughters. Those who did not escape early into matrimony, to which most aspired, were earmarked as the carers and supporters of parents in their old age. Duty was the virtue invoked and insisted upon, and many a promising career was blighted by a daughter being called back to fulfil the caring role. This custom continued well into the twentieth century, and many of my generation can recall the homebound maiden aunt whose duty it was to care for the elderly. In some families there was even the suspicion that measures had been taken to ensure that would-be suitors of the carer daughter were strongly deterred before the relationship became too strong.

The early lives of some of the most influential Victorian women illustrate the handicaps from which they had to escape before the work for which they are noted could begin. A few examples must suffice to underline the point.

Mary Kingsley (1862–1900) had no formal education. She was the daughter of a doctor who loved to travel, and Mary educated herself by reading her father's travel books. Her mother was sickly and frustrated, and became mentally ill. Mary was chained to them as carer until, when she was thirty, they both died. In relief she began her travels in West Africa. She wrote two books on West Africa but in 1900, depressed by critical reviews of her work, she looked for a way to resume her travels. She chose to go to South Africa, then in the throes of the South African (Boer) War, as a nurse, although she had no formal training. She hoped to become a reporter on the war and then to go north and continue her travels. She found, however, that the need for nurses was so great that she stayed to nurse Boer prisoners. She caught typhoid (enteric fever) from her patients and died (see Birkett 1993).

Jane Waterston (1843–1932) was born in Inverness, Scotland, one of the six children of a bank manager father and a mother who rapidly adopted the hypochondriac existence typical of many upper-class Victorian women. Her three sisters rapidly slipped into the same state of mind. Jane resisted this escapism and became convinced of the need to rescue such women by structured education. She was taught at home by governesses and decided at an early age that she wished to become a missionary. In pursuit of this and against family opposition, she gained some experience as a teacher and as a nurse and midwife. In 1866 she was appointed by the Foreign Missions Committee of the Free Church of

Scotland to serve at Lovedale Mission in Kaffraria, South Africa, to further the education of girls. She arrived there in 1867, and the Girls' Institution which she was to head opened the following year (Bean and van Heyningen 1983: chap. 1). How she moved from this to become a doctor, and the long struggle she had to acquire medical qualifications, I shall explore later.

Emily Davies (1830–1921) and her sister were educated at home by their mother, while her brothers went to public school and university. After her father's death she and her mother moved to London, where Emily began her crusade for the education of women. She became involved in the provision of schools for girls and for their inclusion in examinations that were, at the time, open only to boys. Her attention then turned to providing university education for women, and she was mainly instrumental in opening the first college for women at Cambridge (see Forster 1984: chap. 4).

Florence Nightingale (1820–1910) was another who had no formal education but was taught by her well-read father. Most useful was the weekly essay he set for her and her older sister. He had no intention that his teaching would lead anywhere, and this sent his younger daughter into a raging discontent with domestic life and duties. Florence even rejected the idea of marriage as she felt that it would only trap her into a man's way of life. At the age of twenty-four she asked to be allowed to train as a nurse in a hospital, but her mother and sister became so hysterical that she gave in and spent the next years gaining knowledge of health statistics by studying Blue Books (Boyd 1982: chaps. 7–9). How she gained enough nursing experience to become the 'Lady with a Lamp' in the Crimean War I shall consider later.

Elizabeth Garrett Anderson (1836–1917) and Millicent Garrett Fawcett (1847–1929) were sisters in the remarkable Garrett family of daughters. Both became well known in their fields. Elizabeth was the first woman in Britain to qualify as a doctor. Her younger sister, Millicent, became one of the leaders in the women's suffrage movement, standing out strongly against the suffragettes for the battle to be won only by constitutional means. The daughters of Newson Garrett, a Suffolk businessman, they were educated mainly at home, but Elizabeth and her elder sister spent two years at the Academy for the Daughters of Gentlemen at Blackheath, where they learned little but acquired the taste for more learning. Their father, after the first shock at learning of Elizabeth's determination to become a doctor, was supportive, but her mother, we are told, wept for two days at the thought of her daughter working for money. This, at the time, was taboo among the 'Drawing-Room Class' (Kamm 1966).

Emigration in the Nineteenth Century

One of the indicators that spells out the dilemma faced by middle- and upper-class women in the nineteenth century is the number of such women who left their native countries and emigrated to the newly developing countries of the

British Empire. Of these, the majority went to the New World, seeking a more fulfilling life in Canada from where many crossed the border into the United States. Although the majority of emigrants were families seeking to escape the poverty and poor conditions of an industrialising and urbanising society, many were single women who, for a variety of reasons, were unable to support themselves in Britain. Why were these women leaving their homes and families?

The main cause for this movement among upper-class women was the failure, for whatever reason, to find a marriage partner and the fear of a life of poverty and frustration that would face them if the support of a father or brother should not be forthcoming (Swaisland 1993: 14). As has been noted above in the brief biographies of a group of representative women, few of their class had received an education on the basis of which they could support themselves, except perhaps as underpaid and socially ostracised governesses. Such women spent their days in the schoolroom, accepted neither members of the family nor as equals of the servants below stairs. They were paid such a pittance that when their life's work was done, they often retreated into a parlous state of poverty and loneliness. In 1841 the Governesses' Benevolent Institution was founded and a committee set up to examine the extent of the problem. The members were appalled to discover how many 'educated' women were reduced to destitution.

The plight of middle-class women who became governesses occupied the attention of several women, who recognised how many of them had the greatest difficulty in finding any employment. Maria Rye, the daughter of a London solicitor, had, with various other like-minded women, set up the Society for Promoting the Employment of Women. Rye herself had set up a Law Copying Office, as one of the Society's projects to provide some employment, but when the Society was besieged by so many desperate women whose needs could not be met, she turned her attention to the possibility of emigration as a solution. As a result, in 1862, the first of a series of emigration societies for women was founded. The Female Middle Class Emigration Society (FMCES), despite its firm rules and good intentions (which were to send out only those with adequate education to become governesses and who had a basic knowledge of household skills), was unable to fulfil all its objectives. Especially among these was the promise to make adequate arrangements for reception overseas and to find suitable employment for the emigrants. Despite their hope of finding employment in many fields for educated unemployed women, the Society was disappointed to find itself only in effect a placement agency for governesses (see Swaisland 1993: 108–21).

The later emigration societies that grew out of the FMCES after its final demise in 1884 benefited from various changes in the social scene, not least the improved opportunities for the education of women. Other factors were the revolutions in transport and communications, which enabled the emigrants to reach their destinations more easily and to maintain contact with the societies that had sent them out. As the numbers of women taking this course of action to alleviate their problems grew, it became possible for those already in a territory to help later arrivals in finding posts and in settling into their new lives. The most efficient and successful of these societies in the late nineteenth century was the British Women's Emigration Association (BWEA, 1885–1919), whose records and carefully transcribed letter-books give a clear picture of the circumstances and qualifications of those who applied for help and of their subsequent experiences in their new homes. The final society, in the sequence stretching back over a hundred years, was the Society for the Settlement of British Women (SOSBW). It was finally ended in 1963 as, by then, women were able to cater for their own needs. Instead of the poorly qualified women whose chances of employment were poor in a society that regarded paid employment as demeaning and too much education as possibly damaging physically and morally to the 'weaker sex', the 'new women' were highly qualified professional women, more often seeking chances of promotion in their field that were unavailable in the still overcrowded professions in their home country (Swaisland 1993: 22–28).

Education, Training and Employment

In 1884 Jane Waterston, by then established in Cape Town as the first woman doctor in private practice in South Africa, was asked to present a paper to the Literary Society of the Church of Scotland. She chose to talk on 'The Higher Education of Women' and commented on the great changes that had taken place over the previous ten years in the attitudes to women at such meetings. In the 1870s she had asked to attend a public meeting at a Missionary Conference but was denied entrance as it was not 'proper' for a woman to do so and no woman had ever asked before. She managed to gain entrance by enlisting the help of a male acquaintance, who was prepared to risk the wrath of 'Mrs Grundy' by accompanying her in. No other woman had been present.

What, she asked, were the reasons for such an extraordinary change? The first, she thought, was the revolutionary spirit of the age. In an age of discontent and questioning it would be astonishing if the only people not to react to it were women. She quoted a churchman in Oxford who proclaimed to women, 'Christianity 1800 years ago fixed your place for ever!' Why, she asked, was the Church putting up a bar to larger thought and work as if nothing had changed since the early teachings?

The second influence was the role of the father in forming a daughter's character. Waterston pointed out the dire consequences of a father failing to recognise the needs of a daughter made in his own image. By denying them an outlet for their restless energy and even quoting scripture to assert that a 'good' girl obeys her parents, they might force the daughter's energy to turn in on itself and so lead her into mental conflict. Waterston, quoting an actual case, asserted that it could even lead to a lifelong incarceration in a lunatic asylum. There is no evidence that Jane herself had to fight as hard as this, despite the strong objections of her family to her wishes to become a missionary and later a doctor. She may have been thinking of what she believed to be the wasted lives of her mother and sisters.

The third factor, quoted by Waterston as influential in facilitating the education and training of girls, was the economic situation in Britain in the last quarter of the nineteenth century. A series of bank failures led her to question whether parents were asking themselves if it would not be better to spend some money, while they had it, on giving their daughters an education and training that would enable them to earn their own living if necessary. The alternative would be that 'ladies', especially the unmarried, could be cast on the world in their middle or old age, after a youth of comfort and luxury, knowing nothing thoroughly. What, she asked, was the forfeit of a little gallantry against being able to provide the comforts of life for themselves?

What, Jane Waterston asked, was the meaning of higher education for women? At base, it meant doing away with the 'old, scrappy, tinselly, slovenly kind of stuff that used to be thought enough for a girl's schoolroom'. In its place should be put a thorough knowledge of one, two, or three subjects, with an intelligent grounding in others, on which a woman could work herself as the need arose. Jane believed that on such a foundation a woman could build any accomplishments she needed.

There remained the problem of careers and employment open to women. These were becoming more numerous than in the past, but without exception they did require training: 'The untrained woman is a drug on the market.' The days when this could not be obtained, she believed, were past. There were a variety of trades and professions for which a woman could be trained. She quoted many of the recognised outlets, such as teaching and nursing, and added some less familiar ones such as 'General Booth's lady officers and preachers' (to which my own grandmother aspired in the 1890s). To sum up, Waterston quoted the three things on which all wise friends of womankind were now insisting: a preliminary education as good as the father could afford, followed (if the girl would be destined to work) by a 'careful consideration of her natural bent' before a profession or trade was decided upon, and then a thorough training for the branch of work chosen (see Bean and van Heyningen 1983: Appendix 3).

The question is whether Jane Waterston was too sanguine in her belief that a wide variety of trades and professions were opening up to women in the later nineteenth century. If one looks in more detail at those most often chosen, namely teaching and the medical profession, it becomes clear that, although changes were undoubtedly taking place, there were still many hurdles to be surmounted. Jane herself had to overcome these before she could become a doctor. It was not until the twentieth century that many professions were opened to women as of right.

The Teaching Profession and the Education of Girls

In the absence of other opportunities, teaching was the most sought-after profession and the one in which changes followed one another most rapidly. The campaign to improve the education of upper-class women began in the 1840s with the realisation of the woeful ignorance of a high proportion of the women who offered themselves as governesses when their knowledge was little better than that of their pupils. In an attempt to rectify this, Revd F. D. Denison, Professor of English Literature at King's College, London, proposed the institution of an examination leading to a teaching diploma. The idea was abandoned when it was realised that most of the possible candidates were too uneducated to pass any examination. Professor Denison and his colleagues thus set up a series of lectures that proved so popular, and the need so great, that they were opened to all women. Out of this venture emerged Queen's College for Women, founded in 1848 and open to all from the age of twelve. When the wide age range proved impractical, the younger ones were taught in a house in Bedford Square and became the nucleus for Bedford College. Attending the lectures were certain notable names such as Frances Mary Buss and Dorothea Beale, both of whom became teachers on the courses (Kamm 1966: 49).

It was rapidly becoming apparent that the need at its most basic was for good girls' schools that would give the pupils the grounding already available in many boys' schools. Hence, in 1850, Buss, who was already running a small school of her own, began the task of establishing the North London Collegiate School; it was to be her life's work. Beale, no less convinced of the need for improved education for girls, founded the Cheltenham Ladies College in 1858, into which she wisely incorporated a teacher-training course. Excellent as these two schools proved to be, there was still much to be remedied in other schools for girls. This became apparent when in 1864 a Schools Enquiry Committee into the state of boys' schools began work. After a fierce battle, girls' schools were included. The report concluded that most girls' schools were underfunded and had low standards of education and few good teachers – though many boys' schools were found to be little better.

As more girls began to receive a better education, attention moved to a new battle front. Emily Davies, after the establishment in 1858 of the Oxford and Cambridge Local Examinations, which was at first only for boys, began a campaign to have girls included. In 1863 Cambridge agreed to an unofficial trial of the examination for girls. Raising enough girls for such a test proved difficult but eventually eighty-three were found and did well except in mathematics, the teaching of which proved to be poor and in need of reform. In 1865, after much canvassing, Cambridge opened the examinations to girls on a permanent footing; and this was followed in 1870 by Oxford (Kamm 1966: 46–64). These advances did not go unnoticed by certain conservative elements in society. Not only did some believe that young women would do themselves physical injury, such as hysteria and fainting caused by too much study (neither of which had occurred among the first batches to take the Local Examinations), but one journal even put forward the view that 'a learned young woman is one of the most intolerable monsters in creation' (ibid.: 54).

Having achieved success in the Local Examinations, Emily Davies turned her attention to storming the highest bastions of education. London University was already admitting women to courses but not to degrees. Oxford and Cambridge were doing neither. The first step was to lease a house in 1869 in Hitchin, Herts, and to admit the first five students, who would be prepared for the Cambridge tripos. Sitting the examination, the university ordained, would be informal, and no degrees would be awarded. In 1874 the move to Cambridge took place, and Girton College was incorporated. In 1880 a second college, Newnham, was founded. Many of the students from both colleges achieved impressive results over the years (Kamm 1966: 61–64). One of these was a student from Newnham, Philippa Fawcett, the daughter of Millicent and Henry Fawcett: she was placed as Senior Wrangler, above all the men, but without being awarded a degree (ibid.: 63). Oxford was not far behind Cambridge in founding women's colleges: Somerville College and Lady Margaret Hall were established in 1879 (Brittain 1960: 36).

The Medical Profession: Nursing

While all this activity was proceeding in education, attention was also being focused on the entry of women into other professions, notably into nursing and doctoring. The best-known name in nursing was that of Florence Nightingale. Her early life had been dominated by what she saw as her duty to her family. Her mother and sister were inclined to become hysterical at the thought of a 'lady' undertaking any of the tasks then associated (at the time she reached adulthood, in the middle of the century) with untrained, mainly lower-class women. These women, the 'Mrs Gamps', were little more than domestic servants, although some offered inherited skills in folk medicine and practical knowledge in midwifery and nursing. When Florence Nightingale wished to train as a nurse it was refused, and she was obliged to learn from experience, mainly at first by nursing sick relatives. Other types of nursing included the nursing care given by religious bodies, mainly to the poor. None of these 'nurses' had any systematic training but learned, like Florence Nightingale, by practical experience (see Swaisland 1993: 147 on the low status of nursing in South Africa).

The story of Florence Nightingale and her chosen band of nurses in the hospitals of the Crimean War has become legendary. 'The Lady with a Lamp' is what Nightingale has become known and revered for. In fact, the main service she offered was administrative – in forcing the British Government to supply the woefully lacking basic needs for the injured. When she returned to England, physically and mentally exhausted, she turned her attention to the reformation of the medical services for the Army. On completing this task she retreated into one of the long periods of withdrawal which were to mark the rest of her life (Boyd 1982: 183–91).

It had been expected that Florence Nightingale would turn her attention to setting up a nursing school, and a fund of £45,000 had been raised to train nurses. A committee to administer the fund, on which Florence Nightingale did not sit, found itself uncertain how to proceed on the practical issues of what nurses should be taught and what menial tasks should be expected of them. In

1859 Nightingale produced a booklet, *Notes on Nursing*. It was not a manual but a guide to what nurses should be – practical, but tough and unsqueamish. There was nothing in the *Notes* on procedure or on a course of study. It railed against the contemporary image of women, especially against the impractical nature of women's dress. The diehards in society responded by claiming that nothing needed to be done as women were incapable of understanding such courses and, in any case, doctors needed nothing more than efficient housemaids.

Eventually, in 1860, a nursing school was opened. It was housed within St Thomas's Hospital, which would afford ward experience. A matron was appointed but recruitment at this stage was disappointing and the dropout rate was too high. The lectures offered to complement the training failed because the standard of education of the trainees was so low. Florence Nightingale was disappointed at the number of trainees who dropped out in favour of marriage because, they claimed, they feared they would be labelled as unsexed paragons. However, the struggle to improve the quality of nursing continued, and in 1886 it was proposed that trained nurses, like doctors, should be registered. A series of examinations, marked by an independent body, would entitle those who passed to be placed on a state register. Nightingale, although agreeing in principle with the idea of registration, opposed the move, fearing that with such a scheme registration would simply become automatic. Not only were examination results needed but also the careful scrutiny by qualified persons of each candidate before registration could be granted. The idea of a register was dropped and did not come into being until nine years after Nightingale's death in 1910 at the age of ninety (Forster 1984: 110–23).

The Medical Profession: Women Doctors

The career that required the greatest effort and patience to enter was that of the medical doctor. The battle that Elizabeth Garrett Anderson fought to gain the qualifications she needed is well known in the annals of women's efforts to become doctors. The idea came to her in the late 1850s, when she attended a course of lectures given by Elizabeth Blackwell, who had qualified as a doctor in New York. When she broke the news of her intentions in 1860, her parents were appalled, but her father withdrew his opposition and determined to help his daughter achieve her goal.

Elizabeth's first step was to work for six months in a surgical ward at the Middlesex Hospital. This led to her admission to all wards and to lectures and demonstrations on dissection. Although she passed all the examinations for the lecture courses with honours, no medical school at the time would accept women and award them degrees. She decided to study for the examination of the Society of Apothecaries, which, by its charter, was obliged to accept all who satisfied its requirements. The Society, having never contemplated the possibility that a woman would apply, tried to refuse her permission to sit the examination but backed down when threatened with legal action. To prevent any other women applying the Society rapidly changed its statutes. To consolidate her position, Elizabeth took advantage of the University of Paris opening its medical degrees to women in 1869. She obtained her MD with credit. Elizabeth worked tirelessly to persuade London University to open its degrees to women. She was partially successful when, in 1877, the Royal Free Hospital offered clinical experience to the School of Medicine for Women, which had been founded in 1874. Elizabeth served the new Hospital for Women for thirty years until her retirement in 1902. After her death in 1917, the hospital was renamed the Elizabeth Garrett Anderson Hospital (Kamm 1966: chap. 4 ('The Doctors')).

To return to Jane Waterston, whose words of wisdom on the education of women have already been noted. In 1874, at the age of thirty-one, she decided to become a medical missionary. On returning to Britain, she began her practical training at Somerset House but until the London School of Medicine for Women was founded, there was no place where she could train as a doctor. She was one of the first to benefit from the new school but, as no degrees were then offered, she moved to Ireland. There she first studied midwifery at the Rotunda Lying-in Hospital in Dublin, before completing her training at the College of Physicians with two courses of lectures on surgery.

She returned to London to gain clinical practice at the Royal Free Hospital. After several years back in South Africa she returned to Britain to study for her Licentiate at the Royal College of Surgeons in Edinburgh. In 1888 she was awarded her MD and, in addition, worked for a Certificate in Psychiatric Medicine before returning to South Africa to set up a private practice in Cape Town. She became a well-known and respected figure in the city and died there in 1932 at the age of eighty-nine (on her training see Bean and van Heyningen 1983: 44, 75, 108, 111, 121, 208; on her work in Cape Town see ibid.: 252–4).

The Demand for Women in South Africa

If we return to the question asked at the beginning of this chapter as to why, in 1902, two thousand women applied for the two hundred places for teachers and nurses to serve in the Boer War's so-called concentration camps, the reason now becomes clearer. Despite the good work by many nineteenth-century women in improving the education and employment chances of their fellows, there was still an acute shortage of satisfactory jobs for women and even less opportunity for promotion and better rates of pay. The fact remained that the majority of employed women were trapped in the lower echelons of their professions and were suffering from frustration and boredom. Work overseas was at least different, and they had heard of many earlier migrant women writing home about their satisfaction with their new lives.

The demand for women to go to South Africa began when Emily Hobhouse reacted to the news of the suffering of civilians in the Boer War by setting up the

South African Women's and Children's Distress Fund in Britain. When she went to South Africa with supplies of necessities and comforts for the concentration camps she was appalled by the conditions she found there, and on returning to Britain she did not hesitate to make her views known to the government (Van Reenen 1984: 32–113; Hewison 1989: 187–93). As a result, it was decided to send out a Commission of Inquiry to report on the state of affairs in the camps. Uniquely for the time, the Commission was made up entirely of women and was led by the suffragist Millicent Fawcett (Hewison 1989: 193–94). Among those appointed to serve on it was Jane Waterston, the only colonial to be included. As a pro-Boer she was reluctant to be appointed but felt it was her medical duty to do whatever she could to help improve conditions in the camps (Bean and van Heyningen 1983: 246–48). Emily Hobhouse was not included as her somewhat emotional approach was suspect, and the military in South Africa had taken a distinct dislike to what they considered to be her meddling. In fact, when she tried to re-enter South Africa in 1901, she was forcibly restrained and put back on a ship for England (see Pakenham 1993: 254–55 for a cartoon version of this event). Why Millicent Fawcett was chosen for the work is debatable, but the reason may lie in her measured views on women's suffrage and the fact that she was the widow of a Minister of State, Henry Fawcett, who had served as Postmaster-General. Accompanying her mother as secretary was her daughter, Philippa – the 'Great Philippa Fawcett' to her contemporaries, for her achievement as Senior Wrangler in her Cambridge tripos. Millicent Fawcett was also, as already noted, the younger sister of the known and admired Elizabeth Garrett Anderson.

When the Commission returned to England to write their report they left behind some immediate improvements in the camps, but the report, published in December 1901, made far-reaching recommendations which, when implemented, changed the conditions in the camps to the extent that the death rates fell dramatically (*Blue Book* 1902). The two hundred nurses and teachers arrived to find that permanent buildings had been erected as schools and hospitals and that basic needs for better food, sanitation and comfort had been provided for. After the end of the war, many of the women stayed on in hospitals and schools to help rebuild the country. Some of the teachers trekked back with the families to their home areas and set up farm schools for the children. Philippa Fawcett returned to the Transvaal to reorganise kindergarten education there (Swaisland 1993: 138–39).

The Early Twentieth Century

On the evidence submitted below, the early years of the twentieth century may be seen as constituting a watershed in the lives of women. Although there were few immediate major changes, there are many pointers that indicate changes in attitudes and in the life chances of many women. In nursing, an important advance came with the introduction of state registration in 1919. In education, the introduction of girls' high schools by the Balfour Morant Education Act of 1902 widened opportunities for girls of all classes, who entered them through scholarships or by the payment of relatively modest fees. In higher education, women could already obtain degrees at London University and other newer universities. Oxford University admitted women to degrees and full membership in 1919, but Cambridge made the move to admit them only in 1948.

In other professions not considered here in detail, such as the legal profession, the opposition to the inclusion of women was gradually eroded. The Sexual Discrimination Removal Act of 1919 made it possible for women to enter Parliament for the first time; Lady Astor was the first to do so, in 1921. The suffrage movement, to which all women were wedded – even though there were differing views on how to achieve the vote – was eventually conceded in February 1918 for women over the age of thirty, and followed in 1928 by the so-called 'Flapper Vote' for all women over twenty-one (Kamm 1966: chap. 11).

The First World War changed the lives of women dramatically as a result of the conscription of most of the male population. There was no longer any time for lying feebly on the chaise longue. Women of all classes were called on to fill the places left by the men in the trenches and, in reaction to the massive loss of life, to remain in many of those places after the war was over. In recognition of the part played by women in 'keeping the home fires burning', the voices of the diehards who would have liked to return to the *status quo ante*, were disregarded, and legislation for the legal emancipation of women was rapidly instituted.

The economic depression of the 1930s was undoubtedly a setback and the voices of repression were once more heard, claiming that women in employment were stealing the jobs of men who had families to support. There was, however, no going back to the days of unfulfilling boredom for middle- and upper-class women, who had learned that there was a world of work awaiting them. They were now willing, eager, and able to embrace it.

References

Bean, L. and E. van Heyningen (eds) 1983. *The Letters of Jane Elizabeth Waterston 1886–1905*, Cape Town: Van Riebeeck Society.
Birkett, D. 1993. *Mary Kingsley 1862–1900: A Biographical Bibliography*, Bristol: University of Bristol (for the Royal Africa Society).
Blue Book 1902. CD 893, London: HMSO.
Boyd, N. 1982. *Three Victorian Women Who Changed Their World*, London: Macmillan.
Brittain, V. 1960. *The Women at Oxford*, London: Harrap.
Forster, M. 1984. *Significant Sisters: The Grassroots of Feminism*, New York: Oxford University Press.
Gordon, L. 1994. *Charlotte Brontë: A Passionate Life*, London: Chatto & Windus.
Hewison, H.H. 1989. *Hedge of Wild Almonds: South Africa, the Pro-Boers and the Quaker Conscience*, Portsmouth, New Hampshire: Heinemann; Cape Town: David Philip.

Kamm, J. 1966. *Rapiers and Battleaxes: The Women's Movement and its Aftermath*, London: Allen & Unwin.

Pakenham, T. 1993. *The Boer War* (illustrated edn, abridged by J.W. Buchan), London: Weidenfeld & Nicolson.

Swaisland, C. 1993. *Servants and Gentlewomen: The Emigration of Single Women from Britain to Southern Africa 1820–1939*, Oxford: Berg; Pietermaritzberg: University of Natal Press.

Van Reenen, R. (ed.) 1984. *Emily Hobhouse: Boer War Letters*, Cape Town: Human & Rousseau.

9

A GOOD LADY, ANDROGYNOUS ANGEL, AND INTREPID WOMAN: MARIA CZAPLICKA IN FEMINIST PROFILE

Grażyna Kubica

This essay discusses the Polish-British anthropologist, Maria Czaplicka (born 1884), a contemporary of Bronisław Malinowski, who like him came to England in 1910 and studied under C.G. Seligman at the London School of Economics and Political Science. Later she worked with R.R. Marett and obtained a Diploma in Anthropology from Oxford University. In 1914–15, she led the Jenisei Expedition to Siberia, where she became an experienced fieldworker and made important finds for the Pitt Rivers Museum. While she was the first female lecturer in anthropology at Oxford University, she was also a tragic figure without a secure academic appointment. In 1921 she committed suicide in Bristol, where she had held a temporary teaching position; she was only thirty-seven when she died.[1]

Maria Czaplicka would certainly fit into the collection of women anthropologists edited by Shirley Ardener (1992a; see also Ardener 1992b). I do not intend here, however, to describe Czaplicka's scholarly achievements per se. Instead, I wish to analyse how she constructed her subjectivity in her writings. She represents a time when women were still a very conspicuous novelty in the public arena – and later to be conferred the status of 'honorary men'. My aim is to show how gender was an important factor in the early anthropological project, only to be excluded by the later emergence of positivist models under the pretext of objectivity: autobiographical insights that might have revealed the self of an ethnographer were suppressed in the name of professionalism (Callaway 1992; Okely 1992). Czaplicka's life and writings afford us a glimpse into the world of the self of an anthropologist before the self was forced out from the discourse.

Thus, I am interested in 'engendered knowledge', to use Pat Caplan's phrase (1992), a theme worked on so successfully by Shirley Ardener (e.g., 1975, 1984) and other British scholars. My work here also benefits from American feminist anthropology, as represented by the volume *Women Writing Culture* (Behar and Gordon 1995). My task is a kind of 'critical movement towards home', to confront the invisible processes of the formation of the self, the practice that Kamela Visweswaran called 'homework' in contrast to fieldwork. I am, like her, 'rendering women's subjectivity within the contexts of larger dominant narratives' (Visweswaran 1994: 10). My purpose here is to show how Maria Czaplicka operated within various discourses: the ethos of the Polish gentry–intelligentsia, dilemmas of European feminism, and the civilising mission of British colonialism. All these were intertwined with the academic discourse she gained access to at an early stage of her life. Science was her main and basic choice.

Writing this essay, I have taken the liberty of combining various languages: those of literary theory, feminist philosophy, and anthropology. The oscillation between them enables me, I hope, to describe differentiated and evasive shadows of womanhood. Because womanhood is not, in my opinion, a homogeneous, overarching category: there is no universal model of it. I am writing about a real woman who existed some time ago, and I analyse her through the constructs she created (or re-created) of herself, whether following or contesting the culturally prevalent definitions of womanhood of her time (Moore 1988).

Pedigree

Maria Czaplicka was born on 25 October 1884 in Stara Praga, a location that later became a suburb of Warsaw. The area was then growing very energetically: it was densely populated and chaotically built. There were new, modernist five-storied buildings side by side with slum huts with shingle roofs. The area was inhabited mainly by the working class and poor Jews.

The father of Maria, Felix Czaplicki, was the stationmaster of Terespol railway station (Wawrzykowska-Wierciochowa 1959: 662). For impoverished representatives of the Polish gentry who had some education, working for the railways was one of the few opportunities to earn money. Felix Czaplicki seems to have been just such a case. Probably his parents, after losing their family estate, moved to Warsaw and tried to furnish their children (sons) with the best education they could afford – attendance at gymnasium, followed by some years of university. After that, a young man had to find any paid position he could in order to provide for his family, and the railways offered one such solution. This family history is a typical example of the rise of the intelligentsia, an important social class in eastern Europe.

Felix Czaplicki married Sophie Zawisza and they had three children: one son (who later became a physician) and two daughters. They lived together with their parents, whom they had to support. The Czaplickis were probably not very well off and moved to Russia in 1904 because Felix got a better-paid job there. The family came back a few years later and settled down on Hoża street in the very centre of Warsaw. One can still feel there something of the magnificent grandeur of old Warsaw.

It is very difficult to get any idea of Maria Czaplicka's home and family life. In her letters from England to a writer named Władysław Orkan (the only collection of her private correspondence I have come across) during the years 1910–12, there is hardly any information concerning her family (OP).[2] She did not mention her father at all so it can be supposed that he was probably dead by then; her constant financial problems would support this hypothesis – a widowed mother could not help her much. From the tone of her daughter's writing about her, it would seem that there was some tension between them, some emotional distance. Perhaps the mother did not like the life her daughter had chosen. She might have preferred her to get married and live somewhere near home. Perhaps she even had a suitable match for her. Maria would have said 'no', because she knew that this would have meant the end of her academic aspirations. She opted for further education and earning a living for herself. Or perhaps it was a totally different scenario. A young woman without a dowry could not even dream of a reasonable marriage, so Maria did not have any other choice but to study and find a job.

Education

It should be added here that Poland was not an independent country during the nineteenth century, having been divided up (partitioned, to quote the term commonly used) between its neighbours at the end of the eighteenth century: Warsaw was in Russia. Polish national life was suppressed. Russian was the compulsory language of instruction in education. But an underground, clandestine system of Polish schooling existed at every level: alongside the Russian university in Warsaw there was also a 'Flying University', whose lectures moved between different private flats. It brought about the possibility of higher education for women, although it could not give its students any kind of job qualification. On the other hand, when a girl wanted to study abroad, she had to pass a 'maturity exam' in one of the boys' gymnasia, because girls' schools did not prepare their pupils for that and indeed were not entitled to do so. But, as an effect of the 1905 revolution and a strike by the schools, the situation in educational and academic life improved: a private charitable foundation for the promotion of science, the Kasa Mianowskiego, was established, which in turn led to the creation of the Association of Higher Scientific Courses, a quasi-university.

Education was still treated as a value in itself, not as the basis for a good job. This was the context for the raising of future cadres of 'educational and social activists', as they were called. Such a role did not harm the traditional model of public activity acceptable for women outside the household: on the contrary, at the beginning of the twentieth century, it was teaching that still remained the main occupation for women coming from the impoverished gentry and/or the intelligentsia (Żarnowska 2000).

The case of Maria Czaplicka well reflected this general model. She attended a girls' school (1894–1902), as all young ladies did then, and then took some courses in pedagogy. When the family moved to Russia, she passed her maturity exam at the boys' Government Gymnasium in 1905 and the teachers' exam for geography (according to her curriculum vitae (CzP)). At the same time she worked as a Polish governess. Later she attended the Flying University and went on to become a student of science at the Association of Higher Scientific Courses. As a result of her ambitions and talents, she was able to continue her education, thanks to a Kasa Mianowskiego scholarship (*Sprawozdanie* 1915). Some women had been given grants to do scientific research or to publish their findings, but Czaplicka was the first to receive a considerable amount (nine hundred roubles) enabling her to study abroad. She wanted to study ethno-geography and planned to write a book about different peoples of the world, to be published in the series *Nauka dla wszystkich* (Science for everyone).

Independence

The younger generation of women operating within the patriarchal system of this time strove for more independence. In the Polish conditions of the early twentieth century, women tried to achieve this in various ways. Paradoxically, one way was through matrimony. A married woman had a higher social status, she was not subject to the customary taboos of avoiding certain topics in drawing-room conversation, she had the possibility of unchaperoned trips, etc. A married woman simply had more freedom, and her family was satisfied. This was the solution adopted by one intellectual friend of Czaplicka, the writer Zofia Nałkowska, who married a poet, Leon Rygier.

Another way of obtaining relative autonomy was to go abroad to study. A woman could in this way not only escape strict family control but also achieve a social position equal to her male siblings. Thus educational aspirations went together with emancipation from patriarchal family life (Żarnowska 2000).

For the young scholar, independence meant being alone and earning a living, which, however, brought constant financial problems. In an interview in 1913 Czaplicka complained: 'During three years in Warsaw I was impossibly overworked with various secretarialships, substitutions, lessons, lectures etc. All those paid poorly or not at all. Of course, I remember the University for Everyone and clandestine study classes the best' (SC). She worked as a teacher, but she was also involved in other forms of educational activities.

Czaplicka also worked as a *dame de compagnie* (companion to rich women). She wrote to Orkan from Ostend: 'I take baths and stay with Mrs Gloger, who is nicer to me than Mrs. Epstein was to Rygier-Nałkowska' (OP). Apparently this must have been quite a frequent practice for educated and poor young ladies.

At a certain point Maria Czaplicka started to earn her living by writing. She wrote for *Revival: A Socio-Political, Literary and Artistic Journal*, a Warsaw periodical that appeared in the years 1910–11. It was a radical weekly – 'progressive', to use the contemporary term – which meant socialist, anticlerical, and in favour of the emancipation of the Jews and of women. It argued for Polish political independence and therefore had constant problems with the censors. Czaplicka published her poems there.

In 1910 she enriched her author's portfolio with a 'novel for young people' entitled *Olek Niedziela* (which literally translates as 'Alex Sunday'). She wrote it in Zakopane, a famous health resort in the Tatra mountains, where she spent the whole winter that year. She edited and typed the novel the following summer, staying on an estate where she was giving private lessons to the owners' children. The book was published a year later in Warsaw.

A Good Lady

Maria Czaplicka's novel tells the story of a poor boy who from early childhood wanted to learn. His dream was to become reality when he was eleven years old. It was then that some young lady accepted him for the free schooling she had organised in her own flat for a group of boys. One cannot learn much about the tutoress from the novel: her appearance is not described, her name is unknown, and she is referred to simply as 'Miss'.

The book focuses on the world of the pupils and is written from their point of view – a novelty in literature for young people then – presenting the inner problems and changes of one of them, named Olek (Alex). He was the most talented member of the group, the most sensitive and eager to learn, and he used to ask interesting questions. His family was extremely poor: his mother was a washerwoman, and his father could only plait baskets.

Miss introduces Olek not only to the world of knowledge, but also to the world of art. The book is to a large extent a description of the reaction of a naive boy to the encounter with beauty – the beauty of music, of painting, and also of nature. Olek dreams of becoming a teacher. Miss wants to prepare him to enter gymnasium. Unfortunately, she becomes seriously ill, goes abroad for medical treatment, and leaves Olek in the care of her unsophisticated cousin, who, of course, does not fulfil his duty, and Olek takes on a job in a factory. He resents Miss, who had simply left him. One day he falls into the rollers of a machine. 'As circles that appear on water when a stone is thrown into it, become more and more delicate and then disappear at the edges when they merge with an even surface of water, so inaudibly and almost invisibly Olek Niedziela merged with the machine' (Czaplicka 1911: 123).[3]

The book perhaps lacks an enthralling plot, but there are some well-aimed sociological insights. The worlds of rich and poor are impenetrable to one another. The 'Miss', who wanted to be a mediator, inevitably belongs to her own class; she is not really interested in her pupils' lives and does not even want to understand them. She dragged Olek into her world and provoked his new aspirations. The life he had been living until then now became impossible to sustain: the boy became a hybrid, unable to survive. The responsibility for this lies with the tutoress and her world, not with her pupil.

Undoubtedly, the novel is an augury of the future anthropological talent: the gift of curious observation, the skill of precise and accurate description, the one closest to the facts. But it is not only the way of writing that is relevant here, but also the respect for the people written about and an attempt to understand their position. What the Miss from a noble family cannot conceive of (and does not even try), the author presents and analyses. She tries to see the world through the eyes of a poor working-class boy, tries to inspect the processes launched in his soul by this contact with another world and shows what can go wrong in all that if the boy ends up not being properly cared for by the people involved. What is that if not an anthropological sensitivity? In an important sense it is all very modern, very up to date by our standards.

The earliest construct of womanhood in Maria Czaplicka's writings is the Miss from her novel *Olek Niedziela*. She is the embodiment of the myth of a noble woman: sensitive, emotional, and sympathetic to the poor, extending them help and enlightenment. Another version of this myth was the symbol of the 'Polish Mother', well rooted in Polish culture and which became very powerful especially after the defeats of the Polish uprisings against Russia in the nineteenth century, when many men died or were sent to Siberia. These were the women who had to take on male roles (a similar situation took place in Britain somewhat later, during the Great War). Thus, the Polish Mother served as the educator of future generations of fighters for independence, the guardian of national traditions, and the depository of the nation's most laudable virtues. The role of Polish Mother did not consist so much in giving birth to future generations in the biological sense but rather in giving cultural birth to politically conscious Poles, for whom Poland's independence was the main goal. Therefore the Polish Mother did not necessarily have to be a biological parent, because she was an educator and a curator (see Walczewska 2000).

It is very difficult to assess to what extent the figure of the Miss resembles Maria Czaplicka herself. We know that the social milieu she described in the novel was her own, and we know that she was also involved in clandestine teaching – so it is quite likely that she depicted her own experiences. The narrator of her novel both sympathises with Miss and at the same time criticises her severely.

So, if we could extract the construct of 'right' womanhood from the novel, it would be a good lady deprived of some of the limitations of her gender (weakness, irrationality) and class (egoism, irresponsibility) but enriched with the idea of enlightenment and socialism. It may well be that Czaplicka used to be a normal, good young lady but over the course of her education and political activity she deconstructed this model.

How may we view this construct from today's perspective? The symbol of the Polish Mother (and a good lady) may be seen as a hindrance to the emancipation aspirations of Polish women. They were not individuals with their own needs but only parts of the nation, the collective goals of which were the most important (Walczewska 2000). In fact, this perspective has only recently undergone change, enabling modern Polish feminism to be born. Similarly, the mission of the intelligentsia (not only that of noble women) to enlighten the lower classes – not so far from the mission of civilising the lower races – has only recently come to an end with the radical changes of Polish society in recent years.

Androgynous Angel

Yet another figure looms from Maria Czaplicka's poems. Her lyrical production was very modernist: one can easily see in it the need for investigation of the self, fascination with the problems of sex and love and her own corporeality.

In her poetry one can trace a basic, Cartesian dichotomy between body and mind, a conflict even more dramatic because the author is a woman, traditionally located on the side of the corporeal. In 'On My Journey' she deals with the longing for 'bodily intoxication'. This would be paradise, possible and close at hand – but reason, the 'chill of inertness', points out that crossing through paradise's door would bring subordination. Reason demands independence, where every achievement is arrived at entirely as a result of one's own work ('to have everything, take nothing'). The coexistence of these contrasting elements is thus impossible: when reason wins, the body loses. Right is on the side of reason.

Her problems with her own corporeality are best characterised in the following fragment:

> On the summit of pride and knowledge withers my young body.
> Dull is the flame of my eyes, less sweet is their expression,
> On the summit of act and reason little is a smile for my face –
> > the heart knows nothing of shivers,
> > and caresses. (OP)

Choosing reason means abandoning the body: a sacrifice, the price paid for knowledge.

In her poems we can find a trace of John Locke's concept that all human beings, in every individual case, have to prove their own humanity. Women can show that they are equal to men if they appear rational (Hyży 2003). Maria Czaplicka, like Mary Wollstonecraft before her, pays homage to reason, rejecting emotions and striving for self-control, and, like Simone de Beauvoir after her, exhibits a lack of confidence in her own body – and in effect rejects it (de Beauvoir 1949; Wollstonecraft 1975).

It is characteristic of this mode of thinking to define body and mind as exclusive categories; the body is what the mind has to reject in order to maintain its integrity (Grosz 1994: 6). Czaplicka's suicide can be seen as the true plight of this manner of thinking, a deadly threat to a human being, a woman.

Czaplicka's case can also serve as an example of idealising women's roles. Their work within the household was presented as 'sacrifice' or 'service'. The educational aspirations of women were later to be formulated within the same idiom: as devotion to science. On the altar of 'reason and knowledge' they laid their 'young bodies'.

Czaplicka writes in her poems that she is 'a human being – a woman' (a very Wollstonecraft-like turn of phrase), that she is 'free, far away from fear', strong, possessing pride, knowledge, and rich imagination, but also a 'young body'; she has 'fortresses of her own power' gained through work; her forehead is 'proud and self-assured'; the whole world bows before her; she can seize everything she loves, but reason boggles at her doing so. These sentiments are best seen in the following fragment ('The Truth about my Soul'):

> I possess only a woman's body
> but have an abnormal soul:
> what is a gift for both sexes
> I have to stand in myself.
>
> I have a man's hungry, unsatisfied eagerness,
> and steadfast bravery,
> as well as female vacillation and tenderness
> and permanence of emotions.
> ...
>
> I surpass you with my womanhood,
> yet do not cede in manliness –
> and derisively proud of this monstrousness
> I poison myself with my own laughter.

Her female attributes are corporeal shape, emotionality, and imagination. But she also has a man's strength, activity, bravery, and rationality. However ironically, she reckons herself to be perfect. She is a man and a woman at the same time. She was in fact a model for an androgynous angel painted by Jan Rembowski in Zakopane in 1910. The picture is an illustration of a poem by Juliusz Słowacki, a great romantic poet, 'Angels are Standing in Country Fields'. Its message (and that of the painting) was that Poles should parlay their sufferings into military action in order to regain independence. Czaplicka posed for the main figure in this painting, as a dominating, winged, athletic angel with a Greek profile and long hair, holding a sword in outstretched arms. Similarly, a British journalist wrote in the *Daily Sketch* five years later that she was 'a very charming and brilliant person, not at all the Oxford blue stocking in appearance, and her capacity for assimilating facts and figures of economics and ethnology is little short of marvellous' (SC: 74). Here we have it again: female charm and male brains.

Mircea Eliade has analysed the androgyne motif, describing its various incarnations: literary, mythical, and ritual. He connected them with the unification of oppositions and the 'mystery of the whole', *coincidentia oppositorum*. In archaic cultures an androgyne was regarded as the model (archetypical) image of the perfect human being. Eliade also discusses Balzac's fantastic novel *Séraphita*, which deals with 'un être étrange d'une beauté mobile et mélancholique' (Eliade 1962: 121). The creature is qualitatively different from the rest of mortals, and the difference stems from the very structure of its existence. A woman takes it for a man, while a man takes it for a woman. It displays evidence of unusual erudition and it surpasses normal humans in its talents; it is the perfect human being.

Androgyny has been a frequent theme in feminist writings. For example, Virginia Woolf stressed that a great mind is always androgynous (Woolf 1984: 91–7). Similarly, Elisabeth Badinter strove for the coexistence of male and female traits within any human being and for free expression of these elements (Badinter 1992).

Postmodern feminism points out that the concept of androgyny is based on a synthesis of features *defined* as male and female (exactly as Czaplicka did). But 'male' traits (rationality, objectivism, autonomy) are connected with the rejection of the female body and its differences. At the same time 'female' traits (empathy, care, emotional responsibility) are seen only as epiphenomenal to the structures of male dominance (see Bator 2001).

But let us return to Czaplicka's poems. Their lyrical object is not happy; she is not an incarnation of harmony, she is – like Séraphita – melancholic, because she cannot communicate with mundane mortals. A lover noticing a 'wrinkle between her eyebrows', which discloses the 'world of her thoughts', starts to 'examine the bottom of her knowledge like a rival'. He prizes more her 'corrupt charm' than her mind. Therefore, she will 'close the depths of her eyes' and give him the delusion that he is her 'master and king'. The poem has a symptomatic title: 'Eternal Woman'. Love brings non-satisfaction for the woman; she has to hide her soul, because a man does not want to sympathise with her but to dominate. She will let him feel like this, 'bowing her proud forehead like a meek bindweed'. Bindweed is a symbol of traditional femininity.

Séraphita's melancholy is not to be wondered at: she is sentenced to erotic non-satisfaction. The case shows that gender is not so much the characteristic of an individual but rather the trait of an interaction (West and Zimmerman 1991). Note that it was contact with a man that caused her to remark about her 'nature' that she felt herself to be 'a human being – a woman'. It was that manhood, which packed her into the motionless category of womanhood, that did not suit her. The cultural construct of gender made her think about herself as having male and female traits together. From her point of view it was enriching, but the male saw it as threatening his dominance. Thus 'a human being – a woman' started to pretend to be a bindweed, to play the role of the Eternal Woman.

Das Ewig-Weibliche zieht uns hinan (the Eternal Feminine draws us upward) is the last line of *Faust* by Goethe. The phrase seemed to be a popular bon mot of the time. Malinowski frequently writes about *das Ewig-Weibliche* in his diaries,[4] and through this idea he tries to define the erotic attraction of some women (though he does not describe them but rather their influence on him). According to Czaplicka, the symbol of the Eternal Feminine meant the female physical attraction ('corrupt charm') strengthened by the delusion of male domination ('bowing forehead'). Thus she deconstructed another myth.

Maria Czaplicka's literary subjectivity reveals an androgynous coexistence of male and female characteristics. But they were not treated as equally important. She had a woman's body and a man's reason, but right was on the side of reason. Her intellectual friend, Zofia Nałkowska, adopted a totally different strategy. Her literary programme consisted of identifying womanhood with sexuality and nature, and granting it positive value. The difference between man and woman should not be levelled, but – on the contrary – it should be emphasised. Nałkowska wanted equality in difference, stressing the female side. She proposes 'ostentatious, triumphant acceptance of her own sex' (Podraza-Kwiatkowska 1993: 39). As if arguing with Czaplicka, she wrote in her diary: 'We will never become men altogether, even if we stifle our female traits. Thus it is better to develop them and become more and more eminently and specifically women' (Nałkowska 1975: 117).

Why did these two friends adopt such totally different strategies of constructing their subjectivity? Perhaps it can be traced back to the different relationships they had with their mothers: comforting or conflicting. Another reason was certainly the choice of discourse. As a writer, Nałkowska had better opportunities to take advantage of her womanhood, while Czaplicka's choice of science led her to reject her body and her gender. We can see in these women two examples of contemporary feminisms: liberal (Czaplicka) and postmodern (Nałkowska).

Intrepid Woman

In the early summer of 1914 our heroine led a year-long scientific expedition to the Jenisei valley in Siberia. There were four members of the expedition at the beginning: two anthropologists (Czaplicka and an American, Henry Hall), an artist (Dora Curtis) and an ornithologist (Maud Haviland). Only the first two remained there for the whole year.

The young fieldworker published her book *My Siberian Year* in 1916. It describes her expedition and work among the Tungus and the Samoyed. It was not a scholarly report (that was never published) but a traveller's log, part of the series *My Year* published by Mills and Boon (a publisher now better known for popular romantic novels). This literary project, however, is quite useful for my purpose here, because we can observe the way in which the author constructs her own image.

Let us begin with the figure of Henry Hall, to whom the book is dedicated. One might have expected that he would play the role of a natural partner to the author and would accompany the reader all the time. But in fact this is not the case. Hall appears by name only once or twice, although one can perhaps suspect his presence when Czaplicka writes 'we'. Her general style is to write in a manner that gives the reader the impression that she is basically alone with the natives. Hall is presented rather as a shadow, a person whose presence we have to deduce rather than someone whose presence imprints itself constantly. It was certainly Maria who was the stronger partner in the relationship. But the psychological aspects of the couple and their reversed roles do not exhaust the problem.

In accordance with the fashion of this genre of book, the author describes her various adventures, some of them dangerous, some of them funny or unexpected. One of them was an expedition to collect mammoth bones. They (she together with Hall) went first by boat, then on foot, working their way through the swamps of the tundra. It took them several hours, sustained only by biscuits and some chocolate. Czaplicka does not complain or boast, she just reports, though she does elaborate on the role of their native guide. She says that 'the natives are not fond of walking' and that therefore the guide underestimated their 'capacities as pedestrians' (Czaplicka 1916: 47), expecting them to give up early on. At least that way he could have earned his thirty shillings more easily. Instead, they were tough and persistent, so the expedition managed to arrive at the site (which, however, did not yield much in the way of a mammoth).

She has a dramatic story about how they got lost in a *purga* (blizzard). When the guide stopped their sledges and announced that he did not know where they were, a fit of hysteria struck Michikha (her Tungus *dame de compagnie*, as she used to call her), which Czaplicka commented on as a 'wasteful expenditure of the energy' (ibid.: 122). She found a thermos flask with warm cocoa and poured some for Michikha. By the time she wanted to drink some herself, she found that the 'contents were frozen hard'. The guide went to find help while they stayed where they were. 'I was bitterly cold,' Czaplicka writes, 'I was sore with weariness, but most of all I was hungry.' She became obsessed with thinking about the reindeer as warm-blooded and as edible meat. She was on the point of sticking her pocketknife into one of them when the guide came back with his good news, but all she could think about was how he could help her slaughter the animal. In an hour they were in a warm *chum*, where she ate a huge amount of venison roasted over the fire, while Michikha treated herself to the raw meat.

There are numerous references to Czaplicka's activities in hunting and shooting, such as the case when in Turuhansk a boy ran to where she was staying, asking her to follow him and shoot a quail his father had found. There are many other types of stories, such as the one about inspecting native tombs and nearly being caught red-handed by the natives, or another one about boiling human bones in a kettle and joking that making soup of somebody's grandmother should be done more cautiously (though this was in fact Maud Haviland's gag).

Alongside the stories present in the book, I have to note those that are absent – such as references to weakness, illness, emotions, doubts, inertia, passivity. But there is some evidence on this from other members of the expedition. For example, Dora Curtis wrote to Miss Penrose of Somerville College (Oxford) about Czaplicka's physical strength:

> She has amazing powers of recovery, and on land she seems able to endure more than a normally strong person. Sometimes she astonishes me with the miles she walked on

the tundra which is, I think, the most difficult ground in the world. Every step one takes one is almost up to one's knees in bog. I have known her walk thirty-five versts [equivalent to more than twenty miles] with only a piece of bread and some chocolate to sustain her and at the end appear unfatigued. What I fear for her is that she can accomplish these feats because she has great spirit but afterwards she pays for them dearly. (CzP)

The same author wrote also about a strange and dangerous illness Czaplicka suffered earlier, during their journey on the steamer boat: 'She developed alarming symptoms. She was in great pain in her back and side, was frightfully sick and could eat nothing. Miss Haviland and I had to nurse her night and day, when we arrived at Golchikha she was fairly well and more or less remained so all the time' (CzP, 22 October 1914). During the journey she was also seasick and vomited blood (Collins 1999).

These examples offer a more differentiated picture, enabling us to see more clearly how this Siberian traveller constructed her subjectivity. She presents herself as being as strong as a man, behaving as a man – playing the role of a white man. She was not only stronger than the natives, she was also more clever. In the story about the *purga*, she was calming a hysterical native woman, giving her the warm drink first, and in the end she was ready to kill an animal. She was in this sense a European man, who, in extreme conditions, would act instinctively in order to survive. Thus what we have here is strength, wit, a proactive attitude, a male instinct – but also care of the weak. We have to add several 'scientific' features: rationality, dedication and an unprejudiced, scholarly approach. Her rationality included the ability to see virtue in native behaviour. For instance, she praised the method of educating children not by suppression but rather through experience ('let the children see life as it presents itself to their elders' (Czaplicka 1916: 89)); or she described their different sexual morality: a married woman may have a lover provided she does not leave her husband.

At one point there is a footnote concerning her presence at a native court: she could attend such proceedings because she was not a Tungus woman (ibid.: 165). Presumably the footnote was added in the process of editing, though for the author it seemed pretty obvious. In the case of a white woman 'out there' it was her race that mattered more than her gender.

If anything specifically female is to be found in Maria Czaplicka's book, it is probably in the manner in which the story is told. 'Men's travel accounts are traditionally concerned with What and Where, and women's with How and Why' (Robinson 2001: x). For Czaplicka writing about her winter expedition in Siberia, that How meant, for instance, a very detailed, lengthy description of the clothes she wore: woollen Jaeger underwear and several layers of native fur. This was not the cross-dressing of early travellers (which James Clifford (1997) has written about) but a necessity of the climate.[5] Worth mentioning here is that she was wearing a man's native dress, or rather she did not have the additional frock worn by women. In her book she also commented on the scent of reindeer, which she said permeated everything, and she mentioned the need to change European standards of cleanliness. It was in ways such as these that she described the Siberian wilderness, not only through her dangerous adventures but also by things being 'closer to the body', in both the literal and metaphorical senses of the phrase.

Generally speaking, the role of traveller (discoverer, fieldworker) was a distinctly 'male' role, personalising the concept of control over nature, conquering the unconquered, knowing the unknown. Edward Said (1978) saw this as being at the foundation of the Orientalist discourse. The traveller was the embodiment of energy, activity, strength, and reason. There was no room for weakness, illness, or doubt.

The problem still remains whether Czaplicka's male profile was simply the further process of her own masculinisation, or whether it resulted from the logic of her choices or the grammar of her discourse. Or, to put it differently: was she fashioning herself as a man, or did some structural factors play an important role in the process?

For the sake of comparison, consider another of Czaplicka's contemporaries, namely Karen Blixen. Her book *Out of Africa*[6] was not published until the 1930s but she went to Kenya in 1914 (at the same time that Czaplicka went to Siberia and Malinowski to New Guinea). Blixen's magnificent work is not only 'male', in a fashion actually quite similar to Czaplicka's book, but was also published under a male pseudonym – Isak Dinesen. The author apparently did not feel uncomfortable writing under a male name, she simply *was* a man there: she ran a farm, hunted lions, and took care of the natives. In her book she conveys some explanatory insight: 'The love of woman and womanliness is a masculine characteristic, and the love of man and manliness a feminine characteristic, and there is a susceptibility to the southern countries and races that is a Nordic quality' (Blixen 1954: 24).

I would venture to generalise the above remark and say that a man is to a woman as whites are to natives – and we can incorporate in this relationship both fascination and subordination. Edward Said also reported the similarity between the image of an Oriental and that of a woman. A white woman in colonial conditions was cast in the role of a dominated white, and whites held a privileged position, both politically and with respect to civilisation. Evolutionary theory provided scientific justification for the system (see Urry 1993).

Baroness Blixen's book was probably the first popular description of Africa that presented more than just exoticism and hunting adventures – the world of its native inhabitants and white settlers against the background of the natural rhythms of the continent. She was a good observer because she was at the same time a man and a woman, so she could better scrutinise the external world. Female anthropologists have often raised this point: indeed, Audrey Richards contended that 'women make better anthropologists than men' (cited in Caplan 1992: 79). They have simply a better structural position. They can study both the world of women and that of men. Women benefited from the colonial system but they produced alternative accounts of the imperial presence in colonised countries (Mills 1993).

This is all observable in Czaplicka's case. She was not only a white traveller, she was also a scientist, and these roles were mutually supportive. She herself perceives the world 'out there' and the natives from a dominant position (however mild): she owns the desirable rubber shoes, she has a gun, and she is better than them at going on foot. She also has her own *dame de compagnie*. She has the moral right to inspect native tombs and cook their bones. Yet the dominant position is also a guarantee of her safety as fieldworker (see Clifford 1997). As she says with regard to Michikha:

> Once she remarked, jestingly, that if anything happened to us in the tundra she would come into possession of my aluminum boxes, furs and warm clothing. I knew the Tungus well enough not to be at all impressed by the hint of disagreeable possibilities I knew she meant to convey. Yet, although I never resorted to threats of any kind in my dealings with the natives, I could not refrain from giving her a reminder of the fact she knew quite well that we were under official protection. (Czaplicka 1916: 76)

Michikha doubted that any army would come into the tundra, and capitulated only at the white woman's suggestion that soldiers could arrive by plane.

Here we can see that Czaplicka in fact negotiates her dominant position, which is not evident to her partner. Only the threat of military action works. So in fact it is the English-reading public who shares the author's assumption of the cultural superiority of the Europeans; the natives believe in no such thing. They are not afraid of her, they want to cheat her all the time, they make use of her and her resources. They do not feel inferior. It is the traveller–fieldworker who perceives them in that way.

The role of Western traveller resulted from (or used) a certain grammar of identity. 'Orientalisation constitutes self and other by negative mirror imaging: "what is good in us is lacking in them", but it also adds a subordinate reversal: what is lacking in us is (still) present in them', to cite the formulation of Baumann and Gingrich (2004). Their book analyses circumstances under which the grammar could cease to work. I have wanted to show here how gender adds another dimension to this structure.

On her return to England, Czaplicka took on the role of an intrepid woman. In my archival research I came across the menu of a 'Women Explorers' Dinner', held in the Lyceum Club in London in January 1916, to which Czaplicka and her anthropological colleagues Miss Freire-Marreco and Miss Murrey, together with Mrs Flinders-Pertie, were invited (LP). In the scrapbook of clippings (SC) concerning the public appearances of our heroine, I found dozens of occasions, in Britain and America, when she delivered lectures about her expedition (of the type 'Through Arctic Siberia with my Camera'). So the uniform of a British woman explorer fitted Czaplicka quite well, and thus was she perceived.

Intrepid women of the twentieth century 'were "victims" of class, wealth, status and the perils of hypergamy which left the daughters of the wealthy unable to find a suitable marriage partner. Unmarried by their mid-twenties, they were condemned to spinsterhood, a strange sort of non-productive but not necessarily non-sexual womanhood. With money they could indulge their interests but these were often best indulged away from the strict eye of Victorian society. So these women who were not quite women (given the preference for marriage and reproduction in the definition of womanhood of the period) were permitted to indulge themselves in men's pursuits and often foreign adventures which led some to science and ethnography' (James Urry, personal communication).

Czaplicka, as it turns out however, was another case. She was not a rich spinster who was able to indulge her scientific interests. She was an impoverished Polish intellectual who tried to make anthropology her profession. And it was in this striving for the professionalisation of anthropology for women that she finally became a victim. But that is yet another story. Here I would only stress that the role of a white woman traveller in the colonies was different from the marginalised (albeit conspicuous) role of an intrepid woman back in Britain.

Concluding Remarks

In this essay, I have attempted to show the process of the self-articulation of a feminist subject, one that was carried out in the context of specific cultural and interpersonal backgrounds and within various significant narratives of the time. It also demonstrates how fluid, heterogeneous and variable the subject is and that the woman is often a place of conflict, or at least she might see herself as such.

Maria Czaplicka was the embodiment of Mary Wollstonecraft's ideal woman: strong in body and mind, a slave neither to her own temptations nor to her family. She was more successful than her predecessor, yet only in one thing: her suicide.

I do hope that this essay has enabled some understanding of the motives of that desperate act. There were enough of them. In fact the logic of all the discourses in which she participated led in that direction: the conviction of the (Polish) nobility that suicide is better than loss of class (for example, by becoming engaged in manual labour), the rejection of the body through science and reason, or the action of an early feminist mimicking men's behaviour. In all these models there was no room for poverty, weakness, emotion, or doubt. Those traits could find some room in the models of traditional femininity (good lady or eternal woman), but these she had deconstructed early on. She had found herself in a deadly trap.

Czaplicka resembles Olek of her novel. She was, like him, dragged into the world of science; she opened her mind to the beauty of rational argument, but she was not given the opportunity for further development. She became, like Olek, a hybrid, and she was, like him, smashed by the mechanism of the modern, dull world.

Notes

I would like to thank my friends and colleagues for their comments – especially Krystyna Cech, Beata Kowalska, Krzysztof Kowalski, Marcin Lubaś, James Urry, Jonathan Webber, Michael Young, and Jan Zieliński – as well as Shirley Ardener for her inexhaustible interest in my research. Her friendly, helpful, and encouraging concern has always been much appreciated.

1. The immediate cause of this tragic decision was her catastrophic financial situation and her failure to be awarded the Albert Kahn scholarship at the University of London, which her prospects of winning had seemed good. There is also a hypothesis that her suicide was caused by her companion in Siberia, Henry Hall, marrying another woman. For biographical details see La Rue 1996; Collins and Urry 1997; Collins 1999; Kubica 2002, 2004.
2. 'OP' is an abbreviation for one of the manuscript sources that I consulted during my research on the life of Maria Czaplicka. Both this and three other sources (abbreviated respectively as CzP, LP, and SC) will be encountered later in the text below; details of these sources are listed at the end of this essay.
3. All translations from Polish-language sources in this paper are my own. I am grateful to Krystyna Cech, Aleksander Jakimowicz, and Jonathan Webber for their help.
4. I refer here to the Polish edition of his diaries (Malinowski 2002), which includes parts that have still not been published in English.
5. Even today, reindeer fur is still regarded as the best protection against the cold of Siberia, according to Nikolai Ssorin-Czaikov and Aimar Ventsel, who also carried out research there (personal communication).
6. Note that the Sydney Pollack film of the same title is not an exact report of the book. There are many biographical details added from other sources.

Manuscript sources

CzP   Czaplicka Papers, Somerville College Archive, Oxford, U.K.
LP   Lindgren Papers, Cambridge University Library, U.K.
OP   Orkan Papers, Manuscript Collection, Jagiellonian Library, Cracow, Poland
SC   Scrapbook of clippings concerning M. Czaplicka, Pennsylvania University Museum, U.S.A.

References

Ardener, S. (ed.) 1975. *Perceiving Women*, London: J.M. Dent & Sons.
―――― 1984. 'Gender Orientations in Fieldwork', in R.F. Ellen (ed.), *Ethnographic Research: A Guide to General Conduct*, London: Academic Press, pp. 118–29.
―――― (ed.) 1992a. *Persons and Powers of Women in Diverse Cultures: Essays in Commemoration of Audrey I. Richards, Phyllis Kaberry, and Barbara E. Ward*, New York and Oxford: Berg.
―――― 1992b. 'Persons and Powers of Women: An Introduction', in S. Ardener (ed.), *Persons and Powers of Women in Diverse Cultures: Essays in Commemoration of Audrey I. Richards, Phyllis Kaberry, and Barbara E. Ward*, New York and Oxford: Berg, pp.1–10.
Badinter, E. 1992. *XY: De l'identité masculine*, Paris: Éditions Odile Jacob.

Bator, J. 2001. 'Feminizm wobec kresu Oświecenia', *Kultura i Społeczeństwo* 45 (2), pp. 3–20.
Baumann, G. and A. Gingrich 2004. *Grammars of Identity/Alterity: A Structural Approach*, Oxford: Berghahn.
Behar, R. and D.A. Gordon (eds) 1995. *Women Writing Culture*, Berkeley: University of California Press.
Blixen, K. 1954 (orig. 1937). *Out of Africa*, Harmondsworth: Penguin Books.
Callaway, H. 1992. 'Ethnography and Experience: Gender Implications in Fieldwork and Texts', in J. Okely and H. Callaway (eds), *Anthropology and Autobiography*, London: Routledge.
Caplan, P. 1992. 'Engendering Knowledge: The Politics of Ethnography', in S. Ardener (ed.), *Persons and Powers of Women in Diverse Cultures: Essays in Commemoration of Audrey I. Richards, Phyllis Kaberry, and Barbara E. Ward*, New York and Oxford: Berg.
Clifford, J. 1997. *Routes, Travel and Translation in the Late Twentieth Century*, Cambridge, Mass.: Harvard University Press.
Collins, D. 1999. 'Introduction', in D. Collins (ed.), *Collected Works of M.A. Czaplicka*, vol. 1, Richmond: Curzon.
Collins, D. and J. Urry 1997. 'A Flame Too Intense for Mortal Body to Support', *Anthropology Today* 13 (6), pp. 18–20.
Czaplicka, M. 1911. *Olek Niedziela*, Warsaw: Sadowski.
––––––– 1916. *My Siberian Year*, London: Mills & Boon.
de Beauvoir, S. 1949. *Le Deuxième Sexe*, Paris: Gallimard.
Eliade, M. 1962. *Méphistophélès et l'androgyne*, Paris: Gallimard.
Grosz, E. 1994. *Volatile Bodies: Towards a Corporeal Feminism*, Bloomington: Indiana University Press.
Hyży, E. 2003. *Kobieta, ciało, tożsamość: Teorie podmiotu w filozofii feministycznej końca XX wieku*, Cracow: Universitas.
Kubica, G. 2002. 'Maria Antonina Czaplicka', in B. Malinowski, *Dziennik w ścisłym znaczeniu tego wyrazu* (ed. G. Kubica), Cracow: Wydawnictwo Literackie.
––––––– 2004. 'Maria Antonina Czaplicka', in V. Amid (ed.), *Biographical Dictionary of Social and Cultural Anthropology*, London and New York: Routledge.
La Rue, H. 1996. 'Marie Antoinette Czaplicka', in A. Petch (ed.), *Collectors for the Pitt Rivers Museum*, Oxford: Pitt Rivers Museum.
Malinowski, B. 2002. *Dziennik w ścisłym znaczeniu tego wyrazu* (ed. G. Kubica), Cracow: Wydawnictwo Literackie.
Mills, S. 1993. *Discourses of Difference: An Analysis of Women's Travel Writing and Colonialism*, London: Routledge.
Moore, H. 1988. *Feminism and Anthropology*, Cambridge: Polity Press.
Nałkowska, Z. 1975. *Dzienniki*, vol. 1, Warsaw: Czytelnik.
Okely, J. 1992. 'Anthropology and Autobiography: Participatory Experience and Embodied Knowledge', in J. Okely and H. Callaway (eds), *Anthropology and Autobiography*, London: Routledge.
Podraza-Kwiatkowska, M. 1993. 'Młodopolska femina: Garść uwag', *Teksty drugie* 4–6, pp. 36–53.
Robinson, J. 2001. *Wayward Women: A Guide to Women Travellers*, Oxford: Oxford University Press.
Said, E.W. 1978. *Orientalism*, Harmondsworth: Penguin.
Sprawozdanie 1915. *Sprawozdanie Kasy im. Mianowskiego*, Warsaw.

Urry, J. 1993. *Before Social Anthropology: Essays on the History of British Anthropology*, Chur: Harwood Academic.

Visweswaran, K. 1994. *Fictions of Feminist Ethnography*, Minneapolis and London: University of Minnesota Press.

Walczewska, S. 2000. *Damy, rycerze i feministki: Kobiecy dyskurs emancypacyjny w Polsce*, Cracow: Wydawnictwo eFKa.

Wawrzykowska-Wierciochowa, D. 1959. 'Maria Antonina Czaplicka: zapomniana uczona', *Problemy* 15, pp. 662–64.

West, C. and D.H. Zimmerman 1991. 'Doing Gender', in J. Lorber and S.A. Farrell (eds), *The Social Construction of Gender*, London: Sage.

Wollstonecraft, M. 1975. *A Vindication of the Rights of Woman*, New York: W.W. Norton.

Woolf, V. 1984. *A Room of One's Own and Three Guineas*, London: Hogarth Press.

Żarnowska, A. 2000. 'Praca zarobkowa kobiet i ich aspiracje zawodowe', in A. Żarnowska and A. Szwarc (eds), *Kobieta i praca*, Warsaw: Wydawnictwo DiG.

10
'RITUAL SISTERS' OR FEMALE RULERS? GENDER AND CHIEFSHIP REVISITED IN SOUTHERN AFRICA

Gina Buijs

It is a truism that social anthropologists often arrive in the field with the mores and expectations of the societies they come from. Such embedded baggage may have unforeseen but real consequences which appear in the ethnographic accounts subsequently presented. I have written previously (Buijs 2002a, b) of the ways in which historians, social anthropologists and colonial officials have marginalised some of the customary social and political roles of women in African and especially southern African societies. Mesmerised by the apparent power exercised by men over women in patrilineal African societies as well as their own patriarchal surroundings, Evans-Pritchard, for example, insisted that when a Nuer woman marries another woman, 'she administers her home and herd as a man would do, being treated by her wives and children with the deference they would show to a male husband and father' (1951: 109). Adam Kuper (1987: 112), referring to the Lovedu of South Africa, states: 'political influence is not exercised directly by the queen but by her male advisers'. Such a statement dismisses the very real political influence exercised by the Lovedu queen, influence which is and has been wielded in different degrees by headwomen and female chiefs throughout southern Africa, in the past and today. Indeed, this traditional political influence echoes the present political prominence given to women in South Africa, where important cabinet positions in government, leadership of various provinces, and the post of Speaker in Parliament are occupied by women.

In this chapter I write of the influence of women as rulers, and as sisters and daughters of rulers, as well as of the influence of women's associations in traditional, mainly southern African, societies. While some of the rituals discussed, including a few associated with the Zulu goddess *Nomkhubulwane*, are no longer performed and remain only in the memories of elderly women, others have been refashioned and revitalised to form part of modern beauty pageants and commemorative occasions for traditional culture. While researching this topic, I have been inspired by the insights provided by Shirley Ardener in her Introduction to *Persons and Powers of Women in Diverse Cultures* (1992: 8–9).

Ritual Sisters and Queen Mothers

The role of women designated as 'ritual sisters' or 'queen mothers' has been reported widely in West and East Africa, among, for instance, the Bunyoro of Uganda (Beattie 1958). Referring to the *Kalyota* as the king's 'official sister', he writes:

> [T]he king's official sister was really a kind of chief … she held and administered estates, from which she derived revenue and services like other chiefs. She settled disputes, determined inheritance cases and decided matters of precedence among the Bito women. She was not the queen, if by queen we mean the king's consort. We may best regard her then, as a kind of female counterpart of the king, the head of the Bito women and so the chief lady in the land. (Beattie 1960: 31)

The *Kalyota* had a counterpart in the form of the king's 'official brother', head of the Bito, the ruling clan among the Nyoro men. Beattie notes that 'although there is little place for her [the *Kalyota*] in the modern system' she still holds an official rank and is paid a small salary.

In his book on power and symbolism in ancient Zimbabwe, the archaeologist Tom Huffman (1996) refers repeatedly to the role of 'ritual sister', which he bases on Venda ethnography. Following designs commonly found on the *hakata* (the Shona term for divining dice), he describes the herringbone pattern frequently found in *dzimbahwe* (stone circle) structures as representing senior female status and the check or chevron design as representing male status. Here also the term 'ritual sister' hardly conveys the pragmatic power wielded by holders of these positions, more properly 'female rulers'. That such a term may be considered legitimate can be inferred from Huffman's own account of royal burials at Mapungubwe, arguably among the most splendid in sub-Saharan Africa. Huffman notes that three of twenty-three burial sites excavated by Fouche (1937) and Gardner (1963) were associated with gold objects. The first one he discusses, Number 14, 'was probably that of a woman, buried in a sitting position, facing west. She wore at least a hundred gold wire bangles around her ankles and there were over 12,000 gold beads in her grave.' Huffman notes that high-status people were often buried sitting up and that the three people buried on Mapungubwe hill were rulers, 'possibly a king with a ritual sister or a king with his brother and sister' (1996: 188). Huffman does not suggest that the female burial is that of a ruler in her own right, although the 12,000 gold beads, not found in the other burials, are evidence for this. But later he quotes from Theal (1964 [1898]: 368) 'the *mazarira* (great wife and sister) of the Mutapa king in fact supported Portuguese requests for trade' and adds 'although female status is secondary in a structural sense, actual status would be historically contingent on the forces of individual personalities. Thus there could have been times when a ritual sister and royal mother had greater standing than their male counterparts' (Huffman 1996: 109).

Sister or Ruler? The Role of Father's Sister in Venda and Tonga

In Venda the position of father's sister or *makhadzi* is an important one, especially in matters of chiefly succession. A chief is succeeded by his son, who is appointed by the *makhadzi* and the *khotsimunene*, his father's brother. When these two appoint the new heir, they at the same time appoint one of his sisters to be the *khadzi* and one of his brothers to act as *ndumi* (the official brother of the chief). The respect and obedience due to a chief is transferred upon his death to his 'female father' and 'little father', his father's sister and father's brother, respectively, and, says Stayt (1931: 196), 'until their deaths they have the right to command the person of their late brother's son, whom they have appointed to represent the family'.

The *makhadzi* is the late chief's eldest sister, although she may not be a uterine one. The chief is supposed to consult her and follow her judgement on all matters concerned with the affairs of his people. She lives at the chief's capital, with her husband and children living elsewhere. She receives a percentage of all taxes given to the chief, who must grant all her reasonable requests. She is treated with most of the respect and formality accorded to the chief. Even men, Stayt says, to whom all other women kneel, must kneel to the *makhadzi*. Her food is prepared, like that of the chief, by one of his wives, and presented to her with the same ceremony as it is given to him. All this respect, notes Stayt, is the outward and visible sign of the real power that she wields in the state. In addition, her home is a sanctuary for criminals and murderers, whom she may reprieve, and her consent is necessary before war may be waged. In all these matters her judgement takes precedence over that of the chief and he is bound to submit to her decisions.

Huffman notes that 'a special sister of a Zimbabwe ruler had similar duties to the Venda *makhadzi*, called *VaMoyo* in Rozwi praise poetry' (Hodza and Fortune 1979: 15–17, cited in Huffman 1996: 64). Shona traditions recall the sister of the founding father as the 'great ancestress', the senior female representative of the ruling clan. Each new chiefdom was supposed to begin with the ritual incest of the chief and his sister. Huffman comments that the documentary evidence on whether the chief and his sister ever married is ambiguous, although he cites Bocarro (in Theal 1964 [1898]: vol. 3, 358), who refers to the *Monomotapa* as having many wives, 'most of them are his relatives or sisters … the principal one, called *mazarira* is always one of the king's sisters'.

While the term *makhadzi* has been rendered as 'chief's eldest sister' by the ethnographer of the Venda, Hugh Stayt, and 'paternal aunt' in Van Warmelo's Venda/English dictionary, I was told in an interview with one of the councillors of a female Venda petty chief, Musanda VhoNetshiendeulu, that the term means 'one who commands, or is in control, an adviser.'[1] This usage was reproduced in the local Venda English-language newspaper, *The Mirror*,[2] in an article concerning the dispute over the succession to the chiefship of the Venda royal house of Mphephu. In early 1998 the reigning paramount chief, Khosikhulu Dimbanyika Mphephu, was killed in a car crash. It was reported that the new acting chief, Prince Toni Peter Ramabulana Mphephu, would fulfil the duties of the late king, together with his female aide, Khadzi Mavis Mphephu. Prince Toni and Khadzi Mavis had both been installed as the king's assistants during his inauguration in 1994. Stayt notes that the power of the *makhadzi* to nominate her brother's successor is a source of endless family feuds if the dead man's brothers refuse to recognise the power of the *makhadzi*.

The influence of women in their role as sisters has been well documented in Polynesia and Melanesia (Weiner 1976, 1978). The way in which the authority of the father's sister was diminished by colonial authorities, who considered this brother–sister relationship of collaboration and power as inappropriate, can be seen in Christine Ward-Gailey's (1987) accounts of Tongan kinship in pre- and post-colonial contact periods. A father's sister was never ignored – Tongan women, especially chiefly women, exercised social authority throughout life as sisters. These rights, which she notes were often termed privileges in the literature, included the sister's call on her brother, his household, and his descendants. She and her children were *fahu* to the brother and his children. The term *fahu* subsumed the claims of sisters and sister's children. The term meant 'above the law' or 'beyond custom'. The father's sister, the imposing *mehikitanga*, was the focus of avoidance by the brother and his children, particularly his sons. She arranged and vetoed her brother's children's marriages. She could command the labour and products of her brother's spouses and she had the right to adopt her brother's children. A curse from the *mehikitanga* threatened a brother's children and spouse with painful childbirth.

The role of sister and *fahu* transcended lineage affiliation. Before, during, and after marriage, a sister had the same claims to a brother and his children. The sibling pair was extremely important in inheritance, alliance, and descent. There are numerous examples of similar important roles being played by father's sisters in patrilineal African societies. Hilda Kuper (1947), writing of the Swazi, notes that, after a man's death, a council of kinsmen chooses his successor. The father's full sister and eldest daughter and the eldest full sister of the deceased are members of this council, along with male kinsmen. An important relative who is not summoned to the discussion may understand the omission either as a slur or as an attempt to circumvent the law in order to appoint a favourite. The matter may be taken to the king's court and the decision of the council altered. Kuper (ibid.: 90) notes that in this matter 'the influence of a woman member is as great as any of the men' and she gives the example of the behaviour of the sister of the late Chief Memezi. When his full sister arrived to mourn her brother's death she found that the family council had already chosen the heir, a man named Pulela. The sister claimed that this honour belonged to Joni, the son of a woman of a preferential marriage and said 'she, Memezi's sister, born from one womb, was not married in England [so] that she could not have been fetched for the discussion'. The sister took Joni and his supporters to the king, who told the family council to reconsider their decision.

Van Warmelo and Phophi (1948: para. 121) note that, in discussions about a young man's betrothal among the Venda: 'it is the *makhadzi* whose word carries the most weight, and whose opinion is most readily accepted. If she says the young man should *mala* (provide bridewealth) at such and such a place, the rest usually just agree to what she says.' Sometimes Venda wives may even appeal to their husband's sister for protection against the anger of their spouse:

> Tshidino one day started trouble with his wives when he gave them a leg of baboon to roast and they went away to a beer party at Muhothe's instead, so that the dogs prised open the kitchen door and finished the meat. Upon his return in the evening he asked them where they had been when the meat was stolen and they could not answer. So he sailed in among them with a heavy club and all of them fled to his sister Tshivhiavhuvi. Next morning early Tshivhiavhuvhi returned with them and scolded her brother severely. 'What do you mean by driving out your wives and beating them like this?' she barked, 'and all about the hind leg of a baboon, so that they spent the night walking through the darkness with their children on their backs. Don't let me hear of a similar uproar in this place again. Scandal will fasten upon you! What will people say of you?' Poor Tshidino said nothing in reply but remained silent. (Van Warmelo and Phophi 1949: Part Three (Divorce), 465)

European colonial authorities, whether in Polynesia or Africa, were mistrustful and suspicious of this form of women's traditional exercise of authority and sought to suppress the influence of sisters over their brothers and their brothers' families. The 1867 Tonga legal code tried to limit the influence of the *fahu* and at the same time to strengthen the role of the nuclear family as a social unit. The code consistently stressed the centrality of the conjugal pair and especially the responsibility and authority of husbands over any collateral kin collection. For instance, it was forbidden for anyone 'to interfere to stop a wedding', which effectively eliminated the right of the father's sister to arrange or veto the marriages of her brother's children. The Tongan state later banned all exercise of *fahu* prerogatives, which meant that a woman could not legally call on the labour of her brothers or their wives and made wives more dependent on their husbands, in European fashion (Ward-Gailey 1987: 208–11).

Similarly, the position of the *Kalyota* in colonial Uganda seems to have been viewed with disapproval by the colonial authorities if one reads between the lines of Beattie's comments (emphasis added):

> Nowadays she (the *Kalyota*) is socially overshadowed by the king's true consort, the Omugo, whom he married in Christian marriage and who has borne him several children. It was she, and not the *Kalyota*, who accompanied the Mukama (the king) on his visit to England for Queen Elizabeth's coronation in 1953, and she sits at his side at ceremonies and entertainments *at which Europeans are present*. (Beattie 1960: 31)

The Mystical Power of African Female Rulers

The power of African female rulers is mystical in origin. For Nso', a chiefdom of the central Cameroon plateau, power was identified with spirit, with life-giving and life-taking energies. Both genders, writes Ifeka (1992: 136), exercise multivalent, equivalent powers. The Fon Nso', who has a commoner mother, appoints some women from the royal lineage to be queen mothers to represent the uterine successor of a dead king's mother. These queen mothers may accompany Fon Nso' to the seasonal sacrifices and there represent the royal dynasty's deceased mothers. They sit in the audience court and act as remembrancers. Other queen mothers are selected by the Fon to represent ancient kings buried in the old capital in the forest. These are chosen 'for the forest', as was, Ifeka notes, Phyllis Kaberry, who bore the title '*yaa woo kov*' 'lady of the forest' and of whom Sally Chilver wrote,[3] 'thus she like all Nso' queen mothers, as well as the elderly ladies of the royal gynaecium, was set apart from other women as she now possessed mysterious power'. Among other proscribed actions, the Nso' queen mother had to refrain from uttering angry words lest the wild winds arise to damage farms and houses.

Even among the militarily based kingdoms of the Azande, Evans-Pritchard (1957, quoted in Poewe 1981: 38–9) describes a female hierarchy among the kings' wives that almost paralleled that of the court and the military. Companies of warriors were attached to queens and cultivated in their names. The senior companies paid tribute to the court in the names of these queens and were responsible for the redistribution of garden products and for their conversion into food. Karla Poewe (ibid.: 39) comments 'when it is remembered that these descriptions of Zande court life are based on information coming solely from male informants, we can be encouraged in our belief that had the queens talked we might have seen them wield more power still'.

Writing of the southern African Lovedu queen, Mujaji, the Kriges (1943: 271) note that during the queen's life she is regarded as the changer of the seasons and the guarantor of their regularity. 'When she [the queen] dies the seasons are out of joint and drought is inevitable. Her very emotions affect the rain: if she is dissatisfied, angry or sad, she cannot work well and in 1934–35 when the first rains did not come until December, the drought was attributed to her being upset at her daughter's liaison with a commoner.' Though renowned as the greatest rainmaker in southern Africa, Krige observes that Mujaji never worked alone. She always had a male rainmaker to work with her. The chief function of the rain doctor was to cooperate with the queen in some of the things she could not do. He divined the causes of drought and discovered which forces were hindering the queen's powers from taking effect. Using his own medicines he aided her in removing these causes and setting right what was wrong. The Kriges (ibid.) note that 'the queen is primarily not a ruler but a rainmaker and men rely for their security, not on regimentation, armies and organisation, but on the queen's power to make rain for the tribe and withhold it from its enemies'.

The myths surrounding the arrival of the Lovedu in their present home around Duiwelskloof on the escarpment suggest an origin in Karanga, Zimbabwe, around 1600, when the sons of Monomotapa quarrelled and set themselves up as independent *mambo* or chiefs, dividing ancient Karanga amongst themselves. One of these chiefs had his capital at Maulwi, in present-day Zimbabwe. This chief had a daughter, Dzugudini, who, although unmarried, had an infant son, Makaphimo. The *mambo* wished to punish the seducer of his daughter but Dzugudini and her mother refused to disclose his identity. The mother stole the sacred rain charms and sacred beads belonging to the tribe and Dzugudini fled with them and her son to the south to the Lovedu area, where they settled and formed the Lovedu people. Lovedu tradition records that Makaphimo's father was his mother's brother. The brother remained at Maulwi as chief. The sister, by virtue of the incestuous relationship, justified the creation of a new people, the Lovedu. Several hundred years later, around 1800, one of King Mugodo's daughters gained the upper hand over her brothers. Before the old king died he prophesied the accession of a woman, the raids of black ants on Lovedu territory (Nguni from the south), and the conquest by red ants (Europeans). The daughter of the first Mujaji is said to have been born as a result of an incestuous union between the mother and the mother's father.

At around the same time the daughters of chiefs in areas to the north of the Lovedu were attaining power in their own right. Tshisinavhute of Mianzwi in eastern Venda was a female rainmaker and ruler. Tshisinavhute was the title of the Mbedzi ruler who has been female since at least the end of the eighteenth century and possibly much earlier. The first female Tshisinavhute, Mufanadzo, had been given the gift of rainmaking by her father, but, according to oral tradition, had had to enlist the help of Chief Ligege Tshivhase to drive out and kill her brother who had also been a powerful rainmaker at Mianzwi. Since then, succession to the headship and powers of rainmaking at Mianzwi has passed from mother to daughter. Ralushai and Gray (1977) suggest that the change in succession from male to female in this instance may be partly explained by the increasing incidence of male circumcision in the area, a custom that was introduced by Sotho speakers from the south-west. Ralushai mentions raids on the Mbedzi in search of uncircumcised men. These raids were detrimental to the rainmaking powers of the Mbedzi as males who had been circumcised were not allowed to hold sacred objects. Tshisinavhute, as a woman, was saved from such raids.

In a similar manner to Tshisinavhute, the origin of the Vondwe female chieftaincy appears to lie in a succession dispute involving a sister and her brother, although here the accounts given by local people and that given by the headwoman herself differ considerably. Matshidze (1988: 24) dates the emergence of female chieftaincy at Vondwe to the installation of Nyatshitahela in 1914. In this account Nyatshitahela was the wife of Chief Rammbuda of Dzimauli. Following a succession dispute she fled with her only son to her maternal grandmother's home and, upon the death of her father, Headman

Ramugondo of Vondwe, returned to Vondwe and became headwoman there. Some of Matshidze's informants said that the Vondwe ancestors preferred a female ruler, others that Nyatshitahela had engineered the removal of her classificatory brother, who had been installed as chief shortly after the death of her father. Musanda Gumani, the present headwoman, told me[4] that her ancestor was made headwoman at Vondwe by her brother, a local chief. She said that Nyatshitahela had been married to another chief nearby, who had died. The people of his village blamed his wife for his death and wanted to kill her. To save her, her brother removed her to his own chiefdom and made her headwoman of Vondwe.

Although Nyatshitahela was succeeded by several male descendants, their reigns were inauspicious. One died after having been struck by lightning, and his son, who succeeded him, died childless in 1976. It was at this point that the chief's family and the community reached a decision that there should be a return to female rule, since it seemed that Nyatshitahela, as an ancestor, was asking for a female successor as the males had not fared well. The present headwoman was installed and given the title Gumani at the age of twenty-one in 1976. Musanda Gumani has commemorated her ancestress by naming a local school after her. VhoGumani herself is an educated woman who is a senior officer at the Thohoyandou Central Prison, situated not far from her *khoro* (traditional court), where she hears cases on Sundays in the company of her *vhakoma* or headmen.

Ifeka (1992) relates that both royal women and men in the eastern Grassfields of Bamum, Cameroon, could inflict death on their subjects. Royal women killed fearlessly and were killed in turn. Local people related how one late-nineteenth-century queen mother exercised the supreme kingly role of war chief: 'you kill the criminals with a chopper like a man'. She did so in the manner of an earlier king's sister, who, in pursuit of political ambition, killed retainers and royal wives with blows from lethal sticks (Njoya 1952, quoted in Ifeka 1992: 140).

In times of peace, some women appointed to high office in Cameroon wore necklaces of leopards' teeth and claws. These were the outward symbols of mystically potent 'leopard power'. In this religio-political system, power and gender are complexly related, interdependent, and yet independent social forces: on the one hand, gender constructs power and, on the other hand, gender is constructed by power. The gendered couple symbolised by the Fon Nso' and a queen mother (*yee fon*) represent the authority of socialised power, the capacity of the heterosexual pair to cultivate fecundity.

In southern Africa we find that the dual monarchy of Swaziland provides a striking example of the construction of gendered power. At the summit of the political hierarchy of Swaziland are the king and his mother, each with a hereditary title and special insignia of office. Each ruler has political power sanctioned by ritual and belief. Hilda Kuper notes that the Swazi king is chosen from among the other sons of his father by virtue of his mother's rank, and is regarded as having in his body 'the blood of kingship' from both his father and his mother's ancestors. Marriage cattle contributed by the nation for his mother make her the 'mother of the people of the country' and her son 'the child of the people'.

When the king and his mother are fully installed, she is given the title of *Indlovukati* (lady elephant) and he of *Ingwenyama* (lion).

The king and his mother are the central figures of all national activities in Swaziland. They preside over the highest courts, summon national gatherings, control the age classes, allocate land, disburse national wealth, take precedence in ritual and help to organise important social events. Royal prerogatives are balanced against royal obligations. The monarchs receive complaints, discuss matters of national importance, interview local authorities, listen to major legal cases, represent the people in negotiations with foreign diplomats (there are echoes of the Zimbabwean *mazarira* here), and supervise ceremonies.

The dual monarchy represents a balance of power, legal, ritual, and economic, in the kingdom of Swaziland between the *Ingwenyama* and the *Indlovukati*. He presides over the highest court in the land, but she is in charge of the second highest court and her councillors may take part in discussions at her son's court, while her home is a sanctuary for men sentenced to death. The king controls the army but its commander-in-chief may live in the queen mother's village. The king has the power to distribute land but he and his mother together work the rain magic that fructifies the soil. She is the guardian of the sacred objects of the nation but they are not effective without his cooperation in manipulating them. He represents the line of past kings but she speaks to the dead in the shrine at the capital. The king is made great and rejuvenated in the annual ceremony held at the queen mother's home. She receives special treatment on that occasion and takes precedence over other participants.

Swazi believe that in all activities the king and queen mother should assist and advise each other, for he is *Inkosi* and she is also *Inkosi*. Together they are spoken of as twins (H. Kuper 1947). In like manner, in ritual contexts in Nso' the feminine is marked by association with the left hand, peace, and the body (which is of the earth), while the right hand, war and killing are associated with the masculine dimension. The notion of twin beings expresses the cosmic equilibrium that should be maintained between opposites. Chilver (1978: 8, quoted in Ifeka 1992: 142) notes that in Nso' twins are children of Breath, being two and yet of one uterine substance. They represent the unity and partibility of Breath (divinity). Twin cults thus articulate the Nso' conception of Breath or divinity as simultaneously dual and yet one – the two opposites being linked in heterosexual union.

Nomkhubulwane: Zulu Queen of Rain and Earth Goddess

Further beliefs in the symbolic power of male and female attributes are found among the Zulu, near neighbours to the south of the Swazi. Berglund documents that Zulu are emphatic that rain is sent to earth by *iNkosi yeZulu*. The creator of rain is the Lord of the Sky and he is associated with the Zulu king, known as a rainmaker. The fact that the king was looked on as playing an important part in the timely and good fall of rain is recorded in the ethnographic literature on the Zulu. Some Zulus today attribute what they regard as an increase in drought to the fact that the king no longer functions ritually as formerly. One informant told Berglund (1976: 53) that 'the trouble is that our kings do nothing today. They simply sit in an office, dressed nicely and writing letters.' Rain is regarded by the Zulu rainmakers as the fertilisation of the earth by the sky described by one informant as follows:

> [T]he sky and the earth are twins like my two feet are twins. My right foot and fist are stronger than my left, but they came from the womb at the same time. That is the condition of the sky and the earth. They are twins. They are both from the beginning. One is like the right foot and the right fist, that is the sky. The other is weaker, like the left foot and the left fist, that is the earth. Being twins, they are also husband and wife. The strong one is the husband, the weaker one is the wife. The husband fertilizes the wife, the fertilizer is the water. Rain … is the water of the sky which causes something to happen on the earth. Like no woman can bear a child without the assistance of a man, so the earth cannot produce food if the sky does not work with water on it. (Ibid.: 62)

As *iNkosi yeZulu*, Lord of the Sky is in charge of the rain, so the earth and its fertility is represented by *Nomkhubulwane*, the Heavenly Princess. She is sometimes called the Heavenly Queen but more commonly known as *Inkosazana* (Princess) and the daughter of the Lord of the Sky. Informants agree that she is closely associated with the rainbow, some saying she is the rainbow and she can be heard in the morning mists. 'They are convinced that she has the ability to bring about steady and frequent rains, brought by pleading with her father, the Lord-of-the-Sky' (Berglund 1976: 70). *Nomkhubulwane* was believed to reveal herself in such a way that she could be heard, but not seen, although writers such as Samuelson and Callaway refer to her appearance as that of 'a beautiful landscape, with verdant forests on some parts of her body, grass-covered slopes on others and cultivated fields on the rest' (Samuelson 1929: 303f.) and 'a very little animal as large as a polecat and marked with little white and black stripes; on one side there grows a bed of reeds, a forest and grass; the other side is that of a man' (Callaway 1868: 407f.).

Several of Berglund's informants emphasised that the main duty of the Heavenly Princess on coming to earth was to assist womenfolk and especially marriageable girls in matters relating to choice of partner, children, cultivation of fields, preparation of food, and general welfare. He relates the views of one informant:

> felt strongly along these lines and was of the definite impression that the chief reason for a loss of interest in *Nomkhubulwane* was the fact that 'today one learns everything in the schools, so that Inkosazana has nothing to teach our people. If the white people had not brought schools then *Nomkhubulwane* would have remained our teacher' … my informant's thoughts were generally those of most people of that area. (Berglund 1976: 71)

While Zulus condemned Europeans for the current loss of interest in *Nomkhubulwane*, A.T. Bryant, an English missionary well-known for his ethnographic accounts of Zulu life, strenuously denied that the Sky Princess could be anything except a Mediterranean import:

> to everyone at all familiar with the Bantu mind ... it will be clear that such a notion as a 'Sky princess' can be no spontaneous Bantu creation. The very idea is so utterly foreign, aye! Practically impossible, to their wholly essentially material modes of thought ... the idea of 'heavenly gods and goddesses, is so far as Africa is concerned, essentially Caucasic and impels us automatically to gravitate towards the old North African 'Mediterranean race', towards Egypt and Crete, to Greece and Rome. (Bryant 1949: 668–69)

The main ceremony associated with *Nomkhubulwane* was *uNomdede*. Bryant (1949: 667) notes that, in the same month as ceremonies to get rid of fever (malaria) were held, girls went out to beg gifts of corn from neighbours as an offering to *Nomkhubulwane*. At home the grain was ground into ceremonial millet beer, called, not *utshwala*, the usual term for home-brewed beer, but *uNomdede*. The women then proceeded to hoe 'a garden for the princess', a small patch of ground where seeds were planted and the beer poured as a libation. Young sorghum plants were treated with a sprinkling of red ochre, using sprigs of the *uleti* bush and invoking the princess with the cry, 'Give us corn. What shall we eat?' Sometimes small gourds of ceremonial beer were placed about the fields 'for the princess'. Later in the season the girls would return to the fields to root out plants affected by the stalk grub, when they would also pick some ears of corn 'for the princess', which were later buried in the earth and the grub-ridden stalks were thrown into the river or on an isolated spot. The girls then roasted the corn they had picked for themselves, bathed in the river, danced, and sang songs described by Bryant as 'lewd' (*iziBino*).

If these rites were neglected, it was believed that *Nomkhubulwane* would be offended and the corn would die of blight (*isiWumba*). Global warming has brought dramatic climate changes to Zululand. Elderly rural women associate crop failure with a general increase in selfishness among farmers and a reluctance to make grain offerings. Mrs Mbokazi, an elderly matriarch of Ntandabantu, northern KwaZulu-Natal, said in an interview with Khangi Zwane (May 2003) 'People nowadays don't plant sorghum. Sorghum was not only for making sorghum beer. It was a sign to thank God for a good harvest. Sorghum was a gift to God. But people were selfish, they harvested all the sorghum for their own purposes. That's why we have drought now.' Mrs Mkhwanazi, a neighbour of Mrs Mbokazi's, said that in the past women would climb a mountain and pray for rain to *Nomkhubulwane*: 'Sometimes we planted a plot to thank *Nomkhubulwane* for giving us rain.'

Nomkhubulwane may have been associated with epidemic disease, and Berglund notes that the Swazi version of *Nomkhubulwane* is 'capable of sending sickness to human beings', which Berglund denies the Zulu *Nomkhubulwane* would do: 'she is, on the other hand, able to prevent illness'. A ritual known as *umTshopi* was performed to remove the threat of epidemics and involved a group of girls leaving home at night and spending the night naked outdoors before making elaborate grass skirts, capes and headdresses. Dressed in this fashion, the girls would visit homesteads and leap over the small children, who were thought to be most vulnerable to disease, to remove the threat of the epidemic from them. In the evening the girls would bathe in the river and squirt water from their mouths, saying '*phuma umthakati*' (go away witch), meaning banish the disease. Other rituals related to *Nomkhubulwane* involved girls taking over their brothers' roles as cowherds for a day and driving the cattle out into the countryside, wearing their brother's garments and singing lewd songs. Any male who encountered the girls would be attacked and beaten.

An early account of the Zulu reported that a group of girls who would elect one of their number as 'a sort of queen', without whose consent none of the others would act, and, when this was done, beer was made and drunk near the river.

> When sweet-hearts came to see any of the girls, the matter is reported to the girl-queen, and if she did not wish the damsels to go out with them, they may not go. If they communicate with their sweet-hearts without her knowledge, she will fine them in beads. When, before eating the first-fruits, the girls wish to exchange presents with their sweet-hearts, they must notify the queen by giving her a present. (Fynney 1967: 106)

Fynney adds that there is a superstition that a girl-queen never nurses a child, as all her children die. Hence parents often object to their daughters being elected as queen.

A Swazi girls' organisation, separate from age classes, was known as *umcwasho* and was designed to honour an important young lady, a princess or daughter of a chief. A group of girls living in the same locality choose a daughter of a local chief to be their *inkosazana*. Permission to hold the ceremony is obtained from her father and his important womenfolk. These older women, who have been through *umcwasho* themselves, advise and direct the new group. The main responsibility is in the hands of the girls who 'carry the *umcwasho*', that is, wear the uniform of the *umcwasho*. The princess is assisted by an *indvuna* and a number of other girls, who form a *libandla* or council. While the *umcwasho* was generally a regional affair, Kuper notes that in 1935 it became a national one to honour the king's four elder daughters and the daughter of his most important sister.

On a specified day, between four hundred and five hundred girls, under the leadership of the daughter of a local chief and her *indvuna*, arrived at the capital. They performed tribute labour and were given 'the laws of the *umcwasho*', which were regulations concerning food, clothing, language, morals, and general behaviour. The *umcwasho* was divided into a junior group, too young to take lovers, and seniors. Each had its own colours, food abstentions, and passwords. After singing, dancing, and feasting, the girls returned to their homes, where they obeyed the rules of the *umcwasho*, subject to penalty fines, the most strict of which forbade any physical contact between the sexes. After three months, the girls returned to the capital for a brief period and the ceremony ended the following winter, with a grand display in front of the king and women of the court and dancing, which lasted for five days. The cost of providing food for the girls was borne by the court and their parents, and each feast ended with praises of the royal family in song and dance. Once the *umcwasho* breaks up it never appears again as a social unit. On their return to their own homes, each group danced at the home of the local 'princess' and her father provided a feast.

However, between the inauguration and the second summons, the *umcwasho* came to the attention of missionaries in Swaziland. Although the king had made it clear that attendance was voluntary, some chiefs had coerced parents into sending their daughters. Some parents had forced their children to attend and some girls had left school of their own free will to take part. The missionaries criticised the ceremony as immoral and reactionary and appealed to the Swazi colonial administration to put a stop to it. In the 1990s King Mswati and his advisers felt that a renewal of the *umcwasho* would assist in preventing the spread of the HIV/AIDS epidemic among young people. He issued a decree ordering girls to take part in the ceremony and to adhere to the no sex regulation for the duration. However, the king during this time took another wife. He was heavily criticised by the Swazi people (and fined) for doing so.

The Zulu version of the annual Swazi Incwala, known as the reed dance, managed to avoid this pitfall. The *Zululand Observer* of 19 September 2003 noted that 'traditionally the Reed Dance is where the reigning king chooses his wives, but as Zulu King Zwelethini serves in many HIV/AIDS structures and is a board member of the LoveLife/HIV AIDS campaign, he is leading by example and has stopped this practice.' Reporter Fezeka Khumalo noted that as part of the ceremony a young woman was crowned queen in a beauty contest that honoured the late Zulu Queen Nozodiyo (the mother of King Dinizulu, who acted as Regent when her son was exiled by the British administration to St Helena). 'Makhosi Gabela will serve as cultural ambassador at all Zulu traditional occasions for the year. She will appear at events such as the commemoration of King Shaka held in KwaDukuza annually and the celebration of the Queen of the Rain (*Nomkhubulwane*) which preserves the good image of the Zulu culture.'

Conclusion

Much anthropological and archaeological writing concerning early African civilisations, such as those of Mapungubwe and Zimbabwe, and present-day kingdoms like Swaziland, refers to female holders of chiefly power as 'ritual sisters' or 'queen mothers'. This chapter advances the argument that these are unsatisfactory (and Eurocentric) terms for these holders of important and influential positions, and that they disguise the real power wielded by women holding high office in African and especially southern African societies. While the role of women as objects of exchange in Africa has been written about in detail, relatively little has been said about women who are social actors in their own right.

Women rulers in Africa, and especially southern Africa, have usually been construed as exceptional. In patrilineal, patriarchal societies, women are believed to be outsiders, important mostly for their positions as mothers of future leaders of the lineage. The importance of women as sisters and daughters, rather than wives, has been less examined. In this chapter, I have shown that African women have traditionally exercised power and influence in their societies, but the extent of this influence has been undermined by the activities of colonial officials, missionaries, or anthropologists who found the close relationship of African brother and sister disturbing and wished to replace it with a vision of what they considered the proper place of woman in their own Western family, that of wife. A closer examination of ritual and symbol among the Venda, Swazi, and Zulu peoples shows the importance of sisters in the lives of their brothers and brothers' families. Whether as deity, queen, chief, headwoman, or paternal aunt, the power of the feminine principle in African cosmology is generally acknowledged by male and female members of society.

Notes

1. Interview with Mr David Malelo, Netshieundulu, Venda, 22 Mar. 1998.
2. *The Mirror*, Thohoyandou, 9 Jan. 1998.
3. Unpublished letter written by Sally Chilver in 1984 to Caroline Ifeka, quoted in Ifeka (1992: 143).
4. Interview with Musanda Gumani, Vondwe, 26 Apr. 1998.

References

Ardener, S. (ed.) 1992. *Persons and Powers of Women in Diverse Cultures: Essays in Commemoration of Audrey I. Richards, Phyllis Kaberry, and Barbara E. Ward*, New York and Oxford: Berg.
Beattie, J.H.M. 1958 *Nyoro Kinship, Marriage and Affinity*, London: Oxford University Press.
—— 1960. *Bunyoro: An African Kingdom*, New York: Holt, Rinehart & Winston.
Berglund, A.-I. 1976. *Zulu Thought Patterns and Symbolism*, Cape Town: Hurst.
Bryant, A.T. 1949. *The Zulu People*, Pietermaritzburg: Shooter & Shuter.
Buijs, G. 2002a. 'Gender and Person in African Societies: The Role of Hermeneutics', *AlterNation* 9 (1), pp. 57–73.
—— 2002b. 'Sisters and Their Brothers: An Examination of the Traditional Ritual Roles of Makhadzi in Venda, Northern Province, South Africa', in D. Lebeau and R.J. Gordon (eds), *Challenges for Anthropology in the 'African Renaissance'*, Windhoek: University of Namibia Press, pp. 138–49.

Callaway, H. 1868. *Izinganekwane: Nursery Tales Traditions and History of the Zulus*, London: Trubner.
Chilver, E.M. 1978. 'Phyllis Kaberry: Obituary', *Royal Anthropological Institute News* 24.
Evans-Pritchard, E.E. 1951. *Kinship and Marriage among the Nuer*, Oxford: Oxford University Press.
—— 1957. 'The Zande Royal Court', *Zaire Belgian African Review*, pp. 361–713.
Fouche, L. (ed.) 1937. *Mapungubwe: Ancient Bantu Civilisation on the Limpopo*, Cambridge: Cambridge University Press.
Fynney, F. 1967. *Zululand and the Zulus*, Pretoria: State Library.
Gardner, G.A. 1963. *Mapungubwe*, vol. 2, Pretoria: Van Schaik.
Hodza, A. and G. Fortune 1979. *Shona Praise Poetry*, Oxford: Clarendon Press.
Huffman, T. 1996. *Snakes and Crocodiles: Power and Symbolism in Ancient Zimbabwe*, Johannesburg: Witwatersrand University Press.
Ifeka, C. 1992. 'The Mystical and Political Powers of Queen Mothers, Kings and Commoners in Nso, Cameroon', in S. Ardener (ed.), *Persons and Powers of Women in Diverse Cultures: Essays in Commemoration of Audrey I. Richards, Phyllis Kaberry, and Barbara E. Ward*, New York and Oxford: Berg.
Krige, E.J. and J.D. Krige 1943. *The Realm of a Rain-Queen: A Study of the Pattern of Lovedu Society*, Cape Town: Juta.
Kuper, A. 1987. 'On the Price of Women and the Value of Cattle: A Rejoinder to Luc de Heusch', in A. Kuper, *South Africa and the Anthropologist*, London: Routledge & Kegan Paul.
Kuper, H. 1947. *An African Aristocracy: Rank among the Swazi*, London: Oxford University Press.
Matshidze, P.E. 1988. 'The Role of the Female Ruler in a Traditional Venda Society with Particular Reference to Vondwe', unpublished BA Honours dissertation, University of Venda.
Njoya, S. 1952. *Histoires et Coûtumes des Bamum*, Centre du Cameroon, Série Population, no. 5, Paris: Memoires de l'Institut Française de l'Afrique Noire.
Poewe, K.O. 1981. *Matrilineal Ideology: Male–Female Dynamics in Luapula*, Zambia, London: Academic Press.
Ralushai, N.M.N. and J.R. Gray 1977. 'Ruins and Traditions of the Ngona and Mbedzi among the Venda of the Northern Transvaal', *Rhodesian History* 8 (1), pp. 1–11.
Samuelson, R.C. 1929. *Long, Long Ago*, Durban: Marrianhill Press.
Stayt, H. 1931. *The BaVenda*, Oxford: Oxford University Press.
Theal, G.M. 1898–1903. *Records of South-Eastern Africa* (9 vols.), London; repr. 1964, Cape Town: Struik.
Van Warmelo, N.J. and W.M.D. Phophi 1948, 1949, 1967. *Venda Law*: Part One: *Betrothal*; Part Two: *Married Life*; Part Three: *Divorce*; Part Four: *Inheritance*; Part Five: *Property*, Pretoria: Government Printer.
Ward-Gailey, C. 1987. *Kinship to Kingship: Gender Hierarchy and State Formation in the Tongan Island*, Austin: University of Texas Press.
Weiner, A. 1976. *Women of Value, Men of Renown: New Perspectives in Trobriand Exchange*, Austin: University of Texas Press.
—— 1978. 'Epistemology and Ethnographic Reality: A Trobriand Island Case Study', *American Anthropologist* 80, pp. 752–57.

11

Revolting, Revolutionary, and Rebellious Women: Symbolic Disruption of Traditional Femininity and the Liberation of Femineity and Other Muted Identities

Rhian Loudon and Ronnie Frankenberg

This essay uses some of the Ardeners' seminal/uterine, even vaginal insights to analyse the way that anthropological research can be seen as a cooperative exercise between subjects rather than merely informant and fieldworker – to illuminate such diverse investigations as resistance and struggle in West Africa and images in art and drama. Finally, on the basis of Rhian Loudon's own field research, they inform analysis of the both vulnerable and powerful, dominant and muted, speech and actions of British Asian women, observed in shared multiple simultaneous realities of home and health-service/social-service workplace. It accepts one challenge posed by Ardener's discussions of multiple dimensional situations in *Persons and Powers* (1992: 8), in earlier writings (1978: 13–14) and in Dube et al. (1986).

Preamble

Audrey Richards once told Frankenberg that she and Malinowski usually thought of themselves as merely extending the thinking and methods of the science-led naturalists of their period to human beings and their environments. She was responding to his somewhat simple-minded Marxism. She knew that Frankenberg accepted Gluckman's (1948) views on Malinowski's cultural theories (see Frankenberg 1990). She understated her own fieldwork achievement, which her successors usually fail to equal and are unable to surpass (Richards 1982; see also Robin 1980 and 1981; Strathern 1981 and Richards's Forewords thereto). She was not a Leachian 'butterfly collector', or a traditional evolutionary anthropologist, or one of their present neo-Darwinian successors. Frankenberg's view was similar in his first fieldwork, despite Gluckman's observation that Whites and Blacks enacted a shared set of cultural processes at the opening of a bridge in Natal/Zululand (Gluckman (1968 [1941]). Gluckman had also tried to teach Frankenberg that the anthropologist was unavoidably involved in cultural exchange without the option of standing outside as mere observer. Loudon and Frankenberg were both influenced by Robert Pool's views (1994: 238–39) on the role of language in fieldwork (see also Ardener 1986: 5–13, developing Hastrup 1978).

Loudon's fieldwork, like that of Frankenberg earlier, in Wales, had informants and investigators who spoke in more than one language with different degrees of fluency and with slow but continuous changes of meaning. Villagers and Frankenberg changed one another's use of English, and their attempts to help him speak Welsh changed their own Welsh usage. Similarly the various South Asian languages (as well as English) used by Asians settled in the Midland city change through time and according to setting, gender, habitation, and degree of personal transmigratory experience. The language of the other in any conversation is always strange but nevertheless has to be accommodated to that of the listener self, in order to be heard.

The Ardeners have provided an extended elucidation over the years (following Hardman 1973 on children) of muteness. Shirley Ardener also provides a cogent analysis of the constant intertwining and change of mode between what is vocally spoken as sign and what is dramatically enacted as symbol; it is the approach which we develop in this essay.

Edwin Ardener's (1972) essay, which appeared in a Festschrift for Audrey Richards (La Fontaine 1972), was reprinted in Ardener 1975a. In her introduction to that book, Shirley Ardener reminds us that he considers why it appeared to be the case that social anthropologists, before second-wave feminism, tended to neglect the sayings and acts of half the populations studied. This was not because women did not speak (or act) but because they were not heard (or seen). They were not silenced but muted. He shows that it could be more instructive to present this in terms of analogical linguistic models than in terms of only partially shared, or unshared male and female cultures. He argued that any social situation expressed through speech was structured by paradigms of practice (p-structures), into which syntagms (s-structures) of action were organised. Speech acts of the second kind that could not, in themselves, be organised in terms of the dominant paradigms were not consciously heard, either by male participants or even by competent ethnographers. They could, however, be heard if accompanied by symbolic acts that drew attention to a possible underlying alternative paradigm. Paradoxically, until this situation was brought to light or the symbolic act recognised and/or interpreted, the more culturally competent that long-term outsiders or indigenous actors became, the less likely they were to hear the 'unspeakable' that had, in fact, been spoken.

Shirley Ardener transcends this and at the same time draws attention to an alternative 'cultural' way of describing it (1975b: 46) by developing independently and in an innovative way ideas formulated by de Beauvoir and Firestone: 'men and women are tuned to a different cultural wave length, that in fact there exists a wholly different reality for women' (cited from Firestone 1972: 151).

Furthermore, she puts forward an argument that there may be two principal p-structures for women. One is the currently shared, but male-derived view of femininity as a whole, dominated by what are appropriately called secondary, sexual characteristics, and another which she calls 'femineity', which is specific to women.[1] Although femineity may be influenced and named by or for metaphorical concepts of sisterhood, it is not identical with biological sisterhood. Nor is it identified with motherhood, or being a wife, or the practice of, or desire for, heterosexual sex. Indeed, there are many situations in Cameroon, in West Africa, in Africa as a whole, and more widely where open (even oblique) reference to sexuality and to sexual organs is initiated by women. There are others, like the classic case of Cameroonian *titi ikoli*, where such reference is apparently accidentally, even serendipitously, initiated by men and then adopted, enhanced, and reacted to by women as a challenge to the subordination often imposed on women by men's control and ultimate ownership of femininity. This is in fact most frequently (but not always and everywhere) the symbolic act by which the muted make themselves heard. As Ardener pointed out, ahead of her time, this is both surprisingly common[2] and similar to (in the way it uses body language in the most literal sense) the usage of nigra and nigger by African Americans as tactics of 'negritude' alongside the Black is Beautiful movement. As she puts it (1975b: 47):

> Unaware of this long-standing preoccupation among Bakweri, Greer (1971) arrives independently at a position close to theirs when she recognises the value of such symbolism and seeks its reinstatement. 'The vagina', she complains, 'is obliterated from the imagery of femininity as in the same way that signs of independence and vigour in the rest of her body are suppressed.' It may seem contradictory that women should suppose that vulgarity can be a means of enhancing dignity. It can be one when the obscenities are merely signals conveying a message which is not obscene.

In her conclusion to this paper Shirley Ardener writes:

> The *realien* [specific and contingent forms which different elements in a model assume in any given situation in the so-called 'real world' of events (Ardener 1975b: 52, n. 23)] of the traditional women's militant movements and women's liberation in America and England are, of course, different; may not the springs of action share a common source? We have discussed the opposition of positively and negatively marked patterns of symbolic behaviour in Africa. When stating that 'In extremities of random violence or in the breaking of cultural taboos, feminists turn femininity on its head', Mitchell exemplifies this (1971: 69). Greer speaks (though not approvingly) of those in the

movement who 'mock' and 'taunt' men. This she may not herself do, but does not the mode by which she presents her case sometimes appear to be a verbal display of vulgar parts. 'The key to the strategy of liberation,' she says, 'lies in exposing the situation, and the simplest way to do it is to outrage the pundits and the experts by sheer impudence of speech and gesture.' (1971: 38)

Titi ikoli indeed!

Individual and social symbolic acts involving specifically sexual gestures, Ardener argued, are a day-to-day public and private reality of women's protest and struggle in many societies in the past, as at the present day. For example, Marcia Poynton writes about this in *Naked Authority* (1990: 67), although she interprets the behaviour, rather disparagingly (following Davis 1978), as:

'a form of symbolic sexual inversion that serves to reinforce the existing order, for ... a world turned upside down can only be righted not changed'. ... In the most famous of the testimonies of 1848 [she is referring to that of Victor Hugo; see Clark 1973: 25, 191] we hear how a young woman, beautiful, dishevelled, terrible, appeared on the barricade. This woman, who was a whore, lifted her dress to her waist and shouted to the National Guard: 'Fire, you cowards, if you dare, on the belly of a woman!' A volley of shots knocked the wretched woman to the ground. She fell, letting forth a great cry. Clark defines this reporting as a travesty that is, in part, deliberate invention. 'This is the language and imagery of myth: but a myth travestied and made obscene. The travesty is part deliberate invention, and part response to the real cruelty and exaggeration of June. The image of the whore and the tricolor was not simply a lie or a piece of propaganda; the last report appeared in a left-wing newspaper, *La Democratie pacifique*. It was, in its clumsy way, an attempt to match the horror of events.'

Neither Clark nor Poynton recognise the possibility that a woman is reclaiming her humanity by emphasising femineity, by at once flaunting and flouting her sexuality. Poynton comes nearer to this earlier in the chapter (1990: 63–64), and nearer also to our own time and place, when she writes:

During the British miners' strike of 1984, a *Guardian* correspondent reported seeing a naked woman posing on top of a taxi holding a National Union of Mineworkers poster. This incident – in which an anonymous unclothed woman posed on a public vehicle – demonstrates the abiding power of woman as a symbol in revolutionary politics. The fact that for the participants at the male rally a naked female on a taxi holding a strike-banner probably constituted at best entertainment (a living manifestation of page 3 fantasies)[3] and at worst an example of bad taste, does not alter the fact that the presentation of female nudity or near-nudity in the context of a call to arms has an exceedingly long pedigree. We are not always aware of why we pick on stereotypes at particular moments; the explanation lies in the general cultural consciousness. The *Guardian* reporter found it 'bizarre' but in fact this woman raised above a crowd and bearing the insignia of the insurgents was a twentieth-century version of a living allegory, signifying an alliance of the erotic and the political, which would have been readily recognised in nineteenth-century France. Whether or not she, as an individual, had any connection with the National Union of Mineworkers was immaterial; her role was symbolic. While absence of clothing may, at one level, signify the erotic, at another level – especially when accompanied by a banner or flag into which the identity of the bearer is subsumed – nakedness symbolises Truth. ... And the well-recognised iconography of Truth in Western culture bears this out. The anonymous woman on the taxi, as well as the named women who participated in picket-line activity, were particular and individual women. But they are valorised in discourse not for who they are but as aspects of womanhood culturally constructed.

In her chapter (in Caplan 1987), Ardener carries her argument about Cameroon society and its processual, ritualised practices (liminal rituals) into the more segregated Cultural (with a capital C) practices (liminoid ceremonials) (Turner and Turner 1978) of Western societies from the sectarian ritual dramas and sculptural artefacts of classical Greece until the present. She takes from Zeitlin (1982) the Greek example of anasyrma, in which women ritually expose their inner selves, their vulva and vagina, in a complex but ambiguous symbolism.

At the time at which she was writing 'vaginal iconography' was beginning, especially, but not uniquely, through the work of Judy Chicago in the United States, to be an important feature of feminist-inspired art, although not an uncontroversial one even for feminists (see the increasing success as drama and text of Ensler 2001).

> We suggest that gender contains sexuality in all three senses; it encompasses, it restrains, and it hides it from view. When sexuality is made to emerge in whatever form, gender as a social relation becomes uniquely visible. The whole point is that the actors can have it both ways. They can, in these circumstances, rightly profess that it is all in the eye of the beholder. (Ardener 1987: 123)

Such revelatory demonstrations shock the witnesses towards whom the act is hostile, but they can at the same time proclaim the honour of that which is exposed. This is true of ancient or modern anasyrmaic self-exposure, the vaginal exhibitionism of some feminist and queer art, the supposed non-availability for marriage of some Midland Muslim women (their sexuality is revealed and emphasised by its non-marketability in the currency of kinship and family), and even in Bernard Shaw's no longer shocking epithet which in 1914 gave a new phrase to the English language: 'Not Pygmalion likely' (see the entry under Pygmalion in the *Oxford English Dictionary*).

Pygmalion, Myth, Art, and Drama

Marcia Poynton (1990: chap. 1, 'Reading the Body') has pointed out how the Greek myth of Pygmalion was a central feature of late nineteenth-century art, contributed to famously by Burne-Jones and Gerome. Whatever its ostensible object, it has the outcome not only that:

woman's special position in the nature/culture debate is most clearly adumbrated in Western art in images within which the female nude is posited as a cipher for male creativity, but also that ... the female body is the sign for male creativity, for that which can 'bring to life' inert material by imaginative projection. Furthermore, in such works, woman is twice removed from the point of production; she is represented within a re-presentation. This insistence upon her presence as re-presentation is precisely what lends legitimacy to the concept of the artist as 'real', as living, breathing flesh, as the creator of art creating more art. (Ibid.: 23–4)

At first sight, Bernard Shaw[4] seems merely to be transferring this trope to the activities of his favourite linguistic craftsmen – teachers of linguistics and especially phonetics.[5] The plot of his play begins with a wager between two such as to whether one of them, Professor Higgins, could forcefully train a common 'girl' to change her speech patterns and thereby change a noisy but muted Piccadilly flower girl into a quiet but articulate, coherent conversationalist with society ladies and gentlemen. She might even ultimately interact on equal terms with duchesses. He did not name Galatea, the statue brought to life by Aphrodite, but, with characteristically unconscious male insouciance (see Ardener 1986), he named his play after Pygmalion, the sculptor. His players and their audiences failed to notice the inversion of the myth in general, or even the point in Act III where, as remarked earlier, contrary cultural expectations are interrupted by an obscenity, and the women, especially Eliza/Galatea, take charge. Although from the outset of the play it was clear that the housekeeper had considerable power of action, this did not challenge the audience, since, like the situation in their own homes, it was unperceived. Servants were culturally muted by being unseen, even when in full view. Royal remnant survivals have reminded us of this as some actors are raised and some lowered in status by formerly unimaginable, or merely unimagined, symbolic body actions, an alleged homosexual relation between royal and servant, and a similar breakdown of intimate conversational and mutual knowledge taboos between a princess and a butler. The play and later film were popular because its anti-romantic argument was undermined in performance.

As did the Webbs, Shaw put great faith in statistics and advocated what we would now call an evidence-based state medical service. It was, however, to be controlled by a General Medical Council from which physicians would be excluded except as assessors, and work under the jurisdiction of a Bureau of Statistics based on the ideas of Karl Pearson (Shaw 1932, 1944, 1946, 1950; Boxill 1969; Frankenberg 1974). He, anthropological playwright, researched by grass-roots participant experience in local government, and he used his experience there in his plays. In contrast to the more sociological and statistical Webbs, he was a social anthropologist 'at home'. His 'field research' and its conclusions were almost invariably summarised in prefaces as well as presented on stage (see Shaw 1934).[6] In *Pygmalion*, Shaw sought to invert a masculinist myth derived from plastic and pictorial art. Feminist writers compared this favourably with Shakespeare's *The Taming of the Shrew*, although some have argued that Higgins's behaviour was as arrogant for his time as Petrucchio's was for his (Pedersen 1977). In 2003, *The Taming of the Shrew* was presented at the Globe Theatre in London by an all-female company, the Company of Women. Kathryn Hunter made Kate's final speech a tour de force so that:

> It turned into a harangue, a tongue in cheek lecture on the obedience owed by women which embarrassed her [on-stage] listeners and which they were powerless to stop. She even climbed onto the table for a more emphatic delivery so that Petrucchio was left nervously tugging at her skirts, wanting her to come down. To illustrate her point about the supposed softness and passivity of women's bodies, she lifted up her dress and shocked Petrucchio into trying to cover her up with a coat. ... The 'men' ... had lost control of the stage. ... I had not realised quite how exciting and positive it would be to see them cast as people, regardless of gender. (Gilfillan 2003)

A high-culture *titi ikoli* ?

Shaw was a prolific writer and rarely curbed his speech but despite the clarity of his argument, he too was muted. In 1915 he was forced to write a prose sequel to *Pygmalion* in an unsuccessful attempt to save his argument. His 'proof' that Eliza had married Freddy and not Higgins and Shaw's pleading failed to prevent Gabriel Pascal giving a romantic ending to the film, and the disaster was compounded when, after Shaw's death, *Pygmalion* emerged as the romantic Hollywood musical, *My Fair Lady* (Shaw and Lerner 1956), with added songs.

The crucial 'demonstration' scene in Act III of the play *Pygmalion*, when Eliza's transformation from fla'hr gel (saying li'dy) to lady comes to grief, first, when she makes inappropriate scientific statements about the weather in her new impeccable accent, and then, even more crucially, when, lacking the insight that enjoying uncompelled exercise is one of the *differentia specifica* of leisure-class females under the leadership of their males, she rejects the romantic choice of walking across the park as against the newly realistic possibility of going by taxi. She says: 'Not bloody likely.' This expletive spoken by a woman had in 1914 as much disruptive power as a four-letter description of female genitals still had until 2003. (See *Guardian* Friday Review of 2 Jan. 2004, where it appears as the capitalised name, in the plural and preceded by Selfish, of a popular 'group' who on U.K. radio are identified only by songs with relatively inoffensive titles. See also McEwen 2001, a novel based on its supposedly 'inappropriate' use, and Allen 2005 for a recent discussion.) Shaw's naturalistic imitation of the grammar and pronunciation of 'kerbside' speech in Act I (1941: 7) did not dare to do more than hint at expletives deleted, lest he incurred censorship and the failure of his shock effect in Act III (ibid.: 80). The production company had difficulty in procuring an actress prepared to risk her career by speaking the word at the Drury Lane Theatre. John Jay Lerner in *My Fair Lady* moved it from a private to a public place (Ascot racecourse). Eliza lapsed into her original accent, euphemised it to blooming, and applied it to a horse as 'Move yer bloomin' arse.'

Interacting with British Asian Women in a Midland City: Managing a Multiplicity of Identities

This section is derived from Loudon's fieldwork and its discussion between the authors. Like other fieldworkers and their object/subjects of study, we have been engaged in mutual ethnography of one another and our respective milieux with the intention of producing texts separately and together. Loudon is a qualified medical practitioner and had taught in a university department of primary health care. Frankenberg joined the physician (who acted as internal supervisor in her own university) as a paid external anthropologist adviser/supervisor to her field-study of the experience (as users, providers or observers) of health services by a specific set of South Asians resident in a Midland city.

A Case Study[7]

Mumtaz: Self-producer as a Muslim woman, as qualified professional and ultimately graduate, friend, overcomer of disability, creator of her own support network, conqueror of both inadequacy of health services as well as uncertainty, and partially absent family support.

Native-born, resident, migrant, and transnational men and women, with links to South Asia, but of many nationalities derived from at least three continents (Africa, Europe, and Asia), live in various numbers in various parts of Britain (Census 2001; White 2002: 7). At some time or another, most of them have certainly experienced disadvantage arising from racial and other forms of discrimination against them in work, housing, and availability of public services,[8] and this has in turn generated an enormous literature by a wide variety of specialist academics, journalists, and administrators. Through her own detailed future reports on her research on the health services in a Midland city, Loudon hopes to contribute to new and creative ways of analysing this literature. We believe the argument of this chapter radically rethinks our shared and separate earlier work. In this final section we give one example of our working together on Loudon's material in the light of Ardener's work.

We do not claim that the situation of the men and women who participated in this study are in any way typical of an 'Asian community' in a generalised sense. Readers tempted to see it in this way could prevent or cure their sickness with Gardner (2002), Gupta (2003), Werbner (2002) or commentaries on the successive National Surveys (Coleman and Salt 1996; Peach 1996; Radcliffe 1996; Census 2001; White 2002). It is important to note also that Loudon's research is that of a direct participant in the health services she is studying and that her subjects are also participants, although in more varied ways, from patients to managers and physicians.[9]

The general argument pursued, in exploring our debt to Ardener's analyses, has been to recognise the simultaneous existence of diverse interlocking identities, including those derived from femineity and femininity, and to demonstrate the way that sudden shifts in the cultural language of individuals and social groups have been triggered by more overtly corporeal symbolic acts than mere linguistic vocalisation. Up to this point, our examples have been both overtly sexual and sensational in several senses. These characteristics are still present in our final example but are either implicit or muted.

Mumtaz describes her experience of engaging with medical and educational networks as a young, British, Muslim woman now with, but earlier without, a visual impairment. She describes her experience of an illness that affected many parts of her body and had a significant effect on her ability to carry out basic activities, like walking and eating, and, given her particular network of social relations prior to her illness, her ability to participate in daily life. Doctors, Asian and less Asian, in general practice and at hospitals, were initially unable to recognise that Mumtaz was ill, let alone the nature of her illness, and then spent many months, creeping into years, trying to label her illness and even ultimately failing to find an effective treatment to what had become a disability.

> Well when I lost my sight first at the time cos so much, like I was anorexic, I had problems with my leg, I had so much going on, I didn't really think about the sight loss, at that time. I just used to think about my problems and that the pain I was in. But coming to think of my sight when I, I've just like recently just you know thought about the sight thing and to be honest with you I don't think I'd ever get over my sight loss, I don't think. That, that's something that I could never ... because if I was born with a visual impairment or disability or if I had some sort of family background or suffered something and due to that, you know, it caused my sight loss, I would have, I would have come to terms with it but to just go to sleep one night and wake up the following morning and your sight, I'm sad to say, I just can't, I just can't get hold of the fact and at that time I thought my life ended. I stayed in the house for a year, I didn't even go to my front door, I didn't come downstairs, virtually in my bedroom, bedroom to the bathroom, bathroom back to the bedroom. I just, I just didn't know how to face the outside world, I just couldn't do it, because ... I mean if I was told 'Oh right this is what your eye condition is, you lost your sight because the nerves did this or something like that', you know, there's something there, there's a definition, there's no definition.
>
> And I thought it life had ended, and you know when you get the teachers from school coming, I didn't want to know, but you know all you know when you have dreams of going to college and then university, I thought that's it, I can't do it, you know, I lost my confident, I weren't Independent. I just, it's just one of those things you know.

Mumtaz did not receive any clear guidelines about how to manage the transition from sighted student to blind woman – either from her family or from her health advisers or anywhere else. When staff from her school visited with work she couldn't see the point of engaging with them.

She formulated her initial despair at her sight loss in terms of the loss of educational opportunities that she perceived as inevitably accompanying her physical impairment. To many Asians, though not all, in addition to the initial perception of loss of educational and employment opportunities, she is also perceived to have become a less desirable marriage partner due to her impairment. 'I don't think the family are looking at me with any marriage sort of thing.'

She goes on to say:

> If you look at the Asians, if you look at the Asians as a whole, looking at someone with a disability getting married, it's not on. I don't, personally they've never said anything to me at all but I think I know because I think personally it'd be that no, they wouldn't expect because no Asian guy is like getting married in the Asian community, Asian guy, would really take on someone with a visual impairment. Yet I know Asian guys that will but I'm looking at my parents' view but they think oh no why would somebody want someone that can't see.

And subsequently:

> cos I think if I had sight, no disrespect to anybody with a visual impairment, don't get me wrong, I wouldn't want to be with someone that was totally blind. I'll be honest with you.

Ayesha, a married, professional worker who lived with her parents and who had met her husband at university, outlined her perception of the effect of disability on a woman's marriage prospects:

> Because it's, it's horrible, but they are looking for a fit and healthy person because to be a mother, to perform the role of a wife it is just not one, a one to one marriage. You are looking after a family, you've got a lot of social events to attend, and a person who's looking for a wife whether they are educated or not the parents go out and look for that wife, and if it is a disability it is held against you, and the parents of the girl, especially the girl, have to disclose if there's a medical problem. And and most of the times people just shun away so then the subject, the girl is free to get on with her life because they know that marriage is not gonna happen very quickly.

This change in 'marriageability' status, a change in one's perceived 'femininity' (Ardener 1975b: 46), due to disability is a source of distress to members of Mumtaz's family, given that in most Pakistani families there are indeed community and family pressures on girls to marry. As Tahira said:

> I'm 22, for Asians like when you're 16 you know they're already getting wedding plans organised and stuff. It was my Mum's fault really. I told her, I, I said, said to them, you know, from the start I said 'If you're trying to get me married you're going to be in trouble.' And she said 'No no no, nothing's going to happen.' And then we got over there [to Pakistan], I don't know and I thought, my sister said it, she didn't want me to go cos she said they'll gang up on you over there and you know what it's like, you'll get pressured into it. And it's true, you do.

Shabir, an older male relative, unwittingly confirmed Mumtaz's assessment of the older generation's perspective in her family:

because now she is a right big girl ... if she had a sight ... she might be married ... but unfortunately she lost sight. I don't know what's her view about the marriage ... but the other thing is that ... I don't think anybody is really liked to have a married with a blind person ... but most blind womans are married as well you know. ... I don't know how [to] ... describe that because if anybody you know asked us... that they want to marry we are ready to ... give every possible facility to make it possible to marry her ... but I don't know what she decides.

Shabir refers to the new uncertainty surrounding Mumtaz's status since it has been changed by her physical impairment. However, in the extract presented above, he does comment that 'most blind womans are married', and indeed Mumtaz separately recounts her knowledge of an Asian woman with a visual impairment who had an arranged marriage.

For Ayesha, whilst marriage for a woman with a disability or negative past medical history is presented as delayed, there is the suggestion of potentially positive consequences: 'the girl is free to get on with her life because they know that marriage is not gonna happen very quickly'.

For Mumtaz, brought up in the U.K., her disability and now ambiguous connection to marriageable networks changes her 'femininity' status; it has a liberating effect. She literally embodies the lack of translation between the sets of 'woman' and 'marriage partner' and in so doing potentially creates a 'positive ruck in the social fabric' (Ardener 1978: 34–43). As Mumtaz said, 'I've got more freedom than anyone in my bloody family, boys or girls.' The atypical but positive 'femineity' nature of Mumtaz's new situation is recognised by her friends and cousins:

> They go 'You've got so much freedom, God you're so lucky', and I go yeah but I've got, I've got, maybe I'm lucky but I can't see at the end of the day, I still don't, I mean you can take me to 'Victoria Park' and say this is Finland and I'd say yeah it's Finland. But they go, God, though everyone I speak to like my cousins and everyone they go you're just so lucky, cos I said, I go you go here, you go there, you're just absolutely lucky cos you've got the opportunity.

Despite the positive connotations of impairment Mumtaz simultaneously pre-empts a discussion as to how far one can sustain this idea that physical impairment may be positive or liberating (see Haraway's 'material-semiotic' actors (Haraway 1991: 183–201)). Although biological perspectives are important in Mumtaz's thinking, it makes little sense to separate them from specific sets of social relations. For example, Mumtaz favourably compares her own position as a woman with a visual impairment, but with strong family support, to others she meets through college who have a similar impairment but do not appear to have the benefit of her family background.

> But I really, you know, when I was really ill and I stayed inside, no one can go through the pain that I went through, but after going to the college and speaking to so many

people, I just think God, I'm glad I'm not in their position and I really my heart goes out to them because I've been talking to every student's there and I think, you know, you feel so bad 'cos I've just, I feel absolutely sorry for them. But I mean most of the parents have neglected them and they're like after college, they've been going to flats and everything and I'm thinking oh no they've got no support at all.

Ironically, not all young men who meet Mumtaz through college and charitable activities in fact perceive her as an undesirable partner. She describes her reaction to the reported feelings of an (admittedly non-Asian) student from overseas:

And yeah apparently one of the students fell in love with me, I thought oh my God. I thought, I, I just turned around and I thought I had to be really formal and I said to one of the staff, 'Oh he's a very nice young gentleman' but the fact, I really, unfortunately I don't have the same feelings for him, but that was the best thing I could come out with.

She represents herself in the context of a conversation with Loudon as an Asian woman with a disability and strong material family support.

It's brilliant I'm telling ya. There is no diff, I think if anything they've got more freedom, more, there's more activities, there's more outgoing things. I mean I've never gone bowling in my entire life and I went last week and I said I'm not gonna go. I've never held the ball in my, you know this ball thing in my hand and I did a strike first time, first go. You should have seen them clapping, cheering, I thought oh my God how embarrassing ...
Well I'm definitely going to university and I do want to do my degree, first I want to do my degree in social policy.

Older members of her family perceive Mumtaz to be excluded or certainly distanced from a marriageable set or network. Parts of her social network frame her having a physical impairment in terms of dependence and caring rather than independence and autonomy. They do not necessarily accept her valuing education either as adding to family prestige or as personal protection in the event of divorce. She described her family's perception that the 'Asian community' at large would condemn families such as hers if they allowed a young Asian woman with acquired sight loss to live away from them in lodgings associated with an educational institution for those with a disability. Shabir, the older male relative, did think that the family status would be changed because of her behaviour and the perceptions and beliefs of local people. Mumtaz reported:

He goes, it's mainly what people are going to think, they'll all think that she's just lost her sight, her family don't want to know her and they've just dumped her. That's how the Asian community would just look at it, so it's silly.

Mumtaz presented herself as someone with a visual impairment whom the Asian community felt should be dependent and for whom seeking independence through education will be interpreted as family failure and detrimental to her family's status. Should Mumtaz succeed in living independently the family would not be seen to be performing its family identity in an acceptable way using socially available symbols.

Mumtaz herself valued employment and education for women, and her experience within an educational network for people with a visual impairment seems to have been a copybook example of how to promote self-efficacy – the belief that one's intervention can make a difference (Bandura 1995). This concept from social psychology calls for safe 'mastery' experiences with a degree of challenge so that one becomes used to success, identifiable role models, verbal encouragement, and positive explanation of emotions and bodily experiences.

Mumtaz tried to bolster her argument for continuing her education, which would necessitate living in college accommodation, by appealing to quantifiable notions of progress. She is someone who is perceived by funding agencies to be benefiting from education.

> Because I study at the college, cos I study at the college it's £30,000 a year bearing in mind I've been there since '97, but because there has been so much progress, that's why they keep on funding me, otherwise they won't fund me. That they look at the progress as well.

Her objective in pursuing education and pursuing independence means the family will be perceived as shameful and uncaring. Although they might have welcomed her living away from home if she had remained sighted and a prospective marriage partner, they opposed it because of her impairment. Mumtaz did use arguments based on family relationships to advance her case. She said that her mother commented that she should think about the effect that her behaviour of seeking help would have on others, and that she should think of what a mother will feel at the loss of her daughter: 'She [her mother] goes to me you've not thought about what's gonna go through me.' To further her cause, Mumtaz then invoked the responsibilities of a mother to prioritise her children's happiness, in this case her daughter over her own and other normative conceptions of what is natural and unchangeable: parents die before their children, the funding for the course is only being offered at this moment in time, travel and early starts make one tired.

Conclusions

Mumtaz drew attention to the hypocrisy of 'people' espousing the importance of support and social models of illness, but with little intention of making an effort to do the work that such social models entail. The familiar idea that we all want other people to make sacrifices for the common good, or to further the image we wish to project of ourselves – families look after their own, we all support each other – but only if this involves minimal effort on our own part. We are all for patient-centred care, or indeed user participation in research, as long as it doesn't make us compromise our most cherished values. We might be too busy ourselves to participate in neighbourhood renewal but for those in poverty it must be a good thing.

Mumtaz's attempts to advance her education were in conflict with existing notions, in some parts of her social network, of appropriate 'femininity' behaviour for a woman with a disability. One might say that she sought to differentiate the signifier, a woman with a visual impairment, from the signified, the need to be looked after at home. She successfully negotiated a postmodern identity and in doing so shaped the value and meaning of education; what it is to be a person with a disability; and what it is to be a woman to some in her social network.

The specific instance of her choosing first to perform and then to present disability in this way and gain independence through education meant that education becomes valued as an end in itself, as well as in terms of how it might be an asset for the family group. Mumtaz's response to sickness presupposes that someone with a visual impairment can live apart from their family and eventually seek employment. The label of a woman with a disability no longer means someone who is dependent and needs to be cared for at home. What would have been negated as forbidden and impossible, at least for someone of her class in Pakistan, and a contradiction in the situation of early diaspora now in postmodernity can be presented merely as a welcome irony or indeed as femineity's triumph over femininity.

The description of a crisis in family relations also demonstrates how shifting one's self and the other into different identities derived from different systems of classification justifies and reinforces actions and, as Derrida (1994a, b) suggests, brings to life relevant spectres of the past, artefactualities in the present, and intentions for the future.

Notes

1. It is interesting that Coleridge's original usage of it was negative, namely that 'Of all men I ever knew Wordsworth had the least femineity in his mind', and that Oliver Wendell Holmes in the same set of citations from the *Oxford English Dictionary* distinguishes it from muliebrity, with its overtones of motherhood.
2. Frankenberg first observed it when, as an undergraduate in 1948 who travelled regularly on a weekend cross-country bus from Cambridge to Birmingham, he discovered a woman who regularly 'flashed' her ex-boyfriend and his new lover (her ex-friend) as the bus passed. The other passengers found the incident unremarkable and understandable, and the woman herself later confirmed to him that it was a protest against their unjust treatment of her. He last observed it in the 1970s, when two women who encountered a well-known and blatantly sexist TV presenter at a railway station behaved similarly.
3. See Ayto 1999: 491. A 'page three girl' (a phrase which is first reported in 1975) is a scantily clad or nude female model whose picture appears as a pin-up in the popular press.

The term was originally applied specifically to such a girl regularly featured on page three of the British tabloid *Sun* (and the term Page Three was registered as a proprietary name by the *Sun*'s owners). The breakthrough display of nipples in a mass-market newspaper brought the *Sun* great commercial success in the 1970s and 1980s, but towards the end of the 1990s its proprietors judged that the readers were jaded and craved greater seriousness, so the nipples disappeared.

4. George Bernard Shaw (1856–1950) was a major playwright, intellectual and prominent political activist and writer during the last quarter of the nineteenth and first half of the twentieth centuries. His biography in the Penguin paperback version (Holroyd 1990, 1991, 1993a) runs to three volumes and 1,450 pages with a fourth volume (1993b) of 135 pages describing the posthumous adventures of his final wishes. He was a noted feminist (Weintraub 1977) and co-founder, amongst other things, of the Independent Labour Party with Keir Hardie and of the Fabian Society with Sydney and Beatrice Webb. Together with the last two, he worked out a programme of social study and reform, of which the London School of Economics (LSE) was a side product. Shaw (1949: 65) says, 'This was the ablest man in England: Sidney Webb' and on the next page: 'The difference between Shaw with Webb's brains, knowledge and official experience and Shaw by himself was enormous. But as I was and am an incorrigible histrionic mountebank, and Webb was the simplest of geniuses, I was often in the centre of the stage whilst he was invisible in the prompter's box.'

5. After personal legacies, Bernard Shaw left the residue of his estate and its future income for the reform of language along phonetic lines. How this was frustrated is described in Holroyd 1993b, appropriately called *The Last Laugh*.

6. Collected in one volume in 1934.

7. All names apart from those of the researchers are fictitious. Interviews quoted are from verbatim recordings, reproduced and transcribed as phonetically as possible by Loudon, who as general practitioner, researcher, and teacher, is thoroughly at home with local speech forms.

8. In this study, for example, one participant in a discussion group, Afzal, described the experience of having a metal object thrown at him one day at work: 'I was outside the factory. I was burning a bit of … paper into the dustbin that was my job and I was working there you know. I don't know I just bent down to pick up something and there was some people in a van … I didn't see them but they throw a piece of metal and very sharp it was, very sharp. And I was bending down whether you can say it racialist or whatever he throw it at me while I was standing. By luck I just bent down at that time. Luckily you know and I picked that metal up and I seen they were white guys in the van. I'm not against anybody, we're all people. They hit me and they run away in the van. I didn't have a chance to note the number. I went inside to see my gaffer I told him that's what happ[ened] … people throws at me. I was doing my job outside. They throw at me and they run away in the van, I couldn't note the number. I didn't have a chance to note it.' Paul Gilroy (1987) warns of the dangers of setting anti-racism wholly in the context of an anti-fascism that ignores forms of institutional racism (see also for example Macpherson (1999: Part 6, 34), whose report reignited a discussion in the public sector about institutional racism and indirect discrimination, which in fact was outlawed in the 1976 Race Relations Act). However, Gilroy also argues cogently that approaches to race relations 'must not have the effect of appearing to reduce the complexity of black life to an effect of racism' (Gilroy 1987: 150).

9. In contrast, after most of this chapter was written, Frankenberg recalled that a quarter of a century ago he had supervised a postgraduate student who had been hired by the health

authority in the same city. She was one of two nurses, one Scottish and White, the other British and of Asian origin, who were asked as research fellows to administer a set of formal interview questions to Asian patients. It was assumed not to be the concern of those of Asian origin employed in the health service at any level. These questions had already been written. The attempts of the research workers to discuss them were labelled as not pertinent, and the very request to do so as impertinent. The patients themselves were reluctant to be interviewed, since this was by no means the first set of interviews, and the earlier ones had been accompanied by promises to improve services, which had not been fulfilled. Subsequently local leaders had also opposed the project. Both nurses, with the help of their professional association, eventually managed to withdraw, and Frankenberg's student completed her higher degree on another topic.

References

Allen, K. 2005. 'Taboo for Who?' http://www.thefword.org.uk, accessed 26 Aug. 2005.
Ardener, E. 1972. 'Belief and the Problem of Women', in J.S. La Fontaine (ed.), *The Interpretation of Ritual*, London: Tavistock.
Ardener, S. (ed.) 1975a. *Perceiving Women*, London: J.M. Dent & Sons.
——— 1975b. 'Sexual Insult and Female Militancy', in S. Ardener (ed.), *Perceiving Women*, London: J.M. Dent & Sons, pp. 29–53.
——— 1978. 'Introduction: The Nature of Women in Society', in S. Ardener (ed.), *Defining Females: The Nature of Women in Society*, London and New York: Croom Helm and St Martin's Press, pp. 9–48.
——— 1986. 'The Representation of Women in Academic Models', in L. Dube, E. Leacock and S. Ardener (eds), *Visibility and Power: Essays on Women in Society and Development*, Delhi: Oxford University Press, pp. 3–14.
——— 1987. 'A Note on Gender Iconography: The Vagina', in P. Caplan (ed.), *The Cultural Construction of Sexuality*, London: Routledge, pp. 113–42.
——— 1992. 'Persons and Powers of Women: An Introduction', in S. Ardener (ed.), *Persons and Powers of Women in Diverse Cultures: Essays in Commemoration of Audrey I. Richards, Phyllis Kaberry, and Barbara E. Ward*, New York and Oxford: Berg, pp. 1–10.
Ayto, J. 1999. *Twentieth Century Words*, Oxford: Oxford University Press.
Bandura, A. 1995. 'Exercise of Personal and Collective Efficacy in Changing Societies', in A. Bandura (ed.), *Self-Efficacy in Changing Societies*, Cambridge: Cambridge University Press, pp. 1–45.
Boxill, R. 1969. *Shaw and the Doctors*, New York and London: Basic Books.
Caplan, P. (ed.) 1987. *The Cultural Construction of Sexuality*, London: Routledge.
Census 2001. Office for National Statistics, General Register Office for Scotland, Northern Ireland Statistics and Research Agency http://www.statistics.gov.uk/cci/nugget.asp?id=457, accessed 9 Jan. 2004.
Clark, T.J. 1973. *The Absolute Bourgeois: Artists and Politics in France, 1848–1851*, London: Thames & Hudson.
Coleman, D. and J. Salt (eds) 1996. *Ethnicity in the 1991 Census*: Vol. 1. *Demographic Characteristics of the Ethnic Minority Populations*, London: OPCS.
Davis, N. 1978. 'Women on Top: Symbolic Sexual Inversion and Political Disorder in Early Modern Europe', in B.A. Babcock (ed.), *The Reversible World: Symbolic Inversion in Art and Society*, Ithaca, New York, and London: Cornell University Press.

Derrida, J. 1994a. *Specters of Marx*, New York and London: Routledge.

——— 1994b. 'The Deconstruction of Actuality: An Interview with Jacques Derrida', *Radical Philosophy* 68, pp. 28–41.

Dube, L., E. Leacock and S. Ardener (eds) 1986. *Visibility and Power: Essays on Women in Society and Development*, Delhi: Oxford University Press.

Ensler, E. 2001 (orig. 1998). *The Vagina Monologues*, London: Virago Press.

Firestone, S. 1972. *The Dialectic of Sex*, London: Palatine.

Frankenberg, R. 1974. 'Functionalism and After: Theory and Developments in Social Science Applied to the Health Field', *International Journal of Health Services* 4 (3), pp. 411–27.

——— 1990 (orig. 1989). 'Village on the Border: A Text Revisited', in R. Frankenberg, *Village on the Border* (orig. 1957), Prospect Heights, Illinois: Waveland Press, pp. 169–93.

Gardner, K. 2002. *Age, Narrative and Migration: The Life Course and Life Histories of Bengali Elders in London*, Oxford and New York: Berg.

Gilfillan, E. 2003. Review of *Taming of the Shrew*, Company of Women, Globe Theatre [London] 2003, in *The F Word: Contemporary U.K. Feminism*. http://www.thefword.org.uk Review/events/taming.live, accessed 22 Dec. 2003.

Gilroy, P. 1987. *There Ain't No Black in the Union Jack*, London: Routledge.

Gluckman, M. 1948. *Malinowski's Sociological Theories*, Lusaka and Manchester: Manchester University Press (Rhodes-Livingstone Paper no. 16).

——— 1968 (orig. 1941). *Analysis of a Social Situation in Modern Zululand*, Manchester and Lusaka: Manchester University Press (Rhodes-Livingstone Paper no. 28).

Greer, Germaine 1971. 'The Smell Sell', *Sunday Times* (London), 25 July, p. 28.

Gupta, R. 2003. *From Homebreakers to Jailbreakers: Southall Black Sisters*, London: Zed Books.

Haraway, D.J. (ed.) 1991. *Simians, Cyborgs, and Women*, London: Free Association Books.

Hardman, C. 1973. 'Can There Be an Anthropology of Children?' *Journal of the Anthropology Society of Oxford* 4, pp. 85–89.

Hastrup, Kirsten 1978. 'The Semantics of Biology: Virginity', in S. Ardener (ed.), *Defining Females: The Nature of Women in Society*, London and New York: Croom Helm and St Martin's Press.

Holroyd, M. 1990 (orig. 1988). *Bernard Shaw*. Vol. 1, *1856–1898: The Search for Love*, London: Penguin Books.

——— 1991 (orig. 1989). *Bernard Shaw*. Vol. 2, *1898–1918: The Pursuit of Power*, London: Penguin Books.

——— 1993a (orig. 1991). *Bernard Shaw*. Vol. 3, *1918–1950: The Lure of Fantasy*, London: Penguin Books.

——— 1993b (orig. 1992). *Bernard Shaw*. Vol. 4, *1950–1991: The Last Laugh*, London: Penguin Books.

La Fontaine, J.S. (ed.) 1972. *The Interpretation of Ritual*, London: Tavistock.

McEwen, I. 2001. *Atonement*, London: Jonathan Cape.

Macpherson, W. 1999. *The Stephen Lawrence Inquiry: Report of an Inquiry by Sir William Macpherson of Cluny*, London: The Stationery Office.

Mitchell, J. 1971. *Woman's Estate*, Harmondsworth: Penguin Books.

Peach, C. (ed.) 1996. *Ethnicity in the 1991 Census*: Vol. 2. *The Ethnic Minority Populations of Great Britain*, London: OPCS.

Pedersen, L. 1977. 'Shakespeare's The *Taming of the Shrew* vs. Shaw's *Pygmalion*: Male Chauvinism vs. Women's Lib?' in R. Weintraub (ed.), *Fabian Feminist: Bernard Shaw and Woman*, University Park and London: Pennsylvania University Press.

Pool, R. 1994. *Dialogue and the Interpretation of Illness: Conversations in a Cameroon Village*, Oxford and Providence: Berg.

Poynton, M. 1990. *Naked Authority: The Body in Western Painting: 1830–1908*, Cambridge: Cambridge University Press.

Radcliffe, P. (ed.) 1996. *Ethnicity in the 1991 Census*: Vol. 3. *Social Geography and Ethnicity in Britain: Geographical Spread, Spatial Concentration and Internal Migration*, London: Office for National Statistics.

Richards, A. 1982 (orig. 1956). *Chisungu: A Girl's Initiation Ceremony among the Bemba of Zambia* (2nd edn, with author's Preface and Introduction by J. La Fontaine), London and New York: Tavistock Publications.

Robin, J. 1980. *Elmdon: Continuity and Change in a North-West Essex Village 1861–1964* (with a Foreword by A. Richards), Cambridge: Cambridge University Press.

Shaw, G.B. 1932. *Doctors' Delusions, Crude Criminology, Sham Education*, London: Constable.

—— 1934. *Prefaces by Bernard Shaw*, London: Constable.

—— 1941 (orig. 1916). *Pygmalion*, Harmondsworth: Penguin Books.

—— 1944. Chap. 24, in *Everybody's Political What's What*, London: Constable, pp. 213–25.

—— 1946. *The Doctor's Dilemma*, Harmondsworth: Penguin Books.

—— 1949. *Sixteen Self Sketches by Bernard Shaw*, London: Constable.

—— 1950 (orig. 1932). *Doctors' Delusions*, London: Constable.

Shaw, G.B. and A.J. Lerner 1956. *My Fair Lady: A Musical Play Based on 'Pygmalion' by Bernard Shaw* (adapted and with lyrics by A.J. Lerner), London: Max Reinhard and Constable.

Strathern, M. 1981. *Kinship at the Core: An Anthropology of Elmdon, a Village in North-West Essex in the Nineteen-Sixties* (with a Foreword by A. Richards and Epilogue by F. Oxford, 'Elmdon in 1977'), Cambridge: Cambridge University Press.

Turner, E. and V. Turner 1978. *Image and Pilgrimage in Christian Culture: Anthropological Perspectives*, New York: Columbia University Press.

Weintraub, R. (ed.) 1977. *Fabian Feminist: Bernard Shaw and Woman*, University Park and London: Pennsylvania University Press.

Werbner, P. 2002. *Imagined Diasporas among Manchester Muslims*, Oxford and Santa Fe: James Currey and School of American Research Press.

White A. (ed.) 2002. *Social Focus in Brief: Ethnicity 2002*, London: Office for National Statistics.

Zeitlin, F. 1982. 'Cultic Models of the Female: Rites of Dionysus and Demeter', *American Classical Studies in Honor of J.-P. Vernant, Arethusa* 15 (1 and 2).

12

WHAT WOMEN REALLY WANT: GENDER, ETHNICITY, AND JOB EXPECTATIONS ON AN AUTOMOBILE FACTORY ASSEMBLY LINE

Fiona Moore

Traditionally, social studies of factories have focused on issues of discrimination, oppression, and resistance. The earliest studies in industrial anthropology, the Hawthorne research projects, examined the ways in which workers controlled the production process against the interests of management (Baba 1986). More recently, the work of Roberts et al., *Language and Discrimination* (1992) focused on ways in which English managers unconsciously exclude their non-English workers through the use of language and communication, and Westwood's (1984) *All Day, Every Day* analyses how women from a variety of ethnic origins gain empowerment against their male relatives and bosses through subversive practices. Much of this is influenced, directly or indirectly, by Edwin Ardener's work (1975a, b) on 'muted groups', which demonstrates ways in which non-dominant groups in society, particularly women, have to express themselves through the language of the dominant group and their concerns and interests are thereby 'muted'.

Studies of white-collar workers, however, have been increasingly focusing less on domination and submission and more on the ways in which different groups in the organisation act strategically according to their own interests (Czarniawska 1997; Abrams 2007). The focus of this chapter, a study of how managers perceive and workers experience gender, ethnicity, and labour on the assembly line at a U.K. automobile factory that forms part of a German manufacturing group, might thus reveal whether this sort of complex strategising also occurs in blue-collar settings and, if so, whether the concept of muted groups can be elaborated upon.

In 2002, I approached the manager of an Anglo-German automobile firm with a view to doing fieldwork in cross-cultural management relations. Although he was amenable to the idea, he had another issue in mind: the firm's management were concerned about the fact that the workforce was less than 10 per cent female, despite their reputation as a pro-affirmative-action company. Could I, as an anthropologist, explain to them how the corporation could improve in this area? With these research objectives in mind, I conducted participant-observation fieldwork, spending three months on the line in the Final Assembly Area, colloquially known as 'Assembly'. I worked as a temporary employee of the firm with their full knowledge and permission.[1]

This chapter is based on my participant observation and interviews with management. The first section sets the scene, describing the factory and its labour force, followed by an examination of the work goals of managers and workers and how muting takes place before analysing the nature of muting and how both groups maintain their self-esteem and autonomy, regardless of the process of muting.

People Making Cars: Factory History and Present Situation

The factory under study started life as a small domestic British car manufacturer in 1912 (Newbigging et al. 1998). Until the late 1960s, the plant remained under the same ownership and had become part of the culture of the local town, developing its own sports teams, volunteer fire brigades, bands, amateur dramatic societies, and social club. Children's events and open days were also organised, remembered with fondness by many local people (Newbigging et al. 1998; Bardsley and Laing 1999). Socially, the plant continues to be a focus for organised activity. Sports teams still exist, as do events at the factory's social club. During the period of my fieldwork, the social club hosted a blood drive and two tribute band evenings.

The historic presence of the plant on the site has given it an intimate association with local history and culture. Some of the employees currently working at the plant spoke of having parental and even grandparental connections with the factory. The original owners had actively recruited local farm workers and tradespeople to work in the plant (Ward et al. 1993). Schofield and Noble (1993) note that the advent of the automotive plant created a strong social division in the town between the white-collar workers employed in education and tourism, and the blue-collar workers, largely housed in the eastern part of the town and mostly employed at the automobile plant. This has continued for most of the century, regardless of the plant's changes in ownership and the gradual changes in the area's ethnic make-up (Shaw 1988). The business under study thus has a particularly strong relationship with local working-class identity.

In the mid-1990s, after nearly thirty years of financial difficulties and constantly changing ownership, the company was sold to a German multinational manufacturing group, which was the plant's owner at the time of the study (Scarbrough and Terry 1996). Today, the factory's culture is officially characterised by an emphasis on quality of work and product output, on the one hand, and flexibility of the car models being produced according to the individual orders of clients in a variety of styles on the other.

Less officially, the culture was characterised by a tension between this ideal and the realities of assembly-line work. Workers expressed frustration or resignation at not being able to work to the highest standards at the fast speed of the line, or pride at being able, despite everything, to keep up with the speed of the line. While nostalgia for earlier periods of ownership is present, it is not to an unexpected degree. Considering the recent nature of the change, there was less nostalgia than I anticipated. This is probably due to the attitude of many that the actual ownership and type of production are not an issue, so long as the factory itself remains in operation. The ownership and practices of the plant are less of an issue than whether or not it is open, functioning, and serving the community as a source of employment.

The staff of the Final Assembly Area are known as 'associates', a term meant to imply membership and partnership in the firm as opposed to a particular position in the hierarchical chain of command, but which, interestingly, also implies a degree of detachment from the firm as a whole. The associates fall into two categories: those with a permanent contract and those hired through a temporary labour agency. It is impossible to tell the difference between the two groups in terms of appearance or duties, and there are some temporary associates who have been working at the plant for longer than most contract associates. The difference is largely one of rights and benefits.

While no data were available on temporary employees, it is possible to gain some impression of the general ethnic and gender composition of Assembly from the statistics on contracted associates. At the time of fieldwork, the ethnic composition of contract employees in Assembly was slightly over two-thirds white, with the remaining third being approximately evenly divided between black/Afro-Caribbean and Asian associates (Table 12.1). The gender ratio is slightly over 90 per cent male. From observations, the gender mix of temporary associates was about the same as for permanent employees. There were more

Table 12.1: Ethnic and Gender Composition of the Plant Labour Force (2003)

Ethnic origin	Female	Male	Total
Asian	4	59	63
Black	6	54	60
Black Caribbean		3	3
Black other		1	1
No information available		8	8
Oriental		4	4
Other	1	21	22
White	52	725	777
White European	2	17	19
White other		1	1
White U.K.	5	133	138
TOTAL	70	1026	1096

Source: BMW U.K. Ltd., 2002

black than Asian temporary associates and, in particular, more black than Asian women. I saw several black women working on a daily basis, but no Asian women. A student intern mentioned that he saw one Asian woman in Assembly, but no others. For comparison purposes, it is worth noting that the 1987 gender ratios cited by McCarthy (1990: 55) give the workforce composition as being 93 per cent male. No ethnic statistics were cited, which is in and of itself significant, suggesting that such information has become more important to both social scientists and managers in the past fifteen years.

The statistics given in Table 12.1, however, go only a small way towards capturing the sheer diversity of the workforce. The single category 'black', for instance, covers black British, Jamaican, Haitian, North, South and East African, and many others. The other terms used are similarly inclusive. The workforce is thus ethnically diverse and male-dominated.

According to Ward et al. (1993), the pre-war workforce at the plant was largely white and male. However, between the 1950s and 1970s, more migrants from overseas came to the U.K., although access was initially blocked by both management and labour. By the 1960s non-white workers began to be employed, and by the mid-1960s they were an integrated part both of the workforce and of the unions. The present-day community is an ethnically diverse place, with large Asian and Afro-Caribbean communities, both of which are well represented in the Final Assembly Area (Shaw 1988; Schofield and Noble 1993). In addition, although little documentation exists, anecdotal evidence suggests that refugees and asylum-seekers from the detention centres recently established in the area, once their claims were formally approved, also became part of the workforce. Although ethnic diversity seems to be an accepted fact of life in Assembly, it has a turbulent history, characterised by conflict and prejudice.

Women have been employed at the factory from 1915 onwards and, although their numbers dropped sharply in the interwar period, have maintained a continuous presence ever since (Bardsley and Laing 1999). Although the bulk of women were in gendered jobs between the wars, they were also employed on the assembly lines, forming one-sixth of the total workforce in 1930 (Sweeney 1993). From 1938 to 1979, women were excluded from working on the lines except in the Body Plant. They were, however, active in trade unions and social activity during this time, both of which contributed to their gradual acceptance in other areas (Newbigging et al. 1998). Today, women form 7–10 per cent of the workforce in Assembly. On the weekday (alternating) shifts, virtually all seemed either to be young, childless women (18–30) or older women (45–65). These demographics are significant, as they suggest that women with pre-adolescent children are reluctant to work in the plant. There were also more women on the weekend shift and permanent night shift, which are the ones best fitted around childcare duties within the home. Like non-white associates, then, women may be an accepted feature of plant life today, but this position was not easily gained, and women in general seem to be having more difficulty than men of non-white origin in maintaining a strong presence within the workforce.

Finally, I could obtain no statistics on the gender and ethnic composition of the plant's management, although anecdotal evidence and observation suggested that the management were largely white Europeans, mostly English, with some Germans. The Germans were most in evidence in senior managerial positions. The gender ratio among office managers seemed more balanced but still overwhelmingly, perhaps 70 per cent, male. Most of them had some sort of formal qualification. There was also an unspoken tension between managers who had been with the plant since before the takeover and those who had joined subsequently.

The plant under study thus has a long history of engagement with the local community, a multi-ethnic workforce and an overwhelmingly male-dominated gender ratio, both of which have been the source of conflict between managers and workers over the years. We shall now consider how the managers viewed the present-day workforce with regard to their expectations of gender and ethnicity.

Taking It from the Top: Managers' Beliefs and Expectations

Although the managers I spoke to seemed genuinely concerned about the associates, frequently their beliefs and expectations regarding how gender and ethnicity affected the workforce were strongly at odds with the realities on the line, such that the diversity and gender make-up of the workforce were rendered invisible, muted discourses. This is revealed in an excerpt from my report to the Human Resources department:

> The first thing any visitor to the Final Assembly Area sees is a diorama depicting four mannequins grouped around a nearly-completed automobile: three are dressed as associates from the three shifts, and one as a visitor. All are White; the three associates are men and the visitor is a woman. On the opposite wall is a pair of charts depicting proper attire for associates and visitors; again, the cartoon figures are both White, the associate is male and the visitor is female. Recently, an article ran in the plant's newsletter, describing the diorama and urging all associates and managers to stop by and have a look at it. The message of this diorama is also, unintentionally, reinforced in other ways. Publicity photos, as well as the historical images of the plant on display in the visitor centre and at the entrance to the Final Assembly Area also depict only White male workers, in contrast to the actual historical realities. (described in Newbigging et al. 1998, Bardsley and Laing 1999)

Despite their portrayal in traditional anthropological literature as a force for domination, the managers with whom I spoke did not appear to view the workforce as a sort of hostile 'Other' (Baba 1998). Most seemed genuinely concerned about the state of the workforce, and expressed a desire to understand 'where the workforce are coming from'. The very fact that they were willing to permit me to conduct my study suggests that they are open to taking risks in order to identify their weaknesses in this area. I also heard of cases of managers going out of their way to try and help staff, as when one of the representatives of a temporary labour agency tried to find on-site jobs for associates who had been laid off from her section with other agencies who supplied the company. The temporary labour agencies had particularly close contact with the workforce. Barring the agency that staffed the Paint area, they all had an office on the shop floor.[2] They described their rapport with the staff as good, and the staff were generally positive about them. They felt comfortable coming into the agency office with concerns about pay or uniform supplies. When I left the organisation, the agency representative with whom I spoke asked friendly questions about where I was going and whether I would have enough money to live on in the meantime. The managers were thus sympathetic to the workforce, and did not consciously regard it as a source of conflict.

The ethnic diversity of the workforce, however, did not seem to register with my managerial interviewees. They would frequently slip into talking about 'the English worker' when discussing the peculiarities of the workforce. Although they acknowledged that the workforce was extremely diverse, they did not do so spontaneously. When asked directly, the responses tended to resemble this one given by a young English woman manager:

> We have very different people working here, across every level of the business. We have a lot of Indians, a lot of Asians, a lot of Afro-Caribbeans, more Kosovans and Albanians. ... And you see in our management style, in our management level we have females, not so many females, but we have females, we have Afro-Caribbean managers, we have English managers, we have German managers, there's a huge sort of diversity to work here, so I am very surprised we don't get more issues than we get, but I think it's that we know we have this diversity so we put the training in place first. (Female manager, late thirties, Human Resources department, interviewed 23 March 2003)

Some of the statements made here are problematic given that most training programmes for associates had been suspended in Assembly, and the programmes to which she refers are for managers alone. Nonetheless, the message is clear: as far as she knows, diversity causes no problems, therefore it is a non-issue. Most of the managers with whom I spoke, also, either directly or indirectly expressed the feeling that they felt 'closer to' the workforce than to their senior managerial colleagues. The managers I spoke to were all English (mostly white, with one being Asian, and another being an Asian trainee), and frequently expressed a sense of resentment and frustration against the mainly German senior management. The managers' vision of the workforce thus defines them as English and generally harmonious. Ethnic diversity, as it causes no visible and immediate problems for them, is not an issue.

Women, furthermore, were even less of a visible presence in managers' descriptions of the plant. Gender diversity was, again, seldom mentioned spontaneously by managers and, when they did speak of it, they tended to do so in terms of women being 'better' at certain jobs than men. One temporary labour agency representative said that she would like to hire more women because, first of all, they are 'better at detail work, [and] have better attention to quality', and, secondly, women come to assembly-line work with no expectations, whereas men tend to feel that they 'know cars' and therefore ignore their managers' instructions in favour of their own beliefs about the job. The particular task that I was given on the assembly line was described by my Team Coordinator (TC) as one that 'women do better than men', notwithstanding that male associates seemed more than capable of doing it and, indeed, I was taught the job by a man. The fact that about half the Human Resources (HR) specialists and managers appeared to be female whereas the bulk of the workforce was male was never discussed, but seemed to form part of this discourse of gender as occupational qualification. The realities of women's work on the line were thus obscured by a discourse regarding their 'suitability' for certain jobs as opposed to others.

In other areas, managers seemed to be generalising their own experiences of gender to the workforce rather than considering them as a distinct group. One HR manager, for instance, said that she felt that more women were coming to work at the plant because of government-led initiatives, their need for flexible working time and the introduction of a crèche, even though flexible working time provisions were rare and the crèche did not actually open early enough for assembly-line workers to put their children into it. There was no statistical proof that the number of women in the workforce was rising. Another manager tried to explain the lack of equal-opportunities cases as follows:

> I don't think we've ever had a major equal-opportunities grievance that we've had admitted to us ... you know everybody's treated fairly and consistently and nobody's judged because of their gender or anything. And there's flexible working for maternity, paternity and so on, and we've already had quite a few cases for part-time working which we're dealing with, and it looks like they can be accommodated, so I'm not aware of any major equal opportunities problems. ... I think it's mainly [be]cause we do a lot of training for the [Process Area] managers, so the managers are aware if they come to us straight away, they don't just ignore it or push it under the carpet or hope it'll go away. (Female manager, late thirties, HR department, interviewed 23 March 2003)

There is a strong discrepancy in this statement. The manager starts out by saying that she feels that people do not report grievances because they are treated fairly, and then turns this around stating that it is because workers are encouraged to come to managers with grievances. As with ethnic diversity, managers were aware that there were issues relating to gender on the Final Assembly line, and yet explained these away with reference to their own experiences.

This generalisation of managerial experience appeared to extend to other areas beyond gender and ethnicity. One manager spoke effusively about the quality and extent of training programmes, which surprised me in light of the above-mentioned suspension of most such programmes for associates. It later became apparent that she was thinking in terms of managerial education programmes rather than training in general. Another said that promotion opportunities were available to all. When I asked how associates would find out about them, she remarked that they were advertised in the plant newsletter and on a noticeboard in the main canteen. However, few associates read the former and almost none use the latter, preferring the small auxiliary canteen in the Assembly building. The spokespersons tended to assume that the same conditions applied throughout the plant, whereas the situation in other sections was quite different from Assembly in terms of training needs, culture, and staff composition. The managers were all on the plant's Intranet. They did not seem to register that the associates were not, preferring the use of mobile phones and text messaging. The managers' views of the associates' expectations were thus very much based on their own feelings about the work that was done in Assembly and their own experiences of working in the plant offices.

Managers' expectations about the workforce thus involved, unconsciously, the subsuming of associates' issues into managerial concerns. For the most part, gender and ethnicity were not discussed. When they were mentioned, managers tended to explain workers' behaviour according to their own personal experiences of gender and ethnicity in management. Furthermore, their views of ethnic identity were strongly coloured by their own experiences of dealing with the plant's new German senior management, and their views of gender reflected their beliefs about women and men's 'special abilities' on the line. Managers' concerns, and their particular interests, thus conspire to make women and ethnic minority associates into muted groups. However, the lack of a sense of conflict or strongly dominant/subaltern relationship between managers and workforce, as well as the introduction of measures by which associates can better communicate with managers, suggest that there may be more to it than a simple case of voices not being heard. We shall now consider how managers' expectations match up with the lived experience of gender and ethnicity on the line.

Little Women and Invisible Men: Gender and Ethnicity on the Line

Even before women join the workforce, they are unconsciously excluded from participating in its culture, by virtue of the fact that the local culture constructs jobs within the automobile industry as 'men's work', as illustrated in another excerpt from my report:

> When I spoke with colleagues about working on a final assembly line in an automobile plant, the general reaction was surprise that 'a little woman' would be capable of doing such a job. I am 5'4", of average height for a woman in the U.K., and physically active. This attitude was not limited to people in the academic community: one of the women with whom I took the Final Assembly aptitude test during the selection process (a test which concentrates on basic literacy, numeracy, reasoning processes and dexterity), whose previous jobs included twenty years at a printing plant, remarked to me upon seeing the other candidates: 'we don't stand a chance, with all those big strong men.'

A key reason why so few women apply for jobs at the plant was the belief that the only work available in automotive plants is hard, 'dirty' work unsuited for women. There was also a strong preconception that women working in the industry would be subject to harassment from male colleagues. However, the Final Assembly Area was a clean environment, a number of jobs exist which do not require brute strength and the behaviour of male associates is generally courteous.[3] These preconceptions meant that many women did not consider applying, let alone accepting a job on the line. They consequently seem not to realise that they would be capable of doing assembly-line work, and recruiters do not always encourage them to think in this direction.

I had registered with the temporary labour agency responsible for staffing Assembly some time before this project started, but I was never asked whether I would consider doing manual or unskilled labour. This attitude is in fact abetted by the invisibility of women in the company's publicity material (such as the diorama described above), in which women are cast as visitors rather than associates. Ethnic minority men, although they did not face the same social exclusion as women, were also not represented in recruitment-related publicity, and were seemingly recruited mainly because they formed a significant percentage of the working-class population of the town. From the point of view of recruitment, women and ethnic minorities were largely 'invisible'.

On the line itself, gender was also largely obscured in social interaction. Initially, women, particularly younger ones, can expect a 'checking-out period', during which their age and availability are enquired about, more or less discreetly, by male associates. After a couple of weeks, however, women are recategorised as 'colleagues'. Although women still experience prurient talk after this point, the same is true of men with mock accusations of homosexuality and sexual infidelity being common between men on the line. Men would talk about desiring 'pretty girls' in front of female colleagues, and then seem surprised when reminded that their colleague was herself a 'girl'. Women on the line were thus recategorised into a sort of third category, 'women workers', as distinct from 'girls' and 'the missus', the male worker's wife or partner, who are seen as more conventionally female.

Gender-related problems, furthermore, were not subject to discussion. Although women were often patronised by male colleagues in a way that men were not and male trainers seemed happier to be training male colleagues than female ones, gender differentiation was never discussed or even alluded to in jest. Of equal concern is the fact that, as with non-white associates, women were less visible in positions of authority on the assembly line. Ten out of 104 TCs were female and there were no female Process Area Managers (PAMs), although one might realistically expect three or four given that women form 7–10 per cent of the workforce.

Women's difficulties in combining childcare and family responsibilities with work were seldom discussed, despite the fact that childcare issues feature strongly in historical accounts of women's presence in automobile factories (Sweeney 1993; Turetskaia 2003). Studies by Romano (1994), Sousa-Poza (2000) and

Kellaway (2002) indicate that women have different job priorities from men – tending to value the quality of life and relationships over salaries, which would suggest that women who have problems on the line or who feel demoralised by the impersonal nature of line work might be more inclined to leave.[4] Although women face exclusions and behaviour that men do not, this is rarely aired, on the line or in private conversation.

A similar situation existed in the case of ethnic minorities. While working teams are multi-ethnic, friendships seem to form most often along ethnic lines. If a group of associates were sitting together in the canteen, the group would usually either be mono-ethnic or dominated by a single ethnic group. The teams were therefore cross-cut by lines of socialisation that frequently formed along ethnic lines. Despite this, ethnicity was not a topic of discussion on the assembly line. The conversation resolutely centred on universal concerns and pastimes that cross ethnic divides, notably football, hip-hop music, and sex for male workers and hip-hop, sex, and family for female workers. On the occasions when I initiated conversations about ethnicity, I generally received non-committal answers or changes of subject. While this does seem to be a way of informally avoiding the possibility of ethnic division, this is not always the case in multi-ethnic workplaces. My earlier work in City of London banks suggests that there was considerable discussion and bonding over the subject of ethnicity (Moore 1999, 2002). Like women workers, non-white workers also faced similar exclusion from authority. There were no Asian PAMs and only two black PAMs out of a total of forty-one. TCs numbered 104, of which there were only two Asians and one black. Thus, while ethnic distinctions were tacitly recognised, they were not openly discussed or problematised.

Another unspoken issue was differences in attitude towards gender and gender roles between different ethnic groups. As mentioned above, Asian women appeared to be relatively scarce. An Asian male associate of Indian origin whom I asked about this said that he found that within his own family and circle of acquaintances, there was a greater rigidity about gender roles and work than he found among white or black acquaintances. Similarly, men from certain groups seemed to have more difficulty accepting female authority figures than others, which might present problems for a woman in a position of authority over a multi-ethnic team. Also, where, to some ethnic groups, it may be simply a sign of friendship or appreciation to engage in prurient banter with a member of the opposite sex, among others it might be taken as inappropriate, harassment, or an invitation. The impact of ethnicity on gender and the presence of gender discrimination were thus visible but never actually discussed.

It would be easy to attribute this exclusion entirely to the fact that, as noted above, women and ethnic minorities are very much muted groups within the plant. While, for instance, the managers focused strongly on the Germanness of the top management, for many line workers, the issue never came up. To them, a manager was a manager, and as long as the factory was operating the subject only arose when, for instance, attempting to decode a label on an auto part. Although managers were correct in assuming that childcare was a major concern for women on the line, they seemed unaware of the fact that most of the women with children tended to be those whose children were teenagers or grown, and thus it was likely that it was not so much that the factory's childcare provisions were adequate but rather that they were so inadequate that women with childcare responsibilities tended to avoid the factory when looking for work.

The enormous gap between managers' beliefs about gender and ethnicity and the ways in which these were experienced on the shop floor suggests that there is more at issue. Although the managers' attitude to women and minorities does cause their exclusion to some extent, this does not seem to be the full story. The workers on the line did not adopt managerial discourse or priorities while on the line, and consequently cannot have been muted in quite the same way described by earlier studies.

Women and minorities were themselves excluding managers, and indeed male and/or white associates, from their own experiences on the line. Although associates were aware that managers often said that workers should come to see them if they had problems, they rarely did so. Rather than trying to discuss and deal with their problems or personality conflicts at work, most associates either accepted them as part of the job or else quit and looked for work elsewhere. One woman worker, speaking of her fraught relationship with a co-worker, said, 'Eventually you learn to just let it wash over you.'

Staff were angry about the lack of formal training on the line, however, rather than officially confronting the issue by going to their managers, they resorted to more subversive and internal measures, such as informing new associates about 'the way it used to be' on the line, followed by assertions that the change is because the 'managers don't care about us'. In this way new associates were directly warned against going to see the manager. Some felt strongly that the two days officially given to train new associates on the job should be extended but this had not been suggested to management as indicated by one temporary associate: 'They only give you two official days of training – that's a joke. Nobody can learn one of these jobs in two days. They have no idea what it's like down here' (male temporary associate, mid-fifties, 9 May 2003).

The plant's newsletter was read by workers and managers but, where managers tended to read it as a source of information and with an eye on career advancement, the associates read it as a source of entertainment, commenting derisively on overly positive news items and gaining a sense of superiority over management by making fun of the articles. Associates are thus aware of the gap between themselves and the managers. Furthermore, they themselves contribute consciously to this gap, by practising various informal measures to keep managers from becoming more familiar with the real experiences of line workers.

At first glance, this behaviour may be seen as running counter to workers' interests, but there were good reasons why the workers acted in this way. The culture of the assembly line was heavily focused on personal contact, with people doing favours for each other and being expected to use their own personal resources of goods and information to exchange with each other. Managers tend to be treated as resources. Managers known to be helpful to staff were spoken of behind their backs as 'all right', whereas new workers were warned off speaking to less friendly managers. Interestingly, there seemed to be a broad rule that the less time a manager spent on the shop floor or the less directly involved with assembly-line work, the more likely they were to be considered 'all right'. The unspoken conclusion was that the less familiar a manager is with shop-floor culture, the easier it is to obtain resources and favours through them.

This can be seen in the ways in which the workers used the formal channels of communication with the managers. For instance, the plant conducted weekly team meetings during which workers were encouraged to air issues. Managers were not allowed to attend unless actively invited. This provided workers with a 'safe space' in which to raise grievances and decide collectively on a course of action. However, it resulted in managers not being privy to the reasoning behind the decisions that the workers took in these meetings. One manager described how grievances were handled:

> The point is that you must talk to the [Process Area] manager first and if it doesn't get a resolution they can come to see us or the trade union representatives. Usually they favour the trade union representative. Usually they are people we've recruited and they know us so we talk to their manager and sort it out. When we hear from trade union reps it is usually [be]cause someone can't be released from the track, so they call for the rep, who comes to me. (Male manager, thirty-five, HR department, 8 April 2003)

There are two significant points in this statement. The first is the use of personal contacts by staff. The people whom he sees are people whom he has recruited and who 'know' him. Secondly, the fact that the workers often approach the trade union representative, who is an ordinary line worker and therefore part of the system of favours and networking, rather than approaching a manager in times of trouble is significant. By using an intermediary, the manager is kept off the line. As it is not that difficult for a worker to find a way of seeing a manager if they want to, the reference to workers who 'can't be released from the track' is either a rationalisation for staff behaviour or an excuse commonly presented for using an intermediary. The workers thus encouraged lack of communication with managers, in order to safeguard their ability to ask for 'favours' and conduct their own affairs autonomously as they see fit.

> The feeling I get, and I tend to walk around there [the Final Assembly Area] a fair bit, is the feeling that they have nothing in common, even with their PAMs – when decisions are made, there is little communication from the top, aside from newsletters, they get no information about new products, or how they contribute. If they are told there's a change, they aren't told the reasons why. ... Maybe it's the nature of the job, but if there's no communication there's little understanding. (Male manager, thirty-five, HR department, 8 April 2003)

Women collaborate in the erasure of their gender in a similar manner. Conversation on the line tends to stick to neutral topics: house music or more general issues of child-rearing and relationship maintenance. Various women advised me to 'not mind' prurient talk by men. They also talked about how they liked to dress up and wear make-up after work but that there was 'no point' in doing so at the factory. One woman, about to go on a week's leave, remarked that the first thing she was going to do was get a manicure. I discovered personally that, if I wore a new hairstyle or a coloured lip gloss on the line, this would evoke comment from male workers. Femininity was thus seen as something to exclude from line work, part of one's 'after work' life. Similarly, as noted above, mono-ethnic friendship networks tended to form during leisure activities or after work.[5] Although co-ethnic friends would sometimes meet on the line, they would generally part in embarrassment if a colleague from another ethnic group tried to join the conversation. In order to achieve success in a mostly male and mostly white environment, then, women and minorities actively participate in their 'reclassification' as non-gendered, non-ethnic beings, at the cost of having their particular concerns and needs unacknowledged.

In summary, although the managers may attribute motives to the workers that are in line with their personal beliefs and expectations, and which consequently bear little resemblance to the workers' own experiences, the workers themselves also shut out the managers in turn, attributing to them different motivations in line with their own activities. The realities of women and ethnic minorities' experiences at the plant demonstrated broadly that, although they were a group that was muted by both male colleagues and managers of both genders, the muted groups also, in their turn, acted to shut the dominant groups out. In terms of recruitment, interaction between men and women and the role of managers on the line, we see a pattern of exclusion on the part of the workforce as well as the managers. In the next section, we turn to why this is the case and how different group strategies in the factory intersect with each other.

Self-Fulfilment and Non-intersecting Lines of Communication

What clearly emerges from comparing and contrasting the managers' and workers' views and experiences of gender and ethnicity on the line is that there is a well-established informal process of mutual exclusion between the two groups that counteracts the effectiveness of official lines of communication. The reasons for this can be seen when one considers the different world views and strategies of each and the points of conflict between them.

Although it is tempting to identify managers and workers as a dominant group and a muted group, respectively, this is not entirely the case. Through their jokes and topics of discussion, workers demonstrate that they are familiar with management jargon but they choose not to express themselves in the language of the dominant group or have recourse to formal channels for worker redress. The workers are neither victims nor oppressed. The job market at the time of the study was favourable, and those who did not like the system felt free to leave. Most were well aware of their rights, and threats to call in the union representative were invariably made if the associates felt that their rights were being infringed. Few, if any, had any illusions about the plant before joining, and there were a number of informal means of expressing resistance, e.g., through anonymous leaflets. The workers are thus fluent in a number of different modes of speech, including both the managers' and those of the local area, and are acting with their rights and opportunities in mind.

The main difference seems to lie in the fact that managers and associates are seeking different rewards from the factory. Managers tend to regard their jobs as a career, if not for life then for the immediate future, whereas associates view their jobs, for the most part, as a means to an end: a way of obtaining money and informal social resources. These attitudinal differences translate into different approaches to problem-solving and communication. If a manager is unhappy with some aspect of their job, they will try and work out a solution, talk to the people concerned and to their superiors, and generally arrange things so that they can stay in the job and be satisfied. In contrast, an associate is more likely to give in their notice to quit work because, in their view, it is less effort to find another job at a similar rate of pay than to try and resolve the problem.

Managers (including TCs and PAMs), when asked why they had chosen to work at the plant, cited 'pride in the company and the product' above anything else. Associates, on the other hand, cited the high wages and short working week, followed by the working atmosphere. For them, the product they produced was less a source of pride and more a source of humour or frustration related to the assembly line. 'Quality' was a word one heard frequently from managers, but less so from associates. It was not that they did a poor job, but that meeting quality standards was not a matter of pride but rather a necessary part of the job.

Finally, managers were much more concerned about the impact of the takeover than the workers, for whom the new management was largely a non-issue so long as they did not do anything that conflicted with their own interests. One manager, for instance, talking about an earlier set of owners, complained that there was less communication with the management, no meetings, and no HR offices on the shop floor, ending by saying that at least the current owners encouraged communication. Associates place little value on formal lines of communication, rejecting managers' attempts to communicate, not out of malice or conflict, but because they do not want managers having too much control over their activities, particularly with regard to informal networking. Managers interpret associates' actions according to their own standards in order to reinforce their own situation vis-à-vis the new German top management.

Workers, however, talked about how they were more relaxed under the previous regime and that they could 'have a laugh' and relax. As the management of that time were presumably not aware of this, there has thus been a long tradition of excluding the managers, which the newer managers, even the English ones, since the takeover are unfamiliar with. Workers' priorities thus include informal activities, from which they therefore have an interest in excluding managers. Managers, similarly, stand to gain more by not officially knowing about breaches of practice and tolerating these in order to keep the workforce happy than they do by engaging with the workforce directly.

The relationship between the management and the workers was thus not one of direct oppression of one group by another or of a more subtle process of muting. Rather, this exclusion stems, not simply from a desire to maintain power or dominance in a particular area, but from a variety of opportunities, strategies and expectations from the organisation, which differ in fundamental ways depending on one's group.

Conclusion

Through my analysis of the gender composition and interaction of this particular factory, probing the relevance of the concept of muting has helped to shed new light on aspects of group inclusion and exclusion. The gulf between managers and workers in the plant in terms of their expectations and experiences of gender on the line is not a simple case of one group excluding another. Rather, it is a complex, dialogic two-way process between the groups. Their opportunities, strategies, and social networks centre on what each group expects from the organisation. The process of muting a group is thus one in which the group itself can and, in this case, does participate willingly, if it is in accordance with their strategies for success in the working environment. While managers' beliefs and expectations about women and ethnic minorities in the Final Assembly Area cause them to become muted groups, in effect, women and ethnic minorities themselves collaborate in this process of muting, in order to further their own strategies for achieving particular goals and individual work fulfilment.

Notes

1. In addition to participant observation I conducted interviews with thirteen staff members, Team Coordinators (TCs) in charge of groups of ten to twenty workers, and Process Area Managers (PAMs) overseeing groups of forty to one hundred workers and the TCs. Two tours were also taken of the full plant as an outsider. Most formal interviews were recorded, although, in a few cases in which the interviewee was not comfortable with the presence of a tape recorder, shorthand notes were taken instead. In some cases, follow-up interviews were conducted, normally over the telephone. Informal, unrecorded discussions were held with workers on the line during the period of fieldwork. The firm provided me with the statistics used in this article. A Nuffield Foundation Small Grant partially funded this study.
2. The Paint area required protective clothing, and consequently the temporary labour agency chose to make frequent visits rather than have a constant presence.
3. More so than is said to be traditional for British automobile plants (see Sweeney 1993).
4. In the words of one interviewee, 'You don't hear from your manager unless there's a problem.'

5. Interestingly, I learned the most about other associates' experiences of ethnicity in afterwork conversations.

References

Abrams, S., 2007. 'Loyalty and Politics: The Discourses of Liberalisation', in S. Ardener and F. Moore (eds), *Professional Identities: Policy and Practice in Business Bureaucracy*, New York and Oxford: Berghahn Books.

Ardener, E. 1975a. 'Belief and the Problem of Women', in S. Ardener (ed.), *Perceiving Women*, London: Malaby Press, pp. 1–18.

——— 1975b. 'The "Problem" Revisited', in S. Ardener (ed.), *Perceiving Women*, London: Malaby Press, pp. 19–27.

Baba, M.L. 1986. *Business and Industrial Anthropology: An Overview*, Washington: NAPA (NAPA Bulletin no. 2).

——— 1998. 'Anthropology of Work in the Fortune 1000: A Critical Retrospective', *Anthropology of Work Review* 18 (4), pp. 17–28.

Bardsley, G. and S. Laing 1999. *Making Cars at Cowley: From Morris to Rover*, Stroud: British Motor Industry Heritage Trust.

Czarniawska, B. 1997. *Narrating the Organization: Dramas of Institutional Identity*, London: University of Chicago Press.

Kellaway, L. 2002. 'It's Better to be a Woman: Contrary to Common Assumptions, Men are More Likely to be Unhappy with their Jobs', *Financial Times*, 10 March, p. 10.

McCarthy, Lord, of Headington 1990. *The Future of Cowley: Report of the Independent Inquiry into the Rover Cowley Works Closure Proposals*, Oxford: Oxford City Council.

Moore, F. 1999. 'Ethnicity, Transnationalism and the Workplace: Expressions of Identity among German Business Expatriates', unpublished M.Phil. thesis, Institute of Social and Cultural Anthropology, University of Oxford.

——— 2002. 'Global Elites and Local People: Images of Germanness and Cosmopolitanism in the Self-Presentation of German Transnational Businesspeople in London', unpublished D.Phil. thesis, Institute of Social and Cultural Anthropology, University of Oxford.

Newbigging, C., S. Shatford and T. Williams 1998. *The Changing Faces of Cowley Works*, Witney: Robert Boyd Publications.

Roberts, C., E. Davies and T. Jupp 1992. *Language and Discrimination: A Study of Communication in Multi-Ethnic Workplaces*, Harlow: Longman.

Romano, C. 1994. 'It Looks Like Men are from Mars, Women are from Venus', *Management Review* 83 (10), p. 7.

Scarbrough, H. and M. Terry 1996. *Industrial Relations and the Reorganization of Production in the U.K. Motor Vehicle Industry: A Study of the Rover Group*, Coventry: University of Warwick (Warwick Papers in Industrial Relations no. 58).

Schofield, A. and M. Noble 1993. 'Communities and Corporations: Rethinking the Connections', in T. Hayter and D. Harvey (eds), *The Factory and the City: The Story of the Cowley Automobile Workers in Oxford*, London: Mansell, pp. 256–74.

Shaw, A. 1988. *A Pakistani Community in Britain*, Oxford: Blackwell.

Sousa-Poza, A. 2000. 'Taking Another Look at the Gender/Job-Satisfaction Paradox', *Kyklos* 53 (2), pp. 135–53.

Sweeney, A.-M. 1993. 'Women Making Cars, Making Trouble, Making History', in T. Hayter and D. Harvey (eds), *The Factory and the City: The Story of the Cowley Automobile Workers in Oxford*, London: Mansell, pp. 116–39.

Turetskaia, G.V. 2003. 'The Family and Women's Business Activities', *Sociological Research* 42 (3), pp. 53–66.

Ward, S., O. Stuart and E. Swingedouw 1993. 'Cowley in the Oxford Economy', in T. Hayter and D. Harvey (eds), *The Factory and the City: The Story of the Cowley Automobile Workers in Oxford*, London: Mansell, pp. 67–92.

Westwood, S. 1984. *All Day, Every Day: Factory and the Family in the Making of Women's Lives*, London: Pluto Press.

13

CAN YOU CALL THIS FIELDWORK? SEPTEMBER IN VENICE

Lidia D. Sciama

Reflexive anthropology, anthropology 'at home' or 'half-way home', and the recognition of the researcher's as well as her informants' subjectivity have dominated much of anthropology since the 1970s. All are intimately bound with feminist critiques of ethnographic approaches and have been guiding principles in research conducted within the framework of Oxford's Centre for Cross-Cultural Research on Women (E. Ardener 1975; S. Ardener 1975; Ardener and Burman 1995). To reach a closer understanding of women's lives, it proved essential to focus on the contacts and active interactions of women in the societies we studied. Indeed, one of the questions we posed in several of the seminar meetings that eventually led to the creation of the Centre was to what extent women were in control of their own social relations. Did women in different societies create and maintain networks of exchange, information, friendship and business? To what extent were they free from the constraints posed by kinship and patriarchal control? As with other aspects of women's lives, these issues, we felt, had been left unexplored by earlier observers.

Reflection, subjectivity, and women's agency in the creation of social networks will accordingly be the topics discussed in this essay. And, given that 'revisiting' inevitably demands introspection and inclusion of the personal, I shall write, in the first person, of the different phases of my fieldwork from its beginning to the present (Haraway 1988: 583; Okely and Callaway 1992). Because of the complex interweaving of present and past, changing perspectives, and accounts of fieldwork in different locations, each an example of the diverse interplay of the local and the global, my argument proceeds along two separate lines: one begins in a northern lagoon island, Burano, and relates to my early work in the 1980s and the other is Venice's historic centre with its international arts and musical festivals in 2003. As George Marcus writes, the result of such double-sited research, conducted 'in the conditions of postmodernity', may be a 'messy text', a 'collage', 'open and incomplete' (Marcus 1998: 187–89; Hannerz 1980: 174–78; Hannerz 1987, quoted in Marcus 1998: 51). However, a focus on network relations shows that the two lines touch and intersect. Indeed, they have long been woven together, and in recent years they have increasingly converged (Sciama 2003).

The Fieldwork

My title, 'Can You Call This Fieldwork? September in Venice', echoes remarks by some of my colleagues who, used to associating fieldwork with the hardships of life in a tropical jungle or on a Pacific island, viewed my research in Italy as a protracted holiday. Others, knowing that I was born and raised in Venice, asked me whether mine was 'anthropology at home'.[1] But it is also a question I asked myself during my recent visit to Venice in September 2003, when I tried to make anthropological sense of my life there in ways I shall describe in the second part of this chapter.

As I had spent most of that academic year in Oxford, writing about Venice and its peripheral islands, I had had ample opportunity to reflect and to critically rework much I had learnt and written about during years of fieldwork. It is therefore no surprise that, when I was there on a visit in the autumn, I should have liked to begin working in a different area. But, as I started concentrating on new 'realities' (in Edwin Ardener's definition (1975: 4), 'a term of art for what fieldwork reveals'), I came to the conclusion that my observations took on greater significance when seen against the background of the past and with the benefit of past experience.

Eventually, an invitation to contribute to an International Gender Studies Centre (IGS) seminar series on 'Fieldwork and Field Notes Revisited: The Local in a Globalised World'[2] forced me to look again at my notebooks, although I had already celebrated the fact that I would never need to do so, once my ethnography was completed. So there I was in Venice again, trying to formulate a new project, but could I leave Burano, my main fieldwork location, altogether, distance myself, and bring that part of my professional life to a closure?

To go back to the beginning, my decision to do my research in insular Venice was due to a number of different reasons, some to do with anthropological discourses, others with Venetian life, and others still with my personal circumstances and with reflections on Cambridge academia I discussed in 'The Problem of Privacy in Mediterranean Anthropology' (1981: 90–91, 105–110) and 'Ambivalence and Dedication: Academic Wives in Cambridge University' (1984). At that stage my programme was by no means well defined. However, the direction of my research was inevitably guided by earlier anthropological studies. In particular, writings on Mediterranean Europe had opened problems and perspectives I had never encountered in my earlier days as a student of literature. I was intrigued with what then seemed to me a peculiarly English and American fascination with southern European mores – especially sexual mores, gender divisions, and notions of honour.

At the same time, a critique of 1950s and 1960s ethnographies, as lacking historical depth and describing the communities studied (mostly villages) as isolates with little contact with the wider societies and nations of which they were part, encouraged me to proceed with a study of the city as a whole (Crump 1975; Davis 1977). My research would therefore develop on two levels: to examine the nature of morality and the force of gender divisions, I would conduct intensive fieldwork in one of Venice's neighbourhoods, while at the same time I would examine the life of the city, especially in its political and cultural aspects.

However, my choice of fieldwork location can also be described as 'event-centred', given that my focus on Venetian life was due partly to events and contingencies that had taken place since the late 1960s (Frankenberg 1966: 142–48). For Venice, the critical event was a dangerously high and invasive tide in 1966, which led to widespread concern over its future. In the context of the social protest and political unrest of the late 1960s, Venice had become a foremost example of environmental damage, industrial pollution, and social inequalities. Concern over its art treasures and its architectural fabric had led to the creation of local as well as international committees and networks of people dedicated to its rescue and its restoration. The 'problem of Venice' was often referred to in debates on global dilemmas such as the contrast between conservation and development; aesthetic and historical values as against aggressive economic enterprise; globalisation versus local values; and, not least, the city's identity.

Initially, my plan was to analyse the ways in which such debates concerning the city's future entered local politics, at that time strongly polarised between a materialistic and development-oriented right wing and a divided left. Local politicians were concerned about decaying housing and the rising costs of restoration, which caused a large-scale exodus of the working population towards inland areas, where they could settle in less expensive and more comfortable homes. The city council was committed to a programme of urban renewal, but Venice's complex architectural structure made planning difficult and inefficient.

In contrast, housing on the island of Burano, while in desperate need of renewal, presented few technical problems. My first approach to fieldwork, therefore, was an attempt to identify the islanders' priorities and examine their uses both of domestic and of public spaces. Above all, I hoped to understand their arguments for moving to the hinterland, as against staying in Burano, given that at that time many of them contrasted life on the island with their own, somewhat nightmarish, 'lonely crowd' visions of a more physically constricting and socially alienating existence in the dry hinterland. One of my informants explained, 'I do not want to become a number in some unfriendly, cold and dangerous city.' Another recalled that, when he once decided to take up a salaried job in a factory in Marghera, he soon found that his breathing was badly affected, 'I was choking from morning till night; I just had to go back to the open air, back to lagoon fishing, however poor that might leave me!'

As I see from many a dialogue I reported in my notebooks, for Burano's people discussions of housing always involved full accounts of family and neighbourly relations, as well as encounters with Venetian officialdom and affirmations of a separate and idiosyncratic island identity. My initial interest in restoration of the island's built environment thus led me naturally to a full anthropological study. I therefore continued to work mostly in Burano, which is in fact part of the Venetian municipality, but in the 1980s was still a small, compact area, as yet little disturbed by mass tourism. My gender and age were significant, as pleas for new homes (by people who naively credited me with influence and power) were often closed with 'You understand, you are a woman.' Indeed, because Buranelli were well aware that life in a new environment – and one so radically different from that of their island village in the lagoon – would affect men and women in different ways, I hoped to establish to what extent outlooks and reasons given for or against moving varied according to gender.

For example, given that most of Burano's cottages are directly off the street and kitchens are on the ground floors, women's interactions with neighbours are usually active and cordial. A young woman who was under some pressure from her husband to move to Mestre feared that life in some anonymous apartment block would amount to 'solitary confinement', while others gave greater weight to the fact that on dry land, their kitchens and living rooms would not be invaded by tidal water. Some men associated life on dry land with modernity; for example, they considered that possession and use of a car would enhance their masculinity and independence. Others thought they could not live away from their fishing, their mates and their piazza. Discourses about life in or away from the island thus did not appear to be consistent with gender divisions.

Arriving in Burano at the height of a housing crisis, I suffered from the very problem I was trying to research: there was no way I could rent any form of lodging. There were a few empty cottages, but people were reluctant to let anyone live in them, because laws adverse to landlords made it very difficult to regain possession. Buranelli felt that their island was crowded and did not wish for any new people to settle there. They nonetheless valued relationships with Venetians, especially with professionals, like doctors or lawyers, on whom they might at some time have to rely (Boissevain 1974). And, while at that time the profession of 'anthropologist' was not a familiar notion, I was variously assigned to different categories, such as 'teacher', 'researcher', 'linguist', 'historian', or 'social worker'.

Eventually a home was found for me, thanks to a Venetian friend, a woman doctor who often worked in Burano and who encouraged one of her patients to let me have a room in her house. Indeed, the doctor and her patient, Marisa, were the first links in a chain of relationships that, in some ways, conditioned my subsequent choices and the direction of my work. In time, I learnt that connections between the two women were long-standing and complex: they were part of an enduring network rooted in a nineteenth-century relation of labour and dependence: the family with whom I lodged were originally from the agricultural area of Tre Porti, where the parents of my landlady's husband had been the tenant farmers on lands owned by the parents and grandparents of the doctor's husband.

By the late 1960s, the landlords, who had entered different professions, sold most of the land to their farmers, but they retained their farmhouses as weekend retreats and they generally continued in their friendly relations and exchanges of hospitality with the neighbouring landowning families. Their interactions with their erstwhile *mezzadri* are now cordial and free from the exacting and authoritarian excesses that characterised those of their parents and grandparents, but they still bear shades and overtones of patronage – a type of relationship that I tried as best I could to see that it should never enter my dealings with my hosts in Burano, Toni, Marisa, and their family. But my determination was put to the test when friends of the doctor who had introduced me to Marisa invited us all to join a Sunday lunch party in Marisa's village. As we arrived, I found that two tables had been laid, one, for the former *contadini*, was near the kitchen door, another, under a leafy grapevine, further removed from the house, was clearly for the landlord and his family, myself, and our Venetian friends. Although it was the latter that had introduced me to our hosts, I stubbornly stuck with my fieldwork family, and only later, as they wandered off to visit other acquaintances, did I take coffee with their past employers and their friends. On the way back, ever alert and observant, Marisa remarked, 'There they are, all ardent communists and socialists, but they would never dream of eating with us!'

In Burano, Marisa, who had soon grown very interested in my work, was incredibly generous in introducing me to people she thought would be helpful. Only now, reflecting upon aspects of my work I have left unexplored in earlier publications, do I fully realise how, in the early stages of fieldwork, I was just following her around, writing my notes, and trying to make sense of social relations, outlooks, and kinship patterns. Eventually I developed my own contacts and formed new relationships – not without some resistance on the part of Marisa, who would have preferred for me to find informants among her trusted friends and acquaintances. As a respected and responsible member of Burano's society, she was part of a well-established network of people, whom she regarded as fundamental to the maintenance of moral values and norms and, indeed, critical in bringing about inclusions or exclusions and thus determining prestige in her community.

Over the years, Marisa has become a firm friend and her house moves and family vicissitudes are central to my interests: her original area, Tre Porti, has become part of my fieldwork and it has proved an important testing ground for Buranelli's affirmations of their unique and different character, especially their sharp distinction between themselves as an 'urban' community and the people of Tre Porti or St Erasmo, whom they viewed as unsophisticated 'peasants'. By the same token, awareness of not being a native of Burano had made Marisa an acute, if sometimes very critical, observer. Her family history, to which I have briefly referred above, and which I learnt in much greater depth and detail through time in my different visits, is a good illustration of radical changes that have occurred throughout the Venetian countryside during the last four or five generations. Both Marisa and her husband were born in the 1930s and spent their early years in extended three-generation peasant households. Both have painful memories of unrelenting and unrewarding agricultural labour. They moved to Burano soon after their marriage, in the 1950s, when extended families were generally breaking up, since many people fought against patriarchal authority and preferred to live neolocally.

Revisiting my Field Notes

I have in my study three filing cabinets full of notebooks in different shapes and sizes – some of them bought from Burano's tobacconist when my supply was finished. I have not looked at them for some time, except occasionally, mainly to jog my memory or to recover statistical data I had industriously collected. In writing my thesis and then my book, the main themes and topics had taken on fairly clear outlines, as had uncertainties and unresolved problems. Therefore, I relied mainly on my 'headnotes' (Jackson 1990: 3; Ottenberg 1990: 144–6; Sanjek 1990, *passim*), but my reluctance to turn back to my untidy and over-detailed notes was also due to a fear of starting on a tidying-up operation that might become far too absorbing. The notebooks are intensely disordered; some have been lost or discarded, but I still have too many cluttering up my workroom – and my plan to reread and then throw them away is usually superseded by some apparently more innovative and tempting activity.

For some of the notes I have also neater second versions but these are by no means exact replicas, because they have obviously undergone some attempts at selection and classification. Now, browsing into a few of my original notebooks I have taken out at random, I see that some are undated, others, written in pencil, are beginning to fade, and fieldwork notes are mixed with personal scribblings. Yet they contain far more, and more varied, material than I could possibly have included in my publications.[3] Notes on regattas include detailed accounts of networks and solidarities based on rowing-club membership, while reports of discussions of nakedness, teenage pregnancy, and property rights, are interrupted with analyses of notions of honour in the early works of Dante, notes from a colleague's seminar paper on Indian mythology, and another on Hong Kong's merchant bankers, which obviously mark one of my visits back to Oxford. These are followed by informants' gossip and remarks about suspicions of father/daughter incest, witchcraft beliefs, and fear of the dead, as well as accounts of feuds and relationships with affines. There is, in other words, an attempt at reporting in real time information pouring in at an unmanageable rate.

The writing is spontaneous and each topic is vividly illustrated with case histories, exemplary tales, proverbs, and fascinating words and expressions in dialect. There are full reports of conversations between informants, with myself just listening or putting in a few words to justify my presence, introduce a new subject, or moderate some difference that was turning too lively – indeed, the stuff that might satisfy some postmodernist anthropologists' pleas for dialogic ethnographies (Clifford 1983: 132 and *passim*; Rabinow 1986: 244). It was, however, a mode of writing already long practised by feminist ethnographers, as we find, for example, in Judith Okely's riveting reports of conversations with Gypsy women (1975: 55–82; and see Caplan 1988: 8–12; Callaway 1992: 44).[4]

Venice, September 2003: The Local, the Global, and the Hybrid

September in Venice is one of the favourite months for the most discriminating and sophisticated travellers and holidaymakers. The school holidays have come to an end and so has the general shutdown of offices and university libraries, which usually lasts for a large part of August. The stifling heat has ended but the days are still warm, sunny, and luminous. In Venice, September is crowded with cultural events, commemorations, literary prizes, concerts, debates, and international conferences. Some Venetians regard all of that with a degree of irony and detachment, but they nonetheless participate, comment, and reflect. I too generally take part in a few meetings and often find that even the most mundane of such gatherings may turn out to be of great anthropological interest.

For example, as I was then struggling with the notion of hybridity, a much debated term in literary criticism and cultural studies, which some writers seem to regard as a panacea for all divisions and hostilities – whether between nations or between academic departments (Herzfeld 2001: 172, 297–98; De Angelis 2002: 40) – I was struck by the strong presence of cognate themes in the Venice Arts Biennale. Statements against intolerance and against the evil of boundaries were put across in a number of crude installations – undoubtedly well-intentioned but very poor artefacts, in which art seemed to have given way to political rhetoric. At the same time, journalists and commentators repeatedly put forward a vision of Venice itself as an early example of mixing, where architectural styles, cultures, and people had met and fused. The International Contemporary Music Festival that followed the Arts Biennale, under the title 'Re-Mix', was similarly dominated by the themes of multiculturalism, peace, universal values and the overcoming of boundaries.

David Krakauer, described in the Festival's programme as 'a superb clarinetist in the Yiddish tradition [who] can boast of some vertiginous collaborations with Berio, Goebbels and Cage', presented a wonderful mix of ancient and classical music with European avant-garde, as well as jazz and rock funk. The composition that was most relevant to my current preoccupation with hybridity (Sciama 2004) was Teitelbaum's *Scenes from Z'vi*, performed by Jewish and Muslim musicians, Jacob Ben Zion Mendelson, Omar Faruk Tekbilek, Zafer Tawil and David Krakauer. Again, to quote the programme, Teitelbaum's work 'is oriented to the integration of live electronics with the music of other cultures. ... Questions of identity, transgression, heterodoxy, religious syncretism, and the dream of a universal peace and redemption are at the bases of his interests, rendered sharper by the events of 11 September 2001.'

The opera begins in a *shtetl* with fragments from Singer's poignant narrative of a brutal massacre in 1648 Poland. In the second scene, on a sabbath in 1665, among the Sephardi Jews of Izmir, Z'vi sings a prayer in memory of a rabbi killed in the massacre. Then, embracing a Torah scroll, he sings the Spanish-Jewish song Melisenda, mixed in with passages from the Psalms and the Song of Songs; he explains the connections of those texts with the Shekhinah, and proclaims himself the Messiah. In the final scene, in Istanbul, seat of the Ottoman Sultan and of the Sufis, Teitelbaum shows Z'vi learning about Islam through the tolerant philosophy, the hymns, and the ecstatic music of the Sufis and attempting to formulate a syncretic religion that might teach universal brotherhood.[5]

The music was spellbinding, but not so the libretto: some of the audience were at the same time elated and indignant. A woman sitting next to me commented gruffly in a strong German accent, 'So, we shall have no more Muslims and no more Jews! Why can't they both learn to respect the other's civilisation?' As I mentioned, for me too, hybridity remains a problematic concept, for, while it certainly can be viewed as a valuable counter to essentialism, it is, as Piasere writes (2002: *passim*), an 'unhappy analogy' that replicates the bodily metaphors dear to functionalist anthropologists, and it inevitably carries unfortunate biological and racist connotations. Anthropological opinion is divided: Michael Herzfeld describes critics of hybridity as 'Romantic purists' 2001: 297–98) and 'hybrids [as] a threat to dominant modes of classification' (ibid.: 172). On the other hand, Martin Stokes notes the struggles in world music discourse:

> to secure the meaning of key [contradictory] notions such as authenticity, roots, hybridity, and the local. ... Study of musical hybridity ... provides evidence of ... cultural and political strategies in which migrants, refugees and diaspora populations detached from nation-states situate themselves in global flows. ... From this theoretical perspective, music enables a 'politics of the multiple'. However, the celebration of hybridity ... shared in certain areas of anthropological and ethnomusicological literature, also erodes important and necessary aesthetic, political and social distinctions. (Stokes 2004: 47)

However, that was just a digression. What is more to the point here is my observation that such occasions are in fact integral to the life of the city; to view them as alien and aggressive invasions of the global against a supposedly more authentic local life and culture is actually an error, since many Venetians, be they composers, organisers, or students, do participate and consider them a natural part of their occupational and intellectual lives. The extent of their involvement and the nature of their reciprocities are of great anthropological interest. For my part, although my initial plan to conduct research in the city had been left in abeyance, while I focused mainly on Burano, at the same time, throughout the 1990s, my stays in Venice have become more frequent and sometimes prolonged. I was returning to the city – that is, 'returning' both in a personal and in a professional sense. With the experience of fieldwork in Burano's compact face-to-face community, I was finding that my life in Venice was fragmented, my interests too diverse, and my position as observer potentially alienating; it isolated me. I thought, 'No wonder members of an earlier generation [E. Marx, personal communication] thought that urban anthropology was impossible.' But can we ever stop observing and trying to construct coherent descriptions of reality, once we have acquired the skill and habit of doing so? Then why not study the history of Venice's early tourist industry and long-distance trade as forerunners of globalisation? Or examine the contrast between the city's well-documented folk culture and some of its leaders' aspirations to refashion and re-present it as a focus of attraction for a (partly imagined) international elite – a locus for the creation of new (but sometimes ephemeral) transnational intimacies, vested interests, and global networks (Hannerz 1980, 1992; Sciama 1996; Marcus 1998)?

At that time, thinking over potential developments of my work in the city, even the most elementary of ethnographic 'research methods' I had implicitly absorbed during years of apprenticeship certainly turned out to be useful or, at least, encouraging. But, while the area of my first fieldwork, Burano, simply by virtue of being an island, was ideally well defined and bounded, the 'territory' I was then planning to study was entirely open-ended, 'mapped by [myself as] ethnographer … moving and acting within it' (Marcus 1998: 188–89).[6] In my attempts to make sense of new experiences, I was occasionally jotting down a few notes (old habits die hard) and, to overcome a sense of overwhelming disorder, I tried to list and group my different areas of interest and activities under separate subheadings. After about two weeks of feeling cut off, I began to see that fragments of experience were in fact coming together and areas of social life were beginning to take on clear outlines.

For the first subheading, which I provisionally called 'anthropology begins near home', a preliminary result of my attempt to discern some pattern in the city's life came in the shape of an (inevitably ego-centred) diagram. This includes a variety of people with whom I am connected, grouped in ways that reflect our shared interests and social spheres. A focus on network connections was thus beginning to prove very useful. As the diagram shows, a network of lines joins the different circles and thus illustrates the interconnectedness of Venetians, affirming a strong sense of local identity (Figure 13.1).

One of the circles represents Venice University, which was the place of work of some of my friends and where I did some occasional teaching. Another includes friends and acquaintances from Burano, which takes me back briefly to that island and to changes in the lives of members of Marisa's family whose history I followed after my fieldwork was 'officially' completed. Research in the city remains to be written. Instead, to answer the question on 'Fieldwork revisited', I shall concentrate on the circle that includes persons I first met in Tre Porti and Burano.

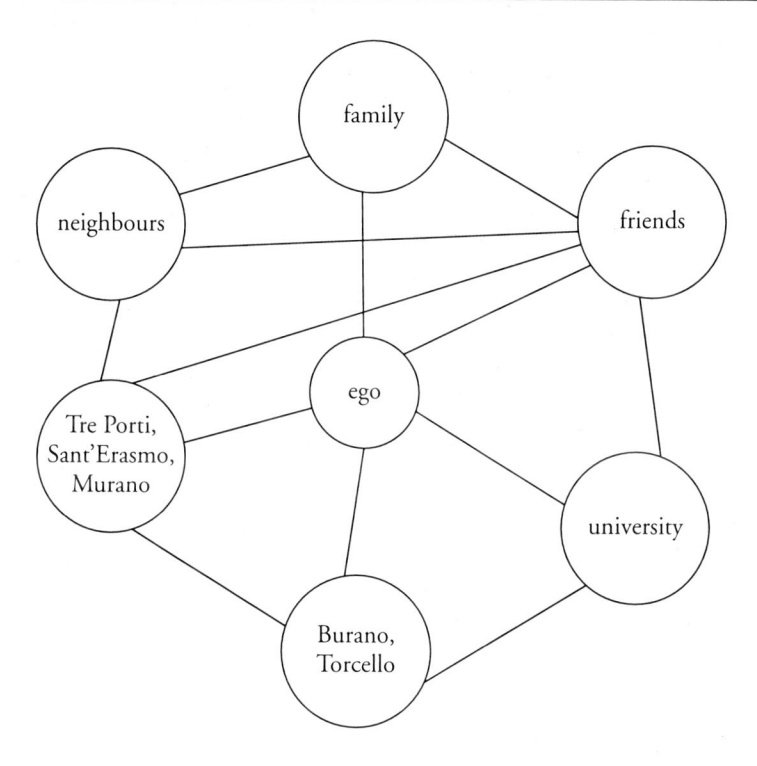

Figure 13.1: Social groupings, based on kinship, friendship, location, profession, or trade, are joined in a complex web of relationships and interactions

Burano Revisited

While anthropologists working in a distant area may find it relatively simple to bring their fieldwork to an end, for those working near home, it is sometimes very difficult to find a natural closure. Indeed, throughout the 1990s, I continued to visit Burano and Tre Porti and some of the relationships I formed during fieldwork have become permanent and enduring (see Kenna 2001). Repeated visits proved of great value, not only in keeping me in touch with changes, but also in deepening my knowledge of several families' and of the community's past, which gradually unfolded as mutual trust developed over the years. My fieldwork was thus extended in both time and space.

Change in Burano and Tre Porti has proceeded in pace with change in the whole of insular Venice. The number of inhabitants has gone down from *circa* 5,000 to 3,500. The housing crisis, therefore, has found its own resolution. Many homes have been transformed into shops, mostly selling lace (Sciama 2003: 155–56); however, much of the lace sold is no longer the valued handicraft of the local women, but somewhat coarser products imported from various Far Eastern countries. Like Venice, Burano is often invaded by large groups of tourists, who confuse and dominate its public spaces, breaking up far older customs in the uses of space and long-standing patterns of encounters and networking. While this has enriched a few people and increased the number of restaurants and shops, for many Buranelli it is a source of irritation. As a man said to me rather wistfully, 'They have taken over all the cafés; now the price of coffee has gone up, so our old men have lost their places of rest and recreation and they just walk up and down the piazza like miserable apes' (see also Davis and Marvin 2004).

A few houses have been sold to foreign buyers. For example, a French fashion designer has bought two cottages he plans to restore, but stereotyping has not ceased: he still defines Burano as 'an island of fishermen and lacemakers'. Instead, most Buranelli now work in Murano, Venice or Mestre and are not as socially distant from the city as they were in the past. There nonetheless remains a sense of difference, expressed mainly by Venetians and often coloured by prejudice. Buranelli are teased on account of the distinctive lilt of their dialect and they are said to be quarrelsome, touchy, and slow in problem-solving. They, on the other hand, say that they find people in the city unpredictable and rude, that authority is exercised in other ways and with other idioms from those they are used to on their island, and that the difficulties they encounter are altogether different from those their fathers met when they were fishermen or craftsmen, and the problems they faced were, on the whole, predictable.

Such dynamic social and economic change as has taken place since the 1970s and 1980s, however, has inevitably brought about a degree of intergenerational tension; older people, especially men, are sometimes critical of their offspring's freedom and spending habits: 'Now they are all millionaires, they know everything, they travel far and wide; Russia, Brazil, even China, you name it! We called ourselves lucky if we reached as far as Iesolo, or, at the most, the coast of Croatia.'

As I followed the moves of Buranelli who have left the island over the last twenty years to seek employment and modern accommodation, I found that most of them had gone to live in villages near Mestre, the Lido, or Ca' Savio on the Cavallino peninsula. For example, a family I knew well during my early fieldwork in the 1980s, Marisa, her husband Toni, and their three teenage sons and one daughter, are now dispersed in different areas. They had lived and worked in Burano for about thirty years. Their youngest son, who is the first member of the family to have completed his secondary school education, is now working for an insurance company in Venice. Another is a librarian. Their oldest son, a sensitive landscape painter, also holds a white-collar job in the city. His wife is a native of Burano, and they have a daughter and a son, now both university students.

What is of interest from the point of view of my early research on housing and people's exodus from Burano is that all of Marisa's offspring have moved from that island, but they have remained in insular areas: two sons have moved to the Lido, one to Ca' Savio, and the daughter, Angela, now lives and works in Venice's historical centre. Marisa herself has moved back to her original Tre Porti with her husband, and she is a regular visitor to her offspring and grandchildren.

Conclusion

As I taught a course at the University of Venice, a colleague asked me if I was willing to supervise a student, Elena, who had proposed to write a thesis on Burano's lacemakers. She had recently completed her undergraduate course in the humanities and was planning to specialise in anthropology. She explained that she was actually born in Burano, but her parents had moved to Venice when she was nine years old. Her description of the street and the house where she was born at once brought back memories of conversations I had enjoyed with a number of women, one of whom I discovered was her late grandmother. At the time of my fieldwork, some of the women were dedicated lacemakers and, as the traditional organisation of that craft required, they formed small collaborative networks, which often led to lifelong bonds of friendship and solidarity.

Like many ethnographers, Elena was in some uncertainty on how to open a dialogue with people in the field, but her mother, herself related to a lacemaking family, helped her to find the right contacts and participated in her initial interviews. Indeed, as Elena explained, her mother was her first and best informant – an approach that initially worried my co-supervisor. Describing the present state of the lacemaking craft, which most young women had abandoned, Elena shrewdly entitled her thesis 'not to lose the thread'. That may have been an expression used by the few remaining lacemakers to explain why they continued to work at their craft, despite its poor rewards. However, the very notion of thread (as of much of women's textile work) is at the same time a rich metaphor for continuity, for narrative, and for the binding together of generations, persons, and events.

From my point of view, Elena, now both colleague and informant, illustrates the value of an all-woman network. She shows the way Venice and Burano have become increasingly close and interrelated, and the way economic change and the spread of education have reduced social distance, while a love of place and a search for a shared identity remain ever puzzling but very real psychological needs.

In conclusion: time and repeated visits to Venice and Burano have added an important dimension to my early fieldwork. Reflecting upon the lives of the women whose histories I have briefly sketched, I have come to see that their success in changing their circumstances has been due not only to their hard work but also to their strong agency in forming new networks of acquaintances and solidary friends. While in some respects the women's strategies include patronage idioms, still embedded in contemporary relational styles despite the strong presence of egalitarian ideologies, they actually enable them to cut across traditional hierarchies and social divisions and become active participants in Venice's economy and culture. My observation of subjective choices, motivated by personal aspirations and based on foresight, social skill, experience, and trust, thus proved very valuable in my attempts to relate individual lives to a broader socio-historical perspective and to document aspects of the dynamic social change that has taken place in 1970s and 1980s Italy.

Notes

1. I usually answered 'not really … only in some ways'. I have come to the conclusion that 'home' is a relative concept: we may think of different places as home at different stages of our life. For some anthropologists, originally 'distant' fieldwork places have eventually become 'home'. For me the matter was complex: speaking the dialect helped to establish communication with great ease and immediacy, but my initial sense of familiarity was deceptive; I had to overcome areas of inattention and simple ignorance on my part, as well as reserve and suspicion on the part of the islanders.
2. The seminar series was convened by Dr Janette Davies and Dr Zoe Morrison in Michaelmas 2003.
3. In one notebook I find extensive discussions about a fourteen-year-old girl who had recently had a baby and was to be married to the father; about a nudist camp in the then Yugoslavia, and speculation about father/daughter incestuous relations – almost condoned for one man who was thought to be 'mad'.
4. Some of the notes are in dialect, but others are in English – written as soon as I was alone after the conversations.
5. The closing words are by the great Sufi mystic Muhyi'oddin ibn al-Arabi.
6. This, in Marcus's view, is one of the conditions of postmodernity, in which 'messy texts' are composed (1998: 188–89).

References

Ardener, E. 1975. 'Belief and the Problem of Women', in S. Ardener (ed.), *Perceiving Women*, London: Malaby Press.

Ardener, S. (ed.) 1975. *Perceiving Women*, London: Malaby Press.

Ardener, S. and S. Burman 1995. *Money-go-rounds: The Importance of Rotating Savings and Credit Associations for Women*, Oxford and Washington, DC: Berg.

Boissevain, J. 1974. *Friends of Friends, Networks, Manipulators and Coalitions*, Oxford: Blackwell.

Callan, H. and S. Ardener (eds) 1984. *The Incorporated Wife*, London: Croom Helm.

Callaway, H. 1992. 'Ethnography and Experience: Gender Implications in Fieldwork and Texts', in J. Okely and H. Callaway (eds), *Anthropology and Autobiography*, London: Routledge, pp. 29–49.

Caplan, P. 1988. 'Engendering Knowledge: The Politics of Ethnography', *Anthropology Today* 4 (5), pp. 8–12, and 4 (6), pp. 14–17.

Clifford, J. 1983. 'Power and Dialogue in Ethnography: Marcel Griaule's Initiation', in G.W. Stocking, Jr (ed.), *Observers Observed: Essays on Ethnographic Fieldwork*, Madison: University of Wisconsin Press.

Crump, T. 1975. 'The Context of European Anthropology: The Lesson from Italy', in J. Boissevain and J. Friedl (eds), *Beyond the Community: Social Process in Europe*, The Hague: Ministry of Education and Science, pp. 2–24.

Davis, J. 1977. *People of the Mediterranean: An Essay in Comparative Social Anthropology*, London: Routledge.

Davis, R.S. and G.R. Marvin 2004. *Venice: The Tourist Maze*, Berkeley: University of California Press.

De Angelis, R. (ed.) 2002. *Between Anthropology and Literature: Interdisciplinary Discourse*, London: Routledge.
Dresch, P., W. James and D. Parkin (eds) 2000. *Anthropologists in a Wider World*, Oxford: Berghahn Books.
Frankenberg, R. 1966. 'British Community Studies: Problems of Synthesis', in M. Banton (ed.), *The Social Anthropology of Complex Societies*, London: Tavistock (ASA Monographs, 4).
Hannerz, U. 1980. *Exploring the City: Inquiries towards an Urban Anthropology*, New York: Columbia University Press.
——— 1987. 'Cosmopolitans and Locals in World Culture', unpublished MS.
——— 1992. *Cultural Complexity: Studies in the Social Organization of Meaning*, New York: Columbia University Press.
Haraway, D. 1988. 'Situated Knowledge: The Science Question in Feminism and the Privilege of Partial Perspective', *Feminist Studies* 14 (3), pp. 579–99.
Herzfeld, M. 2001. *Anthropology: Theoretical Practice in Culture and Society*, Oxford: Blackwell.
Jackson, J.E. 1990. '"I am a Fieldnote": Fieldnotes as a Symbol of Professional Identity', in R. Sanjek (ed.), *Fieldnotes: The Making of Anthropology*, Ithaca: Cornell University Press.
Kenna, M.E. 2001. *Greek Island Life: Fieldwork on Anafi*, Amsterdam: Harwood Academic Publishers.
Marcus, G.E. 1998. *Ethnography through Thick and Thin*, Princeton: Princeton University Press.
Okely, J. 1975. 'Gypsy Women: Models in Conflict', in S. Ardener (ed.), *Perceiving Women*, London: Malaby Press, pp. 55–86.
Okely, J. and H. Callaway (eds) 1992. *Anthropology and Autobiography*, London: Routledge (ASA Monographs, 29).
Ottenberg, S. 1990. 'Thirty Years of Fieldnotes: Changing Relationships to the Text', in R. Sanjek (ed.), *Fieldnotes: The Making of Anthropology*, Ithaca: Cornell University Press.
Piasere, L. 2002. *L'etnografo imperfetto*, Bari: Laterza.
Rabinow, P. 1986. 'Representations are Social Facts: Modernity and Post-Modernity in Anthropology', in J. Clifford and G.E. Marcus (eds), *Writing Culture: The Poetics and Politics of Ethnography*, Berkeley: University of California Press.
Sanjek, R. (ed.) 1990. *Fieldnotes: The Making of Anthropology*, Ithaca: Cornell University Press.
Sciama, L. D. 1981. 'The Problem of Privacy in Mediterranean Anthropology', in S. Ardener (ed.), *Women and Space: Ground Rules and Social Maps*, London: Croom Helm.
——— 1984. 'Ambivalence and Dedication: Academic Wives in Cambridge University', in H. Callan and S. Ardener (eds), *The Incorporated Wife*, London: Croom Helm.
——— 1996. 'The Venice Regatta: From Ritual to Sport', in J. MacClancy (ed.), *Sport, Identity and Ethnicity*, Oxford: Berg.
——— 2003. *A Venetian Island: Environment, History and Change in Burano*, Oxford: Berghahn Books.
——— 2004. 'Review of R. De Angelis (ed.), *Between Anthropology and Literature: Interdisciplinary Discourse* (London, 2002)', *Journal of the Royal Anthropological Institute* 10 (4), pp. 930–32.
Stokes, M. 2004. 'Music and the Global Order', *Annual Review of Anthropology* 33, pp. 47–72.
Tyler, S.A. 1986. 'Post-Modern Ethnography: From Document of the Occult to Occult Document', in J. Clifford and G.E. Marcus (eds), *Writing Culture: The Poetics and Politics of Ethnography*, Berkeley: University of California Press.

14

GENDERED LESSONS IN IVORY TOWERS

Judith Okely

Feminist knowledge entails a theory of power because, as Ramazanoglu and Holland assert in relation to feminist methodology, 'the power to produce authoritative knowledge is not equally open to all' (2002: 13). Certainly this has been my experience as a woman academic. I am confronted with disparities in power. I am obliged to confront my gender because it is made clear to me on a daily basis. In what is ideally presented as a centre for open and rational knowledge, the university is not free of specificity in history and is marked by gender, class, and ethnic differences. Nevertheless, I approached university as a student, as a postgraduate, and then as a lecturer with awe and longing. I wanted to enter the temple of knowledge, something that a person of my era, class, and gender was not supposed to enter even as a novice (see Okely 1978, 2003).

Some aspects of being a woman academic may be taken for granted that were very different in Britain thirty years ago. In this chapter, I explore the changing historical background to the position of women lecturers, drawing on my own experience as a case study. There is an excellent precedent for doing so in the autobiographical work of the sociologist Olive Banks, who recounted her position in academia from the 1940s through to the 1960s (1999). As an anthropologist, I am accustomed to analysing accumulative ethnographic material based on participant observation. Here the culture is that of several British universities, lived by myself as female informant, participant, and later analyst. At the time of each experience, I was only subliminally doing fieldwork in these institutions. I was more a passive recipient of their procedures, taking it for granted that this was normality in an organisation supposedly founded on reason and equity.

In this chapter I review four strands of my experience as a woman anthropologist. The first concerns aspects of the structural and daily reaction of the universities to the presence of a female lecturer. The experience commenced before equal opportunities legislation was recognised as a necessary code of practice and ends with new and unexpected twists in presumed gender equality. Secondly, I examine the institutional reaction to my attempts to introduce and teach courses on women and gender. Earlier examples show the considerable restrictions in gaining approval. After thirty years it seems either that gender studies have become gentrified or that feminism is still marginalised. Thirdly, the significance of supportive colleagues, usually female but some key males, in some male-dominated or hostile contexts is traced. This strand links to the book's networking theme. These network patterns are contrasted with the masculinist or new managerial values that have captured universities. Finally, I consider the production of my feminist publications and how they both influenced and reflected my teaching commitments. In all these strands, Shirley Ardener's influence is ever present through three decades of changing intellectual and academic institutional trends. All four strands can be read as ideas and practices arising from fieldwork in academia.

Institutionalised Experience

Today, there is greater sensitivity towards discrimination, encouraged by compulsory race, if not gender, awareness workshops for senior managers. Over twenty-five years ago, when I started as a lecturer at an English university, there was no such thing. The discrimination was blatant as well as implicit.

In the discipline of social anthropology, the majority of undergraduates were women during the 1970s (which continues to be the case today). Even when women gained first-class degrees, they were less likely to proceed to a doctorate than the male graduates. Women graduates tended to opt for a less ambitious masters and not to progress to a doctorate. Barker (1975) and Caplan (1975), in a study of several anthropology departments in southern England, noted how male graduates were often crucially encouraged by male lecturer patrons to continue. That patronage did not operate to the same degree for women, especially since the proportion of female members of staff to male was increasingly small. Women staff formed a tiny minority and women professors were rare indeed. This gender imbalance was general. A survey in the early 1970s of university teachers in Britain in all disciplines revealed that 12 per cent of lecturers, 6 per cent of senior lecturers and readers and only 1 per cent of professors were women (Blackstone 1973).

Ramazanoglu and Holland, in defending the use of experience for feminist knowledge, argue that 'the passions in struggles over knowledge of difference comes from actual and personal experience of difference' (2002: 123). They confront the criticism of experience as a source of knowledge in that 'any one person's experience will be limited, partial and socially located' (ibid.: 125). It cannot be denied that experience is partial. But detailed accounts may give insights that otherwise remain hidden, especially and precisely because the experience is not that of a majority and the dominant hegemony. They argue that 'experience of power relations can provide information on the realities of people's lives that is otherwise unavailable' and that 'there is a case for grounding feminist knowledge in experience' (ibid.: 127).

Knowledge based on first-hand experience is essential to the discipline of social anthropology. We do fieldwork. I have long argued, especially in the edited volume *Anthropology and Autobiography* (Okely and Callaway 1992), that even though the discipline has traditionally studied groups and cultures, often other than one's own, the anthropologist should confront his/her specificity. The gender, race, age, class, and personality will affect the interaction and ensuing access and knowledge of the people of that culture.

In this case, I am attempting to throw light on the context of the production of knowledge itself through universities. My experience is indeed partial because I have usually researched and lectured in universities where women as permanent academic staff form a tiny minority. But this chapter is intended to add to insights not only into an institution and its members per se but into the way in which we learn about the world generally.

Universities and many public institutions are now often obliged to have an equal opportunities policy, especially in relation to race, disability, and to some extent gender. In the 1970s, such intrusive policies were invisible, but at the same time the universities had intellectual freedoms and institutional autonomy that academics could enjoy.

State intrusions that demand some formal equalities, if not window dressing, have exacted a huge price. The audit culture has brought the madness of counterproductive bureaucracy (Shore and Wright 1999). Academics are less engaged in forging new knowledge than in filling in reports on multiple assessments. Thus the controls on institutional sexism and racism have been a Pyrrhic victory. In so far as the intellectual and original ideas and practices of a university are increasingly constrained, Mary Evans, in discussing the changes undergone by universities since the 1960s, supports feminism's challenge to universalisms. The second battle, she suggests, is 'less to overthrow the ivory tower than retain it' (Evans 1997: 52). She notes 'the gradual transformation of many of the liberal assumptions of universities into questionable habits and the values of the market economy' (ibid.). The managerial attitude brings 'a ruthless belief in policing the behaviour and the "performance" of both students and academic staff and the imposition on the curriculum of unanswerable questions about the "aims of the course" and the "learning outcome"' (ibid.).

The period from the mid-1970s through the 1980s, and with some more general observations about the 1990s and after, reveals some gains in women's appointments and the acceptance of gender studies but also the loss of innovation in research and teaching practice. The gender gains are still marginal. Evans emphasises that 'in the dual sense in which universities are run, that of allocating material resources and deciding the central issues of the curriculum, it is men, and masculine interests, which prevail' (ibid.: 49).

Gendered Ethnography

To commence my ethnography: in the mid-1970s, I applied for both a permanent and a temporary lectureship at a northern and older university, founded in the early nineteenth century. I was shortlisted only for the nine-month temporary job. I had innocently but proudly put on my CV that I was the first woman member of the Oxford Union Debating Society. I had also contributed to the first post-Women's Liberation anthropology volume published in the U.K., *Perceiving Women* (1975), edited by Shirley Ardener. Thus I was marked as someone with feminist interests.

The woman anthropologist on leave had successfully run a course entitled 'Women and Anthropology' the previous year. She had presented it under the general and flexible rubric 'Current Problems in Anthropology' filled in by a lecturer's choice, so it did not require scrutiny by Senate. When the next year's students learned that the woman lecturer would be on leave, they drew up a petition asking if that same course could be made available for their year in her absence. All this was done without my prior knowledge, but was seen by some as a 'feminist conspiracy'. To my surprise, at the interview by an all-male panel, I was asked by a professor, if I would be still interested in the job if I could not teach anything on women. Like a meek schoolgirl, I put my head down and said 'Yes'. The implication in the question was that anthropology was only about men. Thus the teaching and research culture had lines clearly demarcated to exclude any problematisation of gender, as if male hegemony were natural.

I was given the nine-month post and another young woman a six-month temporary post. As the two new women in the department, we conferred about the so-called ban on teaching anything on women and agreed that for the first-year introductory anthropology course we would both introduce gender issues. I put *Woman, Culture and Society* (Rosaldo and Lamphere 1974) on the reading list, together with *Sex, Gender and Society* (Oakley 1972), *Perceiving Women* (Ardener 1975), and *Toward an Anthropology of Women* (Reiter 1974). There were no comments from our senior colleagues, but we were nervous because we felt we had put our jobs on the line, especially if permanent posts were to come up.

Amongst those attending the first-year lectures there was one undergraduate who later became known as a prominent feminist anthropologist in the 1980s. Oblivious to the context in which we had 'daringly' introduced such themes and readings and probably assuming that this was part of some orthodox curriculum, she critiqued such publications as not being feminist because they allegedly focused on women rather than gender (Moore 1988: 6). In fact we would have welcomed any problematisation of masculinity. Some of us women anthropologists were busy challenging the presumed universalisms in male authors who were unwittingly privileging a masculine viewpoint.

At the first departmental social event, I met the two new male permanent lecturers, the second employed as a physical anthropologist and a postgraduate in the department. Several years younger than me, and presumably of a liberal generation, he approached me saying, 'When the man came to paint your name on the office door, we made sure he didn't put Ms in front of your name. We had heard you were a feminist and we told him to put Miss.' I was baffled and replied that I considered it irrelevant. I was merely looking forward to the day when it would say Dr, which in fact happened within a year.

In London I joint-owned a house with my partner, who was supportive of my regular commute every other weekend. The train took a minimum of five hours. My need to have a job far from southern England and what has been termed the 'golden triangle' of Oxford, Cambridge, and London was also a reflection of the competition for university appointments in the more privileged regions and universities. My partner was a philosopher who would not dream of moving north. Like a growing number of women, I had done my anthropological fieldwork 'at home' and in Europe, namely among Gypsies. To the orthodox, anthropology should only be done in exotica far from Europe and the West. Again, this has changed today. Although preceded by others, especially Frankenberg (1990 [1957]), my work has also been seen as pioneering in western Europe in general. Europe and anthropology 'at home' are now territories that men can also cover with career advantages, although there remains hesitation in the golden triangle (Okely 1996: 1).

Masculine Collegiality

Important questions to consider in academia are the extent to which one should form an academic community and, if so, what happens to individuals who are excluded from shared residence and commensality.

Some older universities like Oxford and Cambridge are collegiate, where members reside and eat in colleges. In Oxbridge even teaching is associated with colleges. This was not the case at the collegiate university where I had my first lectureship, but collegiality as shared residence and commensality formed a major power base for networking and domestic support. These major universities were also former theological colleges, with a history of all-male membership and celibacy. Shirley Ardener (1984) and Lidia Sciama (1984) have explored how it was only during the nineteenth century that Oxbridge allowed the all-male 'dons' to marry. Subsequently, the wives of lecturers became a problematic category. In the latter half of the twentieth century, wives had an ambiguous place. But the presence of women academics was even more problematic. They were rare and usually seen as spinsters and 'bluestockings', i.e., sexless nuns of knowledge.[1]

By the late 1960s at least, women academics were seen as rivals or threats to male academics' wives who were expected to act in a service role. We therefore had also to appear unsexed to please all parties. For my first lectureship interview at this hallowed institution, I was advised by the woman whose job had become temporarily vacant that, for the interview, I should look utterly dowdy. At first, I was generally unaware of these conflicting categories, naively believing that an academic, as intellectual, achieved his/her position on merit, regardless of gender. But my feminine gender was marked. There were exclusions. Sandra Harding, drawing also on Hilary Rose, explores parallels with the gendered production of knowledge in science. These 1980s insights reflected my own ambiguous position. Women 'are forced to deny that they are women in order to survive. ... They are prohibited from becoming (masculine) science knowers and also from admitting to being what they are primarily perceived as being: women' (Harding 1986: 143). This 'ancient' university could not cope with women academics – only its wives, who were afforded a marginalised niche as domestic servicers and mothers. Some months into my position, I encountered the token woman lecturer in the geography department, who expressed discontent about the lack of childcare facilities. After a woman lecturer in Senate had bravely suggested a crèche, the geographer described contemptuously how the male establishment had agreed, but only for a couple of hours a day. 'This', she said, 'enabled the academics' wives to go shopping.' It was useless for full-time women academics.

Although universities in the U.K. had begun to accept women academics, it was still rare in the 1970s for any woman academic to have children. Another woman lecturer, appointed in the faculty several years before me, was asked at her interview how she, as a married woman, could continue to be an academic if she had children. Fully prepared in advance, she claimed that she was infertile. Miraculously she conceived some years later. My predecessor returned to her office early from maternity leave, having found an excellent childminder. She was bored. But her line manager's wife, a full-time housewife, telephoned to reprimand the lecturer for being a neglectful mother. Regrettably, at that time, I found maternity to be broadly incompatible with a commuting career. Today, matters have changed in that by EU law, paid maternity leave of six months is available, and the professions, including universities, have come to accept, even be impressed by, commuting marriages of high-profile careers.

Upon my appointment, I needed somewhere to live in this tiny northern city. I approached the staff accommodation office but was told that, since I was not married, they could not supply me with anything. I approached the residential mixed colleges, but again was told that I could not even be a member with dining rights. Apparently, if I had a husband who was a member of such a college, then I would be acceptable. I only once dined in a college in all the years I taught there, and merely as the guest of a male colleague. In contrast, a year or so after my appointment, when two single male lecturers arrived in the department, one was given immediate accommodation in college and the other within months, a flat five minutes from the department. Decades later, I attended two conferences at the university and with accommodation in colleges which I had not previously entered. There were high-ceilinged dining rooms, glass-fronted views of trees, a lake, fountain and herbaceous pathways. In this congenial setting, I enjoyed waves of nostalgia about all the best I had experienced in the past.

Having been unsuccessful with staff accommodation when I was first appointed, I was advised to try the Student Union office. The young man told me that since I was a 'privileged' member of staff, he would give me addresses only ten miles or more from the city. The one available address was an unfurnished terraced house twelve miles away. I took a taxi there to meet the landlady. I grabbed at this windswept house on a hill, even a mile from the centre of the former mining village. I returned in my little Renault Four with blankets, pots, and an old Calor-gas camping cooker that I had used for fieldwork among the Gypsies. In the market I bought a length of foam rubber for a mattress.

This seemingly austere locality turned out to be my escape and sanctuary. One winter night there was a knock on my door, and this woman explained she had been baking and presented me with a plate heaped with meat rolls and cakes. She fled shyly up the path. This was Sue, wife of Dick, a retired miner who lived in that terrace. They were to treat me as an adoptive daughter. I spent wonderful evenings in their home listening to tales of the 1930s and the miners' strikes, past poverty and camaraderie. I in turn took them for drives in my battered Renault. We visited Beamish Museum. Each evening, as I drove away from my office, there was a wondrous moment as I crossed a bridge and turned up a hill. The weight of stress fell away. I was far from the fusty claustrophobia in this university, which had the lowest proportion of women lecturers of any university in Great Britain.

Reception

Back to my entry in the hallowed ivory tower: early in my appointment, I was invited as a new member of staff to a welcoming reception at the Education Department. Wearing a thick red woollen jumper, I drove ten miles from my unheated lodgings on the designated evening. When I eventually found the building, the cleaner turned me away: 'The library's closed.' After explaining I was not a student, I asked where the ladies room was, so I could comb my windswept hair. 'It's locked.' Thus it was assumed that no academic woman would step over the threshold. Already deflated by my genderised access, I walked into the reception room to see about twenty men, all seemingly in grey suits, while I was in scarlet. Everyone, except the director, presumed I was the secretary.

That week I ventured to the main library to collect a staff member's card. The receptionist could not believe I was a member of staff and accused me of fraud. Next, I was barred from the university staffroom and cafeteria as an interloper student. When finally admitted to this haven of men in fading tweed jackets and crumpled grey trousers, I selected lunch at the self-service. The woman at the till stared at my meal. In my anxiety, I had failed to pick up a plate and had spooned all my food straight onto the plastic tray. Thus even the domesticity associated with femininity had failed me in this male-dominated environment.

I can retrospectively appreciate the observation by Morley and Walsh: 'In a culture where emotional literacy is discursively located in opposition to reason, feminist academics frequently have to repress pain and anger, and hide the contradictions and tensions that arise from being members of subordinate groups in powerful institutions' (1995: 2).

The isolation and challenge in becoming a university lecturer brought massive physical side-effects. For months I found that the only food that did not pass straight through me was brown rice. I could not eat fruit, vegetables, or meat. All alcohol was impossible. Colleagues congregating in the pub in the evenings or for lunch teased me about being teetotal. I could not tell them that it was a nervous stomach ailment. On return to my terraced house, I would ask if it was worth putting my body through this agony. Eventually, I visited the local doctor and wept. He gave me tranquillisers.

Teaching Linked to Research

The stress leaked into my teaching plans, but with unexpected consequences, thanks to my good fortune in having David, a supportive colleague. One evening, visiting his family home, I let slip that I was sick with nerves. His sympathetic enquiry opened me up and I sobbed uncontrollably, saying I did not know how to continue. Moreover, I had to give a lecture on Durkheim's *The Elementary Forms of the Religious Life* (1914) the next day. I was now in no mood to run through my notes that evening. In passing, I mentioned my thesis chapter on Gypsy death rituals (Okely 1982: 215–30), where I had argued a different angle on Durkheim's analysis of mortuary rites. David was astonished at my troubled state of mind and smilingly revealed, 'No one could guess. No one has a clue. They think you are so in control, so cool and of course your middle-class accent adds to that impression. ... Meanwhile, why not give a lecture on your own material? Go in there and wow them.'

What wonderful advice. It echoed Shirley Ardener's encouragement in 1973 when she first asked me to think about a paper on Gypsy women (Okely 1975a). Likewise in this new setting, David gave me confidence to use my own research and to hell with the main reading list: let the students in on some original material, as yet unpublished. The next day, I dressed entirely in funereal black and wowed them.

Subsequently, when giving a lecture on Marcel Mauss's *Les Techniques du corps* (1950), which I translated, I used the example of bodily training from my British boarding school. I moved away from the lectern and imitated the military style of marching instilled at my school. Months after, a student told me how this had really inspired them. They saw the modern relevance and application of theories some half a century old to lived experience. All this was thanks to the non-macho sensitivity of my rare male colleague who rescued me from drowning. I was blessed with a brilliant intellectual mentor and friend. At the same time, my use of first-hand autobiographical material drew on the inescapable feminist reflexivity that incorporates experience into wider theory and academic knowledge. After a couple of years, I came to love giving lectures, having been encouraged to innovate and see the occasion as performance.

Pre-audit Innovations

The ironically positive side to the sexism was that it coincided with a general absence of monitoring. Unfortunately, the audit culture has now curtailed the intellectual freedom that a gender- and race-sensitive policy might have liberated. In the 1970s, once appointed as lecturer and indeed only temporary, I was trusted with devising my own reading lists, albeit within the existing course titles. No one questioned the content. I was free to go wherever creative and imaginative ideas took me. At the completion stage of my doctorate, and inspired by my Oxford postgraduate seminars and peer group which included Kirsten Hastrup, Charlotte Hardman, Helen Callaway, Lidia Sciama, Juliet Blair, Jan Oveson, Martin Thom, Paul Heelas, and Malcolm Crick, I could inject experimental ideas and texts into the courses. In those pre-audit days, we were trusted to use our intellects with originality. I had proved my ability through my CV, the interview, and references. Those initial freedoms laid the foundations for all my subsequent lecturing styles. In contrast, today all modules are closely monitored and subject to absurd anti-intellectual constraints. On the horizon, there is standardisation as to the very form of lectures (Okely 2006).

Back then, I gradually became adventurous, in both content and performance. My colleague, David, had already drawn on his first-hand fieldwork among the Bahktiari. I became confident in the feminist emphasis on the personal and subjective. My article 'The Self and Scientism' (Okely 1975b, 1996) argued for the importance of studying Malinowski's posthumous *Diary* (1967). This was used as a major part of a lecture on methods, which I argued should also be taught within the core anthropological theory course.

I would try out ideas and then recount strategies of performance with my colleague David. Before my arrival he had felt intellectually isolated and we, as well as the students, found that our lectures and courses complemented each other. Scandalously, David was mocked by some of his more orthodox colleagues. While a simplistic form of political economy prevailed at that time, few could appreciate his pioneering or reinvigorated interest in religion, dance and performance. One time he arranged for an evening with a hired belly dancer. It inspired us and lived long after the envious mockery that had circulated down the corridors. Years later, our students of that era, an exceptional number of whom are academic anthropologists, including four professors, recall those heady teaching years. On my return to a conference in 2004, we watched a special screening of David's film on the Bahktiari, once nominated for an Oscar, and witnessed the award of a prize in his name for the best dissertation.

As a novice lecturer, I was entrusted with the supervision of several doctoral students, one within days of my first arrival. Marie was studying the women's movement in Iceland. In this non-audit culture, there was not even a second supervisor. I was blissfully unaware how fortunate I was to have as my first student someone who was outstanding and productive from start to completion.

Private Life as Public

The spinster/wife opposing categories continued to haunt women academics. My temporary job was extended to two years. Then the person I was standing in for resigned, and the permanent job was to be advertised. I listened to David's advice and believe that this was correct. He had been in his post for ten years. He said that I should let a rumour spread that I had broken up with my partner in London and that if I got the permanent job I would buy a house in the northern town to which I would be committed. I did just that and got the job. I carried on commuting alternate weekends and in the vacations. A few years on, when my partner in London became seriously ill and was hospitalised, David again advised me not to inform the head of department as it would emphasise my 'lack of commitment' to the university if it was known that I commuted more frequently. Obviously David did not believe in the justice of this but he acted as a useful conduit of the institution's values. The liminal celibate woman was still the preferred female category. Today, in contrast, women and men can publicly celebrate their commuting partnerships.

Gendering Knowledge

Back in the 1970s, the form of knowledge available to students depended on the approval of the dominant male hegemony. The content of the undergraduate degree was profoundly affected by gender specificities and the social context. Some years later, Hilary Rose would articulate in relation to science what I was experiencing in the social sciences, observing that women are 'by and large shut out of the production system of scientific knowledge, with its ideological power to define what is and what is not objective knowledge' (1983: 88). Now a permanent lecturer, I wanted to introduce the gender course for which the students had long petitioned. There was now a serious accumulation of anthropological literature that had moved beyond popularist texts (Okely 1996: 115–38).

Again, I was advised that, for it to be properly instituted and approved by Senate, I had better watch the title. Apparently the Head would be mortified if his department had a course with the word 'women'. I devised a way out by calling the course 'Race and Gender'. No one would dare question the respectability of discussing race.

To my surprise, more men than women signed up and I felt an even greater need to introduce reading on masculinity. It was sparse. The most informative book was Andrew Tolson's (1977) *The Limits of Masculinity*. It grew out of a men's consciousness-raising group. The students were excited by the text and wanted to invite him to speak. Other texts which problematised masculinity included Mead's (1935) classic *Sex and Temperament in Three Primitive Societies* and Margaret Walters' (1978) *The Nude Male*. After checking my order for Walters at the university bookshop, the assistant summoned the manager. He reminded me that the bookshop was a Christian institution which did not stock pornography. I pointed out that many of the centuries old images were of Jesus Christ.

Another unexpected twist was the number of visits by individual male students to the privacy of my office. Each confessed that they were nervous about making statements in front of other students that would cause them to lose face. Here again was practical confirmation of the need for men to present a power-laden front in public. There were parallels with the absence of men's autobiographical and personalised accounts of fieldwork in the anthropological literature. This is something I would explore later in the volume *Anthropology and Autobiography* (Okely and Callaway 1992).

I persuaded David to give several lectures on gender in the Middle East. We had lively arguments in that he would not accept that women were subordinate. He emphasised the power of women, especially in the domestic and sometimes sacred spheres. I now appreciate his focus on what were referred to as lion women among the Bahktiari, who were identified as powerful individual women. He also drew attention to the importance to men of women behaving in a non-shameful way. At the same time, he pointed to the control over male sexuality.

By this time, I had already noticed gender differences in undergraduate essays on non-genderised topics. I had set a first-year question, 'Discuss some of the problems and challenges in studying other cultures.' Without prior assumptions, I found that male students focused on broad and generalised philosophical issues about clashing cosmologies, whereas women used concrete, specific examples and minute aspects of interaction, like body language, dress, movement, and conversation.

An explanation is based on the gendered upbringing of both boys and girls. Both sexes are brought up in early childhood by women, whether or not these are biological mothers, as elaborated in Chodorow (1974). The girl child learns about adult and future femininity by immediate example. But the boy has to learn about masculinity by abstraction. The father figure is more often absent (Tolson 1977), so the boy has to theorise his future masculinity. All this affects each gender's intellectual grasp of the world. Thankfully over the years, I have found some wonderful counter-examples. But invariably, the background of the individual revealed exceptional circumstances.

Women Networking

It has been increasingly recognised that male networks are important in work and professional advancement. Naturally, with the very low proportion of women academics, especially some decades ago, networks were thin and few. But, as I experienced with the isolated women in my first post, the rare contacts were all the more valuable. This had already affected my academic production, publication, and a section of my doctorate. I was fortunate to be a member of the first Women's Anthropology Seminar, when I was a postgraduate at Oxford. It was Shirley Ardener who first suggested that I present a paper on Gypsy women.

Ironically, as a feminist, I had not thought of focusing on women per se in the field. Given my own restricted bourgeois education, I had naively believed that it was a feminist act to go to university and proceed to postgraduate research. I had done fieldwork among a very gender-divided ethnic group. I was too busy trying to get information about both genders. In any case, in those days it was hardly possible to submit a doctorate that focused on women alone – no matter that most monographs written by male anthropologists claimed to research and write about a whole people when in fact they had depended largely on male informants.

At a London women's anthropology conference in the early 1970s, I saw the link between feminist practice and academic work. But it was mainly thanks to Shirley Ardener that I was inspired to write about Gypsy women as a category and in contrast to men.

The same influence occurred when Shirley later urged me to write a paper on my girls' boarding school (Okely 1978, 1996). I had kept in touch with her during my return visits to submit my doctorate. She had noticed that I had frequently referred to my schooling and insisted it was the time to write it up. In Oxford, there was a newly funded interdisciplinary women's seminar forum. I savour the drama of giving my first presentation on the boarding-school theme the day before my doctoral viva. It was doubly dramatic as Shirley was in black, having returned from the funeral of Phyllis Kaberry. I had never and would never have had a request from a male anthropologist mentor to write on such concerns.

Again, there are resonances with my observations on student writing. If women tend to learn about the world through specifics, they are also more open to considering an autobiographical approach to knowledge. If men live gender disguised as the universalised norm, then they do not have to question their specificity. In contrast, women are not brought up in a universalised norm, so they have first to make sense of their place in the world on a subjective level.

However small the numbers in this conservative university where I obtained my lectureship, women formed a crucial potential for sisterly solidarity. I also appreciated two other 'token' women in other departments – one in the English department, and one in the sociology department; the celebrated African National Congress (ANC) activist Ruth First. She likewise could not obtain a job in the 'golden triangle' and commuted weekly to London, where her daughters lived. After my appointment, she went out of her way to contact me. She initiated some alternative female network and we would meet regularly for lunch in a pub/hotel.

The experience of sexism was no longer simply imagined since I could match it with hers. The most distressing memory from those years together was of her description of a staff meeting where she objected to something to her all-male colleagues. As sociologists, they prided themselves on their liberal view of the social world. Ruth said that she was upset about something and a younger male colleague said, 'Perhaps it's your time of life', i.e., the menopause. No one objected to this outrageous reduction to biological causes. Ruth was shattered and we talked at length about her bizarre colleagues. Some later helped raise funds for a memorial in her honour when she was blown up by a letter bomb in Mozambique. Such gestures seemingly only recognised a woman academic's value after her heroic masculinist death.

Move to a New University

My partner in London could be released from the hospital in the early months only if I was at home. So long as I did not miss teaching, no one would notice. Thus personal tragedy was to be concealed. A married man would have been given different treatment if his live-in wife were ill. Eventually, so I could be near my partner and because I wanted to live in southern England, I applied for various posts and was shortlisted for a post in a sociology department in southern England. Here, precisely because I had done field research in the U.K., I could also be classified as a sociologist. Some two hundred sociologists applied and I, the lone anthropologist, got the job. It was exciting to be in a department where, out of seventeen staff, six were women. Finding overlaps with the sociological literature on so-called deviants, I looked forward to ever-expanding intellectual exchange. Although the (all-male) selection committee was unanimous, I learned months after that a leading feminist sociologist initiated a petition protesting against my appointment, in part because I was an anthropologist.

Meanwhile at my previous university, a man was appointed to my vacant lectureship. An eminent married woman applied but was not shortlisted as it was argued that, since her husband did not live in the town, the department would not impose 'the burden of commuting' on her. In contrast, at my new university, there were no enquiries about one's marital or domestic status. As long as the lecturer had a local base, there were no comments about commuting for weekends. The most vivid contrast with my previous university occurred at a staff meeting when a lesbian senior colleague argued successfully for a three-year delay in becoming head of department because her female partner was expecting a baby.

Anthropology in Question

The teaching of gender courses was entirely monopolised by the existing women. However, as in my previous appointment, I introduced gender and feminism into all my teaching. By my third year in this sociology department, I was able to introduce a course entitled 'Social Anthropology', despite some resistance from a feminist Marxist who declared there were 'too many hunter-gatherers' in the outline reading. When I pointed out that the texts by Malinowski, Evans-Pritchard, Geertz, Douglas, Bohannan, Turner, Tambiah, Caplan, Richards, Ardener, La Fontaine and Leach did not concern such groups, the silence revealed that high theoreticians arrogantly labelled any non-urban group beyond Dover as 'hunter-gatherers'. This was the era when pastiche Althusserian mandarins dominated social science. Ethnographic work was denigrated as Anglo-Saxon empiricism. In the same department the alternative was quantitative survey research or symbolic interactionism. It was not understood that anthropology could embrace many theoretical perspectives that were neither positivist nor uniquely desk-bound.

Despite some intellectual gulfs, I eventually had the freedom to set the agenda and introduce aspects of my previous gender course and other anthropological debates. The course was extremely popular. The students enjoyed the ethnographic detail and a cross-cultural perspective, in contrast to theoretical abstractions, which concealed so much Western ethnocentrism. One young woman, now a leading public figure, confided that she resented the Western bias in the mainstream gender courses where high theory ruled.

I also taught so-called 'qualitative methodology' in the core courses, following others who taught quantitative methods. I was free to develop the implications of the gender, ethnicity, race and age of the fieldworker. This interaction between teaching and writing gave me the impetus to bid for the 1989 conference theme of the Association of Social Anthropologists, which I called *Anthropology and Autobiography* (Okely and Callaway 1992).

The research support facilities were outstanding. Secretaries were not as yet engulfed by IT-driven documentation and audit. They typed our books and articles and so had a direct engagement with our work. My book on Simone de Beauvoir (Okely 1986a) was typed entirely in departmental time. Here I could also experiment with changing autobiographical interpretations of her famous texts in order to give the historical setting of different women readers.

My memories through the 1980s were of relative freedom to do my own thing. Teaching on the faculty course 'The Enlightenment' created inspiring cross-disciplinary connections with the humanities. I obtained a major Economic and Social Research Council (ESRC) grant to do research amongst the rural aged in France on condition that I did a comparative study with rural England (Okely 1986b, 1991a). I disappeared to Normandy for months of fieldwork (Okely 1991b, 2001). Some years previously in Oxford, Shirley Ardener had initiated an annual lecture in honour of three women anthropologists, and in 1989 I was invited to give the Phyllis Kaberry Memorial Lecture (Okely 1991b, 1996).

In that second university I made two valuable friendships with women linked to the department. One was a lecturer in development whose first degree in anthropology encouraged a cross-cultural perspective. In addition, she had been to a similar boarding school to mine. It was her reading of my article on that topic which consolidated our friendship. Then there was a mature student who came up to me at a party at the end of my first year to thank me for my teaching. She would become my research officer on another ESRC project. All three of us were born in the same year. The mingling of the personal with the professional was normal. We shared discussions of personal tragedies and joys, relationships, and intellectual pursuits.

After thirteen years as a lecturer and at the top of the scale and having produced three books, numerous articles and gained two major ESRC grants, as well as having introduced postgraduate initiatives, I applied for promotion to a senior lectureship. Casually in the corridor and within earshot of passing students and staff, the female head of department informed me that the department would not be recommending me. This public humiliation undermined any naive belief in collegial sisterhood. I was fortunate to be invited by a male professor to transfer to an anthropology department in another university where I was elected to a Readership within the year and a personal chair a couple of years later.

Postgraduate Culture

It was in this sociology department that I had the experience of supervising my first male doctoral student. As an undergraduate, he had gravitated towards social anthropology, thanks to my one course. In the year of the 1984 miners' strike, I obtained an ESRC-linked Ph.D. award for him to study elderly and retired miners in the north-east of England, near where I had once taught. As someone from a family with a long mining tradition, my Ph.D. student was less likely to have been accepted at my previous university, with its heavy public-school intake. He has recently been appointed to a chair in social anthropology in Australia. I also supervised an Algerian male university lecturer and women from Greece, Bengal, Turkey, and Canada. Here my anthropology was highly relevant to theses concerned with cultures beyond Dover. It was important that I could supervise men in addition to some outstanding women doctoral students and not be expected to be a dominant authority figure. I did not see myself as some authoritarian guru.

When I ran postgraduate seminars in the different universities where I worked, the ambience I sought had been greatly influenced by that generated by the Women's Anthropology Seminar at Oxford. I was deeply impressed by Shirley Ardener's comment that a seminar had been a success because 'everyone had spoken'. The atmosphere was supportive but subtly critical. The participants' questions could point gently to flaws, which eventually the speaker would come round to recognising without being publicly humiliated, let alone destroyed.

This seminar style was to puzzle a male lecturer at my future Scottish university. Apparently he referred to my male postgraduates as 'Judith's eunuchs'. This younger academic believed in the macho mode, where postgraduates were encouraged to perform with aggression and publicly 'destroy' paper givers in a blood letting cockfight. Four of those so-called eunuchs are now university lecturers elsewhere. A fifth became a respected consultant.

From my appointments in the 1970s and 1980s, I moved to become a professor in two other universities. In one, out of some two hundred professors, there were just eight women professors. In my most recent university, for eight years I was the only woman professor in the social sciences. At this institution, the core module in gender was now monopolised by a young male lecturer. As in the past, I brought gender issues into all my teaching.

Female networks across departments continued to be crucial, however sparse. My great privilege was to have a Nigerian sociology colleague, the late Dr Obi Igwara, whom I saw as an ever-optimistic soul sister. Our friendship was a wondrous mixture of the personal, the intellectual, and the academic. While in the 1970s as a (white) woman over thirty, it was presumed I was a mere student, she in the 1990s and over forty had the added experience of being presumed to be a student because of her race. With a confident upbringing in Nigeria, she used various scintillating strategies to confront or ignore racism (cf. Mirza 1995; Rassool 1995).

Gender Institutionalised or Appropriated

Whereas in the 1970s and doubtless before, women were severely disadvantaged in attempting to move into academic spheres beyond that of servant research assistant, by the 1990s there were greater opportunities for women. The old categories of male academic's unwaged wife versus desexed academic spinster are now transformed. There is the increased presence of the academic partner or wife. The latter may provide less domestic servicing for a study-bound husband than was the expectation in the past. Instead, she brings a lucrative salary in her own right for a double-income household. Gone are the days when a woman lecturer had to conceal a commuting relationship. Such split lives are now considered signs of status. It is now illegal for a committee to ask how a woman organises childcare. And women as new mothers will feel free to celebrate their identity as mothers in conferences and public presentations.

The greater sensitivity towards female appointments, driven in part by equal opportunities legislation, has however, been manipulated by male-dominated power structures to put their own women in place.[2] The husband cannot officially be on the appointing committee, but there are informal networks and pressures on colleagues.[3] In Canada the practice is at least transparent through negotiated spouse appointments.

Alternative practices have emerged officially in the name of gender equality, namely the appointment or promotion of unofficial sexual partners to key staff positions. If the relationship is illicit, few dare question those in power about conflict of interest precisely because the liaison is not in the public domain. Thus men may use the modern legal challenge to gender inequalities to continue to strengthen their own power base, while their client women are predictably complicitous. This is to the detriment of other women, who are seen as rivals rather than potential allies.

Conclusion

There are triumphs in the increasing acceptance of gender issues. Disciplines have shown a wondrous flowering in many arenas. Gender is in the academic and intellectual public domain (Davies and Holloway 1995). There are centres of gender studies, degrees, and gender publications in many disciplines. Gone are the early days when I could read gender publications in history, archaeology, literature, languages, art, philosophy, sociology and geography as well as anthropology across all the disciplines. Now, to the credit of gender research, we cannot hope to cover all disciplines, but there remain vital interdisciplinary connections, in contrast to the strict or even antagonistic boundaries between disciplines in so many other intellectual fields.

Women are more visible and with occasional access to academic power. An example was recently recounted by Shirley Ardener. After a special dinner in a prestigious college, she talked with two younger women professors over coffee. Shirley felt that there was something very different that evening. Then she realised it was because the women were happy to talk together as a self-sufficient unit without searching for eye contact and validation among male academics in the vicinity. The women had independent power.

I have argued that not only is the feminist argument 'the personal is political' of value, but also 'the personal is theoretical' (Okely 1992: 9). In this chapter, I have introduced a thread of narrative examples about my experience as a woman academic through a career over decades at several universities. Key incidents, seemingly trivial, give insights into the university power structures. A passing remark can betray the core values and day-to-day practice of academic institutions. The latter I contest are uniquely important, as they are the creators and conveyors of established and new knowledge. Universities are different from industries, which produce physical objects or marketing spin where accuracy and truth are negotiable. As my colleague David once noted, 'We produce human beings' (Okely 2004). Universities guard and create ideas, not mere products. Both the academic staff and students will be affected by the identity and positionality of whoever is producing and transmitting that knowledge.

It is unfortunate that just when U.K. universities have to be sensitive to gender, race, class, and disability, they are under overwhelming pressures to mimic the ideals of the market economy and state-dictated ideas of utility and bureaucratic priorities rather than intellectual creativity. Over a number of decades, Shirley Ardener has been an inspiring example of a woman academic betwixt and between power structures that have moved from gender phobia to audit mania.

Notes

1. This was a path set earlier in my Oxford college, where we women undergraduates had to sign a form agreeing not to marry during our three-year course of study (Okely 1986a).

2. I recall a celebrated woman anthropologist saying how shocked she was when in the 1980s she obtained an Oxbridge fellowship. She was later told that the committee felt safe in her appointment because her husband, a former fellow, had been there before her. The all-male committee needed to know that her 'reliability' had been put to the test by one of the 'chaps'.
3. In one appointment whose procedure I witnessed, a man was allowed to sit on the shortlisting meeting, although it was public departmental knowledge that his mistress was applying. He was permitted to assess another woman's application after he boasted, to shrieks of laddish laughter, of a 'dalliance' with her.

References

Ardener, S. (ed.) 1975. *Perceiving Women*, London: Malaby Press.
——— 1984. 'Incorporation and Exclusion: Oxford Academics' Wives', in H. Callan and S. Ardener (eds), *The Incorporated Wife*, London: Croom Helm, pp. 27–49.
Banks, O. 1999. 'Some Reflections on Gender, Sociology and Women's History', *Women's History Review* 8 (3), pp. 401–10.
Barker, D. 1975. 'Women in the Anthropology Profession – 1', in R. Rohrlich-Leavitt (ed.), *Women Cross-Culturally: Change and Challenge*, The Hague: Mouton Press, pp. 537–46.
Blackstone, T. 1973. 'The Scarce Academics', *Times Higher Education Supplement*, 16 March.
Caplan, P. 1975. 'Women in the Anthropology Profession – 2', in R. Rohrlich-Leavitt (ed.), *Women Cross-Culturally: Change and Challenge*, The Hague: Mouton Press, pp. 547–57.
Chodorow, N. 1974. 'Family Structure and Feminine Personality', in M. Rosaldo and L. Lamphere (eds), *Woman, Culture and Society*, Stanford: Stanford University Press, pp. 43–66.
Davies, C. and P. Holloway 1995. 'Troubling Transformations: Gender Regimes and Organisational Culture in the Academy', in L. Morley and V. Walsh (eds), *Feminist Academics: Creative Agents for Change*, London: Taylor & Francis, pp. 7–21.
Durkheim, E. 1914. *The Elementary Forms of the Religious Life* (trans. J. Ward Swain), London: Allen & Unwin.
Evans, M. 1997. 'Negotiating the Frontier: Women and Resistance in the Contemporary Academy', in L. Stanley (ed.), *Knowing Feminisms*, London: Sage Publications, pp. 46–57.
Frankenberg, R. 1990 (orig. 1957). *Village on the Border*, Prospect Heights: Waverley.
Harding, S. 1986. *The Science Question in Feminism*, Milton Keynes: Open University.
Malinowski, B. 1967. *A Diary in the Strict Sense of the Term*, London: Routledge & Kegan Paul.
Mauss, M. 1950. 'Les Techniques du corps', in M. Mauss, *Sociologie et anthropologie*, Paris: Presses Universitaires de France.
Mead, M. 1935. *Sex and Temperament in Three Primitive Societies*, New York: Morrow.
Mirza, H.S. 1995. 'Black Women in Higher Education: Defining a Space/Finding a Place', in L. Morley and V. Walsh (eds), *Feminist Academics: Creative Agents for Change*, London: Taylor & Francis, pp. 145–55.
Moore, H. 1988. *Feminism and Anthropology*, Cambridge: Polity Press.
Morley, L. and V. Walsh 1995. 'Introduction', in L. Morley and V. Walsh (eds), *Feminist Academics: Creative Agents for Change*, London: Taylor & Francis, pp. 1–6.
Oakley, A. 1972. *Sex, Gender and Society*, London: Temple Smith.
Okely, J. 1975a. 'Gypsy Women: Models in Conflict', in S. Ardener (ed.), *Perceiving Women*, London: Malaby Press, pp. 55–86.

Okely, J. 1975b. 'The Self and Scientism', *Journal of the Anthropological Society of Oxford* (republished in J. Okely, *Own or Other Culture*, London: Routledge, 1996, pp. 27–44).

——— 1978. 'Privileged, Schooled and Finished: Boarding Education for Girls', in S. Ardener (ed.), *Defining Females: The Nature of Women in Society*, London and New York: Croom Helm and St Martin's Press, pp. 109–139 (republished in J. Okely, *Own or Other Culture*, London: Routledge, 1996, pp. 147–74).

——— 1982. *The Traveller Gypsies*, Cambridge: Cambridge University Press.

——— 1986a. *Simone de Beauvoir: A Re-reading*, London: Virago.

——— 1986b. 'The Conditions and Experience of Ageing compared in Rural England and France', Report to the ESRC.

——— 1991a. 'The Ethnographic Method Applied to Rural Transport, Planning and the Elderly', Report to the ESRC.

——— 1991b. 'Defiant Moments: Gender, Resistance and Individuals', *Man* 26 (1), pp. 3–22.

——— 1992. 'Anthropology and Autobiography: Participatory Experience and Embodied Knowledge', in J. Okely and H. Callaway (eds), *Anthropology and Autobiography*, London: Routledge, pp. 1–28.

——— 1996. *Own or Other Culture*, London: Routledge.

——— 2001. 'Visualism and Landscape: Looking and Seeing in Normandy', *Ethnos* 66 (1), pp. 99–120.

——— 2003. 'The Filmed Return of the Natives to a Colonising Territory of Terror', *Journal of Media Practice* 3 (2), pp. 65–74.

——— 2006. 'The Bureaucratisation of Knowledge in Higher Education or What are Universities For?' Paper for the C-SAP workshop, University of Hull, in D. Carter and M. Lord (eds), *Engagements with Learning and Teaching in Higher Education*, Birmingham: University of Birmingham (C-SAP (Sociology, Anthropology, Politics) Monograph Series, no. 4), pp. 127–137.

Okely, J. and H. Callaway (eds) 1992. *Anthropology and Autobiography*, London: Routledge.

Ramazanoglu, C. with J. Holland 2002. *Feminist Methodology: Challenges and Choices*, London: Sage.

Rassool, N. 1995. 'Black Women as the "Other" in the Academy', in L. Morley and V. Walsh (eds), *Feminist Academics: Creative Agents for Change*, London: Taylor & Francis, pp. 22–41.

Reiter, R. 1974. *Toward an Anthropology of Women*, London: Monthly Review Press.

Rosaldo, M. and L. Lamphere (eds) 1974. *Woman, Culture and Society*, Stanford: Stanford University Press.

Rose, H. 1983. 'Hand, Brain and Heart: A Feminist Epistemology for the Natural Sciences', *Signs: Journal of Women in Culture and Society* 9 (1), pp. 73–90.

Sciama, L. 1984. 'Ambivalence and Dedication: Academic Wives in Cambridge University, 1870–1979', in H. Callan and S. Ardener (eds), *The Incorporated Wife*, London: Croom Helm, pp. 50–66.

Shore, C. and S. Wright 1999. 'Audit Culture and Anthropology: Neo-liberalism in British Higher Education', *Journal of the Royal Anthropological Institute* 5 (4), pp. 557–75.

Tolson, A. 1977. *The Limits of Masculinity*, London: Tavistock.

Walters, M. 1978. *The Nude Male*, London: Paddington Press.

AFTERWORDS
IN CELEBRATION
OF SHIRLEY ARDENER

Gendering Oxford: Shirley Ardener and Cross-Cultural Research

Janette Davies and Jacqueline Waldren

Early Beginnings

Since the early 1970s, Shirley Ardener has applied her intellect, creativity and enthusiasm to the development of women's studies at the University of Oxford and further afield. Her contribution to social anthropology and women's studies is revealed in the chapters of this book and in her innumerable publications. She recognised the similarity between the 'consciousness-raising' proposed by Western feminist movements and the social anthropological techniques of 'isolating from their context statements which though trivial in themselves carry assumptions with wider significance' (Ardener 1978: 45, n. 9). The category 'women' was problematised in different contexts; individual cultural models of women – i.e., the set of ideas which together represent women in the minds of those who have generated the model (S. Ardener 1975: xi) – were seen to hold no ultimate theoretical or moral primacy. These approaches increased ways of considering women in society.

Shirley Ardener's paper 'Sexual Insult and Female Militancy', read in February 1971 at the core weekly seminar convened by lecturers John Beattie and Peter Lienhardt at the Institute of Social Anthropology, University of Oxford, discussed patterns of behaviour of Cameroon women and compared these with certain manifestations of the women's liberation movements developing in the West at that time. The paper was met at first by a confused silence in the male-dominated seminar culture (J. Okely, personal communication). Soon afterwards, an informal seminar of women social anthropologists began to meet regularly in Oxford in order to focus on women in cross-cultural perspective and concentrate attention on issues of mutual concern. The professor would not allow a women's seminar to meet at the Institute, so it was convened at Queen Elizabeth House, thus commencing a practice that eventually resulted in the creation of the Centre for the Cross-Cultural Study of Women. At the Decennial Conference of the Association of Social Anthropologists held in Oxford in 1973, anthropologists from different institutions interested in women's studies met for informal discussions. It was clear that a strong sense of localised 'tradition' in different departments of anthropology and limited communication between anthropology departments in various universities were seen to have discouraged innovation and cross-cultural fertilisation of ideas.

Shirley Ardener was in the unique position of being an 'informal' member of the Oxford anthropology circle, an insider/outsider at Oxford.[1] Her knowledge and field experience were recognised but her position in the system remained informal. She was certainly invited to tutor, to give the occasional lecture 'on women', to edit books, and to sit on interview panels; what she also did was to encourage colleagues to organise occasional seminars. A series of regular weekly seminars followed at Queen Elizabeth House, Oxford, outside the official anthropological programme, and as a dialogue developed between contributors, new research on women was presented. It soon became evident that 'the scale of the task of understanding women (or any other defined group in society) was daunting, and perhaps open-minded examination of as many women's models as possible might not only locate interesting differences between them, but might also stumble on possible points of congruence' (S. Ardener 1975: xxi).

The women involved in the early days of the seminar series, entitled the Oxford Women's Social Anthropology Seminar, were pioneering in their academic endeavours to create space for the presentation of research, mostly anthropological and certainly concerning issues of great importance to women worldwide. One aim of the programme was to put those interested in the study of women in touch with one another, by providing an additional forum for discussion. When new papers were to be specially written for a proposed book, some ideas of the themes to be addressed would be provided, although authors were also encouraged to draw on their individual research data and outlook. Titles and topics presented in 1973 such as 'Belief and the Problem of Women' by Edwin Ardener, 'Female Militancy and Colonial Revolt: The Women's War of 1929, Eastern Nigeria' by Caroline Ifeka-Moller, 'Gypsy Women: Models in Conflict' by Judith Okely, 'The Brides of Christ' by Drid Williams, as well as 'Sexual Insult and Female Militancy' by Shirley and 'The Premise of Dedication: Notes toward an Ethnography of Diplomats' Wives' by Hilary Callan, were published two years later in *Perceiving Women* (S. Ardener 1975).

Shirley Ardener (personal communication) remembers in particular how women packed in to hear Judith Okely's paper on boarding-school life and the subsequent excitement of the audience. She also recalls how this graduate seminar series attracted undergraduates who found a supportive milieu for discussion, where participants actually listened to each other in a way not experienced in most seminars around the university. Many of the speakers at these seminars, as well as those who regularly attended them, later went on to become university lecturers and professors in countries such as Britain, Denmark, Indonesia, and the United States, and also in Africa.

Edwin Ardener's pioneering paper entitled 'Belief and the Problem of Women' put forward the idea that 'women may not have been given the kind of attention by anthropologists which is their due as half of most populations, partly because their own societies, and also the world of academic social anthropology, have viewed them under the influence of dominant male systems of perception' (1975: xii). He suggested that women's ideas or models of the world around them might find a way of expression in forms other than direct expository speech, possibly through symbolism in art, myth, ritual, special speech register, and the like. 'The study of symbolism [he wrote] uncovers certain valuations of women. ... I here contend that much of this symbolism in fact enacts that female model of the world which has been lacking' (ibid.: 5). Shirley and others built upon Charlotte Hardman's formulations and Edwin's elaborations that in addition to dominant models – 'dominant modes of expression in any society which have been generated by the dominant structures within it' (S. Ardener 1978: 20) – there are thus also muted models. Edwin's version of the muted-group theory referred to the silence of women, but Shirley pointed out that this was not the only approach to consider: the male and public discourse is encoded by men (Spender 1980), who will be heard and listened to, whereas the 'theory of mutedness ... does not require that the muted group be actually silent' (S. Ardener 1978). However, as in the examples of Mongolian women (Humphrey 1993: 91) and Greek women (Hirschon 1993: 23), Shirley Ardener noted that 'the regulation of women's nomenclature, and their use of language, may go so far as the suppression of speech; thus muting becomes total to the point of silence' (1978: 23). This work influenced research in the 1980s and continues to offer a point of departure for women's studies in general.

In 1976, a few women met to consider forming an interdisciplinary programme focused on the study of women. One of the major concerns was funding. In the introduction to a paper by Sally Chilver, Ardener discusses the problem (1998: 243):

> The preoccupation of so many anthropologists and anthropology departments with securing funding raises many questions about the control of the direction in which anthropological research is going. One is forced to take note not only of the kind and quantity of factual knowledge produced (or ignored), but also the effect this must have on the development of thought in anthropology. There is, of course, an old refrain that research of all kinds must adapt to the needs of society – which leads to the question: who decides what those needs are?

Doubtless influenced by Ardener's perseverance, a small university fund was made available and it was suggested that it be allocated to women's studies. Shirley Ardener noted that 'if the suggestion for a women's studies fund had not met with the approval of the university, the Hebdomadal Council might have been asked to devote the money to the purchase of some dinosaur bones needed by the University Museum'. Fortunately for women, on this occasion, the prehistoric monsters did not win. So precariously do academic concerns advance (Ardener 1978:10).

As more interested persons joined the academic debates, a programme emerged. Some small grants were made to graduates to meet certain research costs. A little money was used to support a bibliographical exercise to locate existing resources in Oxford. The major part of the fund was allocated to meet the costs of an interdisciplinary series of seminars, to run throughout the academic year 1977–78. Following *Perceiving Women*, published in 1975, Shirley's second edited collection of papers in women's studies, *Defining Females*, appeared in 1978, published by Croom Helm in association with the Oxford University Women's Studies Committee. In her Introduction to that volume Shirley described more of the background:

> The study of women at Oxford has been carried out until recently through the personal interest and the individual initiative of workers whose numbers and influence upon their respective fields have varied. Certain academic supervisors have especially encouraged research on women in recent years, and as a result there have been more theses dealing with women. Some seminars have been held. The most extended series of papers has been that organised unofficially by a number of female social anthropologists, who have between them read a new paper each week throughout every academic term since early 1973. Many of these have already been published (in, for example *Perceiving Women*, 1975, and in various issues of the *Journal of the Anthropological Society of Oxford*) and more papers are expected to appear in print in the future. (Ardener 1978: 9)

Weekly seminars continued each term until 1983, when the participants decided to form the Centre for Cross-Cultural Research on Women (CCCRW), with an office at Queen Elizabeth House. The founder members of the Centre were Shirley Ardener; Sandra Burman, a lawyer with socio-legal expertise amongst families in South Africa; Helen Callaway, a social anthropologist who lived and worked in colonial Nigeria; Elizabeth Croll, sinologist and social anthropologist, who was undertaking a project on child welfare in China funded by UNICEF; Alaine Low, a historian conducting research on the Falklands/Maldives dispute; Iona Mayer, a social anthropologist with in-depth knowledge of the Gusii peoples of Kenya; and Alison Smith, a historian working on the Oxford Development Records Project. Later members included Julia Leslie, a specialist on Indian religions, the social anthropologists Renate Barber, Judith Okely, and Soraya Tremayne, and the sociologist Cecillie Swaisland, as well as many others who made vital academic contributions to the seminars during their DPhil studies at Oxford.

Cross-Cultural Research on Women: Gendering Oxford

At the time of the creation of the CCCRW it was clear (certainly now, with hindsight) that women's studies were 'neither a prestigious nor a welcome research area in male-dominated Oxford' (Spaas 1994). The individual and group narration of CCCRW facilitated space and freedom for women to speak out in seminars as never before. These academic women exchanging ideas and debating research experiences were doing so in a climate of advancing Western feminism. They endeavoured to look at women's issues cross-culturally, at a time when such matters were clearly neglected by British anthropology. They were also concerned with their own future and the opportunities for women in academia. The seminars gave them space to present academic papers in the context of a receptive and constructively critical audience.

By the 1980s, the multiplicity of feminisms made it clear that cross-cultural studies were essential in order to deconstruct the meaning of women in a given society. Shirley's edited volume *Defining Females* (1978) was a precursor to approaches that aimed to understand the structural or social position of women in each society studied and how the category 'women' is defined and related to gender in society. Shirley's next edited volume, *Women and Space: Ground Rules and Social Maps*, was published in 1981. It included a study by Sarah Skar of concepts of Andean women's beliefs surrounding space and time, a presentation by Silvia Rodgers of women's space within the 'Men's House', namely the British House of Commons, and a poignant interpretation, by Juliet Blair, of the public and private space of actresses. This publication was wide in geographical perspective. Other papers in this volume included a study of villagers in Iran by Sue Wright, Shi'ite Iran by Jane Khatib-Chahidi, Soviet minorities by Tamara Dragadze, Italy by Lidia Sciama, Greece by Renée Hirschon, Yorubaland by Helen Callaway, and South Africa by Rosemary Ridd.

Curiously enough, a copy of this volume is to be found in the Map Room of the Bodleian Library – probably because of the use of 'Ground Rules and Social Maps' as its subtitle. But where indeed should books on women's studies be placed in libraries? If they are collected together as a section on Women they may very well be looked at only by students directed to that section or those already with an established interest in the subject. There are some advantages of books being misplaced (or could one say muted?) as this opens up alternative channels and modes of communication among a wider readership. Perhaps those from geography or other disciplines searching in the Map Room had the pleasure of discovering new horizons within the covers of *Women and Space*.

In a review of a book in the Oxford University Women's Studies Committee series, *Women's Religious Experience* (ed. Holden 1983), Ronnie Frankenberg, writing in *The Sociological Review* in 1984, opened his remarks by stating that 'Among the greatest of the many benefits that there are to be derived by male sociologists and others from the current concerns of feminism are the various publications coming from the Oxford University Women's Studies Committee'. Along with *Women and Property: Women as Property* (ed. Hirschon 1984), the first three publications were all complimented by Frankenberg: as he said, 'the books are a splendid advertisement for the seminar that gives rise to them, for anthropology and for feminism' (Frankenberg, personal communication). The first three books to appear in that series, all of them multi-author collections, were

Shirley's *Defining Females* (1978), Sandra Burman's *Fit Work for Women* (1979), and Mary Jacobus's *Women Writing and Writing about Women* (1979), all published by Croom Helm.

Led by the editorial vision of Shirley Ardener and Helen Callaway, then deputy director of CCCRW, a new book series, entitled 'Cross-Cultural Perspectives on Women', was set up with Berg Publishers (run by Marion Berghahn from 1984 to 1994). It has been well received. Twenty volumes have been published in this series, now edited by Shirley Ardener and Jacqueline Waldren. They are a clear indication of the importance of understanding gender and of the continued need for academic research that analyses power, history, and the lives of women across all cultures. These books are used worldwide in university departments that encourage students to research into women's and gender issues. Such is the legacy of the CCCRW and, later, its successor, the International Gender Studies Centre (IGS).

As early as 1983, the CCCRW was receiving women Visiting Fellows from around the world, who played an academic role not only within the Centre but also Queen Elizabeth House and the wider University of Oxford. Cooperation with Visiting Fellows after their return to their countries became better consolidated when links were established with UNESCO and the British Council. Joyce Endeley, head of Women's Studies at the University of Buea, Cameroon, hosted a twinning arrangement with CCCRW and the subsequent visits of Shirley Ardener, who gave lectures as well as editorial assistance for a new local journal, Issues in Gender and Development (see Endeley et al. 2004). Marjorie Mbilinyi, Professor of International Development Studies at the University of Dar es Salaam, facilitated the visit of Janette Davies to Tanzania under the same link, where she contributed to the research methods class for masters students and coordinated ongoing links with academics who had been Visiting Fellows at CCCRW (including, for example, Ibrahim Shao, one-time Professor of International Development Studies). In 1995, John Bunch, a CCCRW Visiting Fellow from the Ecole Supérieure de Commerce de Rennes was the first male to come to the Centre in that capacity and thus benefit from its expertise. The now-renamed IGS has facilitated the development and understanding of gender within his anthropological thesis on values attached to goods and female consumers in a cross-cultural perspective. Three Japanese Visiting Fellows strengthened what has become an ongoing link with Tokyo International University and the International Christian University.

The range of issues researched and discussed is noted by Spaas (1994), where she quotes Shirley Ardener: 'If we are going to study women we must not foreclose on any questions.' Spaas suggests that the variety of issues researched resulted from the fact that many of the anthropologists had undertaken extensive fieldwork in many different parts of the world, which guaranteed the cross-culturalism of CCCRW. These women anthropologists and historians were interested in discourse, development, bilingualism, education, and many other topics (Spaas 1994). In 1984, in preparation for the international celebrations of the centenary of the anthropologist Bronislaw Malinowski, his daughter Helena Malinowski

Wayne gave a special lecture at Queen Elizabeth House on the subject 'My Father Bronislaw Malinowski and the Influence of Various Women on his Life and Works'. She found the audience and discussion helpful for her future presentations. A selection of seminars in 1985 shows the width and breadth of such cultural contexts and issues: life among African nuns; protocol among elite Saudi Arabian women; how the United Nations' work on women is organised; the UN conference on women in Nairobi; and rural women in Bangladesh. The study of culture change took anthropologists into the field of modern administrative, social, political, and economic problems, where gender issues were salient in each context. Cross-cultural analysis and comparisons were made. The academic life of the Centre continued apace, not only in its seminar series and commemorative lectures (see below) but also in its facilitation of workshops and conferences based on debates over timely issues, such as 'Medical Missions: Past and Present', 'Culture, the Household and Female Migration to Britain', 'Violence and the Cultural Construction of Sexuality', 'Women and Second Language Use', and 'Women, Drinking and Addiction' – all held between 1985 and 1989.

Soon after its inception, the CCCRW instituted a commemorative series of annual lectures. As Shirley Ardener later went on to describe, in her Preface to a collection of the early commemorative lectures (Ardener 1992):

> Along with the establishing of CCCRW came the decision by members to hold an Annual Commemorative Lecture in honour of three early women anthropologists. The Centre for Cross-Cultural Research on Women was being set up at Queen Elizabeth House, University of Oxford's International Development Centre, in order to secure and enhance work which had been gathering momentum in the House for over a decade. We felt we should mark this step forward by some public event. What better than a gesture recognising our debt to the pioneers in research on women in diverse cultures?

The anthropologists Phyllis Kaberry, Barbara Ward, and Audrey Richards have thus been honoured in the decades since the inception of this series of commemorative lectures. Caroline Ifeka, the first lecturer, gave a paper in 1984 in honour of the work of Phyllis Kaberry, entitled 'The Mystical and Political Powers of Queen Mothers, Kings and Commoners in Nso, Cameroon'. In the following decade, the lecturers included Jean La Fontaine, speaking on 'The Persons of Women', in honour of Audrey Richards; Caroline Humphrey, remembering Barbara Ward's research, who spoke on 'Women and Ideology in Hierarchical Societies in East Asia'; and Judith Okely, who re-examined Phyllis Kaberry's work in a lecture entitled 'Defiant Moments: Gender, Resistance and Individuals'. Sandy Toussaint, a Visiting Fellow in 1996–97, returned in 2000 to present the commemorative lecture, which was about the work of Phyllis Kaberry and entitled 'Interpreting Cultural Narratives: Ethnography, Biography and the Paradox of Memory'. Toussaint's analysis of the link between life stories and ethnographies and how they contribute to the anthropology of knowledge is central to the research conducted and disseminated by the CCCRW and IGS;

and, indeed, the commemorative lectures in general, in re-examining the work of these pioneering women anthropologists, addressed both the era in which they worked and the present relevance of that work. Other scholars who gave commemorative lectures include Wendy James, Sally Chilver, Pat Caplan, Pat Holden, Kirsten Hastrup, Parminder Bhachu, Nancy Lindisfarne, Elizabeth Tonkin, Melissa Leach, and Henrietta Moore.

Shirley Ardener was the founding director of the CCCRW. Later directors included Helen Callaway, Soraya Tremayne, and Lidia Sciama. Maria Jaschok, the current director of the newly renamed IGS, arrived first in 1997–98 as a Visiting Fellow from Monash University, Australia. She gave the 1998 Ward Commemorative Lecture, entitled 'A Mosque of One's Own: Chinese Women, Islam and Sexual Equality'. The strong relationship formed between her and CCCRW proved fortuitous for the Centre when she formally accepted the post of director. Her ongoing research in China and her affiliation as Research Scholar at the Institute of Chinese Studies, University of Oxford, produced two workshops – one on 'Women Organising in China', which resulted in a publication in the Berg series (Hsiung et al. 2001), and more recently a workshop on 'Women and Gender in Chinese Studies', which brought together graduate students in the discipline.

In addition to her work on gender issues, Shirley Ardener, together with co-convenors Jonathan Webber, Tamara Dragadze, Ian Fowler, and Lidia Sciama, continued the Oxford University seminar series 'Ethnicity and Identity', founded over two decades ago by Edwin Ardener. This series focuses on the ethnic, historical, religious, and other elements of culture that give rise to a social sense of belonging, enabling individuals and groups to find meaning both in their own social identities and in what differentiates them from others. The overlap of gender and ethnicity was clear, and a further book series developed from these ongoing seminars.

In 1993 the CCCRW was asked to provide four lectures on gender for a new undergraduate course at Oxford on Archaeology and Anthropology. With the cooperation of other members of the Centre, Shirley Ardener and Jacqueline Waldren designed and coordinated a course entitled 'Gender: Theories and Realities' that would introduce students to theories of gender and feminist critique and aid them in applying these insights to the analysis of anthropological and archaeological research. With a broader understanding of femininities and masculinities and female/male power relations in various contexts, students would be prepared to confront gender issues in the world they inhabit and in the professions they chose to follow. The main themes included reinterpreting social organisation and kinship relations, finding women's places and spaces, the social construction of women's roles, family and household, women's experiences, and muted groups. Also included in the course were reviews of debates on such issues as nature/culture, honour/shame, biology/sex, theories of production and reproduction, and the social construction of sexuality and feminisms in Western, African, Middle Eastern, Asian, and Caribbean societies. The programme was put together on the basis of strategies that had developed from interaction and dialogue with students and colleagues, as well as from an awareness of the misunderstandings that had surrounded women's studies in Oxford and further afield.

Shirley Ardener led her students into areas of thought underlying ordinary everyday life, with a special emphasis on modes of understanding cultural diversity and the socio-political conditions that stimulate change. The initial first-year lectures were developed into a third-year optional paper. Many students wondered why they had not been introduced to gender awareness at the onset of their course (or at school). As Shirley noted, 'The detail and special relevance of women's activities is often indistinguishable from men's in general descriptions although they may not be in reality. Aggregation provides a confusing picture of men's behaviours, of course, no less true, an inference which is an important lesson from women's studies generally' (Ardener and Burman 1995: 11). It was time to understand anthropologically – and particularly through ethnographic research – how dominant forms of 'masculinity' have helped to shape prevailing forms of knowledge, culture, and experience (Cornwall and Lindisfarne 1994).

With the new millennium, the Centre was looking to fresh directions as well as trying to secure sources of funding. One outcome, in 2002, was the Centre's change of name to the International Gender Studies Centre (IGS), with its members emphasising the need to expand cross-cultural research on gender, power relations, the environment, and development. As pointed out in *Persons and Powers of Women in Diverse Cultures* (Ardener 1992), people's experience of inequality needs to be seen through analysis of the relation between gender and power. The subsequent workshops – for example, 'Women and Gender in Chinese Studies', 'Globally Mobile Professional Families: Distance, Age and Gender', and the seminar series 'Gender in Transnational and Transforming Families: Stretching Boundaries and Social Conventions' – provide evidence of the continued commitment to gender research in a changing world.

A sense of social commitment to women's struggles led the Centre to choose Aung San Suu Kyi, the elected leader of Burma, as patron of CCCRW and then the IGS. She accepted this invitation, although under continued house arrest and unable to partake in its activities, and for its part the Centre endeavours to disseminate awareness about her plight in its biannual newsletter and website, as well as on its headed paper. Every time her name is highlighted, the oppression of people in Burma and other areas of the world is brought to the fore.

Shirley Ardener was awarded an OBE in 1989 for 'services to anthropology'. Recognised beyond academia for her many accomplishments, Shirley Ardener gave credit to all who had shared with her and made such an award possible. The creation of an ongoing centre for research is her legacy. The extensive list of her publications, from 1953 and continuing through five decades, attests to her intellectual scope. Her contribution to women's studies and gender awareness also includes the inspiration she has given to many generations of students to attempt new, broader approaches, as well as encouraging graduates to produce papers, convene workshops, publish books and articles, or apply for jobs. Many friends and colleagues will attest to the fact that their academic activities and projects were influenced by Shirley Ardener's experience and support as a gifted teacher, lecturer, and mentor.

Her inspiration is reflected in the articles in this volume and recorded in this history of cross-cultural research in Oxford. It remains a collective effort by a number of committed women (and a few men) over three decades. Gender studies are now an essential component of anthropological studies, and in the midst of seminars and workshops the astute voice of Shirley Ardener continues to provoke thought. This voice is also evident as written word, in particular in the introductions she has written to the numerous publications in the CCCRW/IGS and Ethnicity and Identity series.

Note

1. Jacqueline Waldren discussed the concept of insiders and outsiders in her book *Insiders and Outsiders* (1996). The 'incorporation' of wives into the institutional and moral frameworks associated with their husbands' occupations is discussed in Callan and Ardener (eds) 1984.

References

Ardener, E. 1975 (orig. 1972). 'Belief and the Problem of Women', in S. Ardener (ed.), *Perceiving Women*, London: Malaby Press, pp. 1–27.

Ardener, S. (ed.) 1975. *Perceiving Women*, London: Malaby Press.

——— (ed.) 1978. *Defining Females: The Nature of Women in Society*, London and New York: Croom Helm and St Martin's Press (in association with the Oxford University Women's Studies Committee); revised second edition: Oxford: Berg, 1993.

——— (ed.) 1981. *Women and Space: Ground Rules and Social Maps*, London: Croom Helm (in association with the Oxford University Women's Studies Committee).

——— (ed.) 1992. *Persons and Powers of Women in Diverse Cultures: Essays in Commemoration of Audrey I. Richards, Phyllis Kaberry, and Barbara E. Ward*, New York and Oxford: Berg.

——— 1998. 'The Funding of Social Anthropological Research: A Preliminary Note to a Fragment of History Written by E. M. Chilver in 1955', *Journal of the Anthropological Society of Oxford* 29, pp. 243–50.

Ardener, S. and S. Burman (eds) 1995. *Money-go-Rounds: The Importance of Rotating Savings and Credit Associations for Women*, Oxford and Washington, DC: Berg.

Callan, H. and S. Ardener (eds) 1984. *The Incorporated Wife*, London: Croom Helm (in association with the Oxford University Women's Studies Committee).

Cornwall, A. and N. Lindisfarne (eds) 1994. *Dislocating Masculinity: Comparative Ethnographies*, London: Routledge.

Endeley, J., S. Ardener, R. Goodridge and N. Lyonga (eds) 2004. *New Gender Studies from Cameroon and the Caribbean*, Buea: University of Buea (Issues in Gender and Development, vol. 1).

Hirschon, R. (ed.) 1984. *Women and Property: Women as Property*, Oxford: Berg.

Hirschon, R. 1993. 'Open Body/Closed Space: The Transformation of Female Sexuality', in S. Ardener (ed.), *Defining Females: The Nature of Women in Society* (orig. 1978), Oxford: Berg, pp. 51–72.

Holden, P. (ed.) 1983. *Women's Religious Experience*, London: Croom Helm (in association with the Oxford University Women's Studies Committee).

Hsiung P.-C., M. Jaschok and C. Milwertz, with Red Chan (eds) 2001. *Chinese Women Organizing: Cadres, Feminists, Muslims, Queers*, Oxford: Berg.

Humphrey, C. 1993. 'Women, Taboo and the Suppression of Attention', in S. Ardener (ed.), *Defining Females: The Nature of Women in Society* (orig. 1978), Oxford: Berg, pp. 73–92.

Spaas, L. 1994. 'Defying the "Libido Dominandi" in Feminism: Equality and/or Difference?' *Synthesis: An Interdisciplinary Journal* (special issue), pp. 55–64.

Spender, D. 1980. *Man Made Language*, London: Routledge & Kegan Paul.

Waldren, J. 1996. *Insiders and Outsiders: Paradise and Reality in Mallorca*, Oxford: Berghahn Books.

Shirley Ardener's Habitus

Jonathan Benthall

When I used to think of women anthropologists prominent during the last quarter of the twentieth century, either the profile would come to mind of a figure with arms akimbo ready to pounce on some ill-judged generalisation that I might have let slip, or alternatively a texture of silky meekness charged with static electricity and sheathing a healthy set of claws. The fault for these warped representations was, of course, entirely mine, and was no doubt due to schooling in competitive male boarding institutions where the opposite sex had been a reality only at the margins. Shirley Ardener, however, seemed warm, welcoming and reassuringly fuzzy at the edges: the kind of lady one would have been pleased to encounter at a learned society tea meeting in one of Barbara Pym's novels and turn to with relief from some Ancient Mariner's monologue on his fieldwork, chatting with her enjoyably *de la pluie et du beau temps*. I am ashamed to say that Shirley's habitus resulted in my underestimating her initially – but fortunately not for long. I would not have made the mistake if I had read such papers as 'Sexual Insult and Female Militancy' more carefully.

Shirley's reputation holds its own among her most distinguished contemporaries. It must be encouraging for her – during a life in an Oxford that perhaps once made the same mistake as mine – that 'muted-group theory', first enunciated by her and Edwin Ardener, is still stimulating new research, to which she has recently added on her own account with a sharp analysis of the representation of women and girls in social science graphs and kinship diagrams. In a forthcoming article commissioned by Peter Rivière for his collection *A History of Anthropology at the University of Oxford* (Berghahn 2007), devoted to the period post-1970, I pay tribute to Shirley's contribution to the appreciation of the deep importance of gender in anthropology, which she pioneered in Oxford many years before it became part of the intellectual mainstream. Apart from her own truly original academic work and her tireless support of other women scholars, her non-confrontational style is surely an exemplar for a civilised anthropology.

Circumstance, Personality, and Anthropology

Tamara Dragadze

In the beginning there was turmoil in our Oxford Institute of Social Anthropology the year the Women's Seminar was born, partly because of a controversial appointment and partly because of the cold weather. In this 'winter of discontent' with power shortages, some of us had to bring blankets to our seminars. And there was also the curious Friday Seminar, bringing staff and postgraduate students together. At a time when Wendy James was the only female don as far as the eye could see in our Institute, and when a professor at St Antony's could say to me in the Common Room, 'Tamara, forgive me if I go to speak to those young men to help them get jobs. You see, as a girl, you can always become a dancer or a wife, but they have to have jobs to live' – at that time a question from a female at the Friday Seminar was usually dismissed, perhaps unconsciously by the chairman, but it was.

And so, in the basement of the Institute, the late Juliet Blair, Charlotte Hardman, and I convened a seminar for women only, for and by women only, and wondered what would happen. The late Helen Callaway gave that first paper, showing us her cloths from West Africa. We provided some theory and perspective, and new perspectives opened up.

It is here, however, that Shirley Ardener's presence turned everything around, a tentative adventure turned into a dignified seminar, because she has that incredible gift of taking something at face value and deciding immediately what action to take. By the following week, she personally convened the next meeting at Queen Elizabeth House, faced the consequences – because our women only rule was seen as highly antagonistic – and established her series of books, and with it an increasingly firmer academic base and indeed a women's seminar that has often been the source of new thinking.

Serious women's studies have to be grounded in what Shirley Ardener has in abundance: subtlety. And the touchy protagonists, insecure still as women in a men's world, have been kept together only because of another of her characteristics: discretion.

There is no subterfuge, no calculation of ulterior motives in Shirley Ardener's work; she is dignified in what she writes, scholarly, precise; and she is supportive in what she shares and organises. In short, she is what academia should embody and usually does not.

Shirley in My Mind

Grażyna Kubica

I met Shirley Ardener for the first time in spring 1986, during a ceremonial dinner at St John's College, Oxford. I had come from the Jagiellonian University, Cracow, and had received a grant from the Oxford Colleges Hospitality Scheme for Polish Scholars and was therefore able to spend some time in this magnificent place. St John's contributed to the Scheme by having one person each month. I was thus a piece of the 'Polish sausage', to quote Edwin Ardener's fine turn of phrase. Shirley struck me aesthetically as delightfully eccentric: no make-up, just a dash of red lipstick to mark the festive occasion; a home-made bun of uncoloured hair; dark skirt and a blouse decorated with a bow of something I imagined was a shoelace. Her behaviour – like her appearance – was without any kind of artificiality. She was so open and friendly that I felt enchanted by her from that very moment.

Shirley invited me to her seminar on women at Queen Elizabeth House. I agreed to come, but with some reluctance. I was then very much involved in the activities of the Polish underground movement Solidarity, which was totally preoccupied with the serious issue of Poland's political independence. Feminism was seen simply as a female pastime of rich and free Westerners who had nothing else to worry about, and indeed women's issues were not at all important to me. But I did finally get to the seminar and I still remember it well. The paper was about the cultural context of giving birth. The subject was something I had never heard being discussed in public in Poland at that time, and I was astonished to see how it could be problematised. Shirley led her seminar very professionally and with considerable gusto, raising significant questions and encouraging discussion in which everybody participated. I was suddenly able to feel the intellectually stimulating atmosphere of the female academic gathering, more egalitarian and inclusive than most mixed groups. I am very grateful to Shirley for that experience, and my future conversion to feminism can certainly be traced back to that seminar of hers.

But Shirley Ardener is also for me something else as well – the archetypal anthropologist. The images I have of her focus on her fieldwork stories from the Cameroon, the Land-Rover the Ardeners used to drive even in central Oxford (the original Land-Rover, not the contemporary four-by-four luxury limousines), but above all her true anthropological habitus. I remember when I was leaving Oxford at the end of my first visit I expressed my gratitude to Shirley for her help and friendship. She answered with an English proverb: one must always know how it is to be in someone else's shoes. Yes, this is a simple but very precise formulation of the empathy needed by the ethnographer. And Shirley exercises it with great skill. But there were some limits. During my stay at St John's I organised a 'Polish party', in which I was able to serve delicious Cracovian sausage (unavailable back home, but easy enough to find in the covered market in Oxford) together with well-frozen rye vodka in small glasses. I tried to teach Shirley the right way of drinking it (the whole glass in one shot), but all she did was to sip a little at a time and moreover warmed the glass in her hand.

Shirley sees everything in comparative perspective. When she came to Cracow in 1999 for the conference we held there on the sociology of landscape, we discussed at one point the main Market Square in Cracow. We praised the lively atmosphere after 1989 in what is in fact the largest medieval square in Europe, now with its dozens of open-air coffee bars and restaurants. Shirley counterposed, saying that she remembered from her first visit to Poland the distinctive aesthetic quality of this huge empty square, for which she remained nostalgic.

Since our first meeting we have visited each other quite often, reporting on our personal matters and respective anthropological projects. But we still have one unfinished project which we would like to do together – to write a book about Stefan Szolc-Rogoziński, a brave Pole who explored Cameroon and planned to establish a Polish colony there. We shall certainly write the book, I am sure.

TITI IKOLI IN THE ACADEMY

Sharon Macdonald

Among so many engaging memories of Shirley, one that especially stands out for me is her performance at the Decennial Conference of the Association of Social Anthropologists (ASA), which was held in Cambridge in 1983. I was myself a novice anthropologist at this time, having just completed a year of postgraduate anthropology at Oxford, though I had already had the opportunity to get to know Shirley and maybe shouldn't have been as surprised by her as I was. As an undergraduate, I was partly taught by Shirley and remember being disconcerted at our first meeting at how swiftly she honed in on the conceptual errors in my misguided attempts to be too clever. As a postgraduate, I had come to know her more, having become a regular at the Women's Seminar on Thursdays at Queen Elizabeth House, where, as at the Friday seminar at the Institute of Social Anthropology, I often marvelled at how Shirley would ask questions that came from such unexpected – sometimes apparently tangential – directions, perhaps making what appeared to be peculiar analogies, but which so often threw startling new light on the topic under discussion, and not infrequently fundamentally challenged the presumptions of the speaker. As Edwin was my doctoral supervisor, I regularly visited their home in Walton Street for instruction from Edwin in Scottish Gaelic, where I also had a chance to admire Shirley's excellent paintings, including a portrait of Edwin, which was not only an uncanny likeness but also managed to capture so much more about him, much that is not easy to articulate in words. Shirley and Edwin also visited the student flat of my then boyfriend (now husband) and myself, and one memory that I have – personally disconcerting in light of the 'main memory' that I am about to recount – is of her remarking on my boyfriend's collection of cacti and the collection that I had somehow acquired (without any active agency, I should stress) of pig effigies – mainly toy pigs – and correctly attributing their gendered ownership. (To thank us for a dinner, Shirley later gave me a tiny glass pig.) Altogether then, I had ample reason already to know that Shirley was not only a brilliant, perceptive anthropologist but that she had a real capacity for the unexpected.

All the same, when she stood on stage during what must have been a plenary session at the ASA Decennial and explained that the topic of her talk was 'The Vagina', I found myself taken aback. This was long before *The Vagina Monologues* had become such a hit and it had just as much iconoclastic frisson. As I remember it, the enormous hall was packed with people and the hush of anticipation before she began was more marked than for any other presentation. I seem to recall her referring to herself as 'a bit of a prude' – something that the content of her paper and accompanying slides of vaginal images (some pig-like) in paintings by artists such as Judy Chicago hardly supported. Afterwards it was much talked about, sometimes prudishly no doubt. It wasn't just another conference paper, though. It was a superb performance of intervention into the academy from a person institutionally marginalised and a whole area of study too often overlooked. Bringing the vagina out into the open – right there, in front of all those conventional and predominantly male academic eyes – was a superb instance of the kind of female militancy involving revealing bodily parts about which Shirley has written so insightfully.[1] It was itself a version of what the Bakweri women with whom she had worked call *titi ikoli* – a claiming of honour by presenting what might usually 'be considered vulgar or obscene' (Ardener 1987: 115; see also Ardener 1975). It was, as she was entirely aware (and as she said of another (1975: 49)), *titi ikoli* indeed.

Note

1. Shirley's work on this theme includes 1974, 1975, and 1983, as well as 1987, which is a version of the paper presented in Cambridge. See also the chapter by Rhian Loudon and Ronnie Frankenberg in this volume.

References

Ardener, S. 1974. 'Nudity, Vulgarity and Protest', *New Society* 27 (598), pp. 704–5.
———— 1975 (orig. 1973). 'Sexual Insult and Female Militancy', in S. Ardener (ed.), *Perceiving Women*, London, J.M. Dent & Sons, pp. 29–53.
———— 1983. 'Arson, Nudity and Bombs among the Canadian Doukhobors: A Question of Identity', in G. Breakwell (ed.), *Threatened Identities*, Chichester and New York: John Wiley & Sons, pp. 239–66.
———— 1987. 'A Note on Gender Iconography: The Vagina', in P. Caplan (ed.), *The Cultural Construction of Sexuality*, London: Tavistock, pp. 113–42.

Going the Extra Mile

Sandra Burman

Invited to reminisce about Shirley in a page, I find it difficult to select from some forty years of memories since we first met. It is also difficult to convey briefly her many notable qualities, such as her originality of thought and quiet zest for life that make her such excellent company. But in the end I realise that an underlying feature of all my many recollections of Shirley is her empathy with those she encounters. Although she is a very private person, her concern for people who work with her has led to a greater intermingling of her personal and working life than is common with academics. What follows is a brief reflection on one aspect of her academic work and an example of how she frequently goes the extra mile for friends and colleagues in doing it.

The list of books on women edited by Shirley is substantial but, given the number for which she is actually responsible, it is misleadingly short. Most notably, it does not show her considerable – but often only partially acknowledged – role in the creation of those published under the auspices of the Oxford University Women's Studies Committee and, subsequently, the Centre for Cross-Cultural Research on Women (CCCRW). It was her energy and work that led to both book series coming into existence in the first place, and then her encouragement, ideas, and experience that shaped the seminar series on which they were based. Nor did her help to the editors stop there. I have vivid memories, for example, of my increasingly desperate search for a suitable cover picture for *Fit Work for Women*, which I was editing as second in the series of the Women's Studies Committee. Although I had a clear idea of the duality I wanted portrayed, I could not find anything appropriate, and time was running out. Knowing how generous Shirley always was with her time and ideas, I took the problem to her. The upshot was the idea of a cross-stitch sampler showing a housewife and a schoolteacher, each with children, which we designed with much laughter and which Shirley, with her usual enthusiasm, even volunteered to execute. It was typical of her quiet sense of fun – and also of design – that the figures generated many compliments, and also typical of her modesty that she would not allow me to attribute them to her in the book.

Her Powers of Persuasion

Fiona Moore

I first knew Shirley Ardener as a name in textbooks, in the sections on Africa and on gender studies, and so meeting her for the first time in 1997 was an overwhelming experience. Given that she was such a well-known figure, how could I not agree to her polite request to attend the seminars on Gender and Tourism at Queen Elizabeth House, even though my research interests lay very much in the opposite direction? In doing so, I learned quickly that any seminar series organised by Shirley is sure to have something of interest for any researcher regardless of their area of speciality, and I quickly became a regular at both the CCCRW seminars and the Ethnicity and Identity seminars. Later, I came to learn also that the vibrant nature of the sessions is due, at least in part, to Shirley's incredible knack in getting people to participate: all she has to do is make a few phone calls, and she will have the seminar series, edited volume, or whatever it may be completely arranged, including a few people ready to step in should the original lecturer be unable to make it.

Later, I also became acquainted with Shirley's well-known generous side. If she hears of a friend or acquaintance who needs resources, money, a place to stay or anything else, she always swings into action with a good suggestion or news of a job offer. In 2001, Shirley was instrumental in arranging for me to become a Research Associate at Queen Elizabeth House, a post that provided me with the resources I needed to survive the final writing up of my DPhil and my postdoctoral year. I owe a great deal to Shirley, and I hope that my chapter published in this book goes some way to expressing my appreciation for what she has done.

Shirley Ardener: Mentor and Friend

Paula Heinonen

My relationship with Shirley and Edwin Ardener began in 1977 when I came to Oxford as a Human Sciences undergraduate. My first glimpse of Shirley was in the quad at St John's College when one of my friends pointed her out as one of our anthropology tutors. I blinked and she was gone. For the next few months, the same thing happened. She either flew or zoomed past me on her bike or on foot. Nothing has changed, since I found it hard to keep up with her when we eventually carried out fieldwork together on body piercing in 2003.

Throughout the years Shirley has been my tutor, my mentor, my friend and my role model. It would take more than a few words for me to describe the many instances where she has put me on the right track, including encouraging me to embark on a DPhil in Anthropology as a mature student. I have a vivid recollection of my first tutorial with Shirley. It took place in her house on Walton Street. She opened the door and led me past books in the hallway, books on the stairs, books in the living room and more books in the study where she conducted her tutorials. There are still books everywhere in her present house. While I was reading my essay, she had her face turned away from me, gazing at a squirrel in the garden. I kept looking up and wondering whether she was listening to me. When I finished, there was a short pause and yes, she had heard every word I had uttered. Our tutorial began; she explained where I had got it right, what I had missed out, where I could have said more. All this in the gentlest manner, no put-downs, no 'you have got it all wrong' – all was said in the spirit that I could do even better. Better was still to come when I had Edwin Ardener as my next tutor. After two terms with him, I was hooked on anthropology. My first passions for population genetics and animal behaviour were put on the back burner. I became an anthropologist.

Shirley's work is important to a variety of fields. It has given rise to much scholarship in feminist and women studies. Her books and the Centre for Cross-Cultural Research on Women, which has been renamed the International Gender Studies Centre, are proof that she is a legend in her lifetime. I had the privilege of accompanying her on 31 March 2005 to George Mason University, Washington, DC, for a colloquium celebrating Edwin and her muted-group theory. She gave an excellent paper on the origins and early developments of the theory devised to explain the why and how voices of dominated groups are not heard or distorted: in her own words, 'how in late 1968 Edwin Ardener drew attention to the difficulties anthropologists, of either sex, faced in identifying and articulating models of the world which women might generate, if they did not synchronise well, or accord with, those generated by men'. I do not know what I would have made of the paper on the same theme she gave at an anthropology conference in Cambridge in 1977 entitled 'The Iconography of Gender: the Vagina', which I had not heard when I was an undergraduate. In typical fashion neither she nor Edwin ever pushed their own work on their students. I only realised the enormity of their contribution to anthropology when I became a teacher myself and used their books as required reading for my students and, after our trip to Washington, understood the influence of their muted-group theory on other disciplines.

The Washington colloquium focused on the past, present, and future of muted-group theory. Shirley was joined by both young and mature scholars who have worked with and extended the Ardeners' insights in order to develop new theories: Chris Kramarae, University of Illinois and research associate at the Center for the Study of Women in Society at the University of Oregon, who has extended muted group analysis into communications studies; Julia Wood, University of North Carolina, who has related muted-group theory to feminist standpoint theory; Janette Dates, Howard University, who has connected her work on the exclusion of African Americans from media theory to muted-group theory; Mark Orbe, University of Western Michigan, who has combined muted-group and standpoint theory to develop a 'co-cultural' communication model; Tom Nakayama, Arizona State University, who used muted-group theory in his work on the muting of Asian and gay voices in communication studies. Shirley was filmed, interviewed, and celebrated. She shone. It was heart-warming to see that her many fans included eminent academics from various disciplines.

I had always thought that I would meet Shirley somewhere in Africa, possibly Ethiopia, Kenya, or Cameroon, where our numerous trips have not yet resulted in our paths crossing. It was not to be, but the word 'impossible' does not exist in Shirley's vocabulary. She is now part of my life. I am totally involved in the work and activities of the Centre she created, and I cherish her friendship.

The African Connection in Oxford

Gina Buijs

I first met Shirley in 1990 when I arrived at the CCCRW as a Visiting Fellow from Venda (Limpopo Province), South Africa. When I had applied to the Centre for a fellowship I had thought I would be returning to Venda, but it was not to be, and when I arrived in Oxford I found myself in a hiatus, not at all sure what the future would bring and whether I should return permanently to England, a country I had left for South Africa some twenty years before and where I felt myself to be a stranger. Shirley quickly summed up my dilemma, and in various unobtrusive and tactful ways helped me to feel at home in the Centre and to find my way round the minutiae of English (or at least Oxford) life. She reminded me of the usefulness of the weekly markets held in Gloucester Green for those on a very limited budget such as myself; we sometimes walked back to St Giles laden with fruit after an excursion to this market. Similarly, she let me know that one could get a pizza and half a pint of lager at the Eagle and Child for £1.60, a meal just about within my means, and which I often enjoyed, surrounded by photographs of the Inklings.

My stay at the Centre continued for a fortunate second term and I learned much from Shirley's dedication and perseverance in the face of continual odds. She pointed me in the direction of rewarding university seminars and lectures (and Wednesday morning coffee at the Institute of Social and Cultural Anthropology). She encouraged me to overcome my natural shyness and tendency to hang back and to make the most of the many opportunities the Centre offered to meet with and learn from women scholars in my field from all over the world. After I left Oxford and returned to South Africa, I was glad to be able to remain in touch with Shirley, despite her hectic schedule, now compounded with visits to Cameroon, and with the many friends I had been able to make at the Centre.

SHIRLEY'S AFRICAN ROOTS

Cecillie Swaisland

Shirley Ardener has a long association with West Africa, beginning when she accompanied her husband Edwin Ardener to Nigeria for his fieldwork. They had met when they were students at the LSE together. Subsequently, in the 1950s, Shirley and Edwin Ardener moved to the Cameroons, where Edwin became the Honorary Adviser on Archives and Antiquities (see S. Ardener's introduction to her edited volume, *Kingdom on Mount Cameroon*, Berghahn Books, 1996). So began Shirley's interest and concern with the Cameroons. She acted as Edwin's associate and developed a love of the land, the people and especially the Bakweri in the south. Such connections have remained with her throughout her career.

In the 1960s, Edwin and Shirley Ardener began their association with Queen Elizabeth House, Oxford. Edwin had accepted a post at the Institute of Social Anthropology in Oxford and a Fellowship at St John's College. During this time, Shirley became involved with the Buea Archives set up by Edwin after they discovered that important documents were scattered around the area and in need of collection and preservation. Through the subsequent decades, Shirley continued to work on the files and deepen her involvement in numerous long-term friendships and associations during her regular visits to the Cameroons.

Doubtless, her painstaking attention to detail and profound scholarship, along with her ever-questioning cross-cultural perspective, were first developed in the Cameroons. One of Shirley's first articles on women was about the Bakweri, the Balong, and the Kom in West Cameroon (published in *Man* vol. 8 (3), 1973, pp. 422–40). In this she deployed relevant documentation from Court records. The concern with women, gender, and, indeed, the women's movement blossomed when she embarked on collaboration with women postgraduates at the Institute of Social Anthropology and scholars at Queen Elizabeth House, who began to meet for a weekly seminar. This weekly seminar continues today under the auspices of the International Gender Studies Centre. Her work was officially recognised with the award of an OBE in 1990.

Returning to 'The Mountain'

Peter Geschiere

In 1995, my colleague Piet Konings and I arranged for Shirley's return to Cameroon after more than twenty years. It did not take much persuasion to get her back. Clearly she felt it was time to revisit Buea, where she and Edwin had done so much ethnographic work beginning in the 1950s. The occasion was a conference Piet and I organised with Paul Nkwi, then at the Ministry of Scientific Research in Yaoundé. We were delighted that Shirley had agreed to attend, thus returning to Cameroon after so long.

Of course, there was a deeper reason as well. The archives in Buea (the former capital of German Cameroon and later of the anglophone part of the country), which Shirley and Edwin had built up literally with their own hands, were in a sorry state. Piet and I had spent time on and off over the preceding decade combing through this valuable resource. The staff, notably Primus Forgwe and Prince Henry Mbain, were extremely eager to be helpful. One of the first documents they showed me was a picture from the 1950s, with a very young Shirley sitting on a stool, sorting out a huge pile of papers on her lap, with Edwin hovering in the background.

The archives provide a very quiet place for study and reflection, an exception in present-day Cameroon. Often the building disappears in the fog – Buea is situated halfway up the slopes of Mount Cameroon, one of the wettest places on the earth – and clouds would float through the open windows into the reading-room. No wonder the conservation of the files and the building itself posed serious problems. The decay of the archives seemed to be progressing even more rapidly than that of the Bismarck Brunnen (one of the remaining vestiges of German imperial rule) on the other side of the road. Henry Mbain's sad look when he showed me another pile of papers destroyed by the humidity or another crack appearing in the walls made me finally decide that something had to be done. In fact, it proved to be quite easy to arrange for a KAP (*Klein Ambassade Project*), 'a small embassy project', from the Dutch embassy in Yaoundé, which helped to fund a few very basic repairs to the building. However welcome the embassy's subvention was, it was far too *klein*. When I telephoned Shirley in Oxford to tell her about all of this, her immediate reaction was that more had to be done. I still think this was a major motive for her return to Cameroon.

After the Yaoundé conference, we all set out in a car that I arranged through one of my Maka friends, an official at the Ministry of Environment (the Maka are 'my' people from a very different part of Cameroon). With his younger brother at the wheel, we planned to do the trip in a few hours. However, five Europeans (Phil Burnham and Mike Rowlands came along as well) travelling in an old Peugeot 403 proved to be overly conspicuous. Moreover, we discovered en route that our car belonged to the Ministry and that there was no official permission for the car's use during the journey we were undertaking. And on top of all this, we were travelling at a time when there was official concern about white missionaries driving around without insurance papers. It was my first and last occasion to be addressed by a swaggering policeman as 'mon père'. The result of all this was that we seemed to spend more time negotiating our progression from one roadblock to another than actually driving to our destination.

However, just before Douala, there was a pleasant surprise. The sky, which had been low and grey, opened up and Shirley exclaimed, 'There it is, The Mountain.' Mount Cameroon is one of the world's most spectacular mountains. It rises up directly from the coast to more than 4,000 metres high. It gives the viewer a sense of vertigo: is it possible that there is something so high so close to the sea? I had never seen a view of it emerge before arriving in Douala. The message was clear: this was a very good omen for Shirley's return.

Indeed, Shirley's arrival was a very joyful event. Just after we settled in the Mountain Hotel at Buea, all sorts of old acquaintances came to greet Shirley. For many years this Mountain Hotel was an icon of Buea, dark and damp with big rooms and spacious salons, and outside a beautiful garden overlooking the slopes of the mountain. Now it is abandoned and completely ravaged by squatters and informal parties, since no entrepreneur is prepared to pay the huge rent the government tries to charge for it – a typical example of a basic lesson that so many Cameroonian officials refuse to learn: if you want to 'eat' too much, you destroy the very thing from which you want to 'eat'. Nonetheless, at that time, it was still functioning, and it was good to see Shirley sitting in the garden or on one of the terraces, being welcomed by her old friends and catching up on their news.

However, there was little time for relaxation and chit-chat. Early the next day Shirley insisted on visiting the archives. The staff were nervous with anticipation, eager finally to meet the founder of their archives. I was afraid that the visit might be discouraging for Shirley as she witnessed all the damp files and the sagging building. But she coolly inspected the premises and immediately started making plans. I had to leave two days later for Kribi to visit my students there – which was very convenient for me since it helped me avoid old Samuel Endeley, the new chief of Buea, who was rumoured to be furious with me for publishing an article that contained some less than complimentary quotes from the British files on his predecessors. Therefore I have no idea how things unfolded in any detail. Shirley managed to raise important funding within a few months, and my next visit to the Buea archives revealed a physical transformation: the building was restored, all the offices were tidy and, most importantly, dehumidifiers were ridding the atmosphere of excess moisture in all the storerooms.

Before my departure, I did, however, witness one of the key moments in the transformation process. Shirley immediately purchased a powerful vacuum cleaner, which she presented to the staff the following day. They examined the shiny machine with apprehension. Finally, the youngest member of the staff started fiddling clumsily with it, whereupon Shirley firmly took hold of the suction apparatus and demonstrated how to use it. In no time she had thoroughly vacuumed the first office. I entered the offices only after humbly knocking at the door, and I would not dream of telling the staff what to do. But clearly this was different for Shirley – in many respects these were still her archives, and the staff loved to follow her advice. Up until today, the offices remain cleaner than they had ever been before. A stray remark from one of the staff members, which I overheard when I was recently back in the archives, may explain why. When we noticed a minor problem – in one corner the plaster was crumbling – he whispered to his colleague, 'Yes, we have to ask Mummy about this when she comes next time.' The reader will guess who 'Mummy' was: none other than the establishment's 'founding mother'.

The archives, in their transformed state, have become once again a hub of intellectual activity, with students from the new Buea University filling the reading-room. So let us hope that Shirley will continue to return to 'The Mountain'. Clearly, her proverbial energy worked miracles here also: thanks to her, the archives became again a vibrant place for the production of local history.

Shirley's Magic

Jonathan Webber

Shirley Ardener has taught me some important things in the thirty years I have known her. If I were to pick out just one of them, one that has run like a thread throughout these long years, it would be the theory and practice of magic.

Let me explain. *JASO: Journal of the Anthropological Society of Oxford* was founded by Edwin Ardener in 1970 to disseminate new approaches in social anthropology. Little did I realise, when I became its editor in 1979, just what it meant in practice to be associated so closely with the Ardeners, even though I had been Edwin's doctoral student when I first arrived in Oxford in 1972. Shirley was the treasurer of *JASO*, and I well remember her saying to me, when I took over the journal, that it was simply 'magic' how *JASO* continued to appear regularly, during the last week of each university term. In my naivety I thought that what she meant was that it was a miracle that this publication somehow managed to keep going – without any financial sponsorship but instead relying on the hard work of a relatively small circle of enthusiastic volunteers.

That was my first image of Shirley – her belief in miracles (albeit brought about and necessarily underpinned by hard work). In all the years that have elapsed since then, that paradoxical image has stayed with me – except that I slowly came to understand that there was also another, equally valid, parallel interpretation of the 'magic' word. What that small, informal circle of enthusiastic volunteers was able to create turned out to be magical – something that had a special atmosphere, a special quality, something that could inspire and in its own modest way change the world.

When Edwin died – so young, so unexpectedly – in 1987, Shirley asked me to join her in continuing his Ethnicity and Identity seminar, and so, together with Tamara Dragadze, the three of us indeed ran the seminar and eventually produced a book series based on it. I was involved with the seminar for fifteen years, until I moved to another university in 2002. That seminar was magical – in all possible senses. First of all, we never missed a single one: year in, year out, the seminar continued; we (miraculously) kept going. Secondly, like *JASO*, the seminar was on the margins of the institutional life of the Institute of Social and Cultural Anthropology: it was not officially listed as part of the formal work of the Institute, and so although we used the premises and did manage to obtain some of the travel expenses for our out-of-town speakers, we had no funding. Thirdly, it was a magical series: every term, each with eight seminars, had a different theme. Just to give a sense of the range, the themes included, for example, the social construction of time, bureaucratic identities, land and territoriality, the identity of the fieldworker, the identity of cities, death, linguistic conflicts, the identity of fathers, dress and ethnicity, identity and music, art, tourism. Our participants became devoted to the seminar, and many would regularly say that it was fascinating, one of the best showcases of social and cultural anthropology anywhere in the university. Magical it has always been, broadening and highly stimulating, but the point is that it was very largely Shirley's hard work that made it possible (and has kept it going to this day, along with Ian Fowler, Elisabeth Hsu, Lidia Sciama, and others). Not only was it Shirley who so often came up with next term's theme, she was also able to come up with names of speakers. I have to confess I never really understood how she was able to do it: just give Shirley a topic – anything from animals to medicine, from conflict resolution to artisans – and she would immediately come up with names of specialist speakers, who, moreover, could be found nearby, in Oxford or in the south-east of England. The list would be typed up, and Shirley would then set off round Oxford to pin it up on the noticeboards.

The work was not over. After each term's seminars, the three of us would meet and evaluate the series for its suitability as a publication. Berg Publishers accepted the idea of a series on 'Ethnicity and Identity', of which a dozen titles have been published since 1993; more recently, Marion Berghahn, of Berghahn Books, has relaunched the series as 'Social Identities'. Who was it who took it upon herself to chase the editor of each multi-author volume to come up with a finished work, chase the authors themselves, negotiate royalties with the publishers, read through the manuscripts? It was Shirley throughout, maybe with some help from the enthusiastic volunteers who surround her, but essentially her achievement.

Yes, it has all been a miracle, but due to Shirley's extraordinarily devoted hard work for so many years. All this echoes what she has achieved in the field of women's studies, not to mention her work as an Africanist. Much has been said in this volume about Shirley's wide cross-cultural interests and her tremendous richness and range, particularly in women's studies; but her interests and expertise have also extended far into the full sweep of social and cultural studies, and her ever-perspicacious comments in chairing those seminars in ethnicity and identity consistently demonstrate her intellectual creativity, her lateral thinking, and the sincerity of her openness to new ideas. That is the true teacher in her. So many of us have benefited, in so many ways, from the encounter with her that maybe indeed the word 'magical', in all its various senses, best conveys Shirley's contribution to the world that the authors of this volume inhabit. We are happy to dedicate this book to her in friendship and affection, and with our grateful thanks.

List of Published Works by Shirley Ardener

1953 'The Social and Economic Significance of the Contribution Club among a Section of the Southern Ibo', *Conference Proceedings*, Ibadan: West African Institute of Social and Economic Research.

1958a 'Banana Co-operatives in Victoria Division, the Southern Cameroons', *Conference Proceedings*, Ibadan: Nigerian Institute of Social and Economic Research, pp. 10–25.

1958b 'Wovea Islanders' (with E.W. Ardener), *Nigeria* 59, pp. 309–21.

1960 *Plantation and Village in the Cameroons: Some Economic and Social Studies* (with E.W. Ardener and W.A. Warmington), London: Oxford University Press (for the Nigerian Institute of Social and Economic Research).

1964 'The Comparative Study of Rotating Credit Associations', *Journal of the Royal Anthropological Institute* 94 (2), pp. 201–29 (republished in S. Ardener and S. Burman (eds), *Money-go-rounds: the Importance of Rotating Savings and Credit Associations for Women*, Oxford and Washington, DC: Berg, 1995, pp. 289–317).

1965 'A Directory Study of Social Anthropologists' (with E.W. Ardener), *British Journal of Sociology* 16 (4), pp. 295–314.

1968 *Eye-Witnesses to the Annexation of Cameroon, 1883–1887*, Buea: Government Press.

1969 *Promise*, by J. Asheri (illustrated by S. Ardener), Lagos: African Universities Press.

1972 'Biological Note on John Clarke', in J. Clarke, *Specimens of Dialects* (ed. E.W. Ardener), London: Gregg International Publishers.

1973 'Sexual Insult and Female Militancy', *Man* 8 (3), pp. 422–40 (republished in S. Ardener (ed.), *Perceiving Women*, London: Malaby Press, 1975, pp. 29–53).

1974a 'Nudity, Vulgarity and Protest', *New Society* 27 (598), pp. 704–5.

1974b 'Bakweri', *Family of Man*, London: Marshall Cavendish, 9, pp. 225–28.

1974c 'Fernando Po', *Family of Man*, London: Marshall Cavendish, 31, pp. 850–51.

1974d 'A Note on "Mooning" and "Streaking" as Forms of Non-violent Protest', *Journal of the Anthropological Society of Oxford* 5 (1), pp. 54–7.

1975a   (ed.), *Perceiving Women*, London: Malaby Press; second edition: London: J.M. Dent & Sons.
1975b   'Introduction', in S. Ardener (ed.), *Perceiving Women*, London: Malaby Press, pp. vii–xxiii.
1975c   (orig. 1973). 'Sexual Insult and Female Militancy', in S. Ardener (ed.), *Perceiving Women*, London: Malaby Press, pp. 29–53.
1978a   (ed.), *Defining Females: The Nature of Women in Society*, London and New York: Croom Helm and St Martin's Press (in association with the Oxford University Women's Studies Committee); revised second edition: Oxford: Berg, 1993.
1978b   'Introduction: The Nature of Women in Society', in S. Ardener (ed.), *Defining Females: The Nature of Women in Society*, London and New York: Croom Helm and St Martin's Press (in association with the Oxford University Women's Studies Committee), pp. 9–48 (pp. 1–33 in 1993 edition).
1981a   (ed.), *Women and Space: Ground Rules and Social Maps*, London: Croom Helm (in association with the Oxford University Women's Studies Committee); revised second edition: Oxford: Berg, 1993.
1981b   'Ground Rules and Social Maps for Women: An Introduction', in S. Ardener (ed.), *Women and Space: Ground Rules and Social Maps*, London: Croom Helm (in association with the Oxford University Women's Studies Committee), pp. 11–34 (pp. 1–30 in 1993 edition).
1981c   'Preliminary Chronological Notes for the South [of Cameroon]' (with E.W. Ardener), in C. Tardits (ed.), *The Contribution of Ethnological Research to the History of Cameroon Cultures*, vol. 2, Paris: Éditions du Centre National de la Recherche Scientifique, pp. 563–74.
1983   'Arson, Nudity and Bombs among the Canadian Doukhobors: A Question of Identity', in G. Breakwell (ed.), *Threatened Identities*, Chichester and New York: John Wiley & Sons, pp. 239–66.
1984a   (ed.), *The Incorporated Wife* (with H. Callan), London: Croom Helm (in association with the Oxford University Women's Studies Committee).
1984b   'Preface', in H. Callan and S. Ardener (eds), *The Incorporated Wife*, London: Croom Helm (in association with the Oxford University Women's Studies Committee), pp. i–iii.
1984c   'Incorporation and Exclusion: Oxford Academics' Wives', in H. Callan and S. Ardener (eds), *The Incorporated Wife*, London: Croom Helm (in association with the Oxford University Women's Studies Committee), pp. 27–49.
1984d   'Gender Orientations in Fieldwork', in R.F. Ellen (ed.), *Ethnographic Research: A Guide to General Conduct*, London: Academic Press (ASA Methods series), pp. 118–29.
1985   'The Social Anthropology of Women and Feminist Anthropology', *Anthropology Today* 1 (5), pp. 24–26.

1986a (ed.), *Visibility and Power: Essays on Women in Society and Development* (with L. Dube and E. Leacock), Delhi: Oxford University Press.

1986b 'The Representation of Women in Academic Models', in L. Dube, E. Leacock, and S. Ardener (eds), *Visibility and Power: Essays on Women in Society and Development*, Delhi: Oxford University Press, pp. 3–14.

1987a (ed.), *Images of Women in Peace and War: Cross-cultural and Historical Perspectives* (with S. Macdonald and P. Holden), Basingstoke: Macmillan Education (in association with the Oxford University Women's Studies Committee).

1987b 'Preface' (with P. Holden), in S. Macdonald, P. Holden, and S. Ardener (eds), *Images of Women in Peace and War: Cross-cultural and Historical Perspectives*, Basingstoke: Macmillan Education (in association with the Oxford University Women's Studies Committee), pp. xvii–xx.

1987c 'A Note on Gender Iconography: The Vagina', in P. Caplan (ed.), *The Cultural Construction of Sexuality*, London: Tavistock, pp. 113–42.

1992a (ed.), *Persons and Powers of Women in Diverse Cultures: Essays in Commemoration of Audrey I. Richards, Phyllis Kaberry, and Barbara E. Ward*, New York and Oxford: Berg.

1992b 'Persons and Powers of Women: An Introduction', in S. Ardener (ed.), *Persons and Powers of Women in Diverse Cultures: Essays in Commemoration of Audrey I. Richards, Phyllis Kaberry, and Barbara E. Ward*, New York and Oxford: Berg, pp. 1–10.

1992c 'Editorial Preface', in S. Ardener (ed.), *Persons and Powers of Women in Diverse Cultures: Essays in Commemoration of Audrey I. Richards, Phyllis Kaberry, and Barbara E. Ward*, New York and Oxford: Berg, pp. 11–14.

1993a (ed.), *Women and Missions, Past and Present: Historical and Anthropological Perceptions* (with F. Bowie and D. Kirkwood), Providence and Oxford: Berg.

1993b 'Preface' (with D. Kirkwood), in F. Bowie, D. Kirkwood, and S. Ardener (eds), *Women and Missions, Past and Present: Historical and Anthropological Perceptions*, Providence and Oxford: Berg, pp. xvii–xx.

1994a (ed.), *Bilingual Women: Anthropological Approaches to Second Language Use* (with P. Burton and K.K. Dyson), Oxford and Providence: Berg.

1994b 'Preface', in P. Burton, K.K. Dyson, and S. Ardener (eds), *Bilingual Women: Anthropological Approaches to Second Language Use*, Oxford and Providence: Berg, pp. vii–viii.

1995a (ed.), *Money-go-rounds: The Importance of Rotating Savings and Credit Associations for Women* (with S. Burman), Oxford and Washington, DC: Berg.

1995b 'Preface' (with S. Burman), in S. Ardener and S. Burman (eds), *Money-go-rounds: The Importance of Rotating Savings and Credit Associations for Women*, Oxford and Washington, DC: Berg, pp. vii–x.

1995c 'Women Making Money Go Round: ROSCAS Revisited', in S. Ardener and S. Burman (eds), *Money-go-rounds: The Importance of Rotating*

Savings and Credit Associations for Women, Oxford and Washington, DC: Berg, pp. 1–19.

1995d (orig. 1964). 'The Comparative Study of Rotating Credit Associations', in S. Ardener and S. Burman (eds), *Money-go-rounds: The Importance of Rotating Savings and Credit Associations for Women*, Oxford and Washington, DC: Berg, pp. 289–317.

1996a (ed.), *Kingdom on Mount Cameroon: Studies in the History of the Cameroon Coast, 1500–1970*, by E. Ardener, Providence and Oxford: Berghahn Books.

1996b 'Editor's Introduction', in S. Ardener (ed.), *Kingdom on Mount Cameroon: Studies in the History of the Cameroon Coast, 1500–1970*, by E. Ardener, Providence and Oxford: Berghahn Books, pp. vii–xx.

1996c 'Foreword. The Catalyst: Chilver at the Crossroads', in I. Fowler and D. Zeitlyn (eds), *African Crossroads: Intersections between History and Anthropology in Cameroon*, Providence and Oxford: Berghahn Books, pp. ix–xvi.

1998 'The Funding of Social Anthropological Research: A Preliminary Note to a Fragment of History Written by E.M. Chilver in 1955', *Journal of the Anthropological Society of Oxford* 29, pp. 243–50.

2000a 'Biographical Note', in J.-T. Agbasiere, *Women in Igbo Life and Thought*, London and New York: Routledge, pp. xvii–xxiii.

2000b 'Partition of Space', excerpt from 'Ground Rules and Social Maps for Women: An Introduction' (1993 (orig. 1981b)), in J. Rendell, B. Penner, and I. Borden (eds), *Gender Space Architecture: An Interdisciplinary Introduction*, London and New York: Routledge, pp. 112–17.

2002a (ed. and with commentaries), *Swedish Ventures in Cameroon, 1883–1923: Trade and Travel, People and Politics, The Memoir of Knut Knutson, with Supporting Material*, New York and Oxford: Berghahn Books.

2002b 'Preface: How I Came to Edit the Memoir', in S. Ardener (ed. and with commentaries), *Swedish Ventures in Cameroon, 1883–1923: Trade and Travel, People and Politics, The Memoir of Knut Knutson, with Supporting Material*, New York and Oxford: Berghahn Books, pp. xi–xv.

2004a (ed.), *New Gender Studies from Cameroon and the Caribbean* (with J. Endeley, R. Goodridge, and N. Lyonga), Buea: University of Buea (Issues in Gender and Development, vol. 1).

2004b 'Preface', in J. Endeley, S. Ardener, R. Goodridge, and N. Lyonga (eds), *New Gender Studies from Cameroon and the Caribbean*, Buea: University of Buea (Issues in Gender and Development, vol. 1), pp. xiii–xv.

2004c 'Efforts of International Agencies and National Religious Institutions to Improve Life in Africa' (with L. Fondong), in J. Endeley, S. Ardener, R. Goodridge, and N. Lyonga (eds), *New Gender Studies from Cameroon and the Caribbean*, Buea: University of Buea (Issues in Gender and Development, vol. 1), pp. 17–27.

2004d 'Gender-Inclusive Culture in Higher Education: The Case of the University of Buea' (with J. Endeley), in J. Endeley, S. Ardener, R. Goodridge, and N. Lyonga (eds), *New Gender Studies from Cameroon and the Caribbean*, Buea: University of Buea (Issues in Gender and Development, vol. 1), pp. 61–77.
2005a (ed.), *Changing Sex and Bending Gender* (with A. Shaw), New York and Oxford: Berghahn Books.
2005b 'Preface', in A. Shaw and S. Ardener (eds), *Changing Sex and Bending Gender*, New York and Oxford: Berghahn Books, pp. xi–xii.
2005c 'Male Dames and Female Boys: Cross-dressing in the English Pantomime', in A. Shaw and S. Ardener (eds), *Changing Sex and Bending Gender*, New York and Oxford: Berghahn Books, pp. 119–37.
2005d 'Ardener's "Muted Groups": The Genesis of an Idea and its Praxis', *Women and Language* 28 (2), pp. 1–5.
2006 'Partition of Space', excerpt from 'Ground Rules and Social Maps for Women: An Introduction' (1993 (orig. 1981b)), in M. Taylor and J. Preston (eds), *Intimus: Interior Design Theory Reader*, Chichester: Wiley, pp. 15–21.

Forthcoming 2007 (ed.), *Professional Identities: Policy and Practice in Business Bureaucracy* (with F. Moore), New York and Oxford: Berghahn Books.

In preparation *Selected Papers*, New York and Oxford: Berghahn Books.

Notes on the Contributors

Jonathan Benthall is an honorary research fellow in the Department of Anthropology, University College London. He was Director of the Royal Anthropological Institute between 1974 and 2000, and Founder Editor of *Anthropology Today*. He was awarded the Anthropology in Media Award by the American Anthropological Association in 1993. His publications include *Disasters, Relief and the Media* (1993) and *The Charitable Crescent: Politics of Aid in the Muslim World* (2003, co-authored with Jérôme Bellion-Jourdan).

Deborah Fahy Bryceson is a Research Associate at the International Gender Studies Centre, University of Oxford. A human geographer by training, she became a member of the Centre for Cross-Cultural Research on Women during the 1980s. She is editor of two publications in the Centre's book series: *Women Wielding the Hoe: Lessons from Rural Africa for Feminist Theory and Development Practice* (1995) and, together with Ulla Vuorela, *The Transnational Family: New European Frontiers and Global Networks* (2002). Having held academic positions at the University of Dar es Salaam, the Architectural Association School of Architecture in London, the University of Birmingham, and the University of Leiden, she has concentrated her research on de-agrarianisation and urban economies in Africa. Recently she has been involved in a study of HIV/AIDS and its interactive effects on rural women's livelihood patterns in Malawi.

Gina Buijs is Professor of Anthropology and Development Studies at the University of Zululand, South Africa. She was previously Professor of Anthropology at the University of Venda, South Africa, where much of the research on Venda women on which her chapter is based was carried out. Her research interests include gender, especially the life histories of African rural women in South Africa, and migration (she is the editor of *Migrant Women*, Berg 1993), as well as development issues relating to rotating credit associations, water, and HIV/AIDS. She has also published on ritual and divination associated with traditional healers. Her earlier research focused on South Africans of South Indian origin, with reference to kinship and socio-religious change.

Sandra Burman was a founder member of the Oxford Women's Studies Committee and, subsequently, of the Centre for Cross-Cultural Research on Women. She was a Senior Research Officer at the Centre for Socio-Legal

Research, Wolfson College, Oxford, and a Wingate Research Fellow at Queen Elizabeth House; since 1995 she has been Professor of Socio-Legal Studies and Director of the Centre for Socio-Legal Research at the University of Cape Town, South Africa. Her publications include a number of books and articles on women and children.

Hilary Callan is an anthropologist who, since the early 1970s, has been closely associated with the Centre for Cross-Cultural Research on Women at Oxford, of which Shirley Ardener was the founding director. She contributed articles to *Perceiving Women* (1975) and *Defining Females* (1978), both edited by Ardener; and she was co-editor with Ardener of *The Incorporated Wife* (1984). She has held academic appointments in universities in the U.K., Lebanon and Canada, and from 1993 to 2000 was director of the European Association for International Education based in Amsterdam. Since 2000 she has been director of the Royal Anthropological Institute in London.

Gaynor Cohen studied social anthropology at Manchester under Max Gluckman, obtaining her Ph.D. on education in Sierra Leone in 1973. She was a senior lecturer in social policy at the Civil Service College, followed by work as a government adviser on education and employment policy in the 1980s and 1990s. Post-retirement as a Fellow at the Centre for Education and Industry at the University of Warwick, she has undertaken and published research on partnerships in education and industry and acted as an adviser to the Polish government on their education policy. Apart from many articles, she published *Social Change and the Life-Course* (1987). She moved from London to Oxford in 1985 with Abner Cohen, her late husband, where they were welcomed by Shirley Ardener and became strong supporters of the Centre for Cross-Cultural Research on Women. She had undertaken research with Abner in West Africa in the 1970s and again, in the years before his death in 2001, she worked with him in his research on a Welsh chapel community.

Janette Davies trained initially as a nurse and worked as a health professional in Bolivia, on the Thai/Cambodian border, and in Bangladesh with an NGO (Salvation Army) and international aid agencies, including USAID and UNHCR. She then studied medical anthropology at Brunel and social anthropology at Oxford. Her Ph.D. (Brunel) was a study of elderly people in a residential nursing home in rural Oxfordshire. Her present work combines gender, health, and ageing within a development context at the Oxford Centre for Mission Studies, as a member of the International Gender Studies Centre and as a Research Associate at Queen Elizabeth House, University of Oxford.

Tamara Dragadze, born in England, studied anthropology at the universities of Kent (BA) and Oxford (DPhil), and has taught anthropology and sociology at several British universities. She has over fifty academic publications, mostly on ethnic politics in the former Soviet Union, and also contributed to several volumes in women's studies of which Shirley Ardener is the series editor. She has done research funded by the ESRC, the British Academy, and the Department of Overseas Development. She published a novel and has been awarded residencies at centres for the arts such as Yaddo in the U.S.A. (in Saratoga Springs, New York). She lives in London and writes fiction.

Ronnie Frankenberg, now formally retired, studied medicine at Cambridge in 1947–9, but in his third year he switched to anthropology, which he learnt largely from his fellow third-year students. He met Max Gluckman, who agreed to accept him for the new taught Masters at Manchester University. Supervised by Gluckman and Elizabeth Colson, he then obtained his Ph.D. for fieldwork in North Wales. He also studied a village in South Wales, where he stayed on as Education Officer for the South Wales district of the National Union of Mineworkers. In 1960 he returned as a Lecturer to Manchester, where he stayed until moving to Keele (1969–85). His last three years in Manchester were spent mainly on secondment to the University of Zambia, Lusaka, teaching and researching medical anthropology. From 1985 he worked in that field (AIDS/HIV) at Keele and Brunel and continued his involvement in gender studies and feminism, which had begun at the National School Magazine Society while he was still at school in London.

Peter Geschiere is Professor of the Anthropology of Africa at the University of Amsterdam (and previously at Leiden University). He has worked on state–village relations in various parts of West Africa; on the role of 'witchcraft' in politics (*The Modernity of Witchcraft, Politics and the Occult in Post-colonial Africa*, Virginia University Press, 1997); and on globalisation and cultural difference (*Globalisation and Identity: Dialectics of Flow and Closure*, together with Birgit Meyer, Blackwell 1999/2003). At present, he is working on a book entitled *Autochthony, Citizenship and Exclusion: New Modes in the Politics of Belonging in Africa and Elsewhere*.

Kirsten Hastrup has been Professor of Anthropology at the University of Copenhagen since 1990. She holds a DPhil from Oxford University (1980), and the degree of DrScientSoc from the University of Copenhagen (1990). She was Secretary (1989–91) and Chairperson (1991–93) of the European Association of Social Anthropologists. Her publications comprise thirty books and *c*.200 articles. Among them are monographs on Icelandic history and society, works exploring the foundations of anthropology, edited volumes on human rights, and a number of textbooks. A recent monograph entitled *Action: Anthropology in the Company of Shakespeare* (2004) provides important background for the article presented in this volume.

Paula Heinonen is the coordinator of the Visiting Fellows Programme at the International Gender Studies Centre, University of Oxford. She also contributes to the development of the Centre's pedagogical activities and is tutor for the university's Human Sciences degree as well as being tutor and coordinator of the Gender Option in the Archaeology and Anthropology degree. She was a senior lecturer in anthropology in the Department of Sociology and Social Anthropology, and head of research of the Centre for Training and Research on Women, at the University of Addis Ababa, from 1995 to 2001. Her research interests are in the areas of gender, development, feminism, the anthropology of children, and globalisation. Among her publications is the paper 'Early, Forced Marriage and Abduction and Their Links to Custom/Tradition, FGM, Poverty and HIV/AIDs' (see www.fourliteracies.org/Research.htm).

Maria Jaschok is director of the International Gender Studies Centre, Queen Elizabeth House (Department of International Development), and senior research scholar at the Institute for Chinese Studies, University of Oxford. Her research interests are in the areas of religion, gender, and agency, gendered constructions of memory, feminist ethnographic practice, and marginality and identity in contemporary China. She has conducted collaborative research projects in central China since 1994, addressing issues of religious and secular identity, and the implications of growing female membership of religions for local citizenship and civil society. Maria Jaschok is a founder member of Women's Initiative on International Affairs in Asia and a co-founder of Women and Gender in Chinese Studies Network (WAGNet). She has co-presented and co-authored with her Chinese collaborator, Shui Jingjun, in China and internationally, in Chinese and English, in order to make published findings fully accessible to their respective home audiences.

Grażyna Kubica works at the Department of Social Anthropology, Institute of Sociology, Jagiellonian University, Cracow. One of her research areas is the history of anthropology, especially the life and work of Bronisław Malinowski. She co-edited the volume *Malinowski – Between Two Worlds* (Cambridge University Press, 1988), as well as the Polish *Dzieła* (Completed Works) of the anthropologist, published by PWN, Warsaw (e.g., the Introduction to *Argonauts of the Western Pacific*, or *The Natives of Mailu*). She authored the introduction and edition of the full and comprehensive version of Bronisław Malinowski's diaries in their original language. *Dziennik w ścisłym znaczeniu tego wyrazu* (Wydawnictwo Literackie, Cracow, 2002). The spin-off from this work was a feminist book, *Siostry Malinowskiego* (Malinowski's Sisters) (Wydawnictwo Literackie, Cracow, 2006), concerning several women appearing in the diaries, among them the Polish-British anthropologist Maria Czaplicka. The exhibition of the latter's field photographs and other materials was organised by Grażyna Kubica at the Ethnographic Museum in Cracow, 2003/4.

Rhian Loudon completed her medical degree at the University of Birmingham in 1989. She then undertook vocational training for general practice in Bristol and subsequently worked there as a principal in general practice until 1996. She then moved to a post in the Department of Primary Care at the University of Birmingham, where she remained until 2004. During this second period in Birmingham she worked in a variety of roles, combining academic work with clinical practice in the inner city. From 1999 until 2002 she was the recipient of an NHS Research and Development Primary Care Researcher Development Award. This award allowed her to complete both an MSc in medical anthropology at Brunel and then a Ph.D. awarded by the University of Birmingham in 2003.

Sharon Macdonald read Human Sciences at Oxford University, where Shirley Ardener was one of her inspirational social anthropology tutors. She went on to study for a doctorate in social anthropology with Edwin Ardener and at the same time worked with Shirley on a seminar series for the Centre for Cross-Cultural Research on Women that led to their co-edited volume, with Pat Holden, of *Images of Women in Peace and War: Cross-cultural and Historical Perspectives* (Macmillan, 1987). Her *Inside Identities: Ethnography in Western Europe* (ed., Berg, 1993) and *Reimagining Culture: Histories, Identities and the Gaelic Renaissance* (Berg, 1997) are both published in the Ethnicity and Identity series, edited by Shirley, Tamara Dragadze and Jonathan Webber, and she has contributed to two books in the Cross-Cultural Perspectives on Women series: the second edition of *Defining Females* (Berg, 1993) and *Gender, Drink and Drugs* (ed. Maryon McDonald, Berg, 1994). Sharon has undertaken ethnographic fieldwork in the Scottish Hebrides, at the London Science Museum, and, most recently, in Nuremberg, Germany. She is now Professor of Social Anthropology at the University of Manchester. Her most recent books are *Behind the Scenes at the Science Museum* (Berg, 2002) and the *Companion to Museum Studies* (ed., Blackwell, 2006).

Zdzisław Mach was educated at the Jagiellonian University (MA in sociology, 1978; Ph.D. 1984; Dr habil, 1990), where he is currently Professor of Sociology and Social Anthropology and director of the Centre for European Studies. Between 1993 and 1999, he served as the Dean of the Faculty of Philosophy at the Jagiellonian University. He has held visiting professorships and fellowships at many academic institutions, including the Central European University, Warsaw; Collegium Civitas, Warsaw; the University of Oxford; Université Paul Valéry, Montpellier III; University College Dublin; the European University Institute in Florence; the University of Chicago; the Netherlands Institute for Advanced Studies; and the Institute for Advanced Studies in the Humanities, University of Edinburgh. Two of his main publications are: *Symbols, Conflict and Identity* (Albany, SUNY Press, 1993) and *Niechciane Miasta* (Cracow, Universitas, 1998).

Fiona Moore received her doctorate at the Institute for Social and Cultural Anthropology, University of Oxford, in 2002, based on a study of the uses of identity and strategic self-presentation among employees in a German multinational corporation. Currently she is the Lecturer in International Human

Resource Management at Royal Holloway College, University of London, and is also part of a multidisciplinary team studying Korean businesspeople in the U.K. In 2003–05 she conducted research at an Oxfordshire automobile plant, focusing on the similarities and differences between managers and workers with regard to their conceptions of identity, technology, gender, and ethnicity. She is a member of the International Gender Studies Centre at Queen Elizabeth House, Oxford, has recently published *Transnational Business Cultures: Life and Work in a Multinational Corporation* (Ashgate, 2005), and co-edited with Shirley Ardener *Professional Identities: Policy and Practice in Business Bureaucracy* (Berghahn, forthcoming 2007).

Judith Okely studied at the Sorbonne and at Oxford and Cambridge. She is Emeritus Professor of Social Anthropology, University of Hull; Honorary Research Associate, Oxford Brookes; and deputy director of the International Gender Studies Centre, University of Oxford. Her books include *The Traveller-Gypsies* (1983), *Simone de Beauvoir: A Re-reading* (1986), *Anthropology and Autobiography* (co-editor, 1992), and *Own or Other Culture* (1996). Some recently published articles appear in *Ethnos* (2001), *Anthropological Quarterly* (2003), *The Journal of Mediterranean Studies* (2003) and *The Sociological Review* (2005). She is on the editorial board of *Anthropology Today*. Her research interests include fieldwork practice, Gypsies, feminism, autobiography, visualism, landscape representations, and the aged, mainly within Europe. She has held permanent positions in four U.K. universities, including a Chair at Edinburgh University, and has been Visiting Professor in Denmark, Hungary, Malta, and Kenya. Her work has been translated into Japanese, Hungarian, Polish, Czech, Italian, German, French, and Chinese.

Lidia D. Sciama is a former director of the Centre for Cross-Cultural Research on Women (now International Gender Studies Centre). She has lived in Italy, Israel, England, and the U.S.A., where she taught social anthropology and comparative literature. She studied in Venice at the University of Ca' Foscari, and received an MA in English literature from Cornell University. She then went on to study for a doctorate at the Oxford Institute of Social Anthropology. Her publications include articles on 'academic wives' in *Women and Space* (ed. Shirley Ardener, Croom Helm, 1981), and in *The Incorporated Wife* (eds. Shirley Ardener and Hilary Callan, Croom Helm, 1984), as well as papers in the Ethnicity and Identity book series (eds. Shirley Ardener, Jonathan Webber, and Tamara Dragadze, Berg, 1992 and 1996). With Professor Joanne Eicher, she edited a book on *Beads and Beadmakers* (Berg, 1998). Her monograph, *A Venetian Island: Environment, History and Change in Burano* (Berghahn, 2003), is based on long-term fieldwork. Her main interests are relations between anthropology and literature, narrative, memory, urban anthropology, gender, and crafts.

Shui Jingjun is a sociologist and researcher at the Henan Academy of Social Sciences. She has conducted research on Hui culture and on Chinese religious culture in general. Her first preliminary findings on women's mosques were published as early as 1996, in *Huizu Yanjiu*, a periodical dedicated to research on Chinese Hui Muslim society, religion, and culture. This work was followed by co-authored books and articles in Chinese and English in collaboration with Maria Jaschok.

Cecillie Swaisland has spent much of her life in Africa, living as a child in South Africa. In the 1950s she spent fourteen years in Nigeria, where her husband was an Administrative Officer. On returning to Britain she taught as head of a history department and later as head of sociology in a college of education for mature women. She has held Fellowships at the University of Mauritius and at Rhodes University, South Africa. While teaching she obtained an MSocSci at the University of Birmingham and after retirement read for an MLitt at Oxford. She has maintained her interest in South Africa with regular visits and in 1993, in the run-up to the first elections, both she and her husband served as peace monitors. Cecillie was a Research Associate at the Centre for Cross-Cultural Research on Women until 2000, having become a member of the Centre in the early 1980s at the invitation of Shirley Ardener. Her publications include several chapters in works published by the CCCRW and three books reflecting her overseas experiences and contacts: *Forty Years of Service: The Women's Corona Society 1950–1990* (Corona Society, 1992), which explored the roles of wives and women officers during the colonial period; *Servants and Gentlewomen to the Golden Land: The Emigration of Single Women from Britain to Southern Africa 1820–1939* (Berg and University of Natal University Press, 1993); and *A Lincolnshire Volunteer: The Boer War Letters of Private Walter Barley and Comrades* (Literatim, 2000), based on the letters from South Africa of her great-uncle Walter. As a millennium project she collected a volume of the personal memories of women serving or living overseas during the twentieth century, published privately by the Women's Corona Society, now Corona Worldwide, under the title *A World of Memories 2000*.

Jacqueline Waldren is a social anthropologist who obtained her doctorate at Oxford University. She divides her time between England and Spain, being both the director of the Deia Archaeological Museum and Research Centre in Deia (Mallorca) and a part-time lecturer and tutor at Oxford University and a Research Associate of the International Gender Studies Centre. She is the series editor of New Directions in Anthropology (Berghahn Books) and co-series editor of International Gender Studies (Berg Publishers, for the Centre for Cross-Cultural Research on Women). Her own published books include *Insiders and Outsiders* (Berghahn, 1996), *Tourists and Tourism* (co-edited with Simone Abram and Don MacLeod; Berg, 1997), and *Anthropological Perspectives on Local Development* (co-edited with Simone Abram; Routledge, 1997).

Jonathan Webber studied under Edwin Ardener at the University of Oxford, where he obtained his DPhil in social anthropology in 1979. For the next twenty-five years he was managing editor of *JASO: Journal of the Anthropological Society of Oxford*, and, together with Tamara Dragadze, for fifteen years co-chaired with Shirley Ardener at Oxford a weekly seminar on 'Ethnicity and Identity' at the Institute of Social and Cultural Anthropology. His main scholarly interests lie in the interface between Jewish studies and social anthropology, and among his publications are *Jewish Identities in the New Europe* (London, 1994) and *Auschwitz: A History in Photographs* (Auschwitz State Museum, 1993). From 1983 he was Fellow in Jewish Social Studies at the Oxford Centre for Hebrew and Jewish Studies, and in 2002 he moved to the University of Birmingham, where he holds the UNESCO Chair in Jewish and Interfaith Studies.

INDEX

academics, 15, 118, 119, 180; academic traditions, 105; academic wives, 233; collaboration, 116–19; gendering knowledge, 237–38; masculine collegiality, 232–34; women, 230, 238, 244
Academy for the Daughters of Gentlemen, 135
Africa, 21, 158, 164, 165, 174, 176, 177; East, 165; West, 134, 165, 179, 181, 261, 272; *see also* Bakweri; Boer War; Cameroon; Lovedu; Natal; Nigeria; Nso'; Nuer; Nyoro; Shona; South Africa; Swazi; Transvaal; Venda; Yorubaland; Zambia; Zande; Zimbabwe; Zulu; Zululand
African Americans, 181
Allés, É., 117
anasyrma, 183; *see also* ritual
ancestral custom, 83
androgyny, 15, 153, 154; androgyne/androgynous, 8, 152–55
anthropology, 21, 129, 241; colleagueship, 7, 103–4, 107, 109; feminism/feminist, 27, 130n1, 146, 231, 240; fieldwork, 126–7; gendered, 231–32; at home/reflexive, 107, 117, 118, 126, 130n3, 214; industrial, 197; organisations, 110, 110n3; production of knowledge, 103, 104, 229–32; professionalisation of, 160; theatre and, 38–51; urban, 222
antisemitism, 60, 62, 64, 74, 85, 89n9
Ardener, Edwin, 5, 31, 32, 34, 38, 99, 115, 180, 250, 260, 269, 270, 272, 276
Ardener, Shirley, 3, 5, 10, 11, 15, 16, 21, 26, 32, 38, 91, 99, 110, 115, 129, 146, 165, 179–83, 186, 197, 215, 229, 231, 232, 235, 238–42, 244, 249–58

Aristotle, 43, 48
Association of Higher Scientific Courses, 148, 149
Association of Social Anthropologists, 241, 249, 265
Astor, Lady, 144
audit culture, 230, 236
Auschwitz, 66, 83
Austen, Jane, 133, 134
autobiography, 104, 126

Badinter, Elisabeth, 154
Bakweri, 181, 266, 272
balance of power, 55, 121, 172
Balfour Morant Education Act, 144
Balzac, Honoré de, 153
Banks, Olive, 228
Barker, Linda, 23
Baumann, Gerd, 85, 159
Beattie, John, 165, 168, 249
Berglund, A. I., 172–74
Bethel chapel, 92–100
Bible, Hebrew, 75–82, 88n5; Welsh-language, 97
Billig, Michael, 32
Blair, Juliet, 236, 253, 261
Blair, Tony, 33
Blixen, Karen, 158
Blum, Susan, 116, 117
body, androgynous, 152–5; Cartesian, 15, 44–45, 152; language, 181, 184, 187; masculinisation of female, 158, 160, 171–73; in theatre, 47
Boer War, 7, 14, 133, 134, 142
Bohannan, Paul, 240
Bohannon, Laura, 24
Bolsheviks, 62, 69
borders, 55, 60, 63, 68

Bourdieu, P., 46
Bowie, Fiona, 91
bricolage, Levi-Strauss's concept of, 24, 32
Britain, 6, 14, 15, 26, 29, 91, 143, 186, 229; DIY culture in, 23–32, 35n3, 36n7; welfare state in, 100; women in, 135–38, 151, 228, 234, 255; *see also* United Kingdom
British, 22, 23, 24, 26; Asians, 3, 7, 179, 186–92, 200; Black British women, 200; Chief Rabbi, 76, 77; empire, 136; feminists, 6, 7, 12, 14; identities, 200; women, 133, 137, 159
British Women's Emigration Association (BWEA), 136
Brontë, Charlotte, 133
business, 62, 105, 198, 202, 214

Callaway, Helen, 173, 236, 252–54, 256, 261
Cambridge, 15, 135, 139, 143, 144, 215, 232, 265, 270
Cameroon, 10, 169, 171, 181, 183, 249, 254–55, 263–64, 270–74
Caplan, Pat, 146, 229, 240, 256
Catholicism, 4, 5, 13, 56, 60, 65
Centre for Cross-Cultural Research on Women (CCCRW), 214, 249, 252, 254–58, 267–69, 271
Chapman, Malcolm, 31
Cheltenham Ladies College, 139
Chicago, Judy, 183, 266
Chilver, Sally, 169, 172, 251, 256
China, 3, 5, 7, 16, 85, 115–19, 121–24, 127, 129, 224, 252, 256; ethnicity in, 116; intellectuals in, 121; research in, 117; *see also* Chinese Communist Party; Chinese Muslim culture; Han Chinese; Henan Province; Hui Chinese
Chinese Communist Party, 116, 123, 128
Chinese Muslim culture, 7, 125, 128
Chmielnicki massacres, 82
Chopin, Frederick, 57, 59
civil society, 11, 70
class, 3, 10, 12, 14, 31, 56; in Poland, 58–59, 68; women and, 133–47, 159–60, 185, 192; working-class, 30, 59, 91, 96, 133, 147, 151, 198, 205
Clifford, James, 157

Cohen, Abner, 92, 98, 99
Cohen, Anthony, 49
Cohen, Gaynor, 4, 5, 7, 10, 12, 13
colleagues/colleagueship, 32, 101, 129, 139, 159, 161, 202, 204–5, 209, 215, 229, 231, 236; ethnography of, 103–110, 110n2; idiom of, 106; shared notion of, 106
colonialism/colonial conditions, 147, 158
communication, 8, 46, 64, 100, 106, 116, 120, 160, 197, 207–10, 222, 226n1, 253, 270
communities, as a source of employment, 199; of discourse, 104; of practice, 16, 105
conflict, 66, 160; political, 59; resolution, 25, 277
corporeal/corporeality, 15, 151, 152, 187
Cracow, 82, 83, 86, 263, 264
creativity, 30, 244; collective, 122; male, 184
Crick, Malcolm, 236
Crimean War, 135, 140
Croll, Elizabeth, 252
culture, 22, 34; DIY, 28–34; Chinese Muslim, 125, 128; European, 69, 70; female religious, 116, 123, 124; intercultural communication, 109; intercultural competence, 109; Jewish, 14, 62–66, 75, 76, 77, 81, 86, 87, 89; material, 54; male-dominated, 249; political, 16, 105; Polish, 56–60, 71, 151; popular, 23; third culture, 107; Western, 43, 183; women writing, 146
Curtis, Dora, 155, 156
Czaplicka, Maria, 8, 15, 146–60
Częstochowa, 59, 68

daughters, 16, 100, 138, 147, 159, 177; chiefs/kings, 164, 170, 175, 176; father's influence on, 133, 134, 135
Davies, Emily, 134, 139
Davis, J., 104
de Beauvoir, Simone, 15, 152, 181, 241
dialogue, 50, 51, 70; cross-cultural, 107; dialogical ethnographies, 216, 225; and shared understanding, 50–51, 109, 115, 116, 118, 120, 125; strategic, 126, 127, 129, 130n
diasporas, 5, 81, 192, 221; American-Chinese, 128; diasporic identities, 83; Jewish, 58, 82–86

disability, 7, 9, 186–90, 192, 230, 244
discrimination, 62–63; female, 144, 186, 193, 197; gender-based, 206, 229
diversity, 11, 124, 125; cultural, 13, 257; ethnic/gender, 200–3
DIY, 6, 23, 28–30, 33, 35; DIY culture, 28–34
dominance, 25, 116, 123, 210; male, 154
Douglas, Mary, 105, 240
Dragadze, Tamara, 253, 256, 276
Dublin, 142
Durkheim, Emile, 235

education/training, 28, 62, 63; bilingual, 91, 100–1, 100n3; Jewish, 62–63; managerial, 203; in Poland, 56–58, 60, 69, 147–49; Welsh-language, 91–98, 101n3; women, 133–43, 152, 190–92
Egypt, 77, 78, 79, 82, 174
Eliade, Mircea, 153
emigration, female, 136–37, 144n1, 255
employment, 12, 93, 95, 101, 192; community as a source of, 199; women, 136–78, 142, 144
Enlightenment, 15, 39, 42, 70, 241
ethnicity, 22; in China, 116; as collective identity, 38; ethnic minorities, 58, 66; ethnic revival, 67; gender and, 197, 201–2, 204–9, 239; Ukrainians in Poland, 65; workforce, 205–6, 211; women, 209
ethnographers, 128, 180, 220, 225; ethnography 'at home', 104
etiquette, 106
European Association for International Education (EAIE), 104, 106–9
European Commission, 108
European Union (EU), 69, 105, 233
Evans, Mary, 230
Evans-Pritchard, E.E., 164, 169, 240
exchange, 9, 10, 175, 214, 240; cultural, 16, 180; ethnographic, 107; women as objects of, 177
exile, 5, 13, 82, 83, 84, 85, 89n9; sociology of, 80
expletives, 185

family, 134–37; British Asian, 186–92; control, 140; and cultural identity, 65; history, 119, 122, 126, 147; in Venice, 224–25; Welsh-speaking, 92–100
Female Middle-Class Emigration Society (FMCES), 136
female subordination, 7
femineity, 181, 182, 187, 189, 192, 192n1
femininity, 192, 238; workplace, 209, 234
feminism, 27, 125, 155, 229, 230, 253; European, 147; gender and, 240; Liberal, 128; Polish, 151; postmodern, 154; Western, 128, 253
feminists, 1, 3, 119, 121, 125, 126, 129, 160, 183; anthropology, 117, 129, 146, 160, 183, 188, 231; British, 6, 7, 12, 14; methodology, 115, 188, 228; Muslim, 128; and reflexivity, 235; Western, 120, 128; writing, 154, 184
fieldwork, 2, 8, 22, 107, 109, 115, 120, 126–27, 129, 180, 186, 197, 215, 223–25; ethnographic, 45; historicising, 121; and language, 180; multi-sited, 21; notes, 219; participant observation, 198
First World War, 7, 63, 144, 151
Florence, 6, 135, 140, 141
Foucault, Michel, 127
Frankenberg, Ronnie, 7, 9, 16, 179–80, 184, 186, 232, 253
Free Church of Scotland, 134
friendship, 100, as network, 203, 225; notions of, 107; representation of, 103
Fukuyama, F., 1, 4

Garrett Anderson, Elizabeth, 135, 141, 142, 143
Garrett Fawcett, Millicent, 135, 140, 143
Geertz, Clifford, 240
gender, 29, 104, 183, 216; construction of, 120, 154; equality, 228, 243; and ethnicity, 197, 201–2, 204–9, 239; gendering knowledge, 237–38; as occupational qualification, 203; and power, 171; sex and, 45; and sexuality, 183; see also anthropology, gendered
genocide, 55, 64

Germany, 6, 22, 25, 26, 30, 32, 33, 36n8, 59, 61, 62, 63, 74, 85, 96; Germans, 4, 13, 22, 27, 31, 34, 55, 56, 57, 59, 60, 63, 64, 66, 67, 70, 200
Gilroy, Paul, 85
Gingrich, A., 159
Girton College, 139
globalisation, 13, 130n10, 216, 222
Gluckman, Max, 179
governance, 106
Governesses' Benevolent Institution, 136
Granovetter, M., 11
Greer, Germaine, 181
Gypsy/Gypsies, 220, 235, 232, 234, 238, 239, 250

Habsburg monarchy, 57
Han Chinese, 116, 122, 125
Hardman, Charlotte, 180, 236, 251, 261
Hastrup, Kirsten, 3, 9, 14, 15, 107, 109, 119, 129, 236, 256
Hebrides, 21
Heelas, Paul, 236
Henan Province, 115, 126
heritage, 54, 63, 64, 68, 69, 70, 86
Herzfeld, Michael, 221
hierarchy, 7, 8, 12, 103, 104, 106, 129, 130n10, 169, 171
Hill Collins, Patricia, 127
Hirschon, Renée, 253
historical, 39, 40, 56; consciousness, 73, 74–80, 82–87; counter narratives, 86; identity, 57, 61, 66, 86, 259; memory, 5, 74, 79, 80, 81, 82, 86; myths, 70; symbols, 62
historicism, diasporic, 80–84; historicity, 78
history, 39, 47; of antisemitism, 74; as basis of identity, 5, 13, 14, 59, 80; Bible/Torah as, 79, 82; Jewish, 74–78, 84–89, 89n9; Jewish history in Poland, 60; of feminist ethnography, 129; Polish, 56–66, 68; of women's mosques in China, 116, 119, 123, 125, 129
HIV/Aids, 176
Hobhouse, Emily, 142
Holland, J., 228, 229
Holocaust, 14, 63–64, 66, 74–75, 82, 86–87

home, 27, 28, 36; decoration, 28–29, 30, 32, 36n6; as part of identity of the self, 28, 31, 36n5; improvement, 24, 27; see also house
honour, 4, 46; notions of, 215, 219; sister's, 167; women's, 175, 176
house, 5, 6, 23, 25, 29; see also home
Hui Chinese, 115, 116, 117, 122, 123
Huntington, Samuel P., 1
hybridity, 220, 221; cultural, 82; notions of, 220

identity, 45, 48, 50, 55; British, 200; collective, 67, 71; construction of, 54–55, 85, 103–6, 127, 129; cultural, 65, 66, 91; ethnic, 64–68, 123, 204; European, 68–71; gender, 29–31; Jewish, 77, 80, 84–90; memory as part of, 70; Polish national, 55–62, 67–71; postmodern, 43, 192; religious, 125, 126; situated, 117, 121; Welsh cultural, 91, 92, 101; women's, 133, 137, 159; working-class, 198
Ifeka, Caroline, 169, 171, 172, 250, 255
imagery, 110, 181, 182
imagination, philosophy of, 14, 39, 43
intellectuals, 58; Polish, 61, 66; Chinese, 121
intelligentsia, Polish, 147, 148, 151
International Gender Studies Centre, 215, 254, 257, 269, 272
internationalism, 104, 105
Islam, 221; in China, 7, 116, 119, 123–29, 130n9; see also Muslim/Islam
Israel, 64, 76, 80, 85, 86

Jaschok, Maria, 5, 7–9, 16, 115, 119–21, 123, 125–26, 129, 256
Jerusalem, 80, 81, 83
Jews/Jewish, 55, 63, 147, 149, 220, 221; antisemitism, 60, 62–66, 74, 75, 76, 81, 85, 86, 89n9; culture, 14, 62, 64, 77, 81, 87; diaspora, 58, 82–86; education, 62–63; historical consciousness, 74; history, 74–78, 84-9, 89n9; identity, 77, 80, 84–90; Jewish history in Poland, 60; Judaism, 75–77; liturgical calendar, 81, 82, 83; memory, 76, 89n7; as minority, 62, 64, 66; in Poland, 55, 57, 58, 62,

66–67, 71n2; religion, 62, 64, 76; ritual, 71n2, 74–75, 77–81, 84; society, 84, 89
Jones, Llywelyn, 12, 92–100

Kaberry, Phyllis, 169, 239, 241, 255
Kingsley, Mary, 6, 134
kinship, 28, 100; role of, among Midlands Muslim women, 183; Polynesia, 167; Venice, 223
knowledge, 25; engendered, 146; ethnographic, 66, 110; feminist, 228–30; gendering, 237–38; production of, 103, 104, 124, 229–32
Krakauer, David, 220, 235, 236, 237, 238, 244
Krige, E.J. and J.D., 169
Kuper, Adam, 164
Kuper, Hilda, 167, 171, 175

La Fontaine, Jean, 180, 240, 255
Lady Margaret Hall, 140
landlords, 217, 218
landscape, 56, 85, 101, 173, 224, 264
language, 32, 38, 46, 48, 50, 57, 62, 107, 184, 187; body, 181, 238; and culture, 54, 56, 109; as ethnic identity, 13, 67; in fieldwork, 180; and models, 180; and racialism, 91; Welsh, 91–101
Leach, Melissa, 240, 256
leadership, 3, 6–7, 82, 94; female, 123, 164, 175; male, 185; rabbinic, 82, 86
Leutner, Mechthild, 129
Lévi-Strauss, C., 24, 32
Li Xiaojiang, 128
liberalism, 5, 13, 60, 70
liberation, movements, 58, 182; women's, 124, 181, 231, 249
Lienhardt, Peter, 249
London, 1, 12, 22, 25, 51, 96, 134, 136, 139, 142, 159, 185, 206, 232, 237, 239, 240
London School of Economics, 15, 146, 272
London University, 119, 139, 142, 144
Loudon, Rhian, 7, 9, 16, 179, 180, 186, 190
love, 15, 41; and men, 158; and women, 152, 154, 158
Lovedu, 164, 169, 170
Lutheranism, 65

Malinowski, Bronislaw, 15, 146, 154, 158, 176, 179, 236, 240, 254, 255
management/managers, 197–211; managerial values, 229
manliness, 153, 158; *see also* masculinity
manufacturing, 6, 197, 198
Marcus, George, 214
Marett, R.R., 146
marriage, 9, 15; arranged 189; men, 93; women, 135, 136, 147, 159, 160, 167, 173, 183, 188, 189
Marx, E., 222
Marxism, 64, 179
masculinity, 217, 231, 237, 238, 257; *see also* manliness
Mauss, Marcel, 235
Mayer, Iona, 252
McDonald, Maryon, 31
Mead, George Herbert, 43, 237
media, 3, 23, 35, 60, 61, 66, 68, 70, 91, 270
Mediterranean, 174, 215
memory, 63, 64, 74, 76; biblical, 79; collective, 81–82; culture, 89n7; historical, 5, 13, 80, 89; as identity, 76; and Jewish historical consciousness, 74–80; memorability, 83
men, 6, 29–30, 98–99, 166–67, 204–6, 230–32, 234; creativity of, 184; dominance of, 154, 249; ethnic minority, 205; leadership and, 185; love and, 158; and manliness, 153, 158; and marriage, 93; power over women, 164, 181; and religion, 96–99; sexuality of, 238; status of, 165; transnational, 186; uncircumcised, 170; *see also* masculinity
Merleau-Ponty, M., 46
messy texts, 214, 226n6
Middle Ages, 39, 63, 82
migration, 28, 34; forced, 85; female emigration, 136–37, 144n1, 255
mind, 71; /body dichotomy, 15, 44–7, 152, 160
miners' strike, 182, 242
minority, 5, 82; culture, 64; ethnic, 62–68, 74, 130n9, 204, 205, 206, 209, 211; Jewish, 62, 64, 66; German, 64; language, 95; religious, 117; status of, 5, 117; Ukrainian, 65, 67
Mitchell, J., 181

modernity, 217; bureaucratic, 74; Jewish ideology of, 84
Moore, Henrietta, 129, 256
Moses, 76, 77, 78, 79
motherhood, 181, 192n1
Mount Cameroon, 273, 274
mourning, 81, 88n3; ritual, 83
multiculturalism, 220; in Poland, 55, 58
Muslim/Islam, 130, 221; British Midlands Muslim women, 183, 186, 187; women in China, 116, 119, 121–29
muted groups, 3, 5, 99, 130n2, 256, 260; defined, 197, 251, 270; ethnic minorities as, 204, 206, 209, 211; women as, 211, 256; workers as, 209, 211
myth/mythology, 54, 57, 67, 68, 70, 76, 170; Greek, 183–84

nakedness, 219; as truth, 183
Naples, Nancy, 127
narrative(s), 79, 80, 107, 221, 225, 244; aesthetics, 74; biblical, 76; counter, 86; historical, 75–76; identity, 48; master, 74, 79, 87; strategy, 78
Natal, 180
nation, 1, 3–4, 13, 33, 55–63, 68–69, 71, 74, 100, 119, 151, 171–72, 221
national, 22–23, 32, 54, 80, 95, 105, 110n2, 148, 171–72; culture, 56, 57–58; history, 14, 56, 60–61, 77; identity, 5, 13, 55–61, 63, 65; movements, 58, 85; mythology, 68–70; symbols, 59, 61; unity, 2, 56, 57
nationalism, 32; ethnic, 60; German, 62, 67; Polish, 5, 13, 57; Welsh, 5, 91–100
native(s), 120, 138, 156, 157–58, 186, 218, 224; informant, 121, 128; language, 73; women, 128, 157
neighbourhoods, 1, 216
Netherlands, 24
network(s), 2, 10–13, 215; educational, 191; social, 187, 190–92, 218, 222, 229; support, 186–87; women, 217, 225, 239
New Guinea, 158
New York, 141
Newby, Laura, 119, 120
Nigeria, 243, 250, 252, 272

Nightingale, Florence, 6, 135, 140, 141
Nonconformism, 5, 92, 99
North London Collegiate School, 139
Nso', 169, 171, 172
Nuer, 164
nursing, 14, 140, 141, 143; as profession for women, 14, 135, 138, 140–41
Nyoro, 165

Okely, Judith, 3, 8, 15, 38, 117, 126, 127, 220, 250, 252, 255
Oxford, 2, 11, 15, 76, 91, 137, 139, 144, 146, 153, 156, 214–15, 219, 231–32, 236, 238–39, 241–42, 249–50, 252, 254–57, 260–61, 263, 265, 267, 269, 271–73, 276, 277
Oxford University Women's Studies Committee, 115, 252–53, 267

paint, 6, 13, 26, 232
Pakistan, 188, 192
Palestine, 78, 80, 83, 84
Passover rituals, 71n2, 79, 80, 83
past, 56, 59, 61, 66, 87; awareness of, 60, 67, 73–75, 80–83, 86–87, 174; historical/historicised, 73, 77, 86; history, 45, 61
patriarchy/patriarchal, 219; in Africa, 164, 177; control, 214; family life, 149, 125, 128; Islamic, 128; and women, 125, 149
patriotism, 14, 61, 133
personhood, 109
philosophy of imagination, 14, 39, 43
Pitt Rivers Museum, 146
pluralism, 58; cultural 66
pogroms, 83, 85; Chmielnicki massacres, 82, 85; Kielce, 64, 67, 71n2; *see also* Auschwitz
Poland, 54–70, 75, 86, 148, 151, 221, 263, 264; citizenship in, 58–59, 68; class in, 58–59, 68; communism in, 59, 61, 64, 68, 69, 71, 85; Communist Party, 59, 64; culture of, 56–60, 71; feminism in, 151; Flying University, 158, 159; history of, 56–66, 68; intellectuals in, 61, 66; intelligentsia, 147, 148, 151;

multiculturalism in, 55, 58; nationalism, 5, 13, 57; post-communist society in, 59–61; religion in, 57, 65; *see also* Auschwitz; Cracow; Częstochowa
Polynesia, 167, 168
polyphony/polyvocality, 110n1
positivism, 2, 146, 241
postmodern, 11, 129, 192, 214; anthropologist, 219; feminism, 154, 155; identity, 43, 192
power, 39, 89, 165–66, 211, 237, 244; balance of, 55, 121; base, 232, 243; economic, 56; knowledge and, 129; political, 56, 98; religion-based, 65, 99; structures/systems, 55, 123, 243; symbolic, 81; theory of, 228
Poynton, Marcia, 182, 183
prejudice, 122, 200, 224
profession/professional, 74, 105, 223, 238, 241; historians, 74–87; identity, 16, 104; non-governmental professional body, 105; women, 133–60
professionalism, 3, 8,105, 109, 146; colleagueship, 104
Prussia, 55, 56
Pygmalion, 183–85

queen(s), 6, 164; in Africa, 164–69, 170–77; mothers, 6, 44, 165–66, 171, 176
Queen Elizabeth House, 249–50, 252, 254–55, 261, 263, 265, 268, 272

rabbis, 5, 13, 78, 81–84, 86, 89n9
race/racism, 19, 174, 229–30, 236–37, 241; relations, 193n8; women, 157
Ramazanoglu, C., 228, 229
rebellion, 76
reciprocity and colleagueship, 103
reflexivity, 3, 4, 46, 104; feminist, 235
religion, 3, 5, 7, 10–11, 13, 91, 97, 236; Catholic, 69; in China, 122–29, 130n9; Jewish, 62, 74, 76; Lutheran, 65; men and, 96–99; minority, 117; in Poland, 57, 65; power and, 65, 99; syncretic, 221; *see also* Bethel chapel; Bible; Catholicism; Free Church of Scotland; Muslim/Islam; Nonconformism; ritual; Uniate Church; worship
Renaissance, 14, 39, 40, 42, 43, 47
representation, 50, 56, 67, 70, 75, 79, 110n5, 260
research, anthropological, 179, 197; in China, 117; collaborative, 115, 119, 121–25, 127, 128; double-sited, 214
revolution, 59, 69–70, 76, 85, 148
rhetoric, 16, 33, 44, 105, 220
Richards, Audrey, 158, 179, 180, 240, 255
Ridd, Rosemary, 253
ritual, 5, 6, 13, 25, 54; anasyrma, 183; Jewish, 71n2, 74–75, 77–81, 83, 84; religious, 6; sisters, 164–66, 170; in Southern Africa, 165–66, 167, 171–72, 174, 175, 176, 177; status, 81
Rodgers, Silvia, 253
Roman Catholic Church, 56, 60, 64–6, 69, 70
Romania, 32
Rome, 174
Rose, Hilary, 15, 233, 237
Rowlands, Mike, 274
Royal Anthropological Institute, 110n3, 227
rulers, 16; daughters of, 164; female, 164–65, 169–72; sisters of, 164–67; women as, 164, 177
Russia, 55–56, 59, 61, 63, 147, 148, 151, 224; *see also* Soviet Union

sabbath, 77, 78, 79, 88n5, 89n7, 221
Sacks, Jonathan, 76, 77
Said, Edward, 85, 158
St John's College, 263, 269, 272
school curricula, 61
School of Medicine for Women, 142
Sciama, Lidia D., 3, 9, 10, 12, 15, 232, 236, 253, 256, 277
Scotland, 134
Second World War, 7, 58, 63, 65
secularisation, 13, 85
Seligman, C.G., 146
Sexual Discrimination Removal Act, 144
sexuality, 155; in Africa, 181; gender and, 183; male, 238; Muslim women, 183; sexual gestures, 182; sexual inversion, 182; and womanhood, 155–60

Shakespeare, William, 4, 15, 38–44, 46–47, 49, 184
Shaw, Bernard, 183–85
Shona, 165, 166
Shui Jingjun, 3, 5, 7–9, 16, 115–24, 126, 128–29
Siberia, 15, 146, 151, 155, 157–59
significant others, 56, 57, 67
Silesia, 64, 67
simultaneities, 32, 33, 85, 89n9
sister(s), 15, 16, 95, 170, 177; collegial, 242; ritual, 164–66, 170; ruler/chiefs, 166–69, 170–75; sisterhood, 7, 99, 181, 242
social, 32, 38–39, 44, 48, 74; change, 54; class, 12, 92, 147; constructivist relativism, 117; engineering, 55; groups, 55, 122, 187; maps, 25; mobility, 28; relations, 28, 38, 55, 62, 126, 183, 189, 214; space, 24–29
society, 38–39, 46, 77; Cameroon, 183; Chinese, 116–17, 119, 122; Jewish, 84, 89; post-communist Polish, 59–61; as theatre of action, 47–49
Society for Promoting the Employment of Women, 136
Society for the Settlement of British Women (SOSBW), 136
solidarity, 58–59, 91, 105; sisterly, 239
Somerville College, 140, 156
South Africa, 14, 16, 85, 133, 134, 137, 140, 142, 164, 252, 253, 271
South African Women's and Children's Distress Fund, 143
South America, 85
South Asia, 186
Soviet Union, 4, 5, 59, 60, 63, 64, 65, 253; *see also* Russia
spinster, 15, 16, 160, 237, 243
status, 5, 140, 165; mainstream, 23; male, 165; minority, 5, 117; ontological, 39; ritual, 81; social, 63; women, 123, 133, 146, 149, 159, 165, 188–89
stereotypes, 6, 14, 22, 31, 32, 55, 76, 182
Stokes, Martin, 221
strategy, 75, 78, 79, 83, 154, 182
subjectivity, 38, 42, 47, 121, 124; female, 28, 146, 157; informant, 214; literary, 155; scholarly, 122

Swazi, 167, 171–72, 174–77
symbol/symbolic, 60, 154, 165, 171, 181–82; Catholic, 56, 59, 65, 66; cultural, 48, 57–58, 95, 151; historical, 62; identity, 54–55, 65, 67, 171; interaction, 241; Polish national, 59–61, 65, 68, 70
syntagms, 180

Tambiah, Stanley, 240
television, 6, 23, 24, 34, 36n6, 101
territory, 56, 58, 62, 64, 127, 136, 170, 222
Thatcher, Margaret, 6, 33
time, concept of, 73, 88n5; experience of, 74, 76–77, 79; motionless, 82–84, 86
titi ikoli, 181, 185, 266
Transvaal, 143
trauma, 73, 75
Turner, Victor, 240

Ukraine, 60, 82
Uniate Church, 64, 65, 67
unions, 96, 200
United Kingdom, 6, 120, 129, 185, 189, 197, 200, 204, 231, 233, 240, 244; *see also* Britain
United States, 136, 183, 250

vaginal iconography, 183, 270
vaginal insight, 179
Venda, 165, 166, 167, 170, 177, 271
Venice, 215, 216, 220, 222; Arts Biennale, 220; Burano, 214, 223–25; Cavallino peninsula, 224; Tre Porti, 217, 218, 222–24
visual impairment, 187–92
Visweswaran, Kamala, 118, 128, 147

Wales, 5, 91–93, 95–100, 180; Welsh language, 91–101
War, Boer, 133, 134, 142; chiefs', 171; Crimean, 135, 140; First World War, 63, 144; Israeli-Arab, 64; Second World War, 58, 63, 65
Ward, Barbara, 255, 256

Warsaw, 69, 147–50
Waterston, Jane, 7, 134, 137, 138, 142, 143
Webb, Sidney and Beatrice, 193n4
Werbner, P., 186
whites/Europeans, 68, 69, 158, 159, 168, 170, 174, 200, 274
wife/wives, 96, 173, 177, 181, 205; academic, 233; chiefs/kings', 165, 170–71, 176; role of, 188
Williams, Drid, 250
Wollstonecraft, Mary, 152, 153, 160
womanhood, 147, 154; construct of, 151, 183; and sexuality, 155–60
women, 36n6, 136; academic, 230, 238, 244; in Africa, 164–65, 176–77; Black British, 200; British, 133, 137, 159; British Asian, 191, 200; in China, 116, 119, 121–29; and class, 133–47, 159–60, 185, 192; diaspora, 85; education of, 137–38, 140–42, 144–48; emigration of, 136–37, 144n1, 255; and employment, 136–78, 142, 144; and ethnicity, 209; honour of, 167, 175, 176; and leadership, 123, 164; and liberation movements, 124, 181, 231, 249; and love, 152, 154, 158; and marriage, 135, 136, 147, 159, 160, 167, 173, 183, 188, 189; and mosques, 116, 119, 123, 125, 129; movements, 122, 133, 135, 181–83; Muslim, 122, 128, 183, 186, 187; as muted groups, 211, 256; native, 128, 157; networks among, 217, 225, 239; and nursing profession, 14, 135, 138, 140–41; as objects of exchange, 177; patriarchy and, 125, 149; and power, 169–72; professional women, 133–60; racism and, 157; religious culture of, 116, 123, 124; role of, 92, 98–99, 165; as rulers, 164, 177; sexuality of, 155–60, 183; and space, 23, 28, 30; status of, 123, 133, 146, 149, 159, 165, 188–89; subordination of, 7, 181; Victorian, 133–34; and work, 30, 197–211; *see also* daughters; discrimination; female; femineity; femininity; feminism; feminists; motherhood; wife/wives
women's studies, 130, 249, 251, 257, 277
Woolf, Virginia, 154
work, academic, 239, 260; analytical, 103; anthropological, 31, 256; collaborative, 127; environment, 110; research, 117, 127; women, 30, 197–211
worship, 2, 7, 93, 97, 101, 122

Yaoundé, 273, 274
Yerushalmi, Yosef Haim, 76
Yorubaland, 253

Zande, 169
Zimbabwe, 165, 166, 170, 176
Zulu, 164, 172, 174–77
Zululand, 174, 176, 180